Blender Master Class

BLENDER
MASTER CLASS

a hands-on guide to modeling, sculpting, materials, and rendering

Ben Simonds

san francisco

Printed in USA

First printing

17 16 15 14 13   1 2 3 4 5 6 7 8 9

ISBN-10: 1-59327-477-7
ISBN-13: 978-1-59327-477-1

Publisher: William Pollock
Production Editor: Alison Law
Cover Design: Anna Diechtierow
Interior Design and Composition: Riley Hoffman
Developmental Editor: William Pollock
Technical Reviewer: Thomas Dinges
Copyeditor: Julianne Jigour
Proofreader: Paula L. Fleming
Indexer: Nancy Guenther

For information on book distributors or translations, please contact No Starch Press, Inc. directly:

No Starch Press, Inc.
38 Ringold Street, San Francisco, CA 94103
phone: 415.863.9900; fax: 415.863.9950; info@nostarch.com; http://www.nostarch.com/

Library of Congress Cataloging-in-Publication Data
A catalog record of this book is available from the Library of Congress.

This book is dedicated to my parents,
James and Katrina.

ACKNOWLEDGMENTS

This book would not have been possible without patient help from Bill Pollock, Alison Law, and everyone else at No Starch Press who helped put it together.

Thanks also to the minds behind CGTextures (*http://cgtextures.com/*), who have put together a fantastic resource for artists and who kindly gave permission for the textures used in the projects in this book to be included on the DVD.

Most of all, thanks to Ton Roosendaal and all those who have contributed to Blender. It's my favorite piece of software and one around which my livelihood is largely built. I'm very grateful for it. Thanks to Thomas Dinges, who is not only an active developer of Blender but also took the time to do the technical review of this book. Thanks to the Blender community, to the members of the Blender Artists Community (*http://www.blenderartists.org/*), and to everyone who contributes to the Blender wiki and other resources like it. It's great to be a member of such a creative, open, and friendly bunch.

ABOUT THE AUTHOR

Ben Simonds is a 3D artist and co-director of Gecko Animation Ltd., an animation and post-production company based in London, England (*http://geckoanimation.com/*). He first started messing around with Blender back in 2005, when he had no idea it would eventually become a major part of his day job. Since then he's authored a wide variety of tutorials and articles for his own website (*http://bensimonds.com/*) and other Blender community websites, including Blender Cookie and BlenderNation.

At Gecko Animation, he produces visual effects, models, animation, and graphics for TV and advertising. His work has appeared on major UK TV channels like the BBC, Channel 4, and Dave. Gecko Animation's in-house short animation *Assembly: Life in Macrospace* won the 2011 Suzanne Award for Best Designed Short Film at the Blender Conference in Amsterdam.

ABOUT THE TECHNICAL REVIEWER

Thomas Dinges was born in 1991. He started using Blender and became interested in 3D graphics at the age of 16, after seeing the world's first open movie, *Elephants Dream*. In 2009, he started working on Blender as a developer, helping create the new interface for the Blender 2.5x project. He also has organized the German Blender conference, BlenderDay, since 2009. His website is *http://www.dingto.org/*.

BRIEF CONTENTS

CONTENTS IN DETAIL

INTRODUCTION

Welcome! This book is designed to teach you how to create models and environments in 3D, using two pieces of software: Blender, for 3D design and animation, and GIMP, for 2D image editing. In each chapter I take you through a part of the process of creating three complete 3D scenes. You'll learn how to block out and create models, sculpt and detail them, texture and create materials, use lighting, and render finished images. In the course of the book, I discuss the wide array of tools that Blender and GIMP offer and how to use them in real projects.

My goal is to teach you how to approach and finish your own projects in Blender, using three of my own projects to provide the narrative and examples of the tasks required. By the end of this book, you should be able to create your own projects from scratch using the principles demonstrated in the three example projects.

Topics Covered

Here's a brief summary of each chapter in the book.

Chapters 1 and 2 offer an introduction to Blender and GIMP. You learn what they are, where you can get them, and what you can do with them. I also introduce you to their user interfaces and the basics of working with them. Chapter 1 focuses on Blender. We look at adding and manipulating objects, saving and loading, and best practices when working on a project. In Chapter 2 we examine creating images in GIMP using its various brushes and filters, as well as how to work with layers and selections.

Chapter 3 covers gathering reference material, creating concept art and using these materials in Blender to make it easier to bring your ideas to life in 3D. I discuss using orthographic references, creating reference sheets, and importing reference images into Blender's 3D Viewport to use while modeling.

In **Chapters 4 and 5** we move on to blocking in the most important aspects of a scene with simple geometry and then fleshing out these basic forms with more detailed models. We look in-depth at Blender's 3D modeling tools and how to create models with simple, efficient geometry.

Chapter 6 covers Blender's sculpting tools and how to combine them with Blender's Multiresolution modifier to produce a model that can be sculpted like clay—perfect for creating detailed, organic models.

Chapter 7 looks at how to modify the high-resolution, sculpted geometry from Chapter 6 to create simpler geometry. We look at a few of the different methods Blender offers for retopology and how they can be applied to turn our sculpted meshes into final models.

Chapter 8 looks at Blender's UV unwrapping tools that allow you to map 2D images onto the surface of your models. This lets you paint on them and give them colors and textures.

Chapter 9 covers creating strand particle systems with Blender's particle tools. These can be used to generate hair and fur, and Blender's particle mode brushes allow you to comb and cut that hair or fur into many shapes and styles. We look at the various settings for particle systems and how to use Blender's child particles to generate vast numbers of particles from relatively few parents in order to create complex, thick hair and fur with minimum input.

Chapter 10 looks at texture baking, the process of automatically generating textures based on the geometry of a mesh, while **Chapter 11** covers texture painting, which combines the baked textures from Chapter 10 with hand-painted details and photographs using Blender's texture painting tools and GIMP.

Chapters 12 and 13 cover Blender's materials and lighting options. We look at the Blender Internal renderer and the Cycles render engine, and how each impacts the way we set up our lights and materials. In Chapter 12 we learn how to use the textures created in Chapters 10 and 11 to create materials that give realistic results when rendered. Chapter 13 covers creating lights and how to set them up for both the Blender Internal and Cycles engines to get attractive lighting and shadows that render quickly.

In **Chapter 14** we bring together all of the components created in previous chapters, including models, lights, materials, and textures, to render our final images. We discuss the most important render settings for the Blender Internal and Cycles engines, along with how to get the best results quickly. We also examine Blender's node-based compositor and how to use it to further post-process your final renders. Finally, we use GIMP for some extra touch-ups and for painting backgrounds for our images.

In **Chapter 15** we take a final look at the projects covered, and think about what could be done to take things further. I cover adding a few embellishments to the projects and look at them from some different perspectives, before examining ways to take our still images and make them move with Blender's rigging and animation tools.

What Isn't Covered

Blender is an extremely powerful 3D design and animation package. It has tools for modeling, texturing, creating materials, and particle systems, as well as tools for rigging and animation, compositing, and scripting; a full-featured game engine; a non-linear video editor; and some advanced fluid, cloth, and rigid body-simulation tools. This book attempts to deal only with the aspects of Blender that are needed to create, texture, and render models as still images. It doesn't cover Blender's rigging and animation tools, simulation tools, or the game engine. There are a wealth of other resources out there on such topics. If you're interested in finding them, try *http://www.blender.org/education-help/*.

Requirements

To make the most of this book, you will need a reasonably current computer, running a recent version of Microsoft Windows, Mac OS X, or Linux. In particular, when it comes to the sculpting portions of the book, some extra RAM (8GB is good) and a reasonably fast graphics card will prove useful. A pressure sensitive pen tablet (for example a Wacom Bamboo or Intuos) will be really helpful when you reach the texturing and sculpting sections of the book, but it isn't an absolute necessity.

The Projects

In order to provide a common thread as we progress through this book, I've chosen to center the discussion on three projects. Each was chosen to provide different challenges and thus provide you with broad, practical knowledge of the tools and options in Blender and GIMP.

The Bat Creature

The Bat Creature project focuses on organic modeling to create a humanoid, if monstrous, creature (Figure 1). For this project we first create a simple base mesh and then sculpt the more complex, organic forms of the body with Blender's sculpt tools. We complement this by creating fur with Blender's particle systems. We move on to unwrapping and texturing our creature and then create realistic materials for the skin and fur, which feature subsurface scattering and realistic hair. We render this project with the Blender Internal engine in order to use its highly customizable materials and fast, efficient rendering of hair and fur. Finally we create some dramatic lighting in Chapter 13, where you learn how to get the best results from Blender's lights and how to achieve realistic shadows when working with fur.

The Spider Bot

In contrast to the organic forms of the Bat Creature project, the Spider Bot project will show you how to create a mechanical-looking, hard-surface model of a robotic spider (Figure 2). This task requires a different approach at each stage of the project when compared with the Bat Creature. We begin by blocking in basic forms with simple geometry, but we use duplication to create the repeated parts of the model, such as the legs. When sculpting we use Blender's hard-surface brushes to arrive at a smoother, less organic final result. Then we use Blender's retopology tools to refine the model into something smooth and sleek. Finally, we render this project with the Cycles render engine because it offers realistic rendering of shiny materials and complex lighting.

The Jungle Temple

The Jungle Temple project centers on an environment instead of a character: a ruined temple deep in the jungle (Figure 3). We look at blocking in a scene and keeping its composition tailored to the camera. We use duplication, particle systems, and Blender add-ons to create varied vegetation. When texturing,

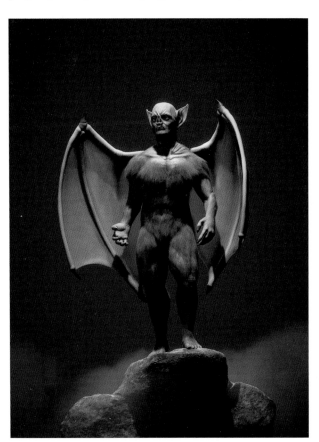

Figure 1: The Bat Creature

Figure 2: The Spider Bot

we focus on creating multiple seamless textures using GIMP, which can be tiled and repeated across multiple objects to allow a wide variety of materials to be created using only a few unique textures. We render this scene with the Cycles engine (which allows for the quick creation of realistic lighting) in Chapter 14, and then use Blender's compositor to add some post-processing. Finally, we use GIMP to paint a background for the scene.

Figure 3: The Jungle Temple

How to Follow the Projects

While the projects form the main narrative of this book, I don't cover every step of creating them. Instead, I focus on the most important or difficult aspects of creating each project at each stage of its development and leave the rest as an exercise for you should you wish to produce a similar result. I hope that this approach will show you how to go about creating all kinds of 3D images with Blender and the thought processes and challenges involved. To help with this goal, most of the chapters in this book also feature supplementary information and tips that offer more general guidance that you should find useful in a wide range of projects.

Resources Accompanying This Book

The DVD accompanying this book contains all the files for the projects in this book, including separate *.blend* files for each project (corresponding to each chapter in the book) and each project in its final state at the end of each chapter (where relevant). These resources should allow you to look in-depth at the workings of each project and to examine how each one takes shape. Creating 3D art is a complex process, and the end product is often a result of some amount of experimentation. These project files are not a literal snapshot of the projects as they progressed; instead, they are an idealized, tidied-up version of what each project would look like at a given stage.

Also included are the textures used for each project, *.blend* files with some useful brushes for sculpting and MatCap materials (see Chapter 6 for more on sculpting and MatCap materials), and the GIMP brush created in Chapter 11 that you can use in your own projects.

You can use these files any way that you like. All are licensed under the Creative Commons non-commercial attribution (CC-BY-NC) license, with the exception of the textures, which are included with the kind permission of CGTextures (*http://www.cgtextures.com/*), a fantastic online resource for finding textures. These may not be distributed unmodified without permission from CGTextures.

Let's Begin

This introduction has hopefully let you know what this book is about and where in the book you can look for the information you need. I've outlined the projects we will be working through and what you can hopefully expect to learn from them. Now we can start getting acquainted with Blender and GIMP, before diving into the projects. If you're already comfortable with the basics of Blender and GIMP, you can skip to Chapter 3. Otherwise, the next two chapters should provide a basic introduction to the workings of the software we will be using in this book.

1

INTRODUCTION TO BLENDER

In this chapter, we will look at the basics of using Blender in order to build a foundation for our work in later chapters. We'll explore its user interface, how to navigate the 3D Viewport, and how to add and interact with objects. Throughout this chapter, I'll point to later parts of the book, where various topics will be covered in greater detail. If you are already comfortable with Blender, feel free to skip to Chapter 2, on GIMP, or Chapter 3, on preparing your projects.

About Blender

Blender is a free open source 3D design and animation package, available for Windows, Linux, and Mac OS X. Originally created as an in-house animation package for Dutch animation studio NeoGeo, it was later released under the GNU General Public License when its developer, NotANumber, went bankrupt and the Blender community raised €100,000 to pay creditors to release the Blender source code.

Since then, Blender has undergone continued development by the Blender community, overseen by the Blender Foundation (headed by Ton Roosendaal, one of the original developers of Blender). The current version (Blender 2.6*x*, as this book goes to press) boasts a wide array of features competitive with many commercial 3D applications and has a committed and enthusiastic community creating art and animation with it.

Blender is used today by many animation studios, game developers, artists, and hobbyists. It has been used to make feature films, short films, and games. Of particular note are the Blender Foundation's open movie projects—community-funded short film projects that are used to drive the development of Blender forward by using it in a production environment. To date, four short films and one game have been completed, each yielding significant improvements and new features in Blender's repertoire. The first short film, *Elephants Dream*, premiered in 2006. It's a surreal tale in which two characters travel through a bizarre mechanical world. It introduced particle-based hair and fur rendering, as well as new animation tools and improvements to Blender's render engine. In 2008, *Big Buck Bunny* introduced improvements to fur rendering, particles, and the render pipeline, as well as more advanced rigging and animation constraints. In 2010, *Sintel*, a tale about a girl and her dragon, brought advanced sculpting tools, new simulation tools, and shading and rendering improvements.

The latest open movie, *Tears of Steel*, focused on adding advanced visual effects tools to Blender. It brought major improvements to the new Cycles render engine and has introduced camera tracking tools, new features for Blender's compositor, improved simulation tools, and better color management.

Current, stable Blender builds for Windows, Linux, and Mac OS X are available from *http://www.blender.org/*. In addition, you can find development builds featuring the latest updates from *http://www.graphicall.org/*. These development builds are designed for more advanced users or those who wish to try new features; they can be unstable, so stick with the official builds for important work.

The Blender User Interface

Blender's user interface (UI) has earned a reputation for being difficult to grasp. In earlier versions, this reputation was somewhat justified, but since Blender 2.5, the interface has seen major updates and is now much more predictable and easier to learn. Plus, with the addition of the search function, if you have trouble finding a particular operator, you can search for it by pressing the spacebar to bring up a search dialog in which you can search for operators by name.

Once you have grasped the UI, you'll find that Blender is very fast and extremely customizable. Most functions have keyboard commands for quicker access, and the interface is non-blocking, which means that windows and dialogs won't be layered on top of one another, obscuring your view.

Layout and UI Terminology

When you first start Blender, the default layout should look something like Figure 1-1. The Blender window is broken into areas called *editors*. These editors include the 3D Viewport, the Properties editor, the Outliner, the Info editor, and the Timeline, as shown in Figure 1-1.

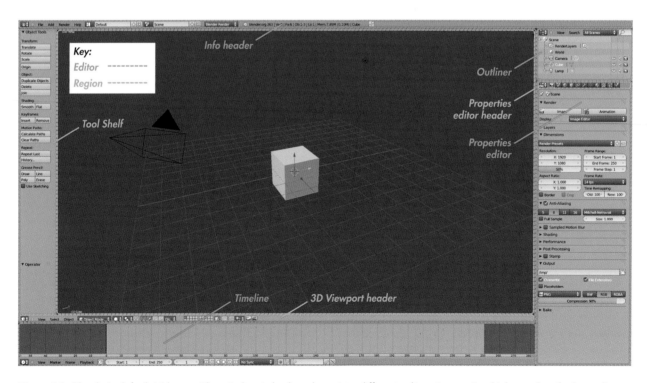

Figure 1-1: Blender's default UI layout. The window is broken down into different editors (orange), which are then further split into regions (green).

Editors are further broken down into *regions*. In the case of the 3D Viewport in Figure 1-1, the regions are the Main region (that is, the 3D view), the Header region at the bottom of the editor, and the Tool Shelf on the left.

Regions that contain buttons and properties—like the Properties editor or the Tool Shelf in the 3D Viewport—are further broken down into *panels*. A panel may contain any number and combination of operator buttons, information, and properties. The panel's name is shown at the top of the panel (see Figure 1-2) and indicates what sort of properties and information the panel contains.

Figure 1-3: Blender's different editor types

Switching Editors and Customizing the UI

Blender's UI layout is highly configurable. You can switch any editor in the current layout to a different editor type by selecting a new one from the drop-down menu at the far left of the Header region (see Figure 1-3).

You can also resize existing editors and add or remove editors by splitting or merging existing ones. To resize an editor (or a region), click and drag on its border. To split or merge editors, right-click the editor's border and choose either Split Area or Merge Area. (In later chapters, we'll use this technique to adjust Blender's layout to better suit various stages of each project.)

Multiple Layouts

Because different UI layouts are suitable for different tasks, Blender allows you to store multiple UI layouts so that you can switch between them as you work. To switch layouts, click the screen layout drop-down menu in the Info editor header (see Figure 1-4).

By default, Blender includes layouts named *Animation*, *Compositing*, *Default*, *Game Logic*, *Scripting*, *UV Editing*, *3D View Full*, *Motion Tracking*, and *Video Editing*, each of which is pretty well suited to the task that it's named for. (Default is the default layout when you start Blender and is good for modeling.) To add your own layout, click the + icon at the right of the drop-down menu to copy the current layout and modify it, or delete the current layout by clicking the **X** icon. Layouts are saved along with your *.blend* file when you save your work, so you can return to them when you reopen the file.

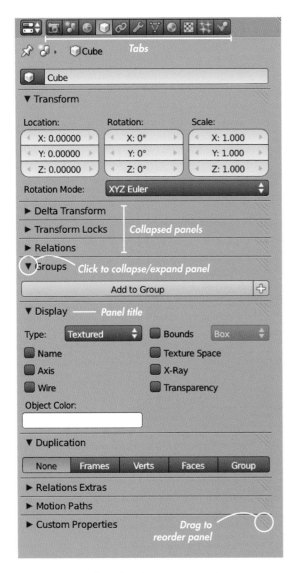

Figure 1-2: Panels within the Properties editor

Figure 1-4: Switching layouts with the screen layout drop-down menu

You can make a layout available by default by saving it as part of the default *.blend* file, the file that is loaded upon starting Blender. To do so, load the default *.blend* file (CTRL-N) and then create the layout

you want using the methods outlined above. Use CTRL-U to save the current file as the new default start-up file. (To restore the original default *.blend* file, select **Load Factory Settings** from the File menu and then save the default *.blend* file again.)

Editor Types

Each of Blender's editors offers a different functionality. Not all editors will be useful to us in the course of this book, so I will discuss just those that are relevant to the projects we'll tackle.

The 3D Viewport

This is Blender's most important editor type. The 3D Viewport (see Figure 1-5) is where you can view your scene and its objects and then move, manipulate, and organize them.

The 3D Viewport has four regions: the main 3D view; the Header, which is found either at the top or bottom of the editor (usually the bottom); the

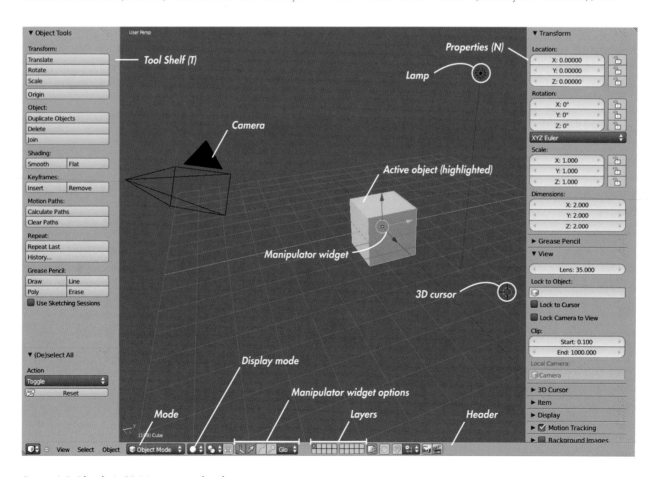

Figure 1-5: Blender's 3D Viewport in detail

Tool Shelf; and the Properties region, the last two of which can be hidden with the hotkeys **T** and **N** while the mouse is over the 3D Viewport editor.

Navigating the 3D Viewport

It's very important to learn to navigate the 3D Viewport, and there are several ways to do so. The simplest is with the mouse. Scrolling the mouse wheel zooms in and out, holding the middle mouse button rotates the view, and SHIFT-middle mouse button pans the view. To center the view on the currently selected object, press NUMPAD . (period), and to reset the view to center on the scene's origin, press SHIFT-C.

 Blender treats the number pad keys and the corresponding keys on the keyboard differently. For example, the number pad (numpad) numbers are used for navigating the 3D view, while the character key numbers are used to toggle visibility of different scene layers.

You can also snap the viewpoint to specific angles using the number pad. NUMPAD 7 snaps to top-down view, NUMPAD 1 snaps to front view, and NUMPAD 3 snaps to side view. NUMPAD 5 switches between a perspective view, where objects in the distance appear smaller (as in real life), and an orthographic view, where objects appear the same size at all distances. When combined with the top, side, and front views, orthographic view is most useful for aligning objects precisely.

The 3D Viewport has multiple display modes that can be selected from the 3D Viewport header (see Figure 1-5). These viewing modes include the default solid view; wireframe; bounding box, which represents objects as simple boxes instead of displaying their geometry; and textured view, which can display shading and texturing. In later chapters, we'll look at customizing the 3D Viewport for different purposes, including using different textured shading modes and working with layers and hiding objects.

Coordinates in 3D and the Grid Floor

If you haven't dealt with 3D graphics before, you may not have thought about how to define a point in space. Of course, 3D models are essentially created by connecting points in space. Thankfully, French philosopher and mathematician René Descartes gave us a solution to this problem several centuries

before we got around to inventing computers and 3D graphics.

To define a point in 3D space, we need information about the point's position in each spatial dimension in relation to a *reference point*. In Blender, this information comes in the form of the point's x-, y-, and z-coordinates, which indicate the point's position along three axes that run perpendicular to one another. These are called Blender's *global coordinates*. The reference point we use is called the scene's *origin*—the point whose coordinates for each of the axes is zero.

By convention, we generally think of the x-axis as being the "left–right" axis, the y-axis as the "forward–back" axis, and z-axis as the "up–down" axis. (The different viewpoints given by the keyboard shortcuts mentioned above conform to this convention—the top-down view looks downward along the z-axis, and so on.)

You can see the x- and y-axes in Blender's 3D Viewport as red and green lines, respectively. Extending from these lines in light gray is the *grid floor*, which we generally use as the ground height of the scene when placing objects. The divisions of the grid are all 1 Blender unit apart by default, giving you a guide to use for placing objects and judging their size. The x- and y-axes and the grid floor are also useful when orienting yourself in Blender's 3D Viewport.

The Properties Editor

The Properties editor is where you can define the settings and properties for a scene or a selected object. The Properties editor is divided into Header and Main regions, with the Main region being split into tabs (as shown in Figure 1-2). Each tab contains a different set of properties that relates to either the current scene or the active object. In order of appearance, the tabs are as follows:

Render The Render tab contains settings for rendering your scene, including render dimensions, shading options, and output formats. (We'll discuss this in more detail in Chapter 14.)

Scene The Scene tab lets you set the properties of your scene, such as the active camera, certain sound settings, and the scene's units (arbitrary Blender units, imperial, or metric).

World The World tab lets you define the scene's background, as well as the world lighting options, such as environment lighting and ambient occlusion. (We'll discuss this in more detail in Chapter 13.)

Object   The Object tab (see Figure 1-2) lets you set an object's transformations manually by using numerical values rather than moving the object about in the 3D Viewport. You can manage an object's group membership as well as how it is displayed. (We'll use groups in Chapter 9 to duplicate multiple objects using particle systems.)

Object Constraints   The Object Constraints tab contains an object's constraints stack. This is useful for animation but not a topic that we'll cover. (See the Blender wiki at *http://wiki.blender .org/* for more on constraints.)

Object Modifiers   This tab contains an object's modifiers stack and lets you add new modifiers. Modifiers are procedural, nondestructive methods for manipulating and generating a mesh's geometry. As you add new modifiers to an object, they are applied in the order they appear in the stack (from top to bottom). (We'll discuss modifiers in more detail in Chapters 4 and 5.)

Object Data   The Object Data tab lets you set which datablock the active object uses and exposes the different sets of data assigned to this datablock (see "Datablocks" on page 10). The contents of this tab vary according to the object's type. For example, in the case of a mesh object, this tab will display the mesh's vertex groups, shape keys, and UV coordinate sets, whereas for a lamp object, it will contain the lamp's color, energy, and shadow settings. The icon for this tab also changes to match the active object's type: For mesh objects, the icon is a cube; for lamps, a light; and so on. The Object Data tab will come up throughout this book.

Material   The Materials tab displays an object's material slots and the materials assigned to them. Here, you can edit the basic properties of the materials you create, turn on or off different shading options, and adjust the properties of an object's material.

Textures   The Textures tab complements the Materials panel. It lets you assign textures to a material, define how textures affect the properties of a material, and determine how they are mapped to an object's surface. (We'll cover this tab in more detail in Chapter 12.) You can also use the Textures tab to assign textures to your world background or to particle systems.

Particles   The Particles tab allows you to assign particle systems to an object and define their properties. Blender has two kinds of particle systems: dynamic emitter particles and hair particles. In Chapter 9, we'll discuss using hair particles to create hair, fur, and foliage, and we'll review the settings for hair particles in more detail.

Physics   The Physics tab contains tools for simulations, allowing you to simulate smoke, fluids, cloth, and rigid and soft body physics. (Learn more about these options on the Blender wiki.)

The Info Editor

The Info editor (see Figure 1-6) looks like a regular menu bar, but it's actually an editor, like the 3D Viewport and the Properties editor. It's usually kept scaled down to show just the header, which is its most important part. The header contains various menus, including the File menu, the Help menu, and menus for adding objects and rendering.

The drop-down menu selectors to the right of these menus let you change the window layout (discussed above) and the current scene (discussed in "Scenes" on page 7). Next to these selectors, a drop-down menu allows you to select which render engine to use. (See Chapters 12, 13, and 14 for discussions of Blender's two native render engines.)

After the render engine drop-down menu, you'll find several pieces of information, including the version of Blender you are using and some information about the scene. From left to right, the scene information includes the vertex count (Verts); face count (Faces); number of objects in the scene (Objects); number of lamps (Lamps); the scene's memory consumption; and the name of the currently selected object.

If you drag down the border of the Info editor, you will see that Blender uses the rest of the editor to provide a log of your actions as Python commands. This information provides a glimpse into the behind-the-scenes workings of Blender's Python API (application programming interface) as you work, and it can be most helpful when creating Python scripts. However, since we won't need Blender's scripting features for any of the projects in this book, it can remain hidden most of the time.

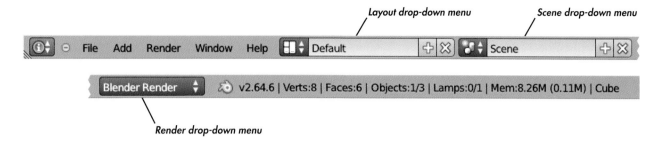

Layout drop-down menu   Scene drop-down menu

Render drop-down menu

Figure 1-6: The Info editor header

The Node Editor

The Node editor is a multipurpose editor for anything that is (or can be) constructed with nodes.
This includes the compositor, which uses nodes
by default, as well as node materials and textures,
which may or may not be node based. You can
switch between viewing Blender's various node setups by clicking icons in the Node editor's header
(see Figure 1-7). The header's main region displays
the current node setup on a grid, allowing you to
add, delete, or move nodes and to view and edit
their connections.

We'll look at the Node editor in more detail in
Chapter 12 when we create node-based materials for
the Cycles render engine and in Chapter 14 when we
create node trees for compositing.

The UV Image Editor

The UV Image editor is the 2D equivalent of the 3D
Viewport. Here, you can view images (Image ▸ Open
Image from the header or select an already loaded
image from the image selector drop-down menu)
and edit the UV coordinates of unwrapped meshes.
While rendering, Blender displays the current render in a UV Image editor. Use the drop-down menu
to view the most recent render or to view the viewer
outputs of compositing node trees. We'll discuss the
UV Image editor in more detail in Chapters 3, 8, 10,
11, and 14.

Other Editors

Blender has several other types of editors. We'll cover
some in this book, but we'll leave out ones like the
Graph editor, which is tailored to animation, and
the Logic editor, which is tailored to Blender's game
engine. For more on these editors, see the Blender
wiki (*http://wiki.blender.org/*).

Using Blender

Now that we have some knowledge of Blender's UI,
we can learn how to actually use Blender. We'll look
at the default *.blend* file and then explore working
with objects in the 3D Viewport and the Properties
editor. We'll also examine how Blender files are constructed, which will help us when working on our
projects.

Scenes

There is a hierarchical structure to *.blend* files (see
"Datablocks" on page 10), at the top of which is
a *scene*. A *.blend* file can contain one scene or many.
Each scene is its own separate 3D space where you
can create objects and build your project, and
each scene has its own settings that define how it
is rendered.

The current scene is shown in the info header at
the top of the Blender window, next to the current
layout (see Figure 1-8). To create a new scene in a

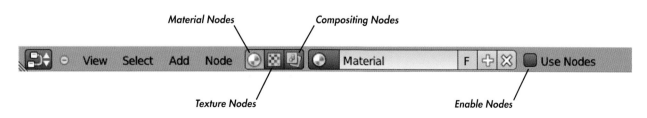

Material Nodes   Compositing Nodes

Texture Nodes   Enable Nodes

Figure 1-7: The Node editor header

.blend file, click the + icon to the right of the current scene's name. Blender will ask you whether you want to create an empty scene or copy data from the current one. Although it can be useful to create extra scenes when working with more complex projects, we'll use one scene per *.blend* file for each project in this book.

Figure 1-8: The current scene is displayed in the info header.

The Default .blend File

When you first open Blender, you are presented with a single, simple scene (as shown in Figure 1-1). By default, this scene contains three objects: a cube, a lamp, and a camera. These objects are all that is required to get a simple render of something more than a blank background. The camera tells Blender what viewpoint it should render, the cube provides something for the camera to view, and the lamp illuminates the cube and makes it appear as more than a simple black silhouette.

However, a gray cube on a gray background doesn't make for the most interesting of renders. To create something more interesting, we need to create our own objects to replace these rather dull ones.

Adding Objects

To add an object to your scene, place your cursor over the 3D Viewport and press SHIFT-A to bring up the Add menu. Here, you can add any object type that Blender supports, including meshes, curves, empties, lamps, cameras, and so on. (We'll discuss these object types as we progress through the book.)

The 3D Cursor

New objects will be added at the location of the 3D cursor, which is Blender's easily configurable way of quickly defining a point in space. The 3D cursor (shown in Figure 1-9) is where new objects will be added by default. You can also set transform operators, such

Figure 1-9: The 3D cursor

as rotation and scaling, to use the 3D cursor as the pivot or origin point for the operator.

By clicking within the 3D Viewport, you can move the 3D cursor to wherever you click (the cursor's distance from your viewpoint will remain the same). You can also move the 3D cursor by changing its location values in the 3D Cursor panel of the Properties region of the 3D Viewport. (If you lose the 3D cursor or simply want to reset it to the scene's origin, press SHIFT-C to reset the 3D Viewport's view and place the 3D cursor at the scene's origin.)

Selecting Objects

To select an object, right-click it. To select multiple objects, SHIFT-right-click them. Selected objects are outlined in orange by default. The most recently selected object is called the *active* object and is outlined in brighter orange than the rest of your selection. The properties of the active object are the ones that will appear in the Properties editor. Most operators use or act on the active object, though some act on your whole selection.

Manipulating Objects

There are several ways to manipulate objects in the 3D Viewport. Perhaps the simplest way is to use the keyboard shortcuts: **G** to move, **R** to rotate, and **S** to scale. You can also use the manipulator widget (see Figure 1-10) to manipulate objects by clicking and dragging one of its three handles to manipulate one axis or by clicking and dragging the white circle in the middle to manipulate the object on any axis.

By default, the manipulator appears as three colored arrows. Click and drag on the arrows to move your selected objects in the directions they point (along the global *x*-, *y*-, and *z*-axes by default). Use the icons in the 3D Viewport header to have the manipulator widget let you rotate or scale objects instead of move them (see Figure 1-10).

By default, when in Object mode, Blender uses the object's local coordinate origin (see Figure 1-11) as the position of the manipulator widget. To change the pivot center of an operator, use the Pivot Center option in the 3D Viewport header. You can switch between using the median point of the selected objects origins (the default), the origin of the active object, the individual origins of each object in your selection, the 3D cursor, and the center of a hypothetical bounding box drawn around all selected objects. This not only moves the manipulator widget but also uses the selected pivot center for any

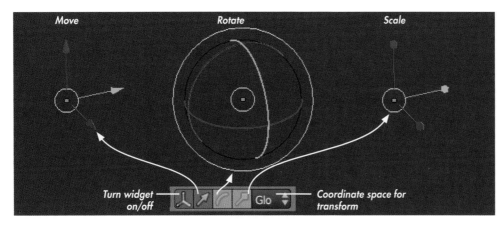

Figure 1-10: The three functions of the manipulator widget: translate, rotate, and scale

Figure 1-11: Choosing different pivot points for the 3D manipulator widget

transformations or operators you do using keyboard shortcuts or the mouse.

In Chapters 4 and 5, we'll examine manipulating objects, meshes, and curves in more detail.

Other Coordinate Systems

The coordinate system described in "Coordinates in 3D and the Grid Floor" on page 5 is defined relative to the scene's origin, and its coordinates are referred to as *global coordinates*. These are universal to the scene. However, objects also have their own individual coordinate systems and their own origins (the latter being indicated by a small orange circle when you have the object selected). These coordinates are called the object's *local coordinates*, and they may match up with the scene's global coordinates or they may not (see Figure 1-12). For example, when you move an object in Object mode, you move its local coordinate origin along with it, and when you scale or rotate it, you scale or rotate its local coordinate axes. This may sound confusing, but it has an important purpose. The positions of the vertices of a mesh (that you can edit in Edit mode) are defined relative to the object's local coordinates. This means that however you move, scale, or rotate an object in

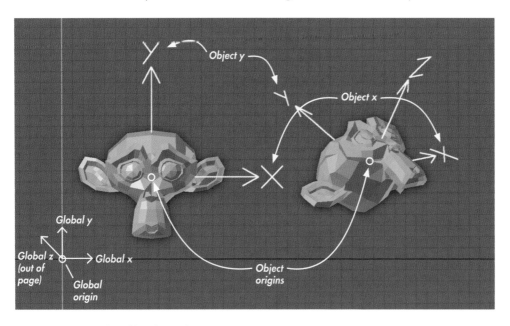

Figure 1-12: Global and local coordinates

Object mode, the mesh's vertices remain unchanged in terms of their local coordinates. We'll use this to our advantage later when creating multiple duplicates of objects, which will share the same mesh data and local coordinates but also be able to be scaled and rotated independently of one another in Blender's global coordinates.

In Figure 1-12, two identical monkey head meshes have been created. The first has been moved in Object mode so that its origin is no longer at the global origin, but its axes still point in the same directions as the global coordinate axes. The second has been moved and also rotated so that neither its origin nor the directions of its local coordinate axes match up with the global coordinates. With respect to the objects' meshes, however, the local coordinates still point in the same directions—the y-axis out of the top of the monkey's head and the x-axis out from its left ear.

You can view an object's local coordinates by going to the Object tab of the Properties editor and enabling the Axis setting in the Display panel.

Operators

Translation, rotation, and scaling are among the simplest ways to interact with an object. Other simple ways include deleting an object (**X**), hiding it (**H**), or duplicating it (SHIFT-D). These and similar actions are all *operators*. We'll cover a much greater range of operators in Chapter 4 when we begin modeling, and we'll continue to expand this repertoire of operators throughout the book.

Datablocks

Everything in Blender is built out of *datablocks*, which are simply chunks of data. All of Blender's objects, meshes, materials, textures, and images are different types of datablocks. Even the scene itself is a datablock that points to the datablocks that make up its contents.

Datablocks are arranged hierarchically. For example, a scene datablock will contain object datablocks, which reference mesh datablocks. Mesh datablocks, in turn, reference material texture blocks, and so on. This structure is shown in Figure 1-13.

The top of the Properties editor's Object Data tab displays the datablock used by the active object. Click the icon to the left of the datablock's name to change the datablock used (see Figure 1-14).

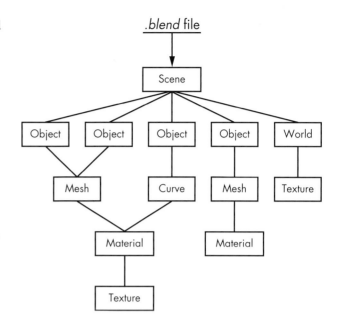

Figure 1-13: Blender's datablock structure

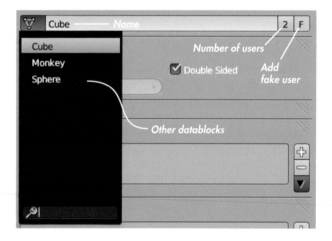

Figure 1-14: Examining object data. Here, a cube object uses a mesh datablock named "Cube." Other datablocks can be selected to change the mesh that the object uses. The number of users a datablock has is shown to the right of its name.

Defining objects as datablocks allows you to easily copy and duplicate objects within Blender. For example, you can create a regular duplicate by pressing SHIFT-D, which creates a new object with a copy of the original's datablock. (You can edit this duplicate without affecting the original.) You can also create a linked duplicate with ALT-D. The linked duplicate uses the *same* datablock as the original, which means that when you edit one duplicate, the other is updated identically. (We'll use this technique in later chapters to save time when working on multiple copies of the same object.)

The same goes for other kinds of datablocks. For example, in the case of materials and textures, you can assign the same material to multiple objects or the same texture to multiple materials, to save time and to avoid having to create unique materials and textures for every object. Of course, this feature also means that we have to keep track of which object is using which datablocks and how many users a datablock has. To see how many users a datablock has, look next to its name in the drop-down menu where it is selected. Datablocks with multiple users will show how many users they have to the right of their name (see Figure 1-14). (Click this number to make a new, unique copy of that datablock.)

Datablocks with no users are deleted when you quit Blender. To keep a datablock that has no users, such as a material you might want to reuse or an earlier version of a mesh datablock, protect it by clicking the **F** icon next to the datablock's name (see Figure 1-14). This creates a "fake" user so that the datablock will be saved along with your file.

Naming Datablocks

To rename a datablock, click its name. When naming datablocks, it's good practice to give them descriptive names to make it easier to pick a particular datablock from a list. Renaming your datablocks with descriptive words, such as *Wood*, *Red Paint*, *Skin*, and so on, will make your scene easier to navigate and understand later on.

Modes

Blender has different modes for editing the different aspects of an object's data. The default is Object mode, which lets you add and delete objects and also move, scale, and rotate them. Other modes let you edit mesh data and particle systems, sculpt on meshes, paint textures, and adjust vertex group weights.

Blender's two most important modes are Object and Edit mode. To switch between them, use the hotkey TAB. To access other modes, click the Modes drop-down menu in the header of the 3D Viewport (see Figure 1-5) and select the mode you want.

In Chapters 4 and 5, we'll use Edit mode extensively for modeling, and in Chapter 6, we'll use Sculpt mode. Then in Chapter 8, we'll use Particle mode and Weight Paint mode to create and comb particle hair and paint vertex groups for controlling fur. Then, in Chapter 11, we'll use Texture Paint mode to paint textures on our models.

Saving and Loading

Saving and loading in Blender works much the same way that it does in any application. Use **File ▸ Save** (CTRL-S) to save and **File ▸ Open** (CTRL-O) to open a file.

Blender saves files in a unique *.blend* format. By default, external files, such as images loaded into Blender, are not saved along with the *.blend* file but are referenced relative to the file. Thus, to open a *.blend* file on another computer, you need to copy over the *.blend* file plus all the other files it references and re-create the same directory structure before opening the *.blend* file. Alternatively, you can "pack" your *.blend* file, which saves external data such as images within the *.blend* file, so that you can then open up the *.blend* file on any machine and have all the data it needs.

Appending and Linking

Blender lacks the standard copy-and-paste functionality for objects or other kinds of datablocks that you might expect from using more conventional applications. To copy an object, you can either duplicate it or simply reference the same datablock using an existing object. But what if you want to bring something in from an external *.blend* file?

That's where the Append and Link features come in. Appending and linking let you bring datablocks from one *.blend* file into another. Append (File ▸ Append) brings the datablock wholly into the current *.blend* file as an independent copy of the original. Linking (File ▸ Link) *references* the original datablock in the other file. Linked datablocks cannot be edited in the *.blend* file they are linked into; rather, they must be edited in the original file.

Appending is useful for quickly bringing an existing resource into your *.blend* file so that you can use and edit it. Linking is useful for combining multiple elements in larger projects when, for example, different people are editing various parts independently. By linking all the elements of a project into one scene, people can work on parts independently in separate *.blend* files, while keeping the final assembly of multiple linked objects up-to-date. (If you link a datablock and wish to edit it locally, make it into a local datablock using the Make Local operator (**L**).)

In Review

This chapter has offered a basic introduction to Blender. You've learned the basics of how to work with Blender's user interface and essential tools. We looked at its UI terminology and its different editor types, explored the basics of adding and manipulating objects, and discussed how objects and datablocks work in Blender. We also looked at how to save and load files and import elements from one *.blend* file into another.

In the next chapter, we will move on to learning a little about GIMP, a free open source image-editing program that makes an ideal companion to Blender when you're working on projects.

2

INTRODUCTION TO GIMP

In this chapter, we'll take a look at the basics of using GIMP: what GIMP is, where to get it, and how to navigate its user interface. Then, I'll cover the basics of actually using GIMP to create and edit images, as well as how to use GIMP's array of brushes and filters, so that we'll be ready to move on to more advanced GIMP features in later chapters.

About GIMP

GIMP is a powerful, free, open source image-editing package, with a wealth of tools for manipulating and painting graphics. GIMP first appeared in 1996 as the project of Spencer Kimball and Peter Matthis, students at the University of California, Berkeley. Originally, the acronym GIMP stood for *General Image Manipulation Program*. Later, this was redefined to stand for *GNU Image Manipulation Program* when, in 1997, GIMP became part of the GNU Project. Since then, GIMP has undergone significant (if sporadic) development, and its current feature set is comparable to that of commercial image-editing packages, like Adobe Photoshop. GIMP has tools

for painting; manipulating colors; and working with selections, layers, paths, and channels. It also offers a wide variety of filters and plug-ins and supports numerous image formats.

GIMP is available for Linux, Mac, and Windows. Official builds for Linux and Mac OS X can be found at *http://www.gimp.org/*. You'll find Windows builds at *http://gimp-win.sourceforge.net/* and unofficial Mac OS X builds (with some useful extra plug-ins and filters) at *http://gimp.lisanet.de/*.

Why GIMP?

You might be wondering why I've chosen to cover GIMP in a book that is primarily about creating 3D art with Blender. The reason is that while Blender is a powerful 3D graphics application, we'll need to do some 2D image editing throughout the book. For example, we'll need to prepare reference images, create textures for models and alphas for sculpting brushes, and add some final tweaks to our final renders. Though Blender does have 2D painting tools within the UV Image editor, we really need something more capable and geared toward editing images.

GIMP is just such a tool, and it makes for an excellent companion application to Blender when creating 3D digital art. In Chapter 3, we will prepare (or even paint) our reference images in GIMP, using guides to align orthographic references and layers to create collages out of multiple images for quick reference. In Chapter 11, we will do some of our texture painting in GIMP, using layers to combine baked images with other elements, such as photos, and we'll use GIMP's painting tools to refine and add to textures we paint in Blender. Finally, in Chapter 14, we will do some touching up of our final renders in GIMP.

The GIMP User Interface

Like that of Blender, GIMP's user interface is known for being a little unorthodox. Primarily, this is due to its default multi-window layout, where the canvas, Toolbox, and other dialogs are split into separate windows. This is easy enough to get used to, but for a tidier layout, switch to the non-blocking, single-window layout by enabling Single-Window mode in the Windows menu (see Figure 2-1). Most of the screenshots in this book use this layout, with extra dialogs added as needed.

The Toolbox

GIMP's main tools are housed in the Toolbox (see Figure 2-1). Click the icon for each tool type to switch to that tool so that you can use it on the current layer on the canvas. GIMP offers the following tools (listed left to right, top to bottom in the Toolbox).

Selection These tools let you make selections in order to restrict the areas of the current layer that you can paint, apply filters to, or copy and paste from (see "Selections" on page 17). The *Rectangle* and *Ellipse Select* tools let you make

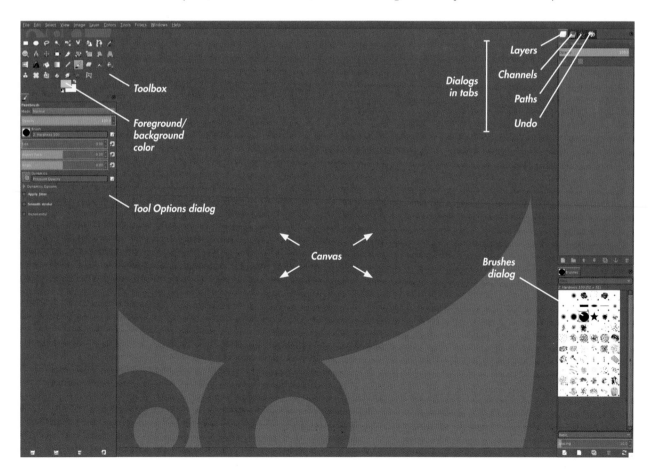

Figure 2-1: Single-Window mode in GIMP arranges all of GIMP's tools and dialogs in a single window. The default single-window layout in GIMP should look something like this.

selections using particular shapes. *Lasso Select* lets you draw freehand selections. *Magic Select* automatically selects areas that are similar to the areas you click on the canvas, and *Select by Color* selects similar colors. *Scissors Select* lets you draw a rough outline around a selection by clicking to place a series of points; then GIMP tries to generate the best selection by detecting edges in the image. *Foreground Select* lets you define a rough foreground area by painting on it, and then it tries to generate a selection using the painted area as a guide.

Paths　This lets you draw paths using Bézier curves. The paths you create can be managed from the Paths dialog, and they can be used to generate selections or be "stroked" to create precise brushstrokes and different effects.

Color Picker　This lets you choose colors from the canvas by clicking them.

Zoom　Use this to zoom in and out of the canvas.

Move　This lets you move layers. By default, it moves the topmost visible layer under your cursor, but you can use the Tool Options dialog to set it to move the active layer instead (regardless of where you click).

Align　This offers several features for aligning layers and selections.

Crop　Use this to crop an image. You can also crop the image to a selection from the Image menu.

Transformation　These tools (including *Rotate, Scale, Shear, Perspective,* and *Flip*) will transform the current layer or selection.

Text　Create text on the canvas as a new layer. Text layers remain editable as strings of text (meaning you can edit an existing text layer with the Text tool) until you paint on or apply filters to them, at which point they are converted to pixels.

Bucket and Blend　Fill the canvas with solid colors or gradients.

Pencil, Paintbrush, Eraser, Airbrush, and Ink　These standard painting tools behave like their real-world equivalents. The Pencil makes sharp, pixelated marks on the canvas, while the Paintbrush makes smoother strokes. The Eraser erases, the Airbrush gradually adds color as you hold down the mouse, and the Ink tool makes flowing, calligraphic lines.

Clone, Heal, and Perspective Clone　These let you "clone" image data from one part of the canvas (the clone source) to another (wherever you paint) and are therefore useful for creating textures and filling in areas. The Heal tool is particularly useful, as it automatically blends together the boundaries of the newly cloned pixels with the original surroundings. CTRL-clicking on the canvas sets the clone source, after which you can stroke normally to clone pixels from the source to another area on the canvas.

Blur and Smudge　These let you blur or smudge pixels.

Dodge/Burn　This lets you selectively brighten (*dodge*) or darken (*burn*) areas of your image, which can be useful for modifying shadows and highlights on an image. Use these effects sparingly because it's easy to be heavy-handed with this tool.

Cage Deform　This lets you draw a cage around part of an image and then freely transform it by adjusting the shape of the cage.

The two color swatches at the bottom of the Toolbox (see Figure 2-1) denote the current foreground and background colors. By default, most brushes paint with the foreground color, with the background color acting as an alternate color that you can quickly switch to by pressing **X**. (Some tools, such as the Gradient tool, use both foreground and background colors at the same time.) The two small icons at the upper right and bottom left of the color swatches allow you to switch between them and reset them to black and white, respectively.

The Canvas

The canvas is where GIMP displays currently open images. You can paint, make selections, and use all of GIMP's other tools by clicking the canvas. Rulers down the left and top edges of the canvas show the position of the cursor with small arrows as you move around. Clicking and dragging out from these rulers creates vertical and horizontal guides that your cursor and selections will snap to by default. This snapping action can come in handy when lining up images for use as reference (as you'll learn in Chapter 3). Along the bottom of the canvas are options for controlling the rulers' units of measurement and the zoom level of the canvas.

Dialogs

Most of the information about your current tool and currently open images is available from GIMP's dialogs. Some dialogs are visible by default when you start GIMP, with others found under Windows ▸ Dockable Dialogs.

Two of GIMP's most important dialogs are the Tool Options and Layers dialogs. You can see both in Figure 2-1, Tool Options on the left below the toolbox, and the Layers dialog on the top right with the Channels, Paths, and Undo dialogs. The Tool Options dialog contains the options for the currently selected tool that define how it works. For example, in the case of the Paint Brush tool, the Tool Options dialog lets you adjust the brush opacity, shape, size, and aspect ratio, as well as allowing you to choose from GIMP's brush dynamics options. The Layers dialog displays the layers that make up the current image and lets you toggle their visibility, lock them to prevent further editing, or edit their blend modes to change how they combine with other layers. The icons at the bottom of the Layers dialog let you add, delete, and duplicate layers, as well as create groups to organize layers. (We'll cover working with and organizing layers in further detail when we discuss painting textures in Chapter 11.)

GIMP allows you to rearrange and reorganize dialogs as you wish. The default dialogs are already grouped and organized into tabs and columns down the sides of the main canvas when in Single-Window mode. To rearrange tabs, click and drag the icon at the top of the dialog either into another group of tabs or to the border between two areas of the UI to place the tab in its own row or column.

Using GIMP

Now we'll explore how to actually use GIMP to create, paint, and edit images. In later chapters, we'll look at much of this in more detail; for now, we'll just look at the basics. As we go along, I'll point to later chapters that go into each feature in more detail.

Creating an Image

Unlike Blender, GIMP does not open any default file at start-up. When you first start the program, you can either open an existing image (File ▸ Open) or create a new one (File ▸ New). When opening images, GIMP normally opens each image as a new file, but you can use File ▸ Open as Layers instead to open images as new layers within the current file.

When you create a new file (see Figure 2-2), GIMP asks you what dimensions you want it to have in pixels and then creates a new, single-layer image with a white background that you can begin painting on.

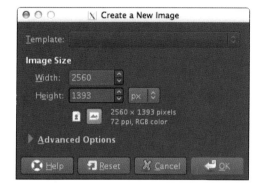

Figure 2-2: Creating a new image in GIMP

Painting and Drawing

Painting and drawing are accomplished in GIMP simply by clicking and dragging strokes on the canvas, using one of the available drawing tools. Your stroke will be drawn using the current foreground color and the brush shape selected in the Tool Options dialog or the Brushes dialog.

Brushes and Brush Dynamics

GIMP has a sophisticated brush engine that uses various inputs to determine the appearance of your strokes. In addition to any settings you apply in the Tool Options dialog, such as opacity or size, you can also choose from a variety of brush shapes in the Brushes dialog (see Figure 2-3). Your strokes will be drawn using the shape you select.

GIMP can also use information such as the speed at which you draw a stroke or the pressure input from a graphics tablet to affect the look of your stroke. These options are called Paint Dynamics in GIMP. You can choose different dynamics from the Tool Options dialog or create and edit your own in the Paint Dynamics Editor dialog. (We will examine this feature in more detail when creating our own brushes in Chapter 11.)

Filters

GIMP's filters act as a procedural way to modify your images by applying an algorithm to the pixels of the current layer to create a new result. There are several filters, including ones for blurring and

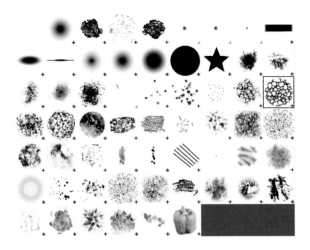

Figure 2-3: Some of GIMP's brush shapes

sharpening images, removing or creating noise, and distorting and deforming images. You will also find filters that apply artistic effects and ones that allow you to create completely new images and patterns from scratch.

Choosing a filter from the Filters menu usually brings up a dialog with some options that adjust how the filter works. For example, if you select the Gaussian Blur filter, the dialog should contain options for the radius of the blur and the blurring method used, as well as a small preview (see Figure 2-4). Clicking OK in this dialog applies the filter to the whole image. (We will use some of these filters when painting textures in Chapter 11.)

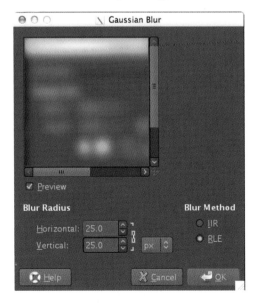

Figure 2-4: Using filters. The Gaussian Blur filter is shown here.

Layers

As a layer-based image editor, GIMP lets you create an image from multiple layers composited on top of one another, combining elements from each. The Layers dialog shows you all the layers in your image and allows you to edit their ordering and how they are combined. By default, each layer replaces the one below it, with any transparent parts letting the layer underneath show through. However, you can also choose from several other ways to blend layers using the Layer Mode drop-down menu at the top of the Layers dialog.

When you paint on the canvas (or use any other tool or filter), your strokes are painted onto the active layer (highlighted in the Layers dialog). We'll cover layers in more detail in Chapter 11.

Selections

One way to restrict the pixels you paint on is to use GIMP's selection tools. With these, you can draw out a selection you wish to work on within the current layer. Brushes, filters, and other tools will then affect only the selected pixels (see Figure 2-5). Selections come in handy when you want to work on an isolated part of an image. They also let you copy (CTRL-C) and paste (CTRL-V) parts of your image or split part of an image off into a new layer. We'll cover these tools in more detail in Chapter 11.

To cancel a selection, click outside of it with a select tool. You can also invert it (CTRL-I), swapping the selected and unselected areas. You can add to or subtract from your current selection by holding the SHIFT or CTRL keys while dragging out a selection. In later chapters, we'll look at other ways to work with selections using tools like GIMP's Quick Mask feature.

Saving and Exporting

GIMP can open almost any image format, but once you have an image open, it distinguishes between saving an image (CTRL-S), which it does only in its native *.xcf* format, and exporting it (CTRL-E) to a more conventional image format, such as a JPEG or Targa. You can choose the image format to export to by adding the correct suffix to the file name (for example, *.jpg* for JPEG and *.tga* for Targa) or by selecting it manually from the list at the bottom of the Save dialog (see Figure 2-6).

When working on the textures and other images for the projects in this book, I both save and export

my textures. Saving the *.xcf* file means I have my texture in a layered format that I can edit later, while exporting it to a normal image format such as *.png* or *.tga* gives me an image that I can open and use in Blender.

In Review

This chapter has offered a basic, high-level introduction to GIMP. We looked a little at GIMP's history, what it does, and where you can get it. We also looked at the layout of GIMP's UI and its available tools, and we covered the basics of how to work with images in GIMP. We explored the basics of working with tools, filters, layers, and selections and discussed saving, loading, and exporting.

In Chapter 3, we'll prepare to work on the different projects in this book before we put GIMP and Blender to work in earnest.

Figure 2-5: Creating a selection (shown highlighted in the top image) lets you restrict GIMP's tools to a particular area of your image.

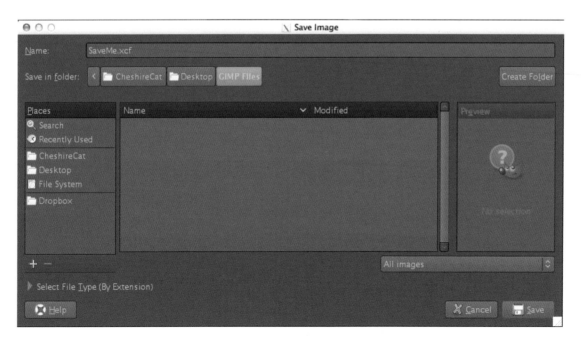

Figure 2-6: Saving images in GIMP

3

PREPARATION

In this chapter, you'll learn how to best lay the groundwork that will make creating projects in Blender easy. This includes gathering and creating references, designing your characters, planning the composition of the final image, and setting up Blender to make the resources you have gathered available while you work. At the end of the chapter, we will be ready to start modeling our projects, with a more solid idea of what it is we want to create and how to go about getting there.

Concept Art and References

Any project requires research and preparation. Before creating the projects in this book, I spent some time thinking about what I really wanted to make, collecting reference images, and creating basic concept art to keep me on track.

When preparing to tackle a particular project, play with various rough ideas and designs, discarding or changing ones that don't work quite right before spending a lot of time on any one. For example, Figure 3-1 shows various sketches

that I made for characters before choosing the Bat Creature design used in this book.

Creating, Finding, and Using References

Concept art serves two purposes: First, it is a quick way to experiment with ideas, and second, it serves as a guide to refer to when creating your project. This means that you don't need to keep the whole of your idea in your head all the time, and you can plan ahead for the different parts of your project, saving you time and effort. Use your sketches each time you begin part of your project as a reminder of your goals. You can use reference images or concept art directly in Blender or GIMP to help with the modeling and texturing process, whether you use them as background images or as a starting point for projecting and baking textures.

When conceptualizing your project, consider whether there are real-world references that you can use. The Internet is a great resource, of course, as are books, objects around you, and your own photographs. For example, when developing the Jungle Ruins project in this book, I began by searching

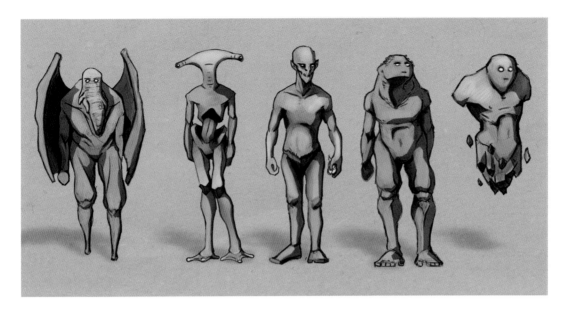

Figure 3-1: Working through different ideas for characters

Flickr and Google Images with phrases like "jungle ruin" and "Mayan temple" and then gathering images I liked. (Obviously, you should make sure that you aren't directly copying someone else's work; gathering inspiration is fine, but copyright violation is not!)

Even when you want to create a completely fictional design, like a dragon or a sci-fi spaceship, it can help to examine real-world objects that share some aspects of your design in order to help better visualize your creation. For example, when creating a dragon, you might search for images of dinosaurs, lizards, large birds, bats, or even mammalian predators, like lions or wolves. Each animal might have some aspect that you can use in your dragon, like the pattern of scales on a lizard or the wing structure of a bird or bat. When creating a spaceship, you could examine existing crafts, like space shuttles, airplanes, industrial vehicles, or even automobiles. Adopting aspects of existing things will help bring realism and believability to your work.

Once you've gathered some references, you could dive straight into modeling, or you might sketch some aspects of your project. Figure 3-2 shows examples of some of my studies of Mayan architecture for the Jungle Ruins project.

If you're not much of a traditional sketcher, consider sculpting a rough concept of your project in Blender from a simple base mesh (see Chapter 6) or block out a rough idea of your scene in 3D in

Blender using simple geometric shapes. Remember that each aspect of any project, whether it's composition, lighting, textures, or models, will affect your concept art, so think about and play with each of these aspects before starting your project in earnest.

What to Look for in Reference Material

When collecting reference material, here are some things to keep in mind.

Subject matter   Try to collect or create as many images as you can that match the subject matter; who knows when one might come in handy. The more reference material you have at your disposal, the better!

Point of view   Try to collect or create reference material that shows your subject from many different angles, both close up and as a whole, to make sure that you won't get stuck when it comes time to create the back of your character or a small object in your scene.

Lighting   Both strongly lit and evenly lit references are useful. When texturing, it can be really handy to have reference material that doesn't show strong lighting or specular highlights, but when you're modeling, you will want those highlights and contrasting lighting to show the shape of your subject. Don't pass up either kind of reference.

Figure 3-2: Sketches of different elements of Mayan architecture

Lens   When using photography, try to collect images taken with as long a lens as possible, especially if you plan to use your reference directly as an orthographic reference in Blender's Viewport for modeling. The shorter the lens, the greater the degree of distortion in the image, and if you blindly incorporate this distortion into your model, you are bound to get some strange results. If you can't get a photograph taken with a long lens, at least try to determine what lens was used when the image was taken and keep this in mind when modeling.

Licensing/copyright   While you can use any image loosely for inspiration or as a jumping-off point, if you plan to use a photo or artwork created by other people, you must comply with their intentions for their work. If an image is protected by copyright, you must get the copyright holder's permission to use it or perhaps contact a licensing third party, like 3d.sk or iStockPhoto. If the image is under a less restrictive license, like Creative Commons, be sure to comply with the specific terms of that license. When in doubt, assume that an image is protected by copyright and don't directly use it in your work.

Above all, remember that all photographic references have their limitations. In addition to manifestations of lens distortion, images may be small, taken from awkward angles, poorly lit, blurry, or incomplete. This doesn't mean that imperfect images aren't useful, but don't be a slave to your references. What matters in the end is that things *look right*, and if they don't, don't let your reference deceive you into making poor artistic decisions. If something doesn't look right, change it.

Composition

When creating any artwork, whether animated or still, it is important to think about composition, and doing so before you start will make it a lot easier to fit together the final elements of your scene. This was particularly true for the Jungle Ruins project, where the goal was to create a final image from a single vantage point. Remember that you want the final results not only to look convincing and detailed but also to be pleasing to the eye when placed within the setting of your final renders.

Composition is a very rich subject, and it is beyond the scope of this book to cover it in detail, but here are some basic principles.

The Rule of Thirds

The rule of thirds principle argues that the points of interest in an image should fall roughly in line with an imaginary grid drawn over the image. This imaginary grid splits the image into thirds along both its length and width. The goal is to carve the image into less symmetrical areas to produce something that is generally more pleasing to the eye, as opposed to an image split right down the middle by the various points of interest. Figure 3-3 shows how I split an image into a total of nine sections, using three rows and three columns.

Figure 3-3: The Jungle Ruins project at the blocking-in stage, with a rule of thirds grid overlaid

For another example of the rule of thirds in action, think of a scene showing the sky and a horizon together with some buildings. Applying the rule of thirds, we would place the horizon at one horizontal division of the image (about one-third of the way up from the bottom or down from the top), with the sky occupying the area above the horizon. If the main points of interest are situated above the horizon, such as a tall building or a lit moon in the night sky, we might place the horizon above the lower third of the image to allow the building and moon to occupy more space. On the other hand, if the main points of the image are below the horizon, say some boats on a lake, placing the horizon at the upper third division would allow us to give the boats more space while creating a balanced composition.

The rule of thirds doesn't always apply to images containing single characters, however. For example, if your image is a portrait or full-body shot of a character, it will likely make more sense to give the subject center stage. But even in these cases, you might apply the rule of thirds to other aspects of the image, such as the character's eyeline or a heavy object carried in his arms.

It's worth pointing out that the rule of thirds isn't the only theory driven by the beauty of asymmetry and imbalance. Other rules, like the golden mean, which places the grid lines according to the golden ratio (approximately 1.618:1), have similar effects and share the goal of not dividing an image into obvious symmetrical halves.

Silhouettes and Negative Space

For your image to read well, it must have a strong *silhouette*. The silhouette is the outline of your subject, as shown in Figure 3-4. If when looking at your image's silhouette you can still tell what the image is, you have a strong design. If the silhouette looks like just a jumble of shapes, however, viewers may have a hard time processing the image, even in its final state. To get a better idea of your model's silhouette, try adding a black material to it with no specularity (see Chapter 12), and render it on its own to see it as a black shape on a plain background (Figure 3-4).

In the same way, the *negative space* around and between your subject and any other objects also affects the appearance of your composition. For example, when placing the horizon on a rule of thirds line, as discussed in the previous section, we are likely to create a pleasing negative space in the form of the sky.

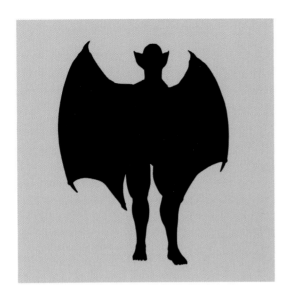

Figure 3-4: Silhouette of the Bat Creature

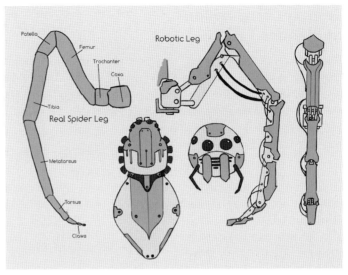

Figure 3-5: Spider concept art. Because the legs are very complex, the design of the body is kept simple to make it easier for the viewer to understand the overall image.

Simplicity and Focus

When creating any image, you should strive to control the viewer's gaze. If your image is busy with too much going on, a viewer may be overwhelmed and not know what to pay attention to. To avoid potential confusion, an image should have some "rest" areas—parts that are simple and don't demand attention so that other, more important parts are not overlooked. For example, if you model and texture a fantastic portrait, you might avoid putting a complex, cluttered background in the negative space behind the portrait because this background might distract the viewer. The negative space in this example is the rest area, but rest areas may simply be less complex and detailed parts of the main image itself.

The same idea applies to all aspects of design: Keep things simple and control the viewer's focus. If you cover the whole of any object in elaborate detail, the result may be an indecipherable mélange of competing focal points. If instead you focus the details in specific areas while keeping others simple, the viewer can more easily understand your design. For example, in the Spider Bot project shown in Figure 3-5, some aspects of the design, like the legs and the mechanical details of the joints between the body segments, are quite detailed, while other areas, like the surface of the body, are kept simple.

Defining areas of focus and simplicity can be accomplished in many ways, the most obvious of which is by placement: Simply leave space between the complex areas in your scene. But there are other ways, too. For example, you can use lighting to put less important areas of a composition in darkness or to overexpose those areas so that they are mostly white, or you can use depth of field to put foreground and background areas of the image out of focus. (We'll touch on these techniques in various chapters, especially in Chapters 13 and 14.)

Visual Path

Most images contain multiple elements. When working with such an image, you should create a path that draws viewers through each element before they look away from the image. By planning this path, you can make your image tell a story and expose more of your scene.

You can use the rule of thirds to create a visual path through an image, as the viewer will naturally look to the intersections of the rule of thirds lines first. You can also use perspective, allowing converging lines in the image to direct the viewer through your composition's various focal points. Or you might frame the points of interest with negative space. In images containing characters, you might have the characters look at the focal point so that the viewer follows their gaze, or you might even just have the characters point at it!

Testing Compositions in Blender

Blender can be useful when blocking in compositions for a scene before going all-out and creating it. For example, in the case of the Jungle Ruins scene, I tried various compositions simply by creating a rough blocking of the scene using cubes, and I then added simple lighting to see how different options would affect the composition.

Blender also has some handy tools for you to use in guiding your composition choices. With your camera selected, you can access these tools from the Object Data tab of the Properties editor, as shown in Figure 3-6. For example, to better see how your image is framed, you can turn up the Alpha value of the Passepartout setting to hide the area outside your camera's view. You'll also find several composition guides that you can toggle to help line up your composition according to the rule of thirds, the golden ratio, or the center lines, as shown in Figure 3-6.

Preparing References in GIMP

Whether you're collecting references for a project from photos or drawing them, it usually pays to invest some time in GIMP making sure that your references will be as useful as possible once you bring them into Blender. For example, you can use GIMP to combine images into reference sheets or to correct distortions in your images to get the best reference possible.

Creating a Reference Sheet

It is generally useful to have multiple images on hand that you can quickly reference when working on your project. For this reason, it helps to combine a lot of images into a single reference sheet that you can then load as a single image into Blender.

To create a reference sheet, choose **File ▸ Open As Layers** in GIMP and then select the images you want to import. Next, increase the size of your canvas using **Image ▸ Canvas Size** so that you can spread out your images and arrange them to fit on the one canvas using the Move tool (**M**), as shown in Figure 3-7. Scale down any images that are significantly larger than others using the Scale tool (SHIFT-T). Finally, add a black background behind the images by adding a new layer, filling it with black, and moving it to the bottom of the layer stack. Save the reference sheet as a *.jpg* file.

Aligning Orthographic References

Orthographic references, or *ortho refs*, are reference images drawn or taken from specific vantage points (front, side, back, or top) with as little perspective as possible. It's easy to reduce perspective when drawing; to reduce perspective with photos, take them as far away from the subject as possible, using a long lens.

If you will be using orthographic photo references or drawings in your project, consider aligning them in GIMP in a single image, as shown in Figure 3-8, before opening them in Blender so that the features of each part line up in each image. By aligning your images, you will be able to follow each feature from more than one viewpoint when modeling.

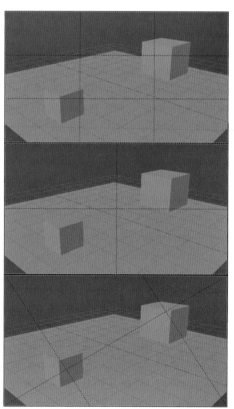

Figure 3-6: Composition guides in Blender

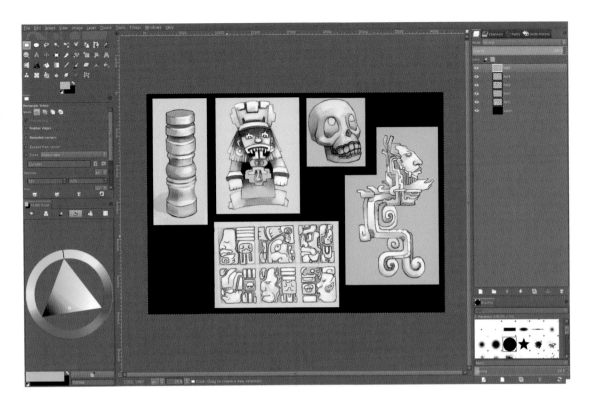

Figure 3-7: Creating a reference sheet in GIMP. You can open multiple images as layers, lay them out with the Move tool, and save the result as a single image that you can then open in Blender.

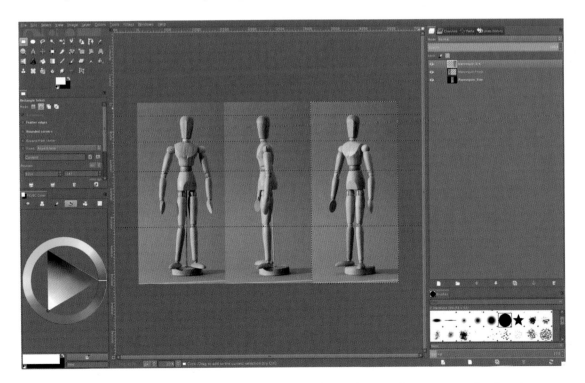

Figure 3-8: Aligning orthographic references in GIMP. Here, photos of an artist's mannequin taken from the front, side, and three-quarter perspectives are being aligned using horizontal guidelines. Each photo has been imported as a separate layer and aligned using the Move tool.

If your reference was taken with a long lens or drawn in orthographic perspective, you should be able to align it easily. To do so, open your images as layers, as described in "Creating a Reference Sheet" on page 24, and then pick one layer to use to align all the others. Use guides (click and drag from the rulers at the side of the image window) to mark the vertical positions of the key features and then use GIMP's Rotate, Scale, and Move tools to position your next layer so that the features line up. By repeating these steps for as many orthographic views of your subject as you have, you'll essentially create a blueprint of your project that you then can use for modeling (see Figure 3-9).

Note that when aligning images with photo references, some features may not line up perfectly in every view due to lens distortion and perspective, particularly if they weren't all the same distance from the camera. While you can correct lens distortion to some extent using GIMP's lens distortion filter (Filters ▸ Distort ▸ Lens Distortion), the result will not be a perfect ortho ref because you still won't be able to correct for perspective. It's easier to simply align the key features as best you can and remember that you aren't shackled to your reference when modeling; you can correct for any errors that you know will be there using your own judgment.

Using Concepts and Reference Images in Blender

Once you've prepared your concept art and reference images, there are several ways to make them available for use as references in Blender. Of course, you can just open your image in your standard image viewer and keep it off to one side of your screen, but you can also use Blender's UV Image editor, background images, or the image display option for an empty object.

UV Image Editor

To open up an image in Blender's UV Image editor, select **Image ▸ Open Image** from the header, navigate to your reference image or concept art in the file browser, and select **Open**. Blender should open your image in the UV Image editor. If you then open another image, you can access any previously opened images, as well as any used by texture datablocks, from the drop-down menu in the header.

When working with several reference images while creating my compositions, I like to combine them all into one big reference sheet in GIMP. I then save that reference sheet as a *.jpg* file and open it in Blender's UV Image editor, as shown in Figure 3-10.

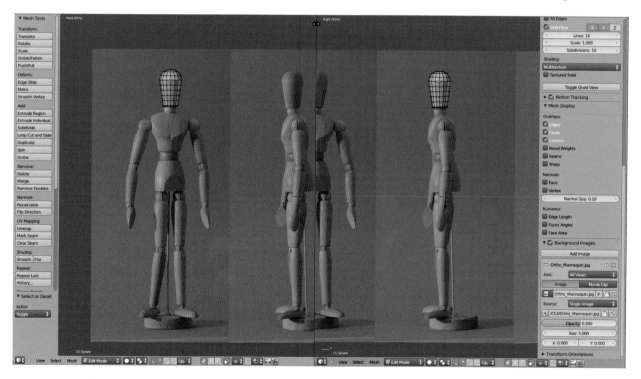

Figure 3-9: Working with orthographic references. The ability to see features from multiple angles makes it easier to model them accurately.

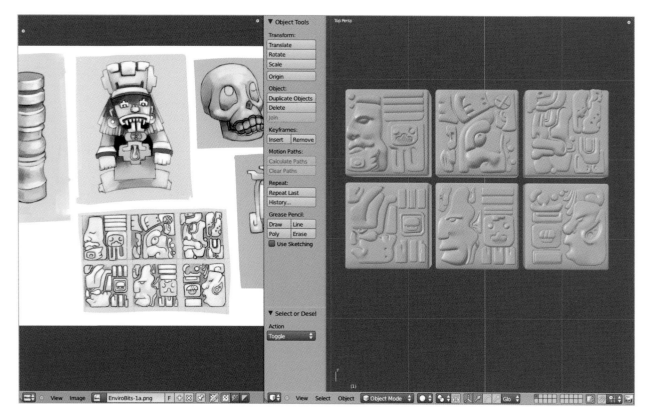

Figure 3-10: Reference collage in UV Image editor in Blender

This reference sheet allows me to pan around the image and zoom in and out to look more closely at specific references without having to load each into Blender separately and switch between them constantly.

Background Images

If you want to display an image in Blender's 3D Viewport, the simplest way is by using background images. With your cursor over the 3D Viewport, press **N** to bring up the Properties region, which contains the Background Images panel (see Figure 3-11). Here you can add images to the 3D Viewport, change their size and location in the 3D View, and define which views they appear from using the Axis setting.

Image Empties

Background images are really useful when modeling from orthographic references because you can set

them to appear only from the correct view or when looking from the camera's viewpoint.

If there's a downside to using background images, it's that they aren't visible when you have perspective enabled in the 3D Viewport. Fortunately, Blender 2.6 allows you to add an image as the draw type for any empty, which you can then position as you like. This makes image empties great both for arbitrarily placing reference images in your scene so you can move them as you please and for setting up orthographic references that can be viewed from any angle.

To use an image empty, create an empty in your scene using SHIFT-A ▶ **Empty**. Then in the Properties editor under the Object Data tab, you can set the empty's display type to **Image** and select an image to display (see Figure 3-12). The empty will now display this image on a plane that you can move, scale, and rotate to place the image in your scene as you would any object, but this object won't interfere with your renders because it will be visible only in the 3D Viewport.

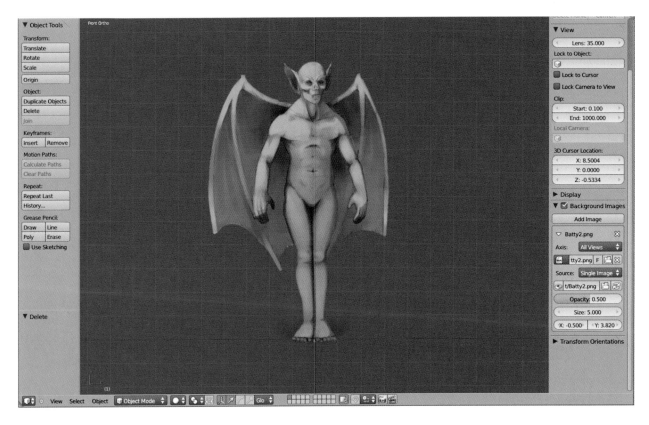

Figure 3-11: Using background images in Blender. You can add further images using the Add Image button, which allows you to see multiple references at once.

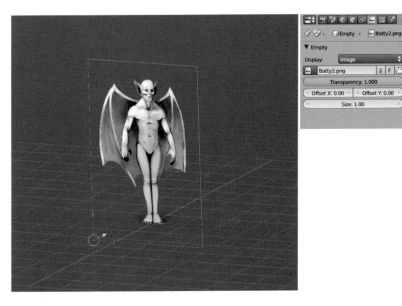

Figure 3-12: The same image used as an image empty can now be viewed from any angle. If your image has an Alpha (transparency) channel, it too will display as a transparent image in the Viewport.

In Review

In this chapter, we have looked at the preparatory steps to think about when working on a project in Blender, including planning what you want to make, collecting reference and concept art, and generating ideas for your final composition. We then moved on to discuss ways to make this information available to you in Blender while you work. In the next chapter, we begin modeling our projects. By blocking out the key elements of our projects, we will develop a foundation on which to build more complex models.

4

BLOCKING IN

With preparation finished and concept art and reference at the ready, we can move on to modeling. *Modeling* is the process of creating a 3D object that is made up of individual points connected to form faces, which in turn make up more complex shapes. There are many ways to create models in Blender, from modifying primitives, like a simple cube or sphere, to building the surface of a mesh face by face or drawing smooth curves that Blender can convert into objects composed of vertices and faces.

Modeling can be a long process, and to save time, it helps to know where you are going with a particular modeling task. Still, you can't model an object all at once; you have to start somewhere, and that's where blocking in comes in. *Blocking in* is the process of adding simple placeholders for the objects you want to create so that you can better plan how they fit together, consider their individual constructions, and spot problems before they become major issues. Once a scene has been blocked in, you can move on to refining, replacing, or adding to each part to create a final model. For example, in the Jungle Temple scene, simple elements like cubes are used as placeholders for key

elements; for other projects, we create simple base meshes for sculpting that act as a foundation for developing the final form of our sculpted models.

Basic Modeling Terms

Before we dive in, here are some definitions of Blender's basic modeling concepts that I'll use throughout this chapter. Table 4-1 lists them in hierarchical order: Vertices make up edges, which make up faces, and so on.

Edit Mode

Edit mode (shown in Figure 4-1) is where the modeling magic happens. With a mesh object selected, you can enter Edit mode by pressing TAB or by clicking the mode drop-down menu in the 3D Viewport header and selecting Edit mode. Once in Edit mode, your selected object is editable (if it is in fact editable—empty objects and lamps, for example, are not). When an object is editable, you can select and manipulate parts as well as create new parts.

Table 4-1: Important Terms for Modeling in Blender's Edit Mode

Term	Description
vertex (plural *vertices*); also known as a *vert*	A single point in 3D space with a specific location. Vertices are connected to construct *meshes*.
edge	A line connecting two vertices.
face (or polygon)	Three or more vertices connected by edges and filled with a flat surface. A polygon formed of three vertices is called a *tri* (short for *triangle*). A polygon formed of four vertices is called a *quad* (short for *quadrangle*). Polygons with more than four vertices are called n-*gons*.
normal	The direction in which a face or vertex points. Imagine a flagpole pointing straight out from the surface of an object. The direction it points is the *face normal*. Vertices and edges can also have normals when they are part of a surface.
mesh	A collection of vertices, faces, and edges that are all part of a single object.
topology	A term that refers to the way the faces of a mesh "flow" over its surface. (See Chapters 5 and 7 for more on topology.)
operator	Any operation you perform on part of a mesh, such as translating, scaling, duplicating, and so on. Operators generally take input from the user (such as the distance and direction you want to move something) and then do something to the selected object as a result.

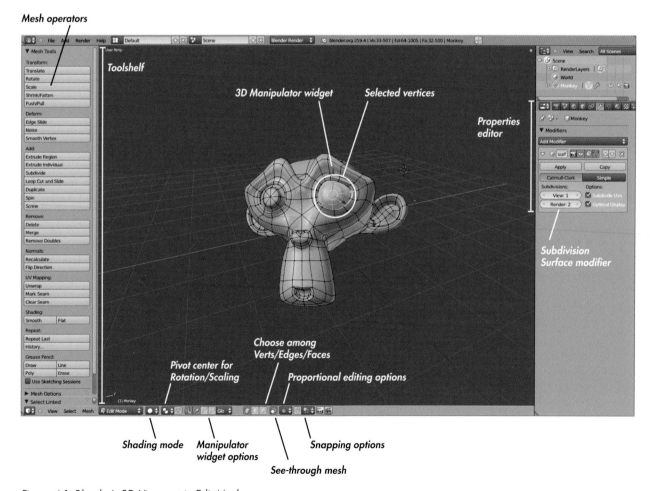

Figure 4-1: Blender's 3D Viewport in Edit Mode

Table 4-2: Frequently Used Operators in Edit Mode

Operators	Hotkey	Description
Delete	X	Deletes the selected vertices, edges, or faces.
Duplicate	SHIFT-D	Duplicates your selection and allows you to move it.
Extrude	E or CTRL-click	Creates new geometry by "pulling" new verts, edges, and faces out from the current selection. The results of extruding depend on what you have selected (see Figure 4-2). CTRL-clicking in Edit mode with nothing selected will create a new vertex wherever you click. Doing so multiple times will create a string of connected vertices.
Fill	F	If two vertices are selected, Fill creates an edge joining them. If three, four, or more vertices are selected, it creates a tri, quad, or *n*-gon from them.
Rotate	R	Rotates the vertices, edges, or faces you have selected. (You can also use the 3D Manipulator widget in Rotate mode.)
Scale	S	Scales the vertices, edges, or faces you have selected, allowing you to resize part or all of a mesh. (You can also use the 3D Manipulator widget in Scale mode to do this.)
Shrink/Fatten	ALT-S	Moves the selected vertices along the direction of their normals to inflate a mesh, almost like a balloon, or to shrink it to make it thinner.
Smooth	W▸Smooth	Smooths sharp angles between edges and faces so that the resulting mesh is smoother.
Subdivide	W▸Subdivide	Divides all selected edges into two and faces into four, creating more dense geometry.
Translate (also known as Grab or Move)	G	Grabs the vertices, edges, or faces you have selected and allows you to move them. (You can also use the 3D Manipulator widget in Translate mode to do this.)
Dissolve	X	An alternative to Delete, this deletes the edges or vertices selected but fills the hole left behind with an *n*-gon.
Connect	J	Connects two vertices that are part of the same face, splitting the face in two in the process.
Cut	K	Gives you a knife tool that lets you cut the selected geometry along the lines you draw. Hold CTRL to snap to vertices and the middle of edges.

❉ *Blender almost always has two ways of performing an action: through the UI and by using a keyboard shortcut and/or Search. In many cases, it pays to learn both because knowing how to quickly perform actions and switch between modes will greatly speed up your work.*

Once in Edit mode, you can select things by right-clicking them. You can extend your selection with SHIFT-right-click. To select or deselect everything in the current mesh, press **A**. To switch between selecting vertices, edges, and faces, click the vertex, edge, or face select buttons in the 3D Viewport header (see Figure 4-1).

Press **L** to select all parts of a mesh connected to the part of the mesh under your cursor. With part of a mesh selected, you can perform various operations on your selection in order to edit your mesh.

Table 4-2 lists the operators that you'll use most often when modeling in Blender. There are many other ways to interact with a mesh, but I'll cover those as we go along.

To learn more about an operator in Blender, search for it on *http://wiki.blender.org/*. You can easily discover more operators (or search for an existing one) using the Search menu (spacebar) or by looking through the header menus and panels of Blender's different editors. You can hover over buttons in Blender to see a tool tip describing what an operator does and whether it has a keyboard shortcut.

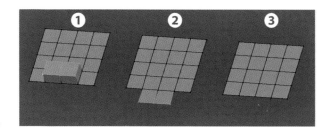

Figure 4-2: Extruding faces ❶, extruding edges ❷, and extruding a single vertex ❸. Extruding operations on different selections will have different results. Extruding vertices will create edges, while extruding edges or faces will create faces. Extruding an entire closed mesh (not shown) will duplicate that mesh.

In Edit mode, the **W** key brings up a menu with a lot of handy tools for modeling. All of the operators you will use in Edit mode can be found in the 3D Viewport. As of Blender 2.5, when you use most operators, the Tool Options panel will appear at the bottom of the Tool Shelf, allowing you to change, retroactively, the parameters of the operator you just used. For example, after applying the Subdivide operator, you can use the Tool Options panel to change how many subdivisions to apply and whether to smooth them.

Other Ways to Model: Curves

You can use Blender to create models in a number of different ways, including using various curves, *metaballs* (which behave somewhat like blobs of clay that stick together when they get close to one another), *NURBS surfaces* (surfaces constructed from cross sections defined by curves), text objects, and Bézier curves. Each has its place in modeling, but the most important (after meshes) are Bézier curves, which we'll use often throughout the modeling sections of this book.

Bézier curves define a path in 3D space and are constructed using control points and handles. They can be used to make both wire- or ribbon-like objects that follow the path of a curve (using closed or open curves) and flat surfaces that are defined by their outline (using closed 2D curves). Each control point has two handles that define how the path flows through that vertex, allowing you to create a wide array of smooth and sharp paths with a curve.

Modeling with curves works very much like using meshes; you can grab, rotate, scale, duplicate, and extrude control points or their handles. (You can't make faces from curves, though; you can only connect each vertex in a curve to two others.)

When working with curves bear the following in mind:

The geometry generated by curves is *procedural*. This means that the curves you define are used to generate a mesh according to the settings you apply to the curve in the Object Data tab (Figure 4-3) of the Properties editor. You can change things like the number of divisions per curve segment and the beveling and extrusion applied to the curve.

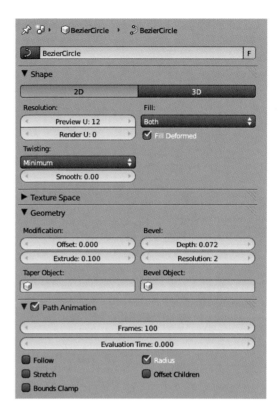

Figure 4-3: The Object Data tab for a curve object allows you to change between a 2D and 3D curve, set the density of the mesh created from that curve (Resolution), and define how the curve is beveled and extruded to create a 3D object (Geometry).

Curves can be open or closed. To close a curve, select its two ends and press **F** to join them. You can delete a segment of a closed curve by selecting two or more connected points and choosing **X ▸ Segment** to make it open again.

Curves can be either 2D or 3D. Points on a 2D curve cannot be moved along the curve object's z-axis, which allows you to create a flat object by defining its outline with a curve. Blender then fills in the shape with faces according to the Fill setting (see Figure 4-3). You can then extrude the outline of a closed curve to create a solid shape using the Geometry settings in the Object Data tab. You can also add details like beveled edges and change the curve's resolution here.

3D curves have a "tilt" that determines the direction of extrusion of the curve, as shown in Figure 4-4. You can see the direction of the tilt from the normals (arrowheads) displayed along the length of 3D curves. You can edit this tilt with CTRL-T, allowing you to create a curve that twists along its length.

Curves can be used to deform meshes. Mesh objects can be stretched along the path taken by a curve by applying a curve modifier to them.

The curve handles can work in one of several ways, as shown in Figure 4-5. The default is usually automatic or aligned, depending on the sort of curve object you add. Automatic handles simply create a smooth path from one control point to the next, with the handles pointing in opposite directions. If you grab one handle and move it, its control point will switch to using aligned handles that point in opposite directions but can be rotated and scaled, allowing you to create more flexible curves. You can change to other handle types using the shortcut **V** (or via the Curve menu in the header). Vector handles create straight lines between points with sharp

corners. Free handles create sharp corners too, but you can also grab them and move them around like aligned handles, allowing you to create curved segments between control points.

Modifiers

Modifiers allow you to procedurally and non-destructively perform operations on your models. They are fundamental to creating just about anything in Blender. Some modifiers generate new geometry, replacing or adding to your mesh, while others deform existing geometry according to certain rules or offer ways to plug simulations and other more complex entities into your scene.

We'll focus mainly on modifiers that generate and deform the meshes they are applied to because they're the most useful for creating models. Some of the most important ones for modeling are listed in Table 4-3. In particular, the Mirror and Subdivision Surface modifiers are used in practically all organic modeling. The effects of the most commonly used generate modifiers are shown on a half-sphere in Figure 4-6.

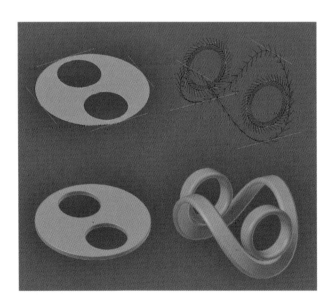

Figure 4-4: Different types of curves. Left: A 2D curve extruded and beveled to make a flat cutout shape. Right: 3D curves extruded to make ribbons. (The tilt of the curve defines how the curve twists.)

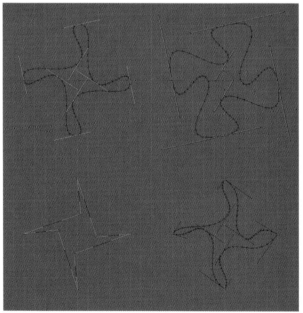

Figure 4-5: Curves with different handle types (clockwise from top left: automatic, aligned, vector, and free)

Table 4-3: Useful Modifiers for Modeling

Type	Modifier	Effect
generate	Mirror	Mirrors the geometry of the mesh along the specified axis, about the object's origin, or of another object. Mirror modifiers are very useful for creating symmetrical objects.
	Array	Copies the mesh geometry and offsets it using a fixed offset relative to the object's size or some other object. Arrays are useful for models with repeating elements.
	Subdivision Surface (Subsurf)	Divides each face of a mesh into four smaller faces and smooths them, creating a smoother mesh with each iteration. Subsurfs are useful for objects with smooth surfaces, particularly organic models.
	Solidify	Extrudes the geometry along its normals to create a solid shell from a surface.
deform	Lattice	Uses a 3D grid of points to smoothly distort the shape of a mesh.
	Shrinkwrap	Projects the mesh onto the surface of another object.
	Curve	Deforms a mesh along the path of a curve.

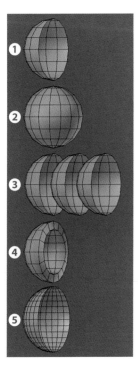

Figure 4-6: Different generate modifiers and their effects. From the top, we see half a sphere ❶, with a Mirror modifier ❷, an Array modifier ❸, a Solidify modifier ❹, and a Subdivision Surface modifier ❺ applied. Modifiers can be combined to create all sorts of shapes more easily than modeling them by hand.

Blocking in the Jungle Temple

Let's consider the Jungle Temple scene. For this project, my initial concern was designing a layout for the environment that lent itself to creating a nice composition. I began with only the main elements in the scene: a door into the interior of the temple and some stone blocks and trees strewn around the ruins.

To create the door, I added a cube in Object mode (SHIFT-A ▶ Mesh ▶ Cube) and scaled it (**S**) to about the size I needed. Once you activate the Scale operator, you can constrain scaling along one axis (by pressing **X**, **Y**, or **Z**) to scale the object in only

one direction. You can also scale on all *but* one axis by pressing SHIFT and **X**, **Y**, or **Z**.

Switching to Edit mode (TAB), I added a hole by extruding in the two outside faces and scaling them on the *x*- and *z*-axes only. Next, I deleted the center faces (**X**) and created new faces around the hole in the center by selecting two open edges at a time and making a face between them (**F**), as shown in Figure 4-7.

Back in Object mode, I added a plane (SHIFT-A ▶ Mesh ▶ Plane) and scaled it up to form the ground plane of the scene. Then I added a camera and moved it to roughly view the door I was looking for. A quick way to do this is to navigate to the view you want just within the 3D Viewport and then press CTRL-ALT-0 to snap the camera to the current view. You can also just move and rotate the camera like any other object. Note that this might result in the camera getting slightly tilted. You can rectify this by manually setting the Y rotation of the camera to 0, using the Rotation properties in the Transform panel of the Properties region (**N**).

From here, I added some simple walls to form the main boundaries of my scene simply by adding, scaling, moving, and extruding cubes. Next, I began adding more cubes, keeping in mind how they would become the final architectural elements of the scene, like stone walls, statues, and loose blocks of stone. This progression is shown in Figure 4-8.

With the simple elements blocked in, I began to add rough proxies for the trees I wanted growing over the ruins. To create these proxies, I added a Bézier curve object and set the handles to automatic. Then I used Blender's Snapping tools to extrude curves resembling the roots and trunks of trees over the surfaces of the placeholder objects (Figure 4-9).

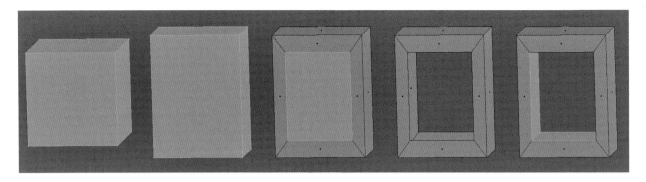

Figure 4-7: Making a simple door

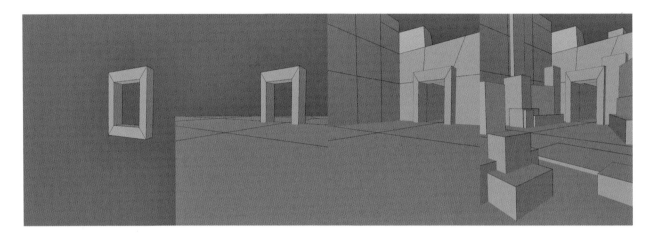

Figure 4-8: Blocking in with simple elements. I began with the door and then added a ground plane, walls, and cubes to represent major elements in the scene.

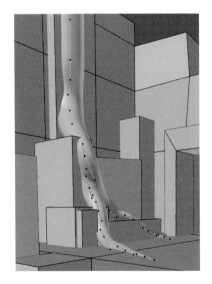

Figure 4-9: By snapping the tree roots to their surroundings, we can quickly block in tree roots crawling over the surface of the ruins.

I accomplished this by turning on Snapping, setting the snapping target to faces, and enabling Project onto Surface (Figure 4-10). This projects the curves onto the other objects in the scene as you move and extrude them, allowing you to "draw out" the trees over the top of the existing scene.

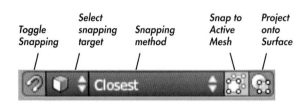

Figure 4-10: Snapping icons

Snapping

Blender has tools for snapping objects, vertices, faces, or edges to all sorts of things. To turn on Snapping, click the Snapping icon (the horseshoe magnet) in the header of the 3D Viewport (see Figure 4-10). Then, from the drop-down menu beside the Snapping icon, select how Blender will snap your selection when it's moved, scaled, or rotated from among the following options:

Increment   Your selection will snap to the nearest increment so that you can construct objects with precisely aligned points. This is useful for modeling things like buildings or mechanical objects where you want perfectly aligned walls and floors with no lumps or bumps. (You can also snap your selection to Blender's grid by pressing SHIFT-S ▸ **Selection to Grid**.)

Vertex/Edge/Face/Volume   Your selection will be snapped to the vertices, edges, faces, or interior of any objects. You can change what Blender chooses to snap to from the drop-down menu that appears. Click the icon to the right of the drop-down menu to rotate the selection so that it aligns with the normal vertices that it snaps to.

One very important snapping option is found in Face Snapping mode. Enabling Face Snapping causes the Project onto Surface icon to appear. Project onto Surface will cause geometry you create to snap onto the surface of existing objects as you move, scale, or rotate them around. This option allows you to create new topology over the surface of an existing object. In Chapter 7, we will be creating new topology over the surface of existing objects to better capture their shapes after we have sculpted the originals.

Base Meshes

To create the Bat Creature, I needed a simple base mesh that could be sculpted on. A base mesh is a simple model that captures the basic shapes of the model you want to sculpt. Once you've created a base mesh, you can add a Multiresolution modifier and begin subdividing and sculpting details in Sculpt mode (see Chapter 6).

Your base mesh should capture the overall proportions of the mesh and be designed to subdivide easily in order to provide a nice even mesh to sculpt on. We can retopologize the sculpted base mesh

later to create the final model, but working with very simple geometry now will leave more freedom for experimentation while sculpting.

A base mesh can have any level of complexity, but try to create topology that will support the forms that you know you want to create, without introducing too many details that you might not be sure about. Depending on how sure you are of what you want your model to look like, you can include topology for features like eyes, mouths, and muscle groups, or you can leave it as simple as a basic sphere or cube if you're just modeling a face.

For the Bat Creature, I aimed for a base mesh that gave topology for the overall body plan but left out fine details, such as the head. I developed the base mesh by setting my concept art as a background image and using it as a guide.

Building the Bat Creature Base Mesh

I started with the torso of the creature to provide a guide for the scale of the rest of the parts, as well as something to attach them to. To begin, I took the default *.blend* file (the scene you are presented with when Blender starts up) and deleted any objects already present. Then I loaded in the concept drawing for the Bat Creature (as shown in Figure 4-11). (For help with this, see "Using Concepts and Reference Images in Blender" on page 26.) While I didn't plan to use this concept to model from exactly, it made a useful guide for judging the proportions as I worked. At this point, I left the wings out of the base mesh for the body, as I planned to model them separately later.

Figure 4-11: Concept art loaded in as a background image

Next, I added a cube, changed to Edit mode (TAB), and scaled it to the rough proportions of the torso. I did this first in overall terms by just scaling it to the right width (**S**). Then I scaled up the *z*-axis (**S ▸ Z**) before scaling in on the *y*-axis (**S ▸ Y**) to make it taller and shallower. By adding horizontal loop cuts (extra rings of edges around the mesh, as discussed below) around the middle of the cube (CTRL-R) and moving them forward a little, I added a bit of curvature to the torso and began refining its shape.

At this point, it was easier to start using a Mirror modifier to keep my mesh symmetrical because the model was becoming more complex. To do so, I added a loop cut vertically around the middle of the torso and deleted its right-hand side. Adding a Mirror modifier then mirrored the geometry of the left-hand side of the body to create a symmetrical whole that only required editing on one side (see Figure 4-12). At the same time, turning on clipping keeps vertices on the midline from straying away from the object's *x* origin, which prevents holes from appearing in the mesh if you accidentally move a vertex slightly away from the line of symmetry.

Loop Cuts and Face and Edge Loops

A *face loop* is a string of quads connected end-to-end in a continuous path, allowing an *edge loop* (a chain of connected vertices) to be cut through the middle.

For example, in Figure 4-13, adding two edge loops around the face loop encircling the cylinder creates a new face loop running around the middle. Technically, an edge/face loop should be one continuous cyclical path, but the term is often used to mean any reasonably long chain of quads/edges.

The Loop Cut tool (CTRL-R) is extremely important because it follows a path of quads through your mesh, cutting through each one to create new edges that flow through the face loop. If you activate the Loop Cut tool and mouse over an edge, Blender will highlight the path in purple. If the path reaches a triangle or an open edge of the mesh, it stops.

Loop cuts are useful because they allow you to add definition to your model while maintaining clean topology. You can create multiple loop cuts by scrolling your mouse wheel after pressing CTRL-R and before choosing an edge to start cutting from (see Figure 4-13).

Blender has other operators for interacting with edge loops and face loops, including ones for deleting the loop (joining the faces on either side together to keep the mesh whole) and sliding the loop up and down the edges parallel to it. You can also select an entire edge loop at once to manipulate it. (If it isn't cyclic, Blender will simply find the longest path that it can.) These operators are detailed in Table 4-4.

As the next step in my project, I extruded down from the hips to make the leg and added loop cuts to flesh out its shape, as shown in

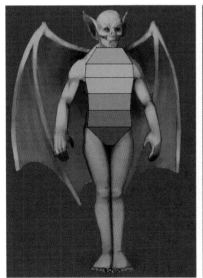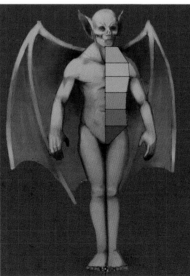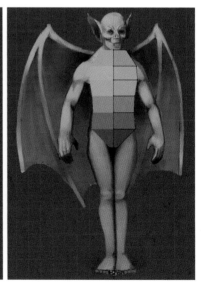

Figure 4-12: Adding a Mirror modifier to the body requires adding an edge loop around the middle and deleting half of the torso first. By default, the mirror modifier mirrors objects around the x-axis, but you can change this to mirror around any combination of the x-, y-, and z-axes, depending on your model.

Figure 4-13: You can add multiple loop cuts by scrolling your mouse wheel or entering a number with the keyboard after pressing CTRL-R. Loop cuts terminate when they reach a triangle or the edge of a mesh.

Table 4-4: Edge Loop Operators

Operator	Hotkey	Function
Delete Edge Loop	X ▸ Edge Loop	Deletes the selected portion of an edge loop, leaving the surface otherwise intact.
Edge Slide	CTRL-E ▸ Edge Slide	Allows you to slide all or part of an edge loop along the edges running perpendicular to it.
Loop Cut	CTRL-R	Creates a new edge loop starting from the edge under the cursor.
Select Edge/Face Loop	ALT-right-click	Selects an edge/face loop (depending on selection mode).

Figure 4-14. For the arms, I added a bend at the shoulder by extruding out from the body and then down from the bottom face of the newly extruded region, as shown in Figure 4-15. This gave the shoulder a nicer, more natural corner than it might have if I'd extruded down directly from the body.

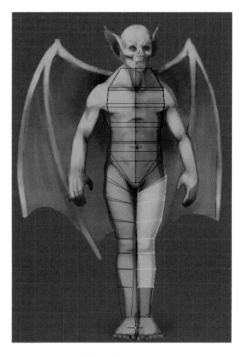

Figure 4-14: Adding loop cuts to the leg gave me more vertices with which to define its shape.

Poses for Modeling Characters

The pose you model a character or creature in is very important to its ultimate look, and your strategy will depend on what you want to use your model for. So far, I've modeled the Bat Creature in a relaxed pose that is close to the classic T pose: arms straight out and legs shoulder width apart. The T pose is useful when *rigging* a character (the process of creating an armature that tells the mesh how to move as if it had bones and joints). However, the T pose looks rather tense and unnatural when modeling, an effect that can stick around when posing a character into other positions. Instead, I wanted the character to look as relaxed and neutral as possible while in the early stages of modeling so that I could progress away from this neutral position later. By relaxing the arms down toward the character's sides, I eliminated this tension to make the character's default pose much more natural.

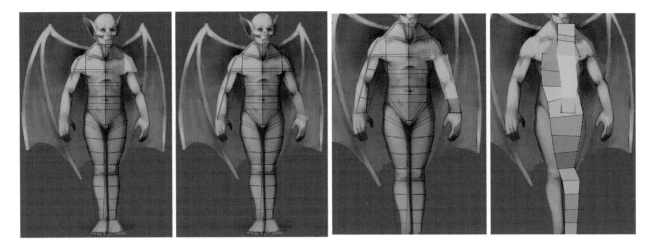

Figure 4-15: Extruding the arms. Creating a corner at the shoulders gave the arm a more natural shape.

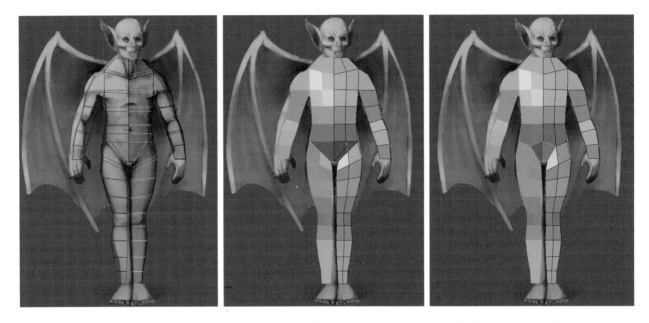

Figure 4-16: Adding an extra edge loop around the torso and legs and merging a couple of edges to clean up the mesh

Though we won't cover rigging in detail, note that there is a reason for the classic T pose. When it comes to rigging, having a character's arms out straight can make it simpler to set up bone chains and constraints. However, continuing improvements in Blender's rigging tools have made it somewhat less necessary to do this. You can always re-pose your model in the T pose after having modeled and sculpted it in a more relaxed pose.

Next, I selected all the edges running down the front and back of the body and legs and subdivided them (**W**) to allow me to refine the shape of the torso and legs. Doing so created some awkward topology at the pelvis, which I fixed by selecting the two new edges and merging them, as shown in Figure 4-16. I did the same for the edges on the backside, too.

I added an edge loop around the middle of the character as seen from the side (Figure 4-17) and running across the chest and down the arms. I then further refined the body shape, tucking in the waist at the back and rounding out the shape of the legs and arms. This step brought the number of vertices around the arms and legs to a total of eight, which would be important when adding hands and feet.

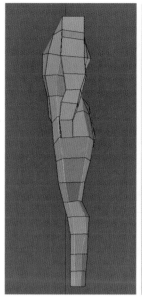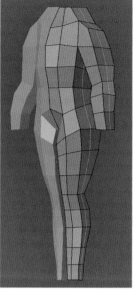

Figure 4-17: Refining the body in side view (left) before adding an edge loop running around the middle (right)

As I went along, I tried to make sure that my mesh was completely composed of quads, and I aimed to keep the size and shape of the quads approximately even and square. This is important when creating a base mesh for sculpting because triangles, *n*-gons, and long, thin faces generally create artifacts when sculpted on.

To create a loop of faces running around the shoulder (Figure 4-18), I selected the faces of the

arm and split them from the body (**Y**). I then shifted the arm out and bridged the edges around the gap using the Bridge operator (W ▶ Bridge Two Edge Loops). This connected two strings or loops of vertices together, filling them in with faces from one to the other. The two must have the same number of vertices to be joined.

Then I added some more loop cuts over various parts of the body, running across the forms, to even out the mesh and give an even distribution of roughly square quads (Figure 4-19). You can adjust the position of an existing edge loop using the Edge Slide operator (CTRL-E ▶ Edge Slide), which lets you slide edge loops up and down.

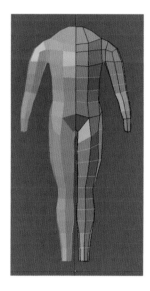

Figure 4-19: Adding some extra edge loops around the legs, arms, and torso

Modeling the Hands and Feet

To model the hands (as shown in Figure 4-20), I began with a cube and flattened it by scaling it down along its *x*-axis to form the basis for the palm ❶. Then I added some loop cuts around the middle and vertically ❷.

At this point, I could have extruded the fingers straight out from each face at the base of the palm. Doing so, however, would have created some nasty topology where the fingers meet each other that would neither sculpt nor deform well when posed. Instead, I did some extruding to add face loops that run between the fingers ❸. For the middle one, I simply selected half of the hand and extruded out. For the outer two gaps, I extruded in the middle 4 faces on the bottom half of the hand on both sides, as well as those connecting the two sides along the bottom, for a total of 10 faces.

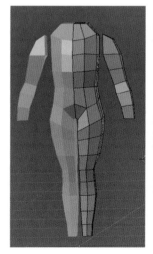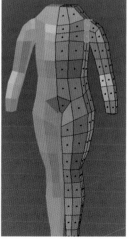

Figure 4-18: Adding a loop of faces around the shoulder. This loop made it easy to reposition the arm in different poses without deforming the chest.

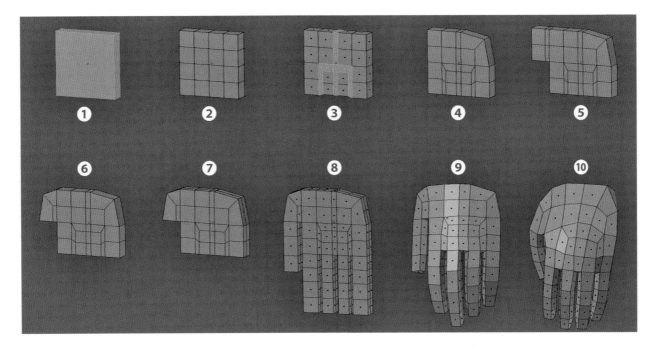

Figure 4-20: Creating the hand

To reduce the number of faces along the top side of the hand (where it will eventually join with the arm), I merged the two pairs of edges on the top corner of the hand opposite the thumb ❹. (Remember I was aiming to have eight vertices to join with the arm, so this area needed to be kept simple.)

For the thumb, I extruded out twice from the faces on the front of the hand ❺ and then merged the vertices on the corner to create a bend ❻. I then added a loop cut running around the outside of the hand ❼, extruded the fingers and the thumb ❽, and smoothed them slightly (W▸Smooth). Next, I gave the fingers and thumb a bit of a curl inward by selecting and first rotating the whole finger, then the last two-thirds, and then just the tip ❾. I also adjusted the shape of the whole hand by selecting parts of the hand from the top view and rotating them with proportional editing turned on to give the palm and thumb a slight curve.

I smoothed the hand slightly (W▸Smooth) to make the fingers and palm a bit less blocky. By selecting the surface of the palm, and with proportional editing turned on, I inflated it slightly (ALT-S) to give the hand a bit more volume ❿. This completes the modeling stages shown in Figure 4-20.

To connect the hand to the arm (Figure 4-21), I deleted the four faces in the middle of the top side of the hand, moved the hand into place, and then joined the hand with the main body in Object mode (CTRL-J). Then in Edit mode, I deleted the corresponding faces at the end of the arm and bridged the loops to connect the hand to the arm.

Because I kept the number of vertices around the end of the arm and the wrist the same, the hand joined to the arm with a minimum of fuss, as shown in Figure 4-21. Because the join now had two edge

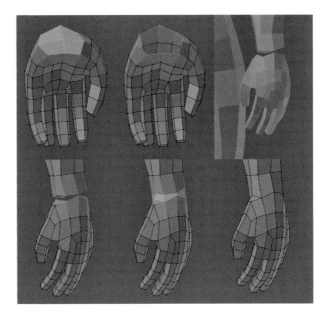

Figure 4-21: Joining the hand to the arm

loops quite close together, I deleted one (selecting it with ALT-right-click, then deleting with X ▸ Edge Loop) to create a more even distribution.

Modeling the feet was much the same, as shown in Figure 4-22. Beginning with a cube, I first extruded the general shape of the foot ❶. I added face loops to produce gaps between the toes (❷ to ❹), extruded the toes ❺, smoothed the foot a little ❻, and then merged the corner edges on the back of the foot to improve the way that the edge loops flow around the back and reduced the overall polycount, as I did with the hand ❼. I used Inflate and proportional editing to make the big toe bigger and refine the slope of the foot, which slopes down forward from the leg and down from the big toe side to the little toe side ❽. Again, because there are eight vertices around the circumference of the leg, I could delete four faces from the top of the foot and bridge the gap with the leg (❾ and ❿). Then

I cleaned up the edge loop distribution along the lower leg by sliding, deleting, or adding edge loops to get more evenly spaced edge loops (⓫ and ⓬).

Modeling the Head

The head began as just a cube extruded out, once at the front and then down at the base to create the chin (Figure 4-23). After adding a few loop cuts, I extruded out from the bottom to create the neck and then smoothed and refined the shape to give it a better silhouette and to make it slightly narrower at the front. I extruded out from the faces on the side of the head to create some geometry for the ears. Then, as with the body, I deleted half and added a Mirror modifier. Next, I connected the head to the body, deleting the faces in between and bridging the gap with the Bridge operator.

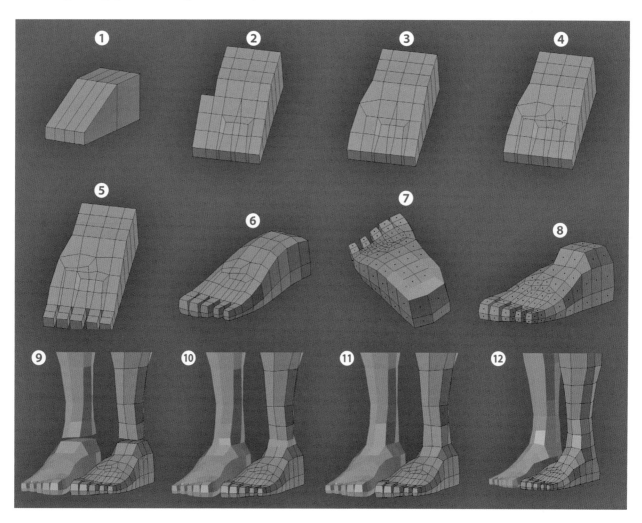

Figure 4-22: Constructing the foot

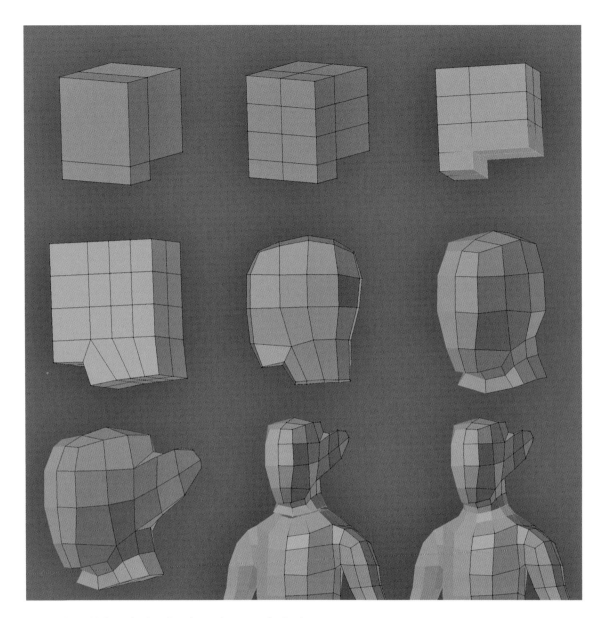

Figure 4-23: Making the head and attaching it to the body

✿ *Be sure that the* x *location of the origin of the head aligns with the body before joining it with* CTRL-J. *If you don't, the Mirror modifier on the body will have a different center than the head, causing it to split the head apart and forcing you to join the faces together again.*

Tweaking the Model with Proportional Editing

If you don't like the proportions of certain areas of your model, you don't have to tweak every vertex individually. Instead, you can use Blender's proportional editing to grab, scale, or rotate one vertex and drag nearby vertices along with it so that changes are made proportionally.

To turn on proportional editing, use the circular icon in the 3D Viewport header (as shown in Figure 4-1) or the shortcut key O. Once proportional editing has been turned on, you can adjust the distance over which the nearby unselected vertices are dragged (along with selected ones), as well as the falloff curve for the effect. To change the radius, scroll your mouse wheel while manipulating your selection. Select the falloff curve from the dropdown menu next to the Proportional Editing icon in the header. You can also set proportional editing to affect only connected vertices (ALT-O), which will drag only nearby vertices in the same mesh as those selected, allowing you to do things like move an arm without affecting your model's waist.

Different falloff settings can significantly impact the effect of transforming part of your mesh. For example, the Sharp Falloff option will create sharp peaks if you grab and move a single vertex, whereas the Sphere Falloff option will create bulbous, spherical shapes. The Random Falloff option is useful for roughening up the surface of a mesh; by grabbing a single vertex and moving it a little, with a wide radius for the falloff, you can add a slight random variation to the surface of a mesh.

Proportional editing is useful for many things besides tweaking proportions. For example, you can use it to create interesting curved or twisted deformations by grabbing or rotating parts of the mesh (Figure 4-24) or for posing characters without having to rig them.

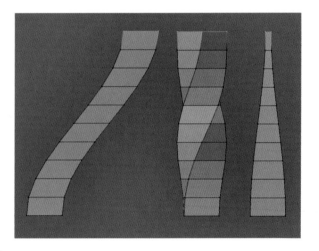

Figure 4-24: Proportional editing has many uses. Here it's used to deform a subdivided column using (left to right) Translate, Rotate, and Scale operations and the standard "smooth" falloff.

I used proportional editing to make a few tweaks to finalize the mesh, such as pulling back the arms and shoulders slightly and narrowing the back where it's level with the waist.

Creating the Wings

To make it easier to sculpt on the body and wings, I created them as separate meshes that I could join later when retopologizing. To create the wings, I first blocked in the skeleton using the reference

as a rough guide, beginning with a small plane and working along the length of the bones (see Figure 4-25). To make it easier to get the topology I wanted, I kept the mesh 2D at this point.

With the basic skeleton blocked in, I began filling in the wings between the bones. To make sure the gap could be filled in neatly, I spaced out the vertices along the bones so that they roughly matched up with one another, adding more as needed or shifting existing ones. Next, I extruded and scaled the edges to create a clean division between the wing and the bones, and I began filling in the gaps. (The extrusion/scaling won't produce perfect results, but you can tweak the position of the vertices manually to get a nicer layout.)

With the gaps filled in, I selected the whole model and extruded it back to give it some thickness, as shown in Figure 4-26 ❶. Next, I selected just the wing membrane areas and used the Shrink/Fatten tool (ALT-S) to make these areas slightly thinner again ❷. At this point, the wing had some thickness but was still very flat looking. To rectify this, I first selected its more central parts and shifted them back slightly to give the wing a bit of a concave shape ❸.

Sometimes Blender will calculate the normals of a mesh incorrectly, which can cause operators like Shrink/Fatten and modifiers like Subdivision Surface or Bevel to behave strangely. You can often see this if you set your mesh to draw smooth, as black boundaries will appear between areas with conflicting normals. To fix this, simply select your whole mesh in Edit mode and use the Recalculate Normals operator (CTRL-N) to force Blender to recalculate the object's normals.

Next I used the Warp operator (SHIFT-W) to give the wing a curve ❹. This operator uses the 3D cursor position as the center of the operation and arranges the selected vertices in a circle around that center. You can define how far the vertices are warped with your cursor; setting the 3D cursor further from the mesh before using the operator will give the curve a wider radius.

As a result of these treatments, I was able to add a nice curve to the wing by switching to the top view and using Warp. Also, by rotating the mesh and using Warp again, I could add a similar curve to the wing's profile ❺.

The Warp operator will often move the mesh about a bit, so I dropped back into Object mode (TAB) and moved the wing back to where I wanted it before applying the transforms (CTRL-A ▶ Apply Location and then repeat for Rotation and Scale, too).

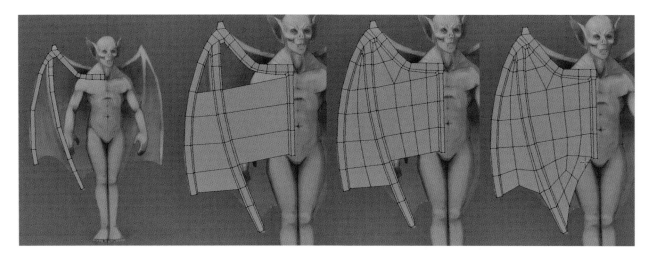

Figure 4-25: Blocking in the wings. Starting with the layout of the wing in 2D keeps things simple and makes it easier to produce the structure we want.

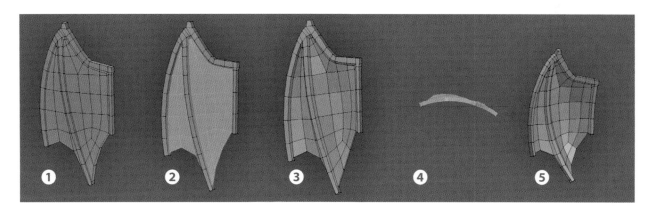

Figure 4-26: Blocking in the wings. The wings are extruded and the membranes between the bones made thinner. Then the whole wing is given some curvature using the Warp tool.

Applying Transforms

Operations like Warp can move your object out of place and require you to rotate, scale, or translate your mesh to put it back in place. It's often easiest to do this by moving the entire mesh at once in Object mode, though doing so will also affect the object's local coordinates, which can lead to strange results when using operators and modifiers. For example, I next wanted to use a Mirror modifier to copy the wings over onto the other side of the base mesh for the Bat Creature, but after using the Warp operator and moving and rotating the wings in Edit mode, adding a Mirror modifier would have given incorrect results (see Figure 4-27). The reason for this is

that by rotating the object in Object mode, I rotated its local coordinates, too. Because the Mirror modifier uses these coordinates to mirror the object, the results were not what you might expect.

To see an object's local coordinates, turn on the Axes setting in the Object tab of the Properties editor (see Figure 4-27). To reset the axes to match the global coordinate system, use each of the Apply Location/Rotation/Scale operators in Object mode (CTRL-A) in turn, which will place the object's origin at the global origin and match the rotation and scaling of its local coordinates to the global coordinates without affecting its shape. As a result, you'll be able to model, add modifiers, and perform other operations with more predictable results.

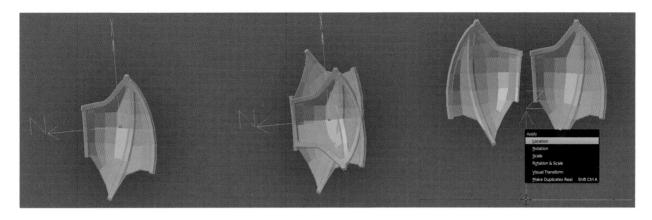

Figure 4-27: With the object's coordinate axes turned on, it becomes obvious why the Mirror modifier isn't producing the desired effects. Applying the transforms on the mesh before applying modifiers produces more predictable results.

Of course, instead of the above, you can manipulate an object's local coordinates to your advantage. For example, you could use a Mirror modifier to create a symmetrical object and then move and rotate it to a position in your scene that doesn't match the global coordinates. As long as you don't apply these transforms in Object mode at this point, the results of the modifier should stay the way you want them to.

Finally, as with the body, I added a Mirror modifier and then used proportional editing to better align the wings with the back and tweak the shape.

At this point, I had completed blocking in the bat's body, as shown in Figure 4-28. We'll create its final topology once the sculpting is finished, as discussed in Chapters 5 and 7.

Shading Modes

Notice that so far in blocking out the projects, I have kept the meshes we have been creating shaded flat—that is, the faces appear faceted and do not blend into one another. The reason for this is that it makes it easier to read at a glance the direction that the faces of a mesh are pointing and to see how the forms of the mesh are progressing. Later on, I will use smooth shading to render some of the models in order to make them look smooth (Figure 4-29), but for now this isn't necessary. To switch between the two, simply select your mesh, and in the Tool Shelf, use the Flat and Smooth operators to switch the shading of your selection between flat and smooth shading. You can do this either in Object mode, which affects the whole of each selected object, or Edit mode, which affects only the selected faces.

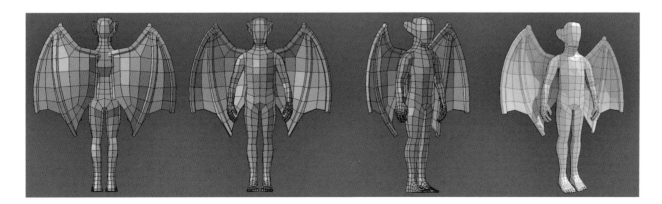

Figure 4-28: The finished body base mesh

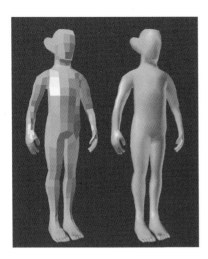

Figure 4-29: Flat and Smooth shading modes. Smooth shading blends between the normals of a mesh's faces to make it look smooth. You can switch between the two modes using the Shade Smooth and Shade Flat operators in either Object or Edit mode.

Creating the Spider Bot

To block in the Spider Bot, I needed only the basic parts of the body and legs. To generate more detailed ideas for the main parts of the body, I used sculpting and then retopologized the results and added more mechanical parts with traditional modeling.

Beginning with two cubes, one for the abdomen (back segment) and the other for the cephalothorax (head and body segment), I scaled them roughly to the correct proportions, as shown in Figure 4-30 ❶. By adding a Subsurf modifier (CTRL-1), I was able to get a more rounded shape without having to add and manually adjust lots of edge loops. Just adding

a couple more edge loops brought me closer to the shapes I needed ❷.

After joining the two cubes into the same object in Object mode (CTRL-J), I applied the Subsurf modifier at subdivision level 1 to give more geometry to play with ❸, but I copied the modifier first to further subdivide the mesh. When a modifier is applied, changes it makes to the mesh are applied to the mesh and thus converted into geometry you can edit. This allowed me to extrude some of the new faces from the front of the body to create a bump for the head ❹. With the extruded faces still selected, I pressed CTRL-+ to grow the selection, fattened it a bit with ALT-S, and then smoothed it a little to complete my base mesh for sculpting the body.

For the legs, I began by laying out my plan for the main part of the leg, consisting of long, flattened, bone-shaped pieces for the long segments of the leg and shield-shaped pieces for the knee and foot segments. I created two slightly different variations of the long segments, one for the first and last pairs of legs and one for the middle two pairs ❺. To create these pieces, I began with a plane, added a Mirror modifier to make the leg symmetrical, and then extruded one edge and added loop cuts to create the top-down plan of the leg. Next, I selected the whole thing (**A**) and extruded it out along its normals by first extruding (**E**) without moving the new faces. I then moved the new faces along their normals (ALT-S) to give the leg segment a uniform thickness. For now, I created only one copy of each piece; after sculpting and retopology, I'll duplicate the finished parts and position them to make the legs. This completes some basic parts for the Spider Bot.

Figure 4-30: Creating base meshes for the Spider Bot

In Review

This chapter laid the foundations for the models. For the Spider Bot and the Bat Creature, this entailed creating base meshes with simple topology that we'll later use to sculpt on and flesh out the designs of our characters. In the case of the Jungle Temple, I blocked in the most important elements of the scene with simple placeholder meshes. In the next chapter, we will replace and expand upon these placeholders, as well as model some extra details for the other two projects and discuss some more in-depth modeling concepts along the way. Then in Chapter 6, we will move on to sculpting the base meshes created in this chapter using Blender's sculpt tools.

5

MODELING THE DETAILS

In Chapter 4, we blocked in the basic elements of the projects, creating the block-in of the Jungle Temple and modeling base meshes for sculpting the Bat Creature and Spider Bot. In this chapter, you'll learn how to flesh out this framework to create finished models.

To create the final models, we need to transform our simple geometry using a mix of techniques. These techniques include using modifiers to add procedural details as well as modeling elements by hand. Our aim should be to end up with clean, well-modeled, detailed meshes, without overcomplicating things or introducing unhelpful geometry that could slow down renders or create artifacts.

Modeling details is great fun, but it can also be quite repetitive, so I won't exhaustively cover the process of making every part. Instead, I'll focus on key aspects of creating certain elements of projects that are the most interesting or tricky and leave the rest to your imagination. We'll begin with some discussion of topology, discuss what constitutes a "good" mesh, and then move on to the actual modeling.

Topology

Topology describes the way that the edges and faces of a mesh connect and flow across its surface. We covered the basics of topology when creating the base meshes for sculpting the Bat Creature and Spider Bot—namely, creating even loops of vertices around the arms and legs and avoiding triangular faces. Now let's talk about why we do things this way.

There are many ways to create meshes that have the same basic shapes but use very different configurations of faces in their construction, as you can see in Figure 5-1.

While the shapes in Figure 5-1 are roughly the same, the middle mesh is the most useful because its geometry flows with the form of the face, creating loops around the eyes and the mouth and running neatly down the neck and over the head. Also, it describes the forms of the head just as well as (or better than) the other meshes, while using fewer faces.

The flowing characteristics of this mesh are also important for animation because they allow the mesh to deform easily and smoothly. For example, closing the eyes or opening the mouth won't stretch edges awkwardly or cause parts of the mesh to intersect unpleasantly. This kind of loop-based topology also helps when creating further variations on the shape, and it makes it easier to place UV seams and to UV unwrap the mesh without too much stretching (see Chapter 8 for more on unwrapping).

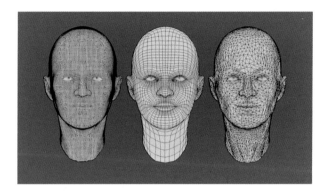

Figure 5-1: The same head shape with three very different meshes

Another reason that the middle mesh in Figure 5-1 is the better choice is that its topology is the best suited for use with the *Subdivision Surface (Subsurf) modifier*. The Subdivision Surface modifier, which we covered in Chapter 4, is used to subdivide and smooth a mesh. The algorithm used by the Subdivision Surface modifier, Catmull-Clark subdivision, works best when given a mesh constructed like this one. When the Subdivision Surface modifier is used with a mesh containing a lot of triangles or long, oddly shaped faces, it can give poor results, but when given well-constructed, flowing topology, it produces very predictable, smooth forms.

What Is Good Topology?

Good topology for animation is usually good for subdivision and vice versa. But what constitutes good topology? While there are no absolute rules, there are a few important principles. It's a mix of art and science.

Avoid triangles and *n*-gons where possible. This is the big one. While triangles are fine in a static mesh that you don't intend to subdivide or in a low-poly object for a game, if you plan to subdivide your mesh, use as few triangles as possible because triangles don't subdivide as well as quads. Equally, *n*-gons are converted to triangles before being subdivided, resulting in the same kinds of problems.

Avoid poles with lots of edges. A *pole* is a vertex where three, five, or more edges meet—that is, a point in a mesh that deviates from a grid-like structure. Like triangles, poles can create artifacts when subdividing a mesh. Poles with three or five edges aren't so bad—indeed, it's just about impossible to create anything but toroids and grids without creating a few poles—but poles with six or more edges subdivide poorly.

Create loops around important forms. This allows you to easily select, deform, and animate your meshes, and it also ensures they will subdivide cleanly. For example, in Figure 5-1, the use of edge loops that flow around the eyes makes it easier to adjust their shape.

Align edges with the form. If your object is roughly cylindrical, the edges of the mesh should flow around its circumference and along its length. If your object is roughly cuboidal, create it by starting from a cube and adding loop cuts. In general, try to create a mesh structure that goes with the "grain" of the shape you are trying to create, as shown in Figure 5-2.

Dealing with Difficult Topology

The rules listed above are simple, but you may run into trouble following them from time to time, especially when trying to eliminate triangles and poles from your models. Here are some tips for dealing with difficult topology:

Plan ahead. Most topology woes can be sidestepped simply by planning ahead. That's why, for example, we made sure there were eight vertices in the loops around the arms and legs when creating the base mesh for the Bat Creature: It made joining the hands easy, as there were no surplus edges to join together when it came to bridging the gap. Powers of 2 (8, 16, or 32) are often a good way to think about this, but regardless, try to keep to even numbers when creating edge loops. If you are new to 3D modeling, it can be helpful to sketch your desired mesh over a photo or your concept art, either in GIMP or on paper, as shown in Figure 5-3.

Two tris make a quad. You can join two adjacent triangles to make a quad, killing two birds with one stone. To convert multiple triangles into quads automatically, select your mesh and press ALT-J to turn suitable pairs of triangles into quads.

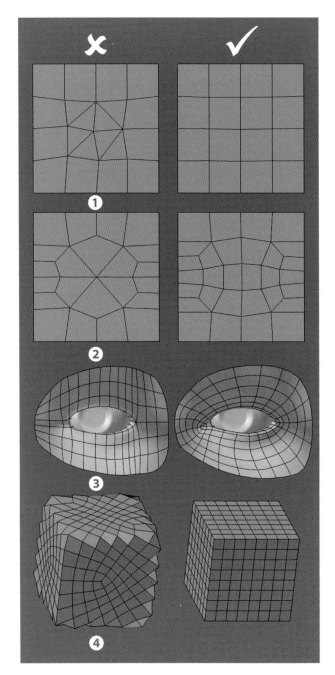

Figure 5-2: Topology dos and don'ts: Avoid triangles ❶, avoid poles ❷, create loops around important forms ❸, and align edges with the forms, not against them ❹.

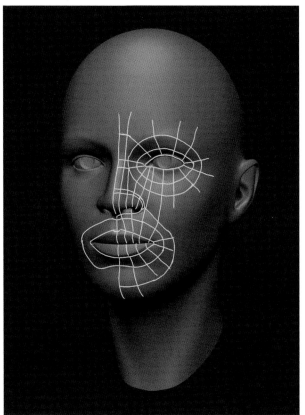

Figure 5-3: Sketching your topology beforehand can help you avoid difficulties.

Rotate edges to move triangles. To rotate or "spin" an edge, select it and press CTRL-E ▶ **Rotate Edge CW/CCW** (clockwise/counterclockwise). This rearranges the faces around that edge, allowing you to move triangles. You can combine this trick with the joining adjacent triangles trick above: By spinning edges to bring two triangles together, you can eliminate them, as shown in Figure 5-4.

Add an edge loop. Adding a loop cut (CTRL-R) that ends on a triangle will turn that triangle into a quad (or two triangles, which you can merge into a quad). If the new edge loop terminates at an open edge, you've eliminated your triangle. If your mesh is closed, it might just move the triangle to the other end of the edge loop, and, if you have triangles at both ends, you can take out two at a time (see Figure 5-5).

Split a pole in two. A pole with six edges can easily be split into two fives by adding a face loop between the two halves. Add further faces for even cleaner topology, as shown in Figure 5-6.

Cut, dissolve, and join. The cut tool (**K**) allows you to arbitrarily cut edges and faces to get the topology you want. You can combine this tool with the Dissolve operator (X ▶ Dissolve)

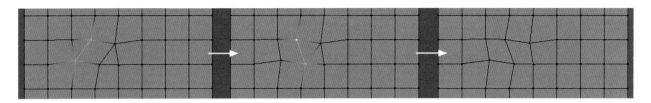

Figure 5-4: Rotating edges to bring two triangles together allows you to eliminate them.

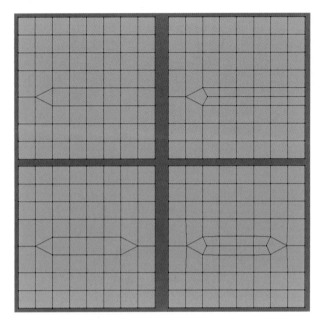

Figure 5-5: Adding edge loops with the Loop Cut tool (CTRL-R) can get rid of triangles. If you add one between two triangles, you can eliminate them both in one go. Alternatively, you could delete one of the edge loops already present with similar effect.

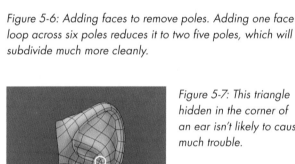

Figure 5-6: Adding faces to remove poles. Adding one face loop across six poles reduces it to two five poles, which will subdivide much more cleanly.

Figure 5-7: This triangle hidden in the corner of an ear isn't likely to cause much trouble.

to get rid of vertices' edges without deleting the faces they are part of. Then use the Join Edges operator to connect two vertices that are already part of a face but do not have an edge connecting them. These tools are great for arbitrarily rearranging difficult topology.

If you can't get rid of it, hide it. If you really can't get rid of a triangle, hide it where it won't cause trouble or create subdivision artifacts, such as inside an ear or nostril or someplace really flat that doesn't need to deform, as shown in Figure 5-7.

When in doubt, start over. If you managed to make something once, chances are you can do it again and get it right. It might take some extra time, but it's usually worth it.

Modeling the Details of the Jungle Temple

The Jungle Temple scene was already blocked in, so next it needed to be refined to make it more final. This process required me to think about the shapes I wanted to create and to model more complex meshes with the shapes I wanted in the final renders.

Walls

For the main walls of the Jungle Temple, I first laid out cubes to form the stone blocks of the wall (see Figure 5-8). Beginning with the bottom row, I added each one by hand and modified its length to give some variation. Next, I built up the higher layers by duplicating and scaling the cubes. To add further variety, I selected blocks at random, moved them in or out from the wall a bit, and rotated them slightly to make the surface of the wall somewhat more uneven. Leaving the basic walls from the blocking-in stage behind the new blocks provided a filler for the gaps between the blocks.

To add a beveled edge to the blocks (see Figure 5-8), I subdivided them a couple of times (select all [A] in Edit mode, then W▶Subdivide) and then added a Bevel modifier and set the "limit" method to Angle. The limit restricts the beveling to edges between faces at a sharp angle, and setting the angle to about 45° gives a nicely rounded bevel that is heavier on the corners of the blocks than at the edges. The sides are left alone.

 When applied, the Bevel modifier can create errors that will turn your geometry into triangles and create a lot of duplicate vertices. To fix this, apply the modifier only once you're finished modeling. Then, in Edit mode, select everything (A) and use the Remove Doubles (W▶Remove Doubles) operator to eliminate duplicated vertices. Next, use the Triangles to Quads operator (ALT-J) to return to a cleaner mesh without so many triangles. You can also bevel individual edges and vertices in Edit mode, using the Bevel operator (W▶Bevel).

Figure 5-8: Creating the stone blocks for the walls. First, I blocked in the walls with simple cubes, which I scaled and moved to build up the wall. Next, I damaged the walls a bit by adding some basic subdivisions and roughening some edges. Finally, I beveled the edges of the blocks using a Bevel modifier limited by angle.

For the block details, I subdivided some of the blocks and then added extra features, such as a crack down the middle, a chunk out of a corner, and a split. I added loop cuts or subdivided specific parts and moved vertices around to create cracks, dents, and chips. Because the mesh won't be subdivided or deformed significantly, there's no need to avoid triangles here; they won't cause problems.

To prevent the blocks from looking faceted, I set their shading mode to Smooth and then added an Edge Split modifier to split the mesh at certain edges in order to produce separate surfaces (see Figure 5-9). The Edge Split modifier breaks the mesh into separate pieces so that when shaded smooth or when further modifiers are applied, the edge between the pieces is preserved. You can set Edge Split to split the mesh either along edges tagged as Sharp in Edit mode (CTRL-E ▶ Mark Sharp) or along edges with sharp enough angles between their faces. Using the angles only with a setting of 30° resulted in nice-looking blocks.

I created the other incidental blocks and paving slabs in the same way as the walls, using the initial block-in cubes as a guide for placement and then deleting the old geometry once the new blocks were placed. The final blocks are shown in Figure 5-10.

Statues

I modeled the statues in the corners by the door of the Jungle Temple using fairly basic building blocks and my concept art as a guide. Each part began with a simple primitive—usually a cube or cylinder—transformed, subdivided, and extruded to create what I need.

As shown in Figure 5-11, each part is fairly simple. To add beveled edges, I used the same method that I used for the wall and floor blocks. Adding some loop cuts around the ends of some pieces (for example, to the "legs" and the ends of the arms) allowed these edges to retain their square shape and sharper corners when beveled, without too much subdivision.

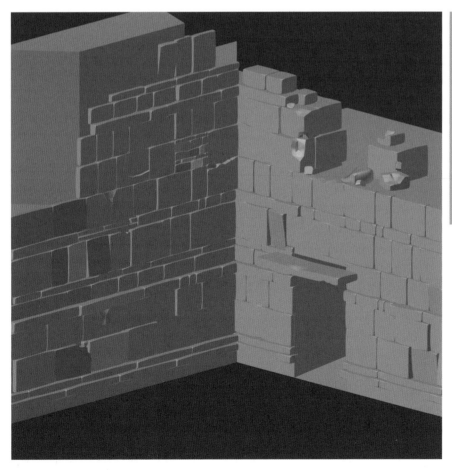

Figure 5-9: The final walls, with a Bevel and an Edge Split modifier to give them beveled edges and flat sides

Figure 5-10: The rest of the stone blocks in the scene were modeled in the same way as the walls.

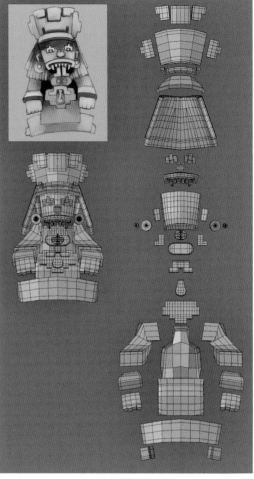

Figure 5-11: The statue model exploded into its constituent parts. Most are derived from simple cubes or cylinders.

Stone Carvings

For the stone glyphs, I used my concept art as a single orthographic reference, loading it as a background image, as discussed in Chapter 3. Then, beginning with a plane, I traced each piece of the designs, sticking primarily to quads where possible. Next, I extruded the whole design downward to give it some thickness and deleted the new faces afterward to leave just the sides and front of the design. By placing edges along the forms of the design's interior elements, I could move the grooves in the design downward to create the details.

To clean up the design, I used creasing (see Figure 5-12). By adding a Subsurf modifier and tagging edges as creased, you can create smooth objects with sharp creases along the tagged edges. Creasing

allowed me to add tight creases to the model without using more polygons than necessary. Adding an Edge Split modifier after the Subsurf modifier then gave a nice smooth mesh with sharp transitions at the creased edges.

With the carvings complete, I moved on to placing them in my scene by replacing some of the rows of stone blocks in the walls with rows of the glyphs. To do this, I lined up all six glyphs in a row and then used an Array modifier to repeat the design to fill the length of the wall (see Figure 5-13).

Tagging Edges

The edges of a mesh can be tagged or marked in a variety of ways, each of which tells different Blender operators and modifiers how to perform operations

Figure 5-12: Creating the stone carvings. I first blocked out the carvings as individual pieces over the concept art, using primarily quads. Next, I tagged some edges as creased (purple) to give sharp edges when subdivided. Finally, I added Subsurf and Edge Split modifiers to give smooth carvings with sharp edges where the edges had been tagged. The result uses fewer polygons and simpler topology than if I had used support loops to produce sharp edges.

on the mesh. The shortcut for Edge operators, including Tagging, in Edit mode is CTRL-E. Edges can be marked as Sharp, which allows operators like Bevel and Edge Split to work only on these edges. They can also be given a *crease* value, either from the CTRL-E menu or with SHIFT-E, which tells the Subsurf modifier not to smooth these edges when doing subdivision, resulting in nice sharp edges.

Sharp Edges and Subdivision

Creasing is one way to achieve a sharp crease in a subdivided mesh; another way is with *support loops*. Support loops work by placing two or more edge loops close together at the edge of a form. When the mesh is subdivided, the new geometry can't be smoothed out as much because the extra geometry defines the corner more tightly (see Figure 5-14).

Both methods have their place. Support loops are the better choice when you're trying to produce nicely beveled edges and need fine control over precisely how your forms look. However, if your goal is to produce very sharp creases or you are working with simpler models with less extra topology, creasing is preferable. You can always mix and match both methods as the situation demands.

Support loops are also useful for ensuring that objects subdivide to give the shapes you want. For example, Figure 5-15 shows a cube with a Subsurf modifier applied and its wireframe visible. With no support loops, the modifier turns it into a sphere. With extra support loops running around the middle of the faces, the object more closely resembles a cube, and shifting these support loops toward the edges of the cube makes the corners sharper. This is useful when modeling all sorts of surfaces.

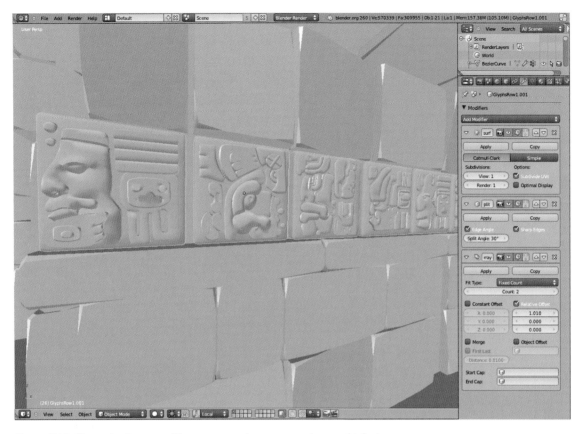

Figure 5-13: Using the Array modifier to repeat the stone carvings multiple times

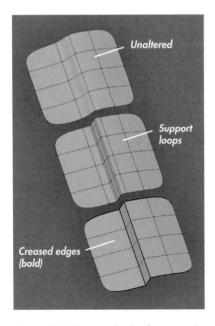

Figure 5-14: Two methods of getting sharp edges when working with a subdivision surface. Top: Unaltered mesh with a gentle slope and a Subdivision Surface modifier applied. Middle: Support loops added to give sharp edges. Bottom: Edges creased to give sharp edges (without extra geometry).

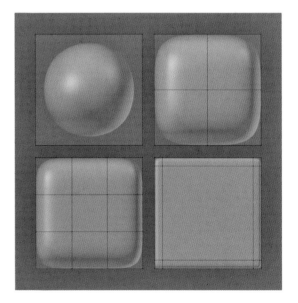

Figure 5-15: Clockwise from top left: A cube with zero loops, one loop, two widely spaced loops, and two evenly spaced loops running around the middle of each side. As the edge loops get closer to the edge, the corners become more sharply defined.

Plants

The plants in this scene are simple. To create them, I began by modeling a few varieties of leaves from planes; I scaled and subdivided the planes into leafy shapes (see Figure 5-16). Next, I started duplicating these different leaf objects and placing them around the scene. By creating linked duplicates with ALT-D, you can create multiple copies of the same mesh that all update together when you change one duplicate, which makes creating UVs and textures much easier because you only have to do so once for each type of plant. By scaling and rotating these duplicates in Object mode and placing them around the scene, you can give the impression of a lot of variation without having to create a lot of different meshes (see Figure 5-17).

There are two ways to duplicate a mesh in Object mode. One way is to create a simple copy, which then becomes a unique object (SHIFT-D); the other is to duplicate a linked copy (ALT-D), which retains the same mesh data and materials as the original and updates along with it. You can still apply different modifiers to a linked duplicate and move, scale, and rotate it independently in Object mode, but its mesh data and materials, as well as other data, will remain linked with the original object; if you edit one, the changes are applied to both.

Both methods are extremely useful for different tasks. Basically, you should use simple duplicates in the following situations:

- You want to edit the new object independently.

- You plan on recombining the new mesh with other elements in the scene.
- You want to keep the old mesh as a backup or alternative.

You should use linked duplicates if the following is true:

- You want to create many copies of a single object and don't want to edit them individually.
- You want only one set of UVs and materials for multiple objects.

When you select a linked duplicate, you can see how many users (copies) of that object are using the same datablock by examining its object data properties in the Properties panel (see Figure 5-18). You can also make the object unique by clicking the number icon next to the datablock's name. Making the object unique creates a new mesh datablock that

Figure 5-17: Duplicating the different plant components and placing them around the scene. Varying the scale and rotation of the duplicates can go a long way toward making them distinctive.

Figure 5-16: The plants were all made with very simple meshes (shown with a Subdivision Surface modifier applied).

is now independent of the one it was copied from, allowing you to edit the object's mesh and change its materials separately (as if it were a simple copy).

IvyGen

The IvyGen add-on for Blender is a procedural generator that allows you to quickly create ivy-like vines that creep over your scene (see Figure 5-19). To use it, first enable it from the User Preferences editor (**File ▸ User Preferences**) and then look under the Add-On tab in the Add Curve category. Once you have enabled the add-on, you should have the option to grow ivy on a selected object via the Add menu (SHIFT-A ▸ **Curve ▸ AddIvyToMesh** in Object mode).

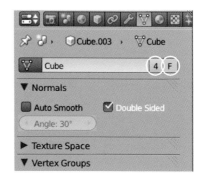

Figure 5-18: Checking the number of users of a mesh datablock. Click the number (4 in this case) next to the datablock's name to create a new copy that you can edit independently. The F icon will create a "fake" user of that datablock, which will save the object and prevent it from being deleted when you save the .blend file, even if there are no instances of that mesh in the scene.

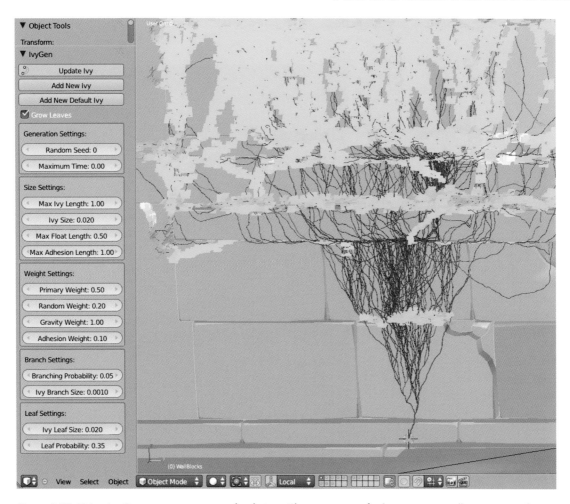

Figure 5-19: Using IvyGen to generate procedural vines. The parameters for how your ivy will grow are in the Tool Options region on the left when using IvyGen. For clarity here, I've added a green material for the leaves and a brown material for the vines.

In order for IvyGen to generate vines, it needs a single mesh object for them to grow over, so we need to create a new mesh that includes all of the geometry we want to grow vines over. To do so, select all of the objects you want the ivy to cover, duplicate them (SHIFT-D), apply any modifiers (using the **Convert to Mesh** operator in Object mode—ALT-C), and merge them into one object (CTRL-J). The result should be one object. If your scene has a high poly count, you might want to skip applying modifiers that increase the poly count a lot in order to give you a lower-poly mesh to grow ivy over; unfortunately, this may come at the cost of some accuracy in how it will grow.

Later, once you've finished growing your ivy, delete this duplicate or move it to another layer so that it doesn't get in your way (**M**).

Next, place the 3D cursor where you want the ivy to start and activate IvyGen with the Add Curve menu (SHIFT-A ▶ **Add Curve** ▶ **Add Ivy To Mesh**). The IvyGen allows you to tweak numerous parameters to determine how the ivy looks, the most important of which are the Max Ivy Length option, which determines how far the ivy spreads, and the Ivy Size and Leaf Size options, which determine the thickness of the vines and the size of the leaves. The leaf probability option determines the leaf density. Other options, like Float Length and Adhesion Length, determine how far the vines can reach out from the wall and how they are affected by gravity.

Keep tweaking IvyGen's settings and pressing **Update Ivy** to regenerate your ivy with any new settings until you're happy with the look of your foliage. Keep in mind that the higher you set the Max Ivy Length, the longer the ivy will take to generate. Also, if you want to cover a large area, it's easier to run IvyGen repeatedly using different starting locations in order to create multiple ivy meshes. For example, in the Jungle Temple scene, I hid the starting locations in the corners of the scene in a couple of different starting locations and let my ivy grow out from there. You can see the final results in Figure 5-21.

IvyGen also creates automatic UV coordinates for the leaves and vines it generates, as

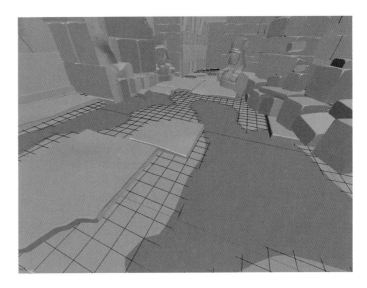

Figure 5-20: Adding puddles to the scene by first creating depressions in the main ground plane mesh and then adding a second flat plane to intersect with it

Figure 5-21: The final modeled Jungle Temple scene

well as assigning material slots to them. This feature will greatly speed up texturing and assigning materials to your ivy later. (See Chapters 8 and 12 for more on UV unwrapping and materials.)

Ground/Soil

To make the ground a bit more interesting, I subdivided it a couple of times and roughened it up a bit with the Sculpt tools, which I'll discuss in detail in Chapter 6. Next, I added a new plane (this time keeping it unsubdivided and perfectly flat) and placed it just below the average height of the ground so that some of the deeper areas poked down through it. This produces the effect of puddles on the ground (see Figure 5-20).

Additionally, I created piles of dirt in the corners of the scene simply by creating a plane, subdividing it several times, and using proportional editing to add lumps. By combining this with a bit of sculpting to build up dirt in the cracks and corners between the blocks and other elements, I was able to give the surroundings more of an aged look. The final scene is shown in Figure 5-21.

 While the following flows from the modeling techniques already discussed, the parts we are creating fit in alongside the sculpted and retopologized meshes we will be working on in Chapters 6 and 7. You can follow along with this part first or skip forward to Chapters 6 and 7 on sculpting and retopology and then return to this later.

Modeling the Details of the Spider Bot

For the Spider Bot, I needed to create the other mechanical parts of the body that will complete the model when combined with the main body and leg pieces I will be sculpting and retopologizing in Chapters 6 and 7. The aim was to create some feasible mechanical-looking parts, such as joints, wires, and so forth, that complete the look of the Spider Bot.

Joints

The joints were all designed from the same basic template: a cylinder for the central part, which allows them to move freely, with struts coming out that attach to the legs (see Figure 5-22). To produce the struts, I began with a curve object to make the

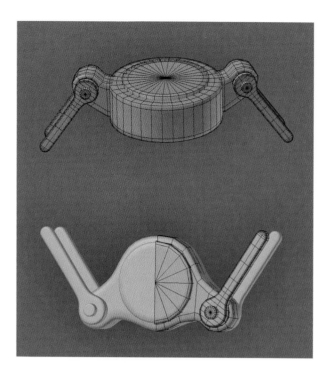

Figure 5-22: The leg joints. Both joints were created using a mix of cylinders for the simple parts and curves (converted into meshes) for the longer pieces. Adding support loops around the edges of the cylindrical parts allows them to subdivide much better.

basic shape a 2D curve, used the Extrude setting to give it some thickness, and then converted it to a mesh. Blender's default curve-filling topology is full of skinny triangles, which do not subdivide at all well, so I deleted these faces and filled in the front and back by hand to produce nicer topology (see Figure 5-23).

Wires

The wires are all created from 3D Bézier curves modeled around the legs and other areas to add interest and connect the parts (see Figure 5-24). To add further detail, I converted some wires to meshes to allow me to add some loop cuts and extrusions (see Figure 5-25).

For some of the more elaborate wires, I combined the Array and Curve modifiers to duplicate a single mesh along a curve (see Figure 5-26). First, I modeled a single unit (the ring-shaped object in Figure 5-26), and then I added an Array modifier and a Curve modifier to duplicate that unit and deform it to the shape of the curve.

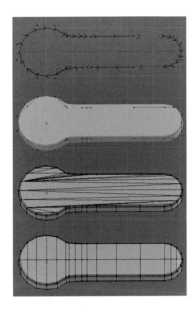

Figure 5-23: Creating the strut elements of the legs with curves and then filling in the flat surfaces of the resulting mesh with cleaner topology

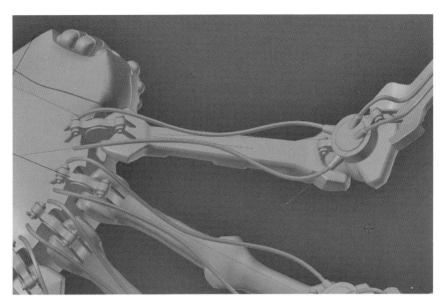

Figure 5-24: Creating the wires for the underside of the legs. These were made with 3D Bézier curves and given thickness using the Bevel setting in the Object Data panel.

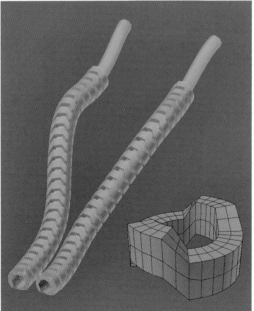

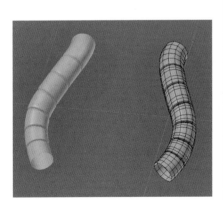

Figure 5-25: Initially, I modeled these tubes using curves. Then I converted the curves to meshes to allow me to add some loop cuts and scale them in to create grooves.

Figure 5-26: A more complex curved object, made by combining an Array modifier to duplicate the base unit (the ring-shaped object) and a Curve modifier to deform the resulting stack along a curve. I also used an Edge Split modifier and a Mirror modifier to mirror the results to the other side of the model.

Coupling

For the coupling between the body and abdomen, I initially created the shape with curves and then duplicated it and converted the duplicate to a mesh (ALT-C). Because Blender's default curve filling creates ugly, long triangles that don't deform well, I fixed the topology by hand by deleting the inside faces and filling in the shape manually (see Figure 5-27).

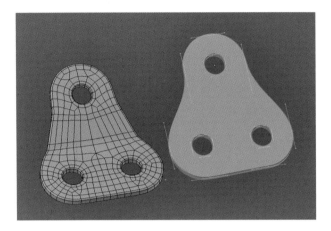

Figure 5-27: Creating the coupling. I converted the curve object (right) into a mesh and then deleted some of the edge loops around the edges to even out the distribution of faces. I filled the inner faces with nicer topology by hand. Then, using proportional editing, I added a bend in the middle.

Other Parts

I placed the Spider Bot's eyes using Blender's Snapping tools: I turned on Snapping to Faces, added spheres in Object mode, and then snapped them to the surface of the head. The fangs are simply cubes, extruded and with loop cuts added to make constrictions where they bend. I added some further embellishments using a mix of Blender's modeling tools and retopology techniques. (See Chapter 7 for these parts and the finished model.)

Modeling the Details of the Bat Creature

The final Bat Creature will consist only of one mesh for the body, which we'll discuss in Chapter 6, but it will need eyes, teeth, and fingernails, too. As these wouldn't be sculpted or retopologized in any way, I aimed straight for the final mesh.

Eyes

There are many ways to model eyes, but in general it helps to model some of the internal structure of the eye first to allow the rendered eye to catch light and reflections realistically. My model for the eye (see Figure 5-28) consisted of an outer layer, which will have a transparent material and which makes up the cornea and the reflective surface of the eye, and an inner layer, which will later be textured with the pupil, iris, and sclera (the white of the eye).

Both the inner and outer layers are made in the same way, beginning with a UV sphere (in Object mode SHIFT-A ▸ Mesh ▸ UVSphere) and then using proportional edit to push in the end of the sphere for the inner part or to push it out a little for the outer part to add a bulge to the cornea. For the inner part, after pushing the surface in with proportional editing, I extruded back the most central faces to create a pit for the pupil. For the cornea, I deleted the end triangular faces of the UV sphere and replaced them with a subdivided plane to avoid artifacts when a Subdivision Surface modifier is added (see the left of Figure 5-27). Using the To Sphere operator (ALT-SHIFT-S) can help you regain the spherical shape of the eye after adjusting its topology.

Teeth and Nails

Both the teeth and nails were derived from cubes (see Figure 5-29). To create the teeth, I began with a cube, scaled it down, and extruded from the bottom. By repeatedly scaling down the bottom of the tooth and then extruding again, I was able to refine the tooth into a point. I then positioned and duplicated the teeth and used a Mirror modifier to fill in the other side of the mouth.

For the nails, I flattened the cube a bit, added a loop cut down the middle, and moved it out a little to give the nail a bit of a curve. I then repeated the same process I had used for the teeth, refining them into a point and then placing them by hand and duplicating as many as I needed.

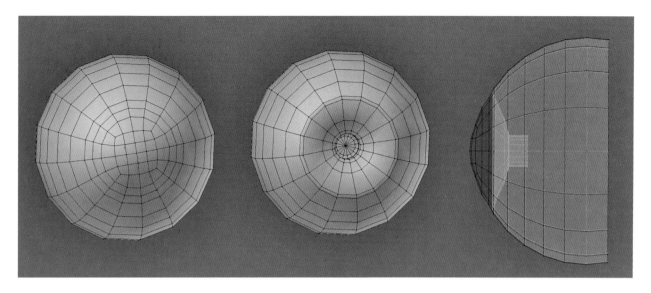

Figure 5-28: Modeling the eye. Left: The outer layer. Note the grid topology at the end of the cornea. Middle: The inner layer. Right: The two combined in wireframe view, shown from the side.

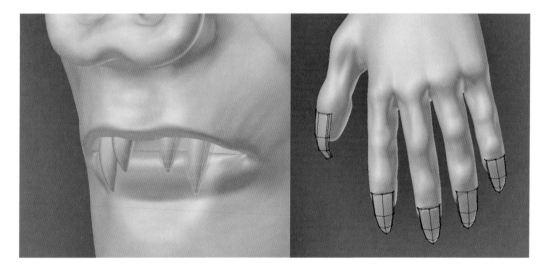

Figure 5-29: Modeling the teeth and nails

In Review

This completes our discussion of modeling the Jungle Temple scene and adding some extra details to the Spider Bot and Bat Creature projects. You've learned how to use a variety of Blender's modeling tools, including modifying existing meshes with modifiers, applying the results of these modifiers so you can edit the results, modeling with curves

and adjusting the results, and modeling parts from scratch using primitives and extrusions to build up complex forms.

In the next chapter, we will move on to sculpting in Blender using the Multiresolution modifier and Sculpt tools to create detailed organic and hard-surface forms. In Chapter 7, you'll learn how to retopologize these forms using Blender's modeling tools in order to create your models.

6

SCULPTING

The addition of sculpting tools to Blender's arsenal has vastly broadened the range of creations possible and the level of detail we can add to our creations. In addition, sculpting allows for much more freedom in the route taken to create a model; prior to its introduction, we had to labor to create topology to support each element of a model. Now, with sculpting, we can start from a much simpler mesh, use multiresolution subdivision to provide the level of control necessary to support the forms we want, and worry about the topology later.

In this chapter, we'll introduce Blender's sculpting tools and show you how to use Sculpt mode. We'll look at customizing the appearance of Sculpt mode and the tools you can use to get the most out of Blender when sculpting. Then, we'll move on to using these tools to start sculpting on the base meshes we created in Chapter 4, taking them from simple, low-res base meshes to highly detailed, sculpted models. Finally, we'll look at some general principles for sculpting.

Sculpt Mode

In order to sculpt in Blender, you'll need to enter Sculpt mode in the 3D Viewport, as shown in Figure 6-1. Once in Sculpt mode, make sure you have the Tool Shelf open (**T**), as this is where you'll find all of Blender's Sculpt mode options and tools.

The familiar Tool Shelf on the left of the Viewport is now home to our Brush options for sculpting, where we can choose between different brushes and adjust their settings. Brush options include the type of brush; whether it will utilize pressure input from a graphics tablet (recommended if you have one); and the size, falloff, and shape of the brush. Figure 6-1 also shows how the 3D Viewport has been set up to make sculpting easier—you use Blender's GLSL shading and enable Only Render to display only objects that will be rendered. This keeps the grid and any superfluous objects in your scene, such as lamps and cameras, out of your way while sculpting. We will cover these settings in more depth in "Customizing the 3D Viewport" on page 73.

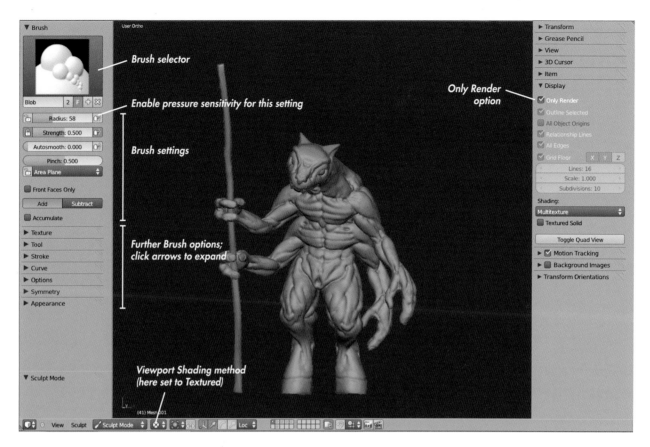

Figure 6-1: Sculpt mode, with the Viewport display mode set to Textured (with GLSL shading) and Only Render enabled. The Tool Shelf, on the left, contains most of Blender's sculpting tools and options.

Brush Options

The Brush options are shown at the left of Figure 6-1. Click a selected mesh in the 3D Viewport to begin sculpting.

Running down the list of panels in the Tool Shelf at the left of Figure 6-1 in order (some are collapsed, but their titles are all visible), we have the following:

Brush   Here, you can select which brush to use; the brush properties, such as radius, strength, and autosmooth; whether the brush should add or subtract from the surface; and some options specific to individual brushes. You can also create new brushes from the Brush selector by clicking the + icon. Doing so will duplicate the current brush, creating a copy that you can modify separately.

Texture   This panel allows you to create strokes with unique shapes and textures or to drag out patterns onto the surface of your mesh.

Brush textures use the brightness of the texture to determine how strongly to apply the brushstroke. While you can use color images for brushes, it's more common to simply use black and white textures to make it easier to judge their effects. (In order to distinguish brush textures from other kinds of textures, I'll often refer to them as *alphas*.)

Tool   While the brushes in the Brush selector have names like Clay and Smooth, you can change these names as you please. The actual behavior of any brush is determined by the choices you make in the drop-down menu in this panel, which allows you to choose from all of the base tool types Blender has to offer before customizing them further.

Stroke   This panel contains options for how your mouse or tablet strokes are converted into sculpting strokes. The default method for most brushes, *Space*, creates a uniform brushstroke. *Anchored* allows you to click and drag out a large stroke over your mesh, centered around the starting point of the stroke and with a radius determined by how far you drag. This option is extremely useful for dragging out textures over the surface of your mesh in order to create surface detail. Another option, *Smooth Stroke*, causes your strokes to lag behind your cursor as you pull it around, resulting in clean, smooth curves.

Curve   This panel lets you choose the brush's fall-off curve (see Figure 6-2) and gives you fine control over how the depth of your strokes fades away from the center. You can either define the curve manually by dragging and clicking to move and adding points to the Curve editor, or you can choose one of the presets from the icons below the Curve editor. The default *Smooth* curve is fine for most brushes, but when dragging out alphas, the flat *Max* curve is useful. For fine creases, the *Sharp* curve is best.

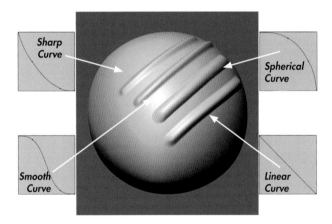

Figure 6-2: Different Falloff settings

Options   This panel contains mainly miscellaneous options. One option is whether to constrain sculpting to individual axes. Another determines whether to keep your brush size and strength universal or to let you set it for each brush. (Maintaining a universal brush size is often less confusing, but it's usually preferable to choose strength for each brush individually, as you may want different strengths for different tools.)

Symmetry   Just as you would use a Mirror modifier for a normal mesh, you can enable Symmetry when sculpting to keep your brushstrokes symmetrical. This is a useful option for a lot of sculpting as most organic creatures are broadly symmetrical.

Appearance   This panel contains some aesthetic options for changing the color of the brush cursor or adding a custom icon for your brush.

Brush Types

The default brush types, which are found in the Tool panel (see Figure 6-3), are discussed below. Some have hotkeys (in brackets) that allow you to quickly cycle through any brushes of that type that you have created. Almost all brushes (Grab, Nudge, Thumb, and Snake Hook are the only exceptions) also have a Subtractive mode (ALT) that usually does the opposite of what the brush does in Additive mode.

Blob   This brush type creates blob-like inflated lumps in the surface of your mesh. This option is a bit of a mix between the Draw and Inflate brushes. Additive mode builds out, while Subtractive cuts in.

Clay (C)   One of the most important brush types, the Clay brush builds up the surface of your mesh evenly, filling valleys first and then building up smoothly from the surface of the mesh.

Figure 6-3: The Tool panel lets you choose between the different base brush types.

You'll find this brush type useful throughout the sculpting process, though beware when adding fine details, as it will build up over them (use the Draw brush instead). Additive mode builds out, and Subtractive mode carves into the mesh.

Crease (SHIFT-C)   This brush type combines the Draw and Pinch brush types, drawing a stroke out on the mesh and then pinching it to make it tighter. It is most useful in Subtractive mode, where it's great for creating wrinkles and creases in a character's skin, but it can also be used in Additive mode to create sharp edges by tracing along the edge of a form.

Draw (D)   The Draw brush type draws a stroke out from the surface, moving the surface without changing the details underneath. If you use Draw early on when sculpting large-scale forms, it may make life difficult, as it can result in a rather lumpy look (which is why the Clay brush is more useful). Later on though, when adding fine details, the Draw brush type is very handy.

Fill   This brush type fills in valleys in the surface of the mesh without touching the peaks. It is useful for smoothing out and filling in concave areas in a mesh without affecting the surrounding areas. Subtractive mode deepens the valleys instead of filling them in.

Flatten   The Flatten brush combines the Fill and Scrape brush types, filling in valleys and scraping away peaks to create a smoother surface. Unlike the Smooth brush type, this brush flattens the surface in addition to smoothing it. In Subtractive mode, this brush type exaggerates the valleys and peaks instead of flattening them.

Grab (G)   This brush type grabs the area under the brush and lets you pull it around. You'll find this to be a very useful brush type.

Inflate (I)   The Inflate brush type inflates the mesh in much the same way the Shrink/Fatten operator does in Edit mode. Inflate is useful for establishing volumes and is sometimes a good alternative to the Draw or Clay brushes, but be sure to keep the strength of this brush low or it can do some damage. Also, be aware that in addition to pushing the surface outward (or inward), this brush usually makes faces bigger, reducing the amount of detail that the modified area can support. In Subtractive mode, this brush shrinks the mesh instead, often causing the mesh to self-intersect. Use it carefully.

Layer (L)   This brush type builds out an even layer from the surface of your mesh or subtracts an even layer in Subtractive mode.

Nudge   Like the Grab brush type, this brush type only nudges the mesh a small distance, and you can keep moving your cursor around to other areas to nudge them as well.

Pinch (P)   This brush type pulls faces under the brush closer together, creating a pinching effect. This brush is useful for tightening creases and wrinkles or for sharpening edges between forms on hard-surface sculpts. In Subtractive mode, this brush pushes the faces farther apart.

Rotate   This brush type rotates the area under the brush around the mesh's origin. I find this pretty useless as a brush type.

Scrape   The Scrape brush type scrapes away the peaks of a mesh without touching the valleys. This brush type is really useful for establishing planes, eliminating lumps and bumps, and smoothing transitions between overlapping forms. Subtractive mode builds the peaks up rather than scraping them down.

Snake Hook   This brush type allows you to pull out a tentacle-like surface from your mesh. Use this brush type sparingly because the topology underneath will probably not support it too well. This option is good for pulling out peaks to look like strands of hair or horns, especially if you plan on correcting the ugly topology later.

Thumb   The Thumb brush type slides the surface of the mesh around under the brush but only on the plane of the direction the surface is facing. This is similar to the Grab brush, except that it allows you only to shift the surface of the mesh around rather than letting you push or pull the surface of the mesh outward or inward.

All of the brushes in Blender's Brush panel (see Figure 6-4) are just variations on the types listed above, with various tweaks to give each brush slightly different effects. For example, the Polish brush is a variation on the Flatten brush with the Autosmooth setting (which adds a smoothing effect to any brushstroke) turned up.

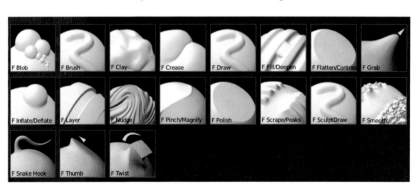

Figure 6-4: Blender's default sculpt brushes

Creating Custom Brushes

Now that we've taken a look at some of Blender's built-in brushes, let's look at how to create custom ones to better suit our needs. As explained earlier, Blender's sculpting brushes are all variations on the same initial set of brush types; the differences come from changing the settings that affect how these brushes function. You'll want to change some settings frequently, like the radius of the brush and its strength. If you end up using a certain set of brush settings often, it's a good idea just to give them their own brush.

To create a new sculpting brush, select an existing one similar to the one you want to create, and then press the + icon in the Brush selector next to its name to create a new, unique brush. Now, modify the new brush by changing its strength, assigning textures and stroke options, and so on.

To demonstrate, let's create a few custom brushes that will come in handy when sculpting.

Clay Tubes

The Clay Tubes brush (see Figure 6-5) will be great for sculpting early on. It works the way traditional clay sculptors work by adding strips of clay to the surface of a sculpture to build up forms. To create a brush that mimics this technique in Blender, take the following steps:

1. Duplicate the default Clay brush.

2. In the Texture panel, add a new texture to use as an alpha for the brush by clicking the + icon in the Texture selector. This creates a new texture and assigns it to the brush. Name it something useful, like *Clay Tubes*.

3. To edit this texture, open the **Texture tab** of the Properties editor (see Figure 6-6), and make sure you have the brush icon selected to edit brush textures.

4. In the Type drop-down menu, choose **Image or Movie** and then select an image to use as a brush texture by opening or adding an image from the Image panel. For this brush, I created a very simple, slightly blurred white square on a black background in GIMP, which I then loaded as the brush texture.

5. With the texture loaded, return to the 3D Viewport Tool Shelf, and set the brush angle setting (in the Texture panel of the Tool Shelf, as shown in Figure 6-5) to **Rake** to make the alpha rotate to match the direction of the stroke. Now we'll have nice square strokes with a slight texture that will be great for building up forms like muscles and wrinkles and for quickly blocking in large shapes.

6. To stop the usual falloff of the brush, set the falloff curve to the flat **Max** preset in the Curve panel.

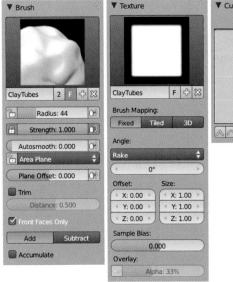
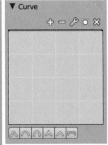
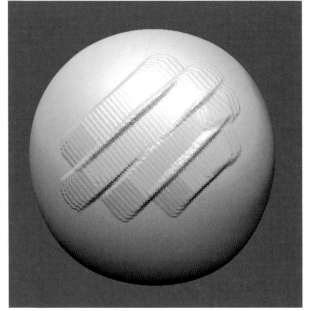

Figure 6-5: The Clay Tubes brush

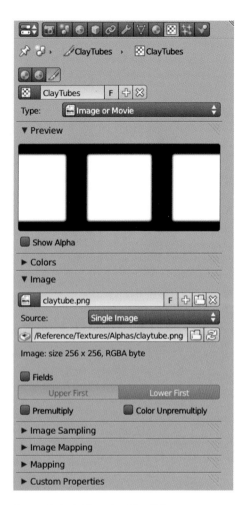

Figure 6-6: Adding the Clay Tubes texture

Rake

Like the Clay Tubes brush, the Rake brush (see Figure 6-7) is based on traditional sculpting. Clay sculptors often use a toothed scraping tool, a *rake*, to scrape away at the clay surface to produce a fine texture and smooth forms. In Blender, the Rake brush is great in both Additive *and* Subtractive modes.

Like the Clay Tubes brush, the Rake brush starts out by duplicating the default Clay brush and then adding a custom alpha, though this time we use a line of blurred dots or squares, as shown in Figure 6-7. To create the Rake brush, take the following steps:

1. Duplicate the Clay brush as you did for the Clay Tubes brush above.

2. Add a texture to the brush, as you did for the Clay Tubes brush. See Figure 6-7 for the kind of texture needed.

3. Set the angle to (surprise!) **Rake**, and enable **Autosmooth** in the Brush panel of the 3D Viewport Tool Shelf, setting its value to about **0.25**. (This adds some smoothing to the brushstrokes to keep the texture from getting out of control.)

4. Set the falloff of the brush to flat (Figure 6-7).

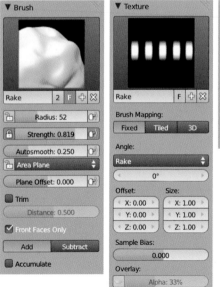

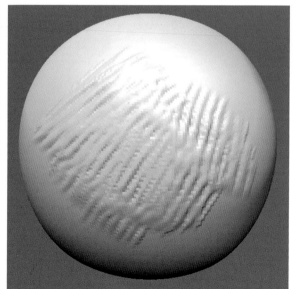

Figure 6-7: The Rake brush

Scrape Flat

The Scrape Flat brush (see Figure 6-8) creates nice flat, faceted surfaces in a mesh. It's great for sculpting jagged rocks and hard, technical surfaces and for quickly establishing clear planes in organic models that you can smooth and refine later.

To create this brush, do the following:

1. Duplicate the Scrape brush.
2. Lock the **Area Plane** of the new brush by clicking the padlock icon next to its option (as shown in Figure 6-8). Now, the surface normal of the surface under the brush when you first begin the stroke will be extended throughout the whole stroke, producing a nice flat surface.
3. Set the brush's Plane Offset to around **0.1** (see Figure 6-8) to make the brush cut more deeply into the surface. This setting determines how deeply the brush affects the surface for positive values or raises its effects away from the surface for negative values.

Try changing the tool type for this brush to the Flatten, Fill, or Clay tools, as they work well with these settings, too.

Figure 6-8: The Scrape Flat brush

Crease Lazy

This brush is a variation of the standard Crease brush. With the Smooth Stroke setting activated, the Crease Lazy brush is good for creating long, smooth creases. To create the Crease Lazy brush, as shown in Figure 6-9, follow these steps:

1. Duplicate the Crease brush and turn on **Smooth Stroke**.
2. For both this and the regular Crease brush, I like to turn up the strength of the brush to between 0.6 and full strength and turn the pinch value down to around 0.1 or 0.2. (I find the default pinch strength a bit heavy.)

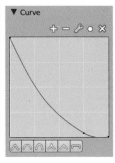
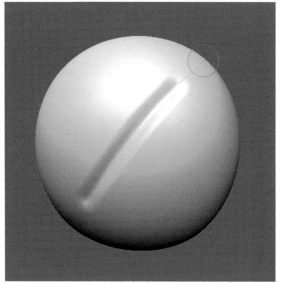

Figure 6-9: The Crease Lazy brush

Drag Alpha

The Drag Alpha brush uses the anchored stroke setting to drag alphas over the surface of a mesh, but otherwise it's just a basic Draw brush. You can create this brush, shown in Figure 6-10, by taking the following steps:

1. Duplicate the Draw brush and add a texture. Most any texture will work; I chose a rocky image.

2. Because you can use all sorts of textures with this brush, different falloff curves are useful. For images with a natural built-in falloff to them, like the Clay Tubes and Rake textures (that are black around the edges), you can set the curve to Flat. For textures that you've created from photos or other images that don't have natural falloff (the pattern covers the whole image), use one of the preset curves. A preset curve creates a nice transition so that the alpha won't produce an obvious edge when drawn out over your mesh.

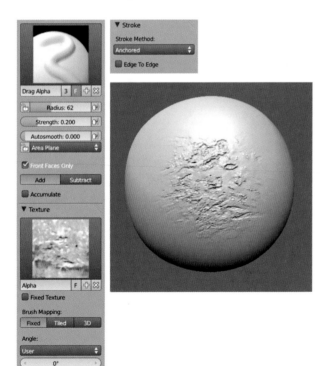

Figure 6-10: The Drag Alpha brush, used here with a rough concrete alpha texture

Making Brushes Available by Default

In order to load your custom brushes by default, you need to include them with your default *.blend* file, the file that loads up every time Blender starts. To do this, create a new *.blend* file, create (or append) any brushes you want to make available by default, and then save the modified file (**File ▶ Save User Settings**). To append into an existing brush, choose **File ▶ Append** (or SHIFT-F1); then select the *.blend* file where you created your brushes, select **Brushes**, choose the brushes you want, and click **Append**. Now your custom brushes will be available whenever you want to sculpt.

Improving Your Sculpting Experience

To get the best from Sculpt mode, you need to tweak Blender's settings a bit. The goals are twofold: to ensure that you get the best performance while sculpting and to configure Blender's 3D Viewport and materials to make it easier to see the effects of your brushstrokes on your model while sculpting.

Optimizing Sculpting Performance

Of course, the best way to improve sculpting performance is to use a powerful computer with a lot of RAM. At minimum, you'll need 4GB of RAM if you plan on going into the millions of polys, but more certainly won't hurt. But barring hardware upgrades, here's how to make the most of what you have.

Close other programs. If you're rendering in another instance of Blender or burning a DVD at the same time, your sculpting performance will suffer!

Enable VBOs (Vertex Buffer Objects). Open Blender's User Preferences (**File ▶ User Preferences** or CTRL-ALT-U), go to the System tab, and select the **VBOs** checkbox. This will boost the performance of the 3D Viewport if your graphics card supports VBOs.

Turn on Fast Navigate. You'll find Fast Navigate in the 3D Viewport Tool Shelf under Options. Fast Navigate causes your model to switch back to a lower subdivision level when you move or rotate the 3D Viewport, speeding up navigation while sculpting.

Subdivide before adding a Multires modifier. If you are working from a reasonably dense base mesh, like the ones we created in Chapter 4, you don't need to perform this step. However, if you intend to start from a cube, add and apply a Subsurf modifier before adding a Multires modifier to speed up sculpting.

This works because, under the hood, Blender looks at how much of the mesh it needs to update based on how many faces of the underlying base mesh were covered by the brushstroke. For example, if your base mesh is only six faces, most strokes will affect a large percentage of faces in the base mesh (at least one-sixth), making it slower for Blender to update its shape. By subdividing first, each stroke will affect a much smaller percentage of faces in the base mesh, so there is less for Blender to update on screen, speeding up you sculpting experience.

Customizing the 3D Viewport

When sculpting, we generally want to see only what we're working on, without distractions like lamps and the grid floor. To turn off these distractions, open the Properties region in the 3D Viewport (**N**) and, in the Display panel, check **Only Render** to show only meshes and other objects at render time. You can also turn off the grid floor and axes guidelines from this panel so that they won't be visible even with Only Render turned off. With Only Render turned on, the background color for the 3D view switches to the background color set in the World Settings tab of the Properties editor. It can be nice when sculpting to set this to a dark gray or black, but use whatever you like.

MatCap Materials

While sculpting, you'll want the look of your mesh in the 3D Viewport to give you as much information as possible about the shape of the surface you are working on. While Blender's open GL shaders do a reasonable job of this (and can be improved for sculpting, as outlined below), using a GLSL material known as a *MatCap* (short for *Material Capture*) that shades your mesh depending on its normals gives a better and more aesthetically pleasing view of your models.

MatCap images use a pre-rendered (or painted/ photographed) image of a sphere to shade your whole object, matching the shading of the sphere

image with the normals of your mesh. The MatCap image used for many of the figures in this chapter is shown in Figure 6-11. I'll cover creating materials in Chapter 12, but I'll outline how to create a MatCap material now.

Figure 6-11: A MatCap image. Blender uses your objects' normals to match the shading of your mesh with the shading of the sphere.

Creating a MatCap Material

To create a MatCap material, do the following:

1. Select the object you want to apply the material to.

2. In the Materials tab of the Properties editor, add a new material by clicking the **+New** button. This will create a new material with the default settings.

3. The only modification you need to make to this is to turn on **Shadeless** in the Shading panel. This stops the material from using lights in GLSL mode and instead only uses color information from the material's textures. (The relevant settings are shown in Figure 6-12.)

4. In the Textures tab, add a new texture to this image. Set its type to **Image or Movie** and then load your MatCap image. By default, this will be used to influence the color of your material, so all you need to do is change the mapping coordinates for the texture (in the Mapping tab) to **Normal**, which will then set your object's normals as texture coordinates.

5. Finally, set the Viewport Shading Method of the 3D Viewport to **Texture** and, in the Display panel of the 3D Viewport, set the shading option to **GLSL**. Your MatCap material should now be visible on your mesh, as shown in Figure 6-12.

Finding MatCap Images

A number of MatCap images are included on the disc accompanying this book, but you can find many more online. Many are available from websites devoted to ZBrush, a powerful commercial sculpting app that was one of the first to implement this kind of shading for sculpting. While many are distributed in the proprietary *.zmt* format, you can often easily find images of MatCap materials to use as textures in Blender. Googling around will turn up plenty of good MatCap textures, too.

It's also worth creating your own MatCap images. Whenever you have a material you like the look of, try applying it to a sphere and rendering it out to use as a MatCap material. (Just remember to crop your image to just inside the outline of the sphere to avoid getting any artifacts around the edges of your mesh.) You can also mix MatCap textures using a material with multiple texture slots. (See Chapter 12 for more on how to do this.)

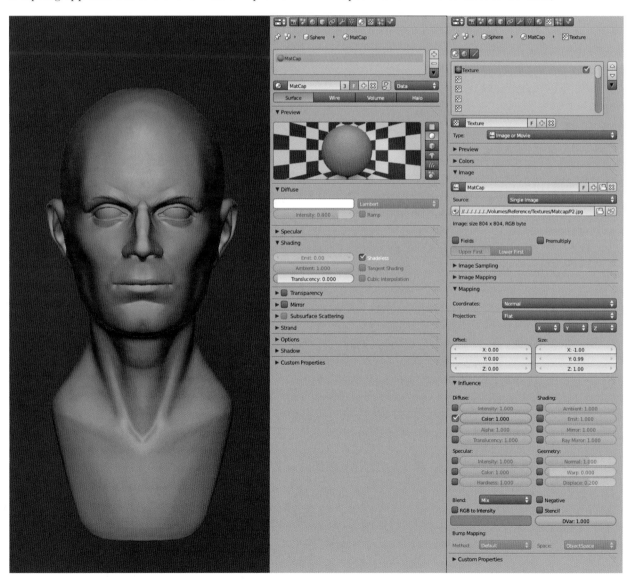

Figure 6-12: A MatCap material setup and the results in Blender's 3D Viewport. With the Normal texture coordinates, the image of the sphere is mapped to the normals of the mesh, mimicking the same shading.

Tweaking OpenGL Shading

While it's nice to sculpt with MatCap materials, once you get into the millions of polygons with your sculpts, Blender's performance may begin to suffer. Switching back to Blender's default OpenGL shading (that is, solid shading) is much faster, but it's quite evenly illuminated and not brilliant for sculpting. Fortunately, you can easily tweak the look of this shading in the System tab of the User Preferences, making it more appropriate for sculpting and increasing the amount of subdivision you can squeeze out of your computer while still maintaining reasonable performance.

In Figure 6-13, I've tweaked Blender's standard OpenGL lighting. To do this yourself, open User Preferences and, in the System tab, locate the Solid OpenGL Lights settings, as shown in Figure 6-13. These settings give you three independent "lights" that determine how meshes are shaded in Blender's default solid shaded view. You can turn these lights on and off using the lightbulb icon, adjust their diffuse and specular colors with the color pickers, and change the direction from which they light the mesh using the spheres on the right.

To make the lighting more amenable to sculpting, I turned off the second and third light sources and set the first light source to point straight at the mesh, giving it a slight tan color. This resulted in the shading on the right in Figure 6-13, which is more directional and gives a better idea of the shape of your mesh while sculpting.

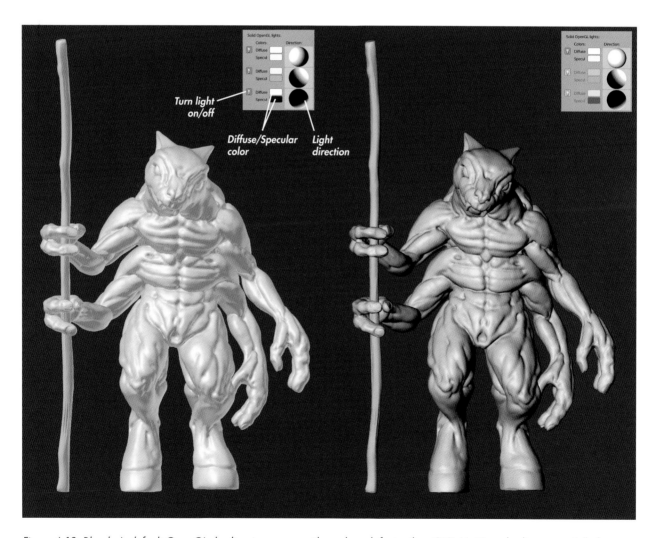

Figure 6-13: Blender's default OpenGL shading is very versatile and much faster than GLSL MatCap shading, especially for higher polygon counts. By adjusting the positions and colors of the three available lights, you can create a variety of lighting setups that are more suitable for sculpting than the default is.

The Multires Modifier

While you can sculpt on any mesh, we need to use the Multires modifier in order to take a sculpt to a high level of detail while maintaining a base mesh that is still simple to edit (see Figure 6-14). The Multires modifier is similar to the Subsurf modifier in that it subdivides your model using either Catmull-Clark or Simple subdivision ❶. However, instead of being purely procedural, the Multires modifier will store further editing of your mesh in Sculpt mode, allowing you to first subdivide your mesh and then use the extra geometry this creates to sculpt in extra detail. This lets us subdivide a fairly basic model into millions of polygons and allows us to sculpt them into whatever shapes and with whatever details we want.

The three settings on the left of the Multires modifier panel (Preview, Sculpt, and Render ❷) determine the level of subdivision shown in different modes. Preview sets the display level for Object mode, Sculpt the level for Sculpt mode, and Render the subdivision level used when rendering the mesh. The Subdivide operator ❸ adds another level of subdivision each time you click it, while the Delete Higher operator ❹ deletes any subdivision levels above the one you are currently working on.

If you happen to export your mesh to another program, or duplicate and edit it separately, you can use the Reshape operator ❺ to reshape your Multires mesh to be the same as that of another selected object. In order to do this, though, both meshes must have identical vertex order and topology, and any deletion or adding of vertices will break this functionality. If you're exporting to another program (like ZBrush or MeshLab), be sure to use the *.obj* format and ensure that the Keep Vertex Order option is checked when importing and exporting.

The Multires modifier does not affect the original shape of your mesh; however, you can use the Apply Base operator ❻ to fit the lowest subdivision level (your original mesh) to the shape of the subdivided mesh. This is useful if you have done a lot of sculpting and want your base mesh to resemble more closely the shape of the sculpted mesh again.

Vertex Order

Blender (and any application that uses mesh objects) stores a mesh as a numbered list of vertices, along with the connections between them that make up the edges and faces. This is the object's *vertex order*, and it must remain unchanged in order for the

Figure 6-14: The Multires modifier

Reshape operator to function. Simple manipulations of these vertices—like moving, rotating, or scaling—will not affect their ordering, but adding or deleting vertices will. Additionally, saving to other formats when exporting or importing may reorder the vertices of a mesh.

Subdivision and Polycounts

When working with the Multires modifier, you can track the polycount of your scene using the Info Editor header (see Figure 6-15). Remember that each subdivision you apply multiplies the polycount of that object by 4, so subdividing a mesh five times increases your polycount by a factor of 1024! Depending on how much RAM you have, you can probably safely subdivide up to a million or more polygons, but the number of subdivision levels that this requires will really depend on the number of polygons in your base mesh.

The Info Editor header contains several useful numbers. These are, from left to right: the version of Blender you are using, the total vertex count (Ve:) of the active layers, the total polygon (face) count (Fa:) of the active layers, the number of objects (Ob:) selected and in total (*selected-total*), the active layer, memory usage, and the name of the active object.

blender.org 259.4 | Ve:393218 | Fa:393216 | Ob:0-3 | La:1 | Mem:62.08M (35.52M) | Cube

Figure 6-15: Keep an eye on the polycount (Fa:) when using the Multires modifier.

Sculpting Concepts

With Blender set up nicely for sculpting, let's get to it. In general, we'll sculpt from coarse to fine, just like sculpture in the real world. By beginning with the broad structure of the final product we want to achieve and working toward the fine details, we reduce the number of steps we need to undo in order to correct errors.

This section will introduce you to some general concepts in the order I think about them when sculpting.

Volumes and proportion   When beginning to sculpt, first set out the rough shape of your subject; in other words, create a rough volume for each component of your overall figure. When sculpting a character, you should block out the volumes of the legs, arms, torso, head, hands, and feet. This is accomplished partly by creating a good base mesh. For example, we already created the basic shape of the Bat Creature character in Chapter 4; however, this can still be refined and improved while sculpting to give a better feel for the size and overall shape of the model.

Gesture   Gesture describes the stance of a character and the flow of forms from one body part to another. This stage applies more to posed characters but is an important part of creating a good neutral pose, and even applies when sculpting inorganic forms. Key at this stage is that the forms of the body are connected by smooth, flowing curves. You should usually be able to draw a smooth curve through your character's pose, as shown in Figure 6-16.

Planes   By planes, I mean breaking down and simplifying the form of the object into flat planes—areas of the object that form broadly flat surfaces rather than polygons. The direction and placement of the planes in your sculpture determine how the surfaces of your objects catch light, creating patterns that in turn play a large part in how we read and recognize shapes.

Even though you'll ultimately smooth out these planes, they'll still influence your finished object. For example, the planes in a human or humanoid character are largely defined by the object's major anatomical landmarks, such as the bony parts of the skull, ribcage, collar bones, and pelvis. In Figure 6-17, the main large planes are defined by the shape of the skull;

Figure 6-16: Try to establish smooth curves that flow through your characters

these planes include those along the side of the head, along the jawline and chin, and down the bridge of the nose. Smaller secondary planes form the shapes of the ears, lips, and nostrils. (You don't actually need to define the planes of your model too rigorously, as they will be smoothed out later, but it is important to know and roughly mark in where they are.)

Coarse details and anatomy   Once you've finished creating the main volumes and planes of your sculpture, you'll find that many of the anatomical details are actually already present, though there are still many anatomical features to be added to the final sculpt. Achieving anatomical realism in your sculpts takes practice and is a matter of gathering and studying anatomical references and then placing and refining those anatomical landmarks on your sculpt.

One way to begin filling in the details is to start with the major muscle groups and skeletal landmarks and then progress to smaller details like the musculature and small features like fingers, ears, eyes, and so on. See "Planes" on page 79 to learn how I accomplished this for the Bat Creature.

Fine details and surface texture   Finally, we progress to fine details, like wrinkles and pores in skin, or technical details in a hard-surface model (see Figure 6-18). This is a fun stage

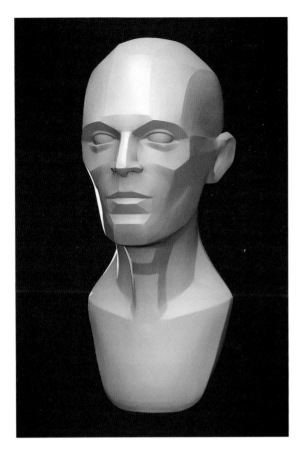

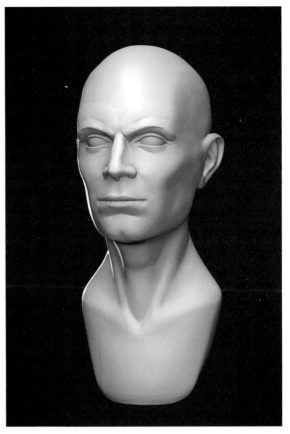

Figure 6-17: The planes of the head. You don't need to define planes to this extent, but keep them in mind.

Figure 6-18: Fine details can be dealt with once the major forms are in place.

that can add a lot of character to a model. One thing to note at this stage is that, particularly with organic characters that aren't heavily muscled, much of the anatomical detail you may have added will need to be toned down. You can either omit these details earlier in the sculpting process (but consider where they will be under the surface nonetheless) or smooth them away in areas where you need a subtler effect. Finally, you can start adding smaller details, like wrinkles, pores, scars, and so on. We can start smoothing and polishing out any artifacts we have created earlier while sculpting and then add more deliberate fine details.

These are the general stages that one goes through when sculpting. They take you from a rough overall shape to something with the key features you are trying to create and then allow you to re-create the finer details. Now let's apply these stages to sculpting the Bat Creature and Spider Bot.

Sculpting the Bat Creature

For the Bat Creature, I began with a couple of simple base meshes that had topology to support most of the features I needed (though nothing for the face). Then I could begin developing the forms of the Bat Creature into something more interesting and add further details, such as some musculature and facial features.

To begin, I took the base mesh and added a Multires modifier and a few subdivisions. The initial aim was to add enough resolution to allow me to begin refining the volumes and defining basic planes and landmarks—but not so much that I would get sucked into adding details too early. When sculpting, try to make the most out of each level of subdivision before adding the next level.

Volumes

I began by adding volume to the legs and arms with the Inflate tool (see Figure 6-19). The Inflate tool is particularly handy at low subdivision levels for enlarging basic masses and giving them a nice rounded shape. The Clay tool is also handy for building up mass in a specific place. (It's easy to make forms thinner again with the Smooth tool or with the Inflate tool in Subtractive mode.)

On the Bat's torso, I began separating the bulk of the ribcage or chest from the pelvis and adding some muscle mass on the back for the shoulders. The Bat Creature is a character with wings coming out of its back, so large muscles on the back are expected.

Planes

Next, I began sculpting the figure's basic planes. Because I was adding more definition at this point, I first added a few more subdivision levels, bringing the overall polycount to a few hundred thousand polygons. The aim here was first to find the bony landmarks of the body, such as the top and bottom of the ribcage, the iliac crests of the pelvis, the knees and elbows, and the skull (see Figure 6-20, Landmarks).

As a first step, you can roughly mark these points with a light impression from the Clay brush. Next, you can place the secondary forms of the major muscle groups using these landmarks as a guide. To do this, simply add and subtract mass with the Clay brushes (Figure 6-20, Masses). Then you can begin flattening these masses out into the main planes of the body using the Flatten, Scrape, and Fill brushes (Figure 6-20, Planes). Using the Crease brush at this stage will allow you to create better divisions between planes in Subtractive mode (the default behavior for this brush); this brush can also be used in Additive mode to add sharp edges to planes that face outward.

A good way to plan and keep track of the details you want to create is to sketch the muscle groups with Blender's grease pencil, using the Surface drawing setting (see Figure 6-21). In Object mode and with your mesh selected, add a new grease pencil layer, set the draw mode to **Surface**, and then draw strokes on the surface of your mesh by

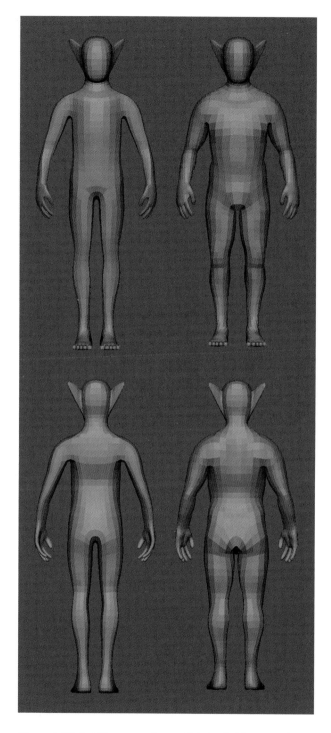

Figure 6-19: Bat Creature volumes: Subdivided base mesh before sculpting volumes (left) and the basic large volumes roughly added using the Grab and Inflate brushes (right). At this stage, I was concerned with refining the overall shape of the character into one with the right volumes and proportions, mainly by inflating and deflating or by smoothing out the forms at a low subdivision level. I could also tweak certain proportions in the base mesh.

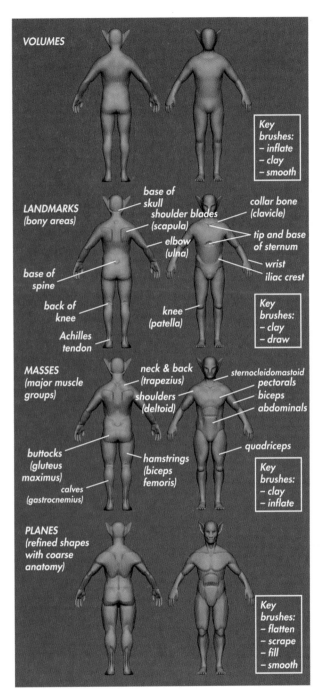

Figure 6-20: Stages in laying out the major planes of the body

VOLUMES

Key brushes:
– inflate
– clay
– smooth

LANDMARKS (bony areas)

base of skull
shoulder blades (scapula)
elbow (ulna)
base of spine
back of knee
Achilles tendon

collar bone (clavicle)
tip and base of sternum
wrist
iliac crest
knee (patella)

Key brushes:
– clay
– draw

MASSES (major muscle groups)

neck & back (trapezius)
shoulders (deltoid)
buttocks (gluteus maximus)
calves (gastrocnemius)
hamstrings (biceps femoris)

sternocleidomastoid
pectorals
biceps
abdominals
quadriceps

Key brushes:
– clay
– inflate

PLANES (refined shapes with coarse anatomy)

Key brushes:
– flatten
– scrape
– fill
– smooth

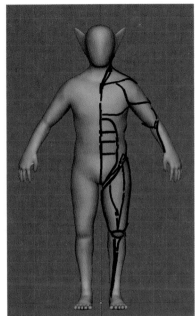

Figure 6-21: Left: Sketching out muscle groups and landmarks with the grease pencil. Right: The Grease Pencil panel, which is found in the Properties region.

Coarse Anatomy

With our planes sketched out, we can move on to further defining the anatomy. References are particularly handy at this stage as we define further anatomical details using brushes like Clay, Clay Tubes, Crease, and Inflate to accentuate individual muscles and the bones of the body and the face (see Figure 6-22).

Sculpting Hard-to-Reach Areas Using Shape Keys

Some areas, like under the armpits or between the legs, can be awkward to reach with your sculpting brushes. To make the task easier, create a new *shape key* for your mesh in Edit mode that will let you reach the area you want to work on.

Shape keys allow you to store different positions for the vertices of your mesh, enabling you, for example, to have one position with the arms up, one with the arms down, or whatever position you wish. Shape keys are fully compatible with Sculpt mode, meaning you can blend them on or off to change your sculpt's pose while sculpting. For example, for this sculpt, I created shape keys with the character's arms and legs held further out to make it easier to reach the armpit and inner leg areas.

holding down **D** and clicking to draw. Now you can sketch any anatomical landmarks on your sculpt before actually sculpting them in. For example, in Figure 6-21, I have sketched out the major muscle groups.

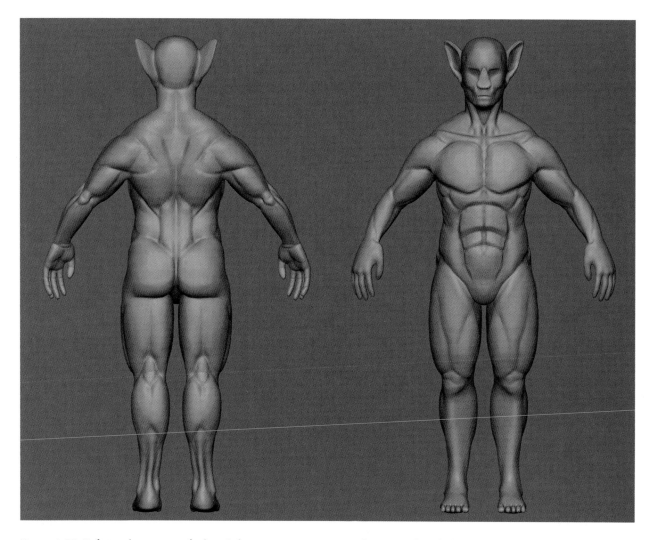

Figure 6-22: Defining the anatomy further. References are important at this stage, though there is room for invention as well.

To create the shape keys, I first added a new shape key in Object mode to hold the new pose. (Click the + icon on the right of the Shape Keys panel twice to set the original shape of the mesh as the default "basis" shape; then click it again to create a new shape with the vertex positions stored relative to the basis shape.) Next, I selected the vertices of the arm in Edit mode and rotated them about the shoulder to bring the arm outward slightly. Then I adjusted the surrounding vertices to refine the new pose (see Figure 6-23). Returning to Sculpt or Object mode, I could then turn this shape key up or down (using the value sliders in the Shape Keys panel) to move the body into a position that would be easier to work on.

Hiding Parts of the Mesh

Another way to reach difficult areas in a sculpt is to hide part of the mesh using the shortcut ALT-B, which lets you drag out a box on the screen to restrict the visible part of your mesh to only what is inside the box (see Figure 6-24). By hiding parts of your mesh, you can concentrate on one small area of your model at a time and also see into more difficult or hidden areas.

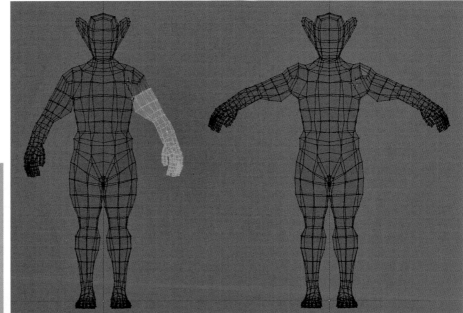

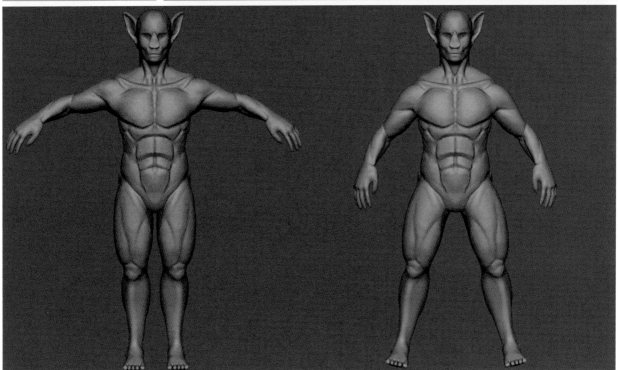

Figure 6-23: Adding shape keys for different poses. Top left: The Shape Keys panel found in the Object Data tab of the Properties editor. Top right: Selecting the arm to move it to a new position to make the previously hidden areas of the arm and chest more accessible. Bottom: The new pose applied in Sculpt mode and a separate, similar shape key for the legs.

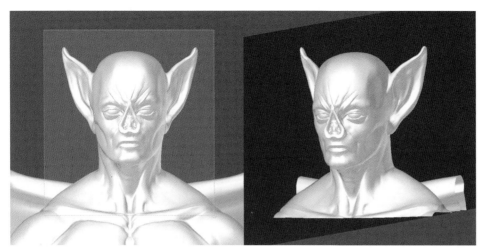

Figure 6-24: Restricting the visible area to a small selection, using the shortcut ALT-B and dragging a rectangle around the area you want to remain visible

Sculpting the Wings

Next I moved on to sculpting the wings (see Figure 6-25). The wings required less work, as the basic shape was closer to the final look I wanted.

I began by using the Inflate brush to add some volume to the wing bones, and then I added some bony landmarks. Next, I refined the planes of the bones and gave them clear boundaries with the Inflate, Crease, Flatten, and Clay brushes. The Crease Lazy brush that we made earlier comes in handy for working on the outlines of the bones and adding ridges to the wing structure.

Basic Details

While I wasn't planning to finalize the fine details covering the Bat's body until retopology, I still needed to add the main features of the head: the eyes, nostrils, mouth, and details of the ears. Returning to the body, I began to add these details. The Crease brush is an excellent way to draw in the outlines of these details—such as the valley between the lips and the creases of the brows and around the nose—before using the Clay brushes to build up the basic forms and the Flatten and Polish brushes to refine them (see Figure 6-26). Later, these would be retopologized and resculpted, so I left them pretty rough for time being, just doing enough to indicate the general shape.

Sculpting Around the Eyes

Eyes can be tricky to sculpt because you need to follow the underlying shape of the eyeball while adding the details of the eyelids and such. To make things easier, first add a new sphere object as a placeholder

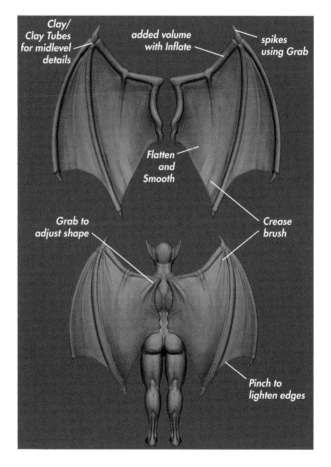

Figure 6-25: The wings were sculpted in the same way as the body. Because the initial base mesh was more defined to begin with, this process was simpler than it was for the body.

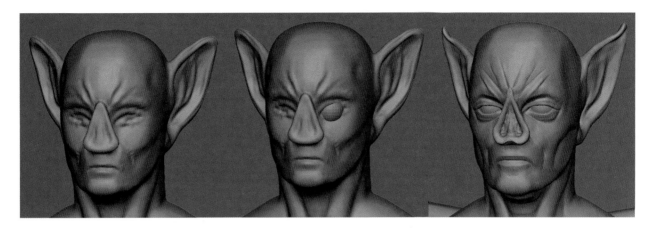

Figure 6-26: Adding an eye to make sculpting the surrounding areas easier and using the Crease brush to mark in key features of the face. Remember when scaling the eye to the correct size that the skull is approximately five eye-widths across and that there should be one eye-width between the two eyes.

for the eyeball (see Figure 6-26), then sculpt the eyelids around the sphere. A Mirror modifier can be used to create the other eye by using the body object as the mirror object in the modifier settings.

Time to Retopologize

At this point, I had reached the stage where adding further subdivisions would be slow and unwieldy with the current topology (the polycount of the body at this point is over 5 million faces). By retopologizing at this stage, you can create a denser and more suitable mesh that gives a higher initial density of polygons in important areas like the face and hands, with better topology to support the coarser details. This will allow you to resume sculpting again after retopologizing and add finer details to the mesh without having to keep increasing the poly-count to ridiculous levels.

Jump to Chapter 7 if you wish to follow along in strict chronological order. From here on, I will be transferring existing details to a new retopologized mesh before moving on to add finer details.

Transferring Sculpted Detail to a New Mesh with a Displacement Map

Having retopologized the sculpt, I was left with transferring the details I had sculpted on the original mesh to the new one. There are several ways to approach this, each with its advantages and disadvantages. One way is to use the Shrink Wrap modifier: first adding a Multires modifier to your new mesh, then subdividing a few times, adding Shrink

Wrap modifier, and setting the original mesh as the target. This can work reasonably well for simpler sculpts, but for more complex objects, it can create some artifacts and errors that will take time to straighten out. As such, for more complex sculpts, a better method is to use a displacement map.

About Displacement Maps

A *displacement map* is an image texture that defines how to displace the surface of a mesh according to the value of the texture: White areas cause the surface to be raised, and black areas are pushed in. By UV unwrapping the mesh and applying a displacement map to the new mesh, you can transfer the details of the old sculpt to the new mesh.

To create a displacement map, use Blender's texture-baking tools to calculate the distances between the surfaces of the original sculpt and the newly retopologized mesh and to bake them into an image. Then, by using the Displace modifier (combined with the Multires modifier to subdivide the mesh), you can apply this displacement to make the new retopologized mesh exactly match the old one. (UV mapping is covered more thoroughly in Chapter 8 and texture baking in Chapter 10, so I will only touch on the basics here.)

I created a simple UV unwrap for my retopologized mesh by tagging some seams (CTRL-E) to split it into easy-to-unwrap patches. Then I unwrapped it using the Unwrap operator (U▸Unwrap) and packed the UV islands into the UV grid. (You can do this automatically with the shortcut CTRL-P.)

Next, I assigned a new image to the object's UV coordinates by selecting the object, entering Edit mode, and, in the UV Image editor, using Image ▸ New Image to create a blank, 4096×4096 image for baking displacement. (Be sure to check the **32-bit float** option for best results when creating this image, as displacement maps with lower bit depths can cause nasty stepping artifacts.)

Finally, I baked the displacement from my original sculpt to the new retopologized mesh (see Figure 6-27) by following these steps:

1. Select the original sculpt.
2. Use SHIFT ▸ **Select the retopologized mesh** and apply a **Subdivision Surface** modifier to it with a render level of **3**. This will subdivide the mesh before calculating the displacement so that later, when we use a Multires modifier to subdivide the mesh, the same displacement can be applied.
3. In the Render tab of the Properties editor, open the **Bake** panel.
4. Make sure that **Selected to Active** is enabled and Bake mode is set to **Displacement**.

5. Leave the Distance parameter set to the default of **0**.
6. Click **Bake** to bake your displacement map.
7. Once it is baked, save your displacement map as an *OpenEXR* file from the UV Image editor by selecting **Image ▸ Save as Image** from the header menu (making sure to set the file type to *EXR* when saving).

Applying Displacement to the Sculpt

Once the displacement map image has been baked, you need to create a texture that uses this image and apply it as the input for a Displacement modifier applied to the new mesh.

 The procedure outlined below is somewhat inelegant because in order to edit a texture's properties, Blender requires you to assign it to a material, world, or brush. To get around this, you can create a "dummy" material to assign the displacement texture to so that you can edit it and then assign it to the displacement modifier. (For more on how images, textures, and materials normally work, skip to Chapters 10, 11, and 12.)

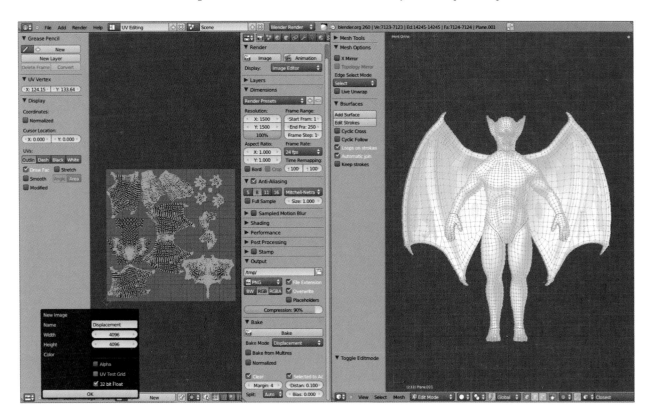

Figure 6-27: Baking the displacement from the old sculpt to the new retopologized mesh. This is often easier to tweak and gives better results than the Shrinkwrap modifier, though it takes some extra effort.

To apply the displacement map to your new retopologized mesh, do the following:

1. Select your retopologized mesh and, in the Materials tab of the Properties Editor, create a new material for it by clicking the **New** button. We won't be using this material to render our mesh later; it's just there as somewhere to hold our texture for now. You can rename this material something like *Displacement_Dummy*. You may also want to create a fake user for this material by clicking the **F** icon next to its name so that when you assign a different material to the object (leaving the dummy material unassigned), the dummy material will not be discarded.

2. Switch to the **Texture tab** of the Properties editor and add a new texture to the material, again by clicking **New**.

3. Set the material type to **Image or Movie** and then, from the Image panel below, click **Open** and load the displacement map you just created. Name this something memorable as well.

4. Delete the Subdivision Surface modifier we added earlier and add a **Multires** modifier to your retopologized mesh instead. Then subdivide it a few times. Aim for roughly the same number of faces as your original mesh for now.

5. Add a **Displacement** modifier. From the Texture selector, choose your displacement material and leave direction set to **Normal**, but change the Coordinates setting to **UV** to use your object's UV coordinates to apply the displacement texture. Because we kept the texture-baking settings mostly on their defaults, the default strength of 1 should be exactly what we need. This should now give your mesh exactly the same shape as the original sculpt.

Controlling Displacement with a Vertex Group

Some areas, like the inside of the mouth, may cause problems when the Displacement modifier is applied. Since the inside of the mouth is completely new topology, it won't have any useful information in the displacement map, and it would be better to exclude these areas from the effects of the Displacement modifier. To fix these areas, you can assign a vertex group to the Displacement modifier to restrict displacement to only certain parts of the mesh, leaving problem areas untouched. Figure 6-28

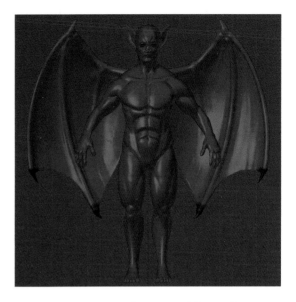

Figure 6-28: Restricting the action of the Displacement modifier with a vertex group (shown here in Weight Paint mode)

shows the vertex group for the Displacement modifier in Weight Paint mode; the inside of the mouth and eyes and the tips of the claws on the wings are not included in the group.

To create a vertex group, take the following steps:

1. Enter **Edit mode**, and in the Object Data tab of the Properties Editor, and click the + icon in the Vertex Groups panel to create a new vertex group.

2. Select the vertices you wish to be included in the group (that is, the parts of the mesh you do want to apply the Displacement modifier to), and click **Assign** in the Vertex Groups panel to assign them to the group.

3. Switch back to **Object mode**, and set this vertex group as the vertex group to use to restrict the effect of the Displacement modifier (the Vertex Group option is in the modifier settings; see Figure 6-29). The modifiers you should now have applied are shown in Figure 6-29.

4. Apply the Displacement modifier by clicking **Apply**. Its effects will be stored by the Multires modifier, allowing you to return to Sculpt mode and continue sculpting and adding details.

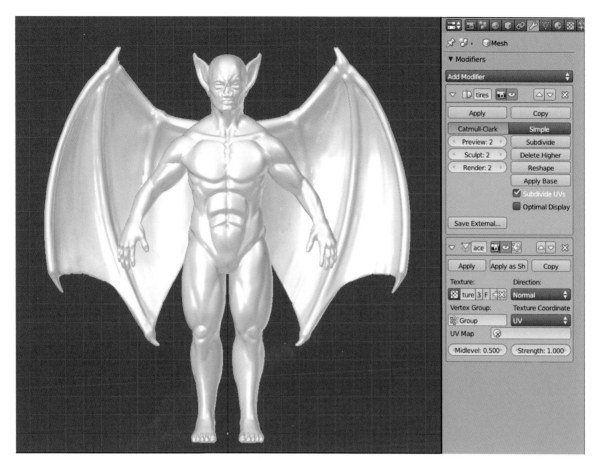

Figure 6-29: Applying the displacement map with the Displacement modifier. Placing the Displacement modifier below a Multires modifier in the modifier stack will allow you to apply the displacement and have the results captured by the Multires modifier so that you can continue sculpting.

Detailing

With the retopologized mesh ready to be sculpted, I began working it over with various brushes and building in the fine details (see Figure 6-30). The Clay and Standard brushes are generally the best for defining the important forms, but alpha textures can be used to add texture much more quickly.

Beginning with the face, I added some of the major wrinkles with the Clay and Draw brushes. Then, I moved on to using alpha textures. Using the Drag Alpha brush discussed earlier in the chapter, together with some skin texture alphas, I began building up the surface texture of the skin.

The rest of the body was covered in the same way: building up texture and fine details using a mix of alpha brushes and small Clay and Draw brushes. In the areas around the shoulders and

wings, I added some creases that flow with the expansion and contraction of the wings, using a mix of alphas, Clay, and Crease brushes, as shown in Figure 6-31.

Procedural Details

While it's best to sculpt the important details of your model by hand, it can be handy to be able to add some generic roughness to the surface of your sculpt. We've used the Displacement modifier to transfer details using a baked displacement map, but we could also use other textures as the input for the Displacement modifier to generate some subtle variation in the surface. Blender has a variety of *procedural textures* (textures generated by various algorithms that do not require images as input) that are ideal for this purpose.

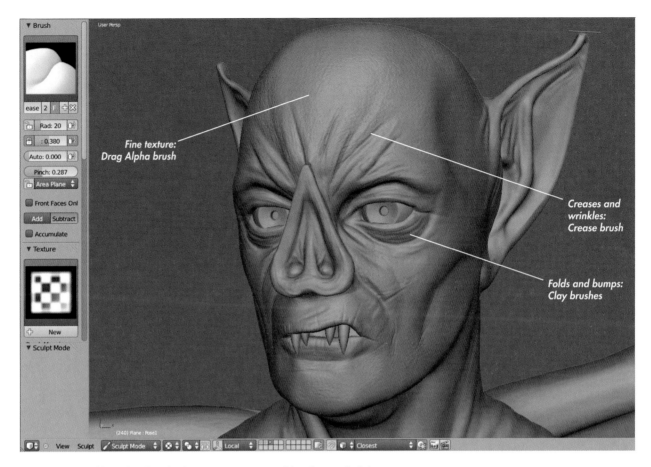

Figure 6-30: Adding detail to the face using a variety of brushes and alphas

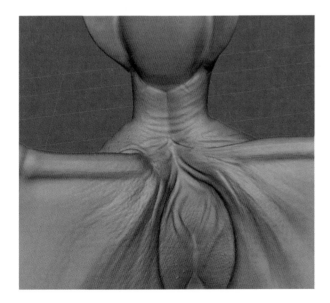

Figure 6-31: Adding detail to the wings and back

To add some surface detail to your sculpt with a procedural cloud texture and the Displacement modifier, do the following and see Figure 6-32:

1. Create a new texture block (we can use the dummy material created earlier to hold it) and set its type to **Cloud**.

2. Add a **Displacement** modifier to your sculpt (after the Multires modifier) in Object mode (Displacement will not be shown in Sculpt mode). Set your new procedural texture as the texture for the modifier.

3. Set the strength of the modifier to something very low. Then switch back to the **Texture tab** of the Properties editor and play with the settings of the Cloud texture, available from the Cloud panel that appears now that you have chosen the Cloud texture type. Try setting the scale of the cloud to something very small and play with the brightness, contrast, and noise basis to produce different effects.

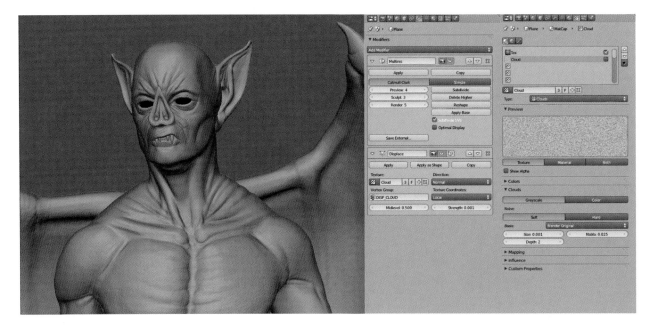

Figure 6-32: Adding procedural detail with a cloud texture and the Displacement modifier

4. As we did when we used a Displacement modifier to transfer details, you can use a vertex group to mask out areas that you don't want to be affected.

5. When you have something you are happy with, apply the modifier to bake the results into the Multires modifier so that you can continue sculpting.

Breaking Symmetry

At this stage, if you keep symmetry enabled, your sculpt may begin to look a little *too* symmetrical. While the bodies and faces of most animals and characters are broadly symmetrical, fine details like pores, wrinkles, scars, and so on are not.

Once you reach the detailing stage, it is usually a good idea to turn symmetry off in the Tool Options. For more far-flung areas, like the ends of the arms and legs, you can leave symmetry on: Because these parts are farther from each other, the symmetry will be less apparent. However, obvious symmetry in the details running down the middle of your character will generally look strange, so turn symmetry off for these areas in particular.

Of course you *can* break symmetry much earlier; most characters and faces have some subtle asymmetry. This level of subtlety can add a lot of believability to your sculpts, so consider disabling symmetry earlier on.

Posing

To create a more interesting pose for my character, I jumped into Edit mode (TAB) and used proportional editing in Connected mode (ALT-O) together with rotating about the 3D cursor to move the limbs (see Figure 6-33). I created a new shape key for the pose and then began adjusting the body. For example, to move a leg, I selected all the vertices in the leg, placed the 3D cursor where the hip joint would be, and then rotated the leg about that point using proportional editing to create a smooth transition. This is a quick and dirty way to pose a character without resorting to rigging it, which is a complex task—and for a still render, more effort than it's worth.

I adjusted the rest of the limbs and the head to pose the character in a more interesting way. Then I returned to Sculpt mode, where I used the Grab and Clay brushes at a low subdivision level to fix any errors with the pose and adjust the look of the musculature. I relaxed muscles that would be extended with the Smooth tool and decreased their volume a bit and conversely inflated and tightened up muscles that would be contracting in the new pose.

Expression

Facial expression is an important part of any character. I added a new shape key to hold the facial expression and used the Grab and Clay brushes to add a bit of a snarl to the Bat's face (visible in

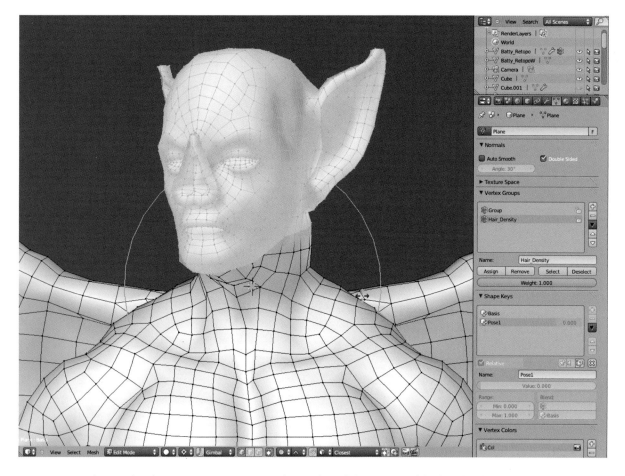

Figure 6-33: Adjusting the character into a new pose. I have selected the vertices of the head and then placed the 3D cursor at the base of the neck to allow me to turn the head slightly by rotating the selection about the 3D cursor with proportional editing enabled. Keeping this new pose as a shape key allows you to change your mind later and return to the standard pose.

Figure 6-32) by grabbing the sides of the nose and shifting them up slightly, pulling up the upper lip a bit, and narrowing the eyes. Adding some creases in those areas where the face is scrunched up and smoothing out stretched areas complements the details already added.

Sculpting the Spider Bot

The Spider Bot was sculpted like the Bat Creature by first blocking out the major forms with the Clay and Grab brushes, then refining planes and adding details. However, in the case of the Spider, I had the added complexity of trying to create hard-surface forms. While you could model these sorts of forms directly (often an excellent approach), sculpting some aspects of hard-surface forms allowed me to be more experimental when creating our model.

While Blender can't quite polish hard surfaces and sharp edges to perfection, you can accomplish a lot with the Flatten and Polish brushes along with the Pinch and Crease brushes. Then you can use retopology to create a finalized model with clean, smooth forms. By focusing on forms first and topology later, you reduce the hassle of trying to model forms you are not yet sure about and get your objects curving smoothly with clean topology later.

Body

Beginning with the Spider Bot's body, I used the Crease tool to roughly mark where I wanted the edges of my hard surfaces to fall. I next used the Clay brushes (the custom Clay Tubes brush is excellent for this purpose) to build up the volumes around these lines, and I used the Polish and Flatten brushes to refine them (see Figure 6-34).

Figure 6-35: The head segment, sculpted in the same way as the body

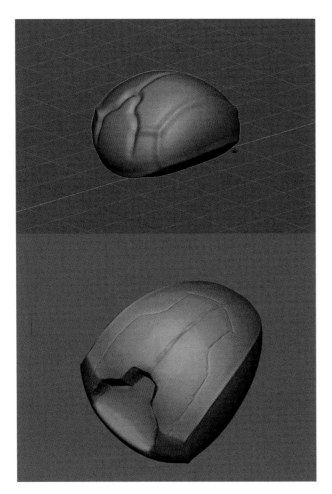

Legs

Sculpting the legs proceeded in much the same manner. I started by polishing the overall shape of the pieces into something flatter and slightly more hard-edged. Then I built up some more interesting shapes on top of that with the Clay and Crease brushes, first drawing out a design and then filling in the shapes. Next, I returned to polishing again to get more tightly defined, smoother shapes (see Figure 6-36).

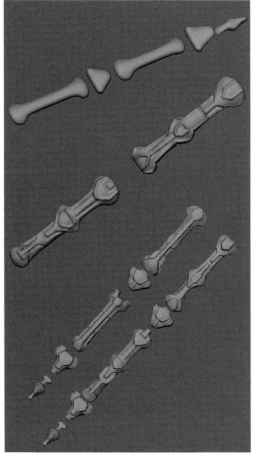

Figure 6-34: First, draw a rough design with the Crease brush. Next, build up masses with the Clay Tubes brush. Finally, refine them with the Polish, Pinch, and Flatten brushes.

To create even finer edges, combine the Crease brushes (the custom Crease Lazy brush we made is good for long, smooth curves) in Additive mode (hold CTRL) to make corners and edges sharper. Then, pinch them together to get a really sharp crease. By steering clear of the edges and using the Flatten brushes on the flat areas, you can achieve a fairly polished result. (Don't go crazy; we'll use retopology later to create a new mesh with smoother forms.)

Head

The head was sculpted the same way (see Figure 6-35), using the Polish brush to produce flatter shapes and the Crease brush to mark in edges and valleys. I also carved in some deep recesses where the legs and fangs will attach to the body.

Figure 6-36: Sculpting the legs using the same technique as for the body. I kept the sculpts for the leg pieces fairly loose, as the final leg parts would be made by retopologizing over the sculpted legs to create clean, smooth geometry.

Again though, there's no need to chase after something perfectly smooth, as we will be fixing these surfaces with retopology in Chapter 7.

❧ *The Polish and Flatten brushes can produce odd effects at sharp corners, creating awkward dents. To fix these, either undo or use the Inflate and Smooth brushes to knock out the dents and then re-crease and polish the surface.*

To get an idea of the look of my sculpt at this point, I duplicated the leg parts (as linked duplicates, ALT-D) and moved and rotated them into place in Object mode (see Figure 6-37). This let me check on the final look of the model, though I didn't bother mirroring the leg pieces over to the other side of the body at this stage.

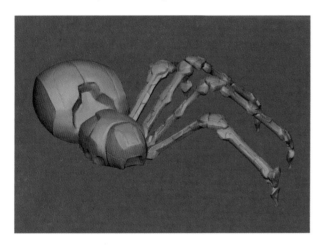

Figure 6-37: The sculpted body parts, duplicated and moved into roughly their final positions

Jungle Temple: Creating Incidental Details

While the ruined temple scene didn't use a lot of sculpting, certain incidental details were easier to sculpt, such as patches of mud and rough ground (see Figure 6-38). I created these areas mainly by using the Clay brushes without a Multires modifier, opting to simply subdivide the mesh a few times in Edit mode instead. I could have sculpted some damage into the stone walls using alphas, but I felt that the relative flatness of the walls contrasted nicely with the chaos of the surrounding foliage, so I left the masonry smooth.

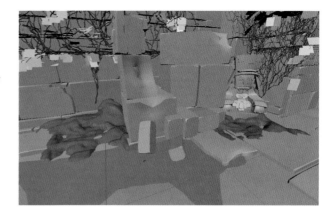

Figure 6-38: Some roughly sculpted patches of mud from the temple scene

Sculpting Natural-Looking Faces

While the Bat Creature *has* a face, it isn't one that you'd call classically handsome. Here are some tips for sculpting more natural-looking faces.

- Focus on the proportions and the large volumes first before diving into the details. Lock down the overall volumes before adding wrinkles, pores, and scars so that you won't have to redo them later when your sculpt doesn't look right (see Figure 6-39).

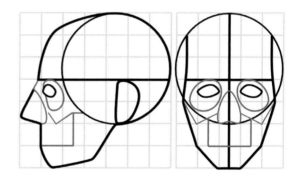

Figure 6-39: Mapping out the proportions of the head. Overall, you can view the head as being constructed around the sphere of the cranium, with the face extending forward and downward from it. Here, the proportions of the head are laid out on a grid scaled to one eye-width per unit. Certain important features of the skull, including the cheekbones, eye sockets, and upper jaw, are marked in red.

- The head is roughly five eye-widths across and approximately seven down (see Figure 6-39). This proves a useful measurement. Keep this measurement in mind and use it to judge the relative distance and size of facial features.

- The mouth is difficult to sculpt. Depending on whether you have an "open" mouth (one with topology that follows round inside the mouth) or a "closed" one (one that is simply "drawn" onto the surface of the face), you will need to adopt different strategies. For open mouths, the Inflate and Smooth brushes are useful for adjusting the shape of the lips and the surrounding areas. For closed mouths, the Crease brush is perfect for drawing in the crease between the two lips, followed by filling out the surrounding areas with the Clay and Clay Tubes brushes. Remember that the upper lip generally has much more definition than the lower lip and has a rough *M* shape to it. The lower lip is more rounded and slightly tucked under the upper lip in most people (see Figure 6-40).

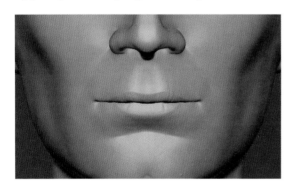

Figure 6-40: The lips

- The anatomy of the face and the landmarks of the skull are important. Try modeling or sculpting a skull, sculpting the facial muscles, and then adding the skin over the top to see how they affect one another (see Figure 6-41).

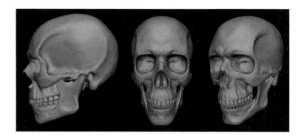

Figure 6-41: The anatomy of the skull is very important in determining how a person looks. In particular, the landmarks of the skull—such as the cheekbones, brows, and chin—have a big impact on the overall appearance of a face.

- Don't add lots of wrinkles and creases unless you want your character to look seriously old. Even a few subtle wrinkles can add a lot of character to a face.

- Few faces are perfectly symmetrical. While sculpting with symmetry turned on will take you a long way, turn it off in the later stages of your sculpt to add a bit of uniqueness to the two sides of the face.

In Review

In this chapter, we have looked at the variety of sculpting tools that Blender has to offer and how to customize them to make the most of their capabilities. Then, we moved on to sculpting the Bat Creature's body and turning the simple base meshes I created both for it and for the Spider Bot project into more detailed, developed models that are now ready for retopology. Finally, we discussed some general principles for sculpting faces.

In the next chapter, we move on to retopologizing our sculpts, bringing the modeling stages of the projects to a close. In later chapters, we'll use our high-poly sculpts again for baking maps and textures for our models before rendering them with displacement and normal maps to recapture the details we created in this chapter.

7

RETOPOLOGY

Sometimes it's easier to create an object's basic form using one method—for example, sculpting or combining simple primitives—before creating the final topology for texturing and the final renders another way, using the basic forms as a guide. This is what retopology allows us to do. *Retopology* is the process of creating new geometry over an existing mesh while maintaining the object's basic shape and rebuilding its topology. Retopology allows us to split the tasks of creating the right shape and creating helpful topology, making it easier to produce the model we want.

In this chapter, you'll learn how to use Blender's Snapping tools and other retopology techniques to model new geometry over the surface of high-poly, sculpted meshes, like the ones we sculpted in Chapter 6. The result will be a final mesh that captures the details of the sculpts with fewer polygons and produces topology that subdivides well and is suitable for rigging and animation.

The Basics

There are several ways to retopologize, but the most direct is to use Blender's projection Snapping tools to create geometry directly on the surface of the mesh you want to retopologize. (See "Snapping" on page 36 for more on these tools.)

Using Snapping to Retopologize

To start retopologizing a mesh, take the following steps:

1. Add a new plane object in Object mode.
2. Enter **Edit mode** and turn on **Snapping**.
3. Change the snapping target to **Faces** and enable **Project onto Surface** (see Figure 4-10 on page 35) to make Blender snap selected vertices and edges onto the surface of other objects by projecting them from the current viewpoint.

4. Scale down the plane until it is the same size you want the faces to be in your final retopologized mesh. Next, grab and place the plane over a region of your mesh where you wish to start retopologizing.

5. Adjust the positions of the existing vertices. Then, select one edge of the face and start extruding out to create new faces, following the contours of the mesh.

6. Whenever you extrude a new face or grab an existing one, it will be projected onto the surface of any other mesh on screen (though other objects you selected before you entered Edit mode will be ignored).

Using the method described above, in a short time you should be able to cover the surface of even a complex mesh with the exact topology you want, creating a new mesh with the same shape as your original.

Alternative Methods for Retopology

There are other useful ways to retopologize quickly that are worth discussing. The first is to use the Shrinkwrap modifier to project simple topology over the surface of a mesh. With this method, you first model a basic cage around the outside of your original model (as shown in Figure 7-1), extruding areas to create the topology you want. The cage needs to match the original shape only roughly because the next step is to add a Subsurf (or Multires) modifier and a Shrinkwrap modifier to the mesh, setting your original model as the target for the Shrinkwrap modifier. The Shrinkwrap modifier then automatically conforms the new mesh to the surface of the old one.

Shrinkwrap has a few methods for doing this, and it's best to experiment to see what works best for your model. I've generally found the most useful methods to be the Nearest Surface Point and Project modes. Note that there are some extra options for Project mode and that you'll need to turn on both Negative and Positive in the direction checkboxes in order for your mesh to project in both directions to conform to the target (unless the surface of the new mesh is always above or below the surface of the target).

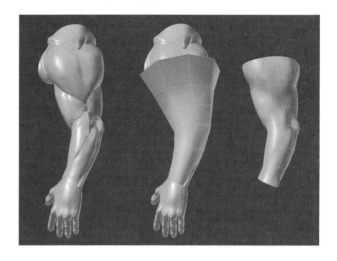

Figure 7-1: Quick retopology with the Shrinkwrap modifier. First, create a simple mesh around your high-poly original. Next, add a Shrinkwrap modifier to project the new mesh onto the original. Here, an arm is retopologized just by extruding a circle along its length, roughly scaling and rotating it into place, and then adding Subsurf and Shrinkwrap modifiers to fit the new mesh to the sculpt.

This method of retopologizing works well when you want to quickly retopologize a sculpt that needs a better base mesh—for example, if you started a head or even a whole body from a cube and then wanted a base mesh with topology that does a better job of supporting the basic forms.

The Shrinkwrap method is also useful for combining models composed of multiple pieces into a single mesh. For example, to create a one-piece version of the Mayan glyphs discussed in Chapter 6, you could project a simple grid mesh onto the glyphs, as shown in Figure 7-2. Notice that I've repeated the Shrinkwrap and Subsurf modifiers to capture all the details. This repeating of modifiers is a useful trick, especially when you are projecting onto a mesh with a lot of sharp corners or deep creases and folds, because the first shrinkwrap will miss details that aren't visible when looking straight at the surface of the target mesh. The resulting mesh can then be easily sculpted or unwrapped and textured without having to work with multiple part meshes.

Another method for retopology uses Blender's Bsurfaces add-on, which has some neat tools for retopology that allow you to draw lines with the grease pencil and have them automatically converted to a mesh, as shown in Figure 7-3.

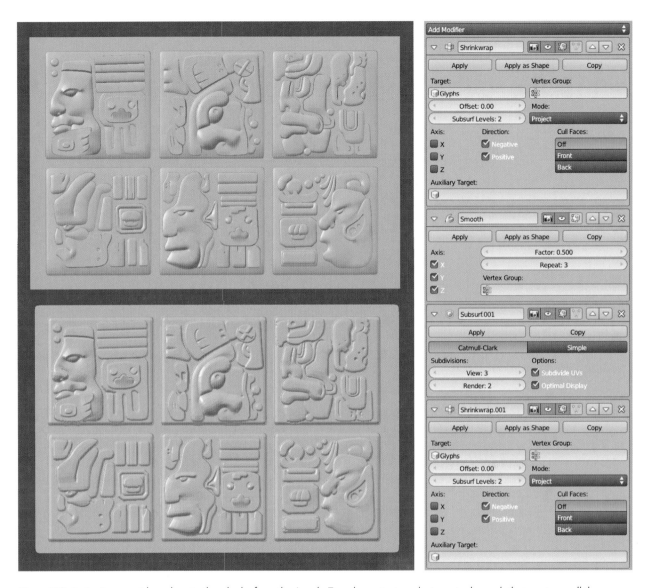

Figure 7-2: Projecting a grid mesh onto the glyphs from the Jungle Temple project results in a single mesh that captures all the details. This technique would make UV unwrapping and texturing very simple, but it would produce a much higher poly count. Top: The original glyphs. Bottom: The grid, projected onto the glyphs. Right: The modifier stack. The Shrinkwrap modifiers are repeated with a Subdivision Surface modifier and a Smooth modifier in between to help the second shrinkwrap get into all the tight corners.

Retopologizing the Jungle Temple Trees

I created most of the Jungle Temple project using traditional modeling methods, without a lot of retopology. However, when blocking out the trees, I came up with nice placeholders by snapping curves over the surface of the background objects. These placeholder curves can easily be turned into more finished meshes using retopology. To apply this technique, take the following steps:

1. Create a duplicate (unlinked, SHIFT-D) of the tree placeholder. Then, convert it to a mesh with ALT-C ▶ **Mesh From Curve/Meta/Text**. This creates a mesh with roughly the topology we want, except that the roots and trunk are separate meshes.

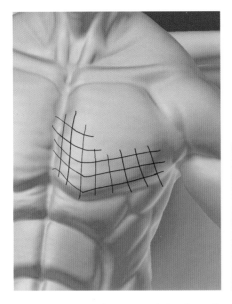
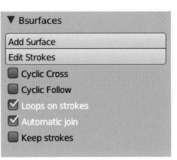
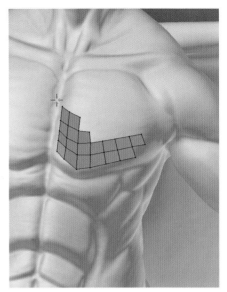

Figure 7-3: Retopologizing with Bsurfaces by drawing polygons with the grease pencil. First, draw your desired mesh with the grease pencil, crossing strokes where you want a vertex to be created. Then, use the Add Surface button (in Edit mode) to create a mesh from your strokes. Using the surface option for the grease pencil strokes will allow you to draw directly onto your sculpt, creating a mesh that follows its shape.

2. Join the roots to the trunk by deleting the vertices in the areas where the two should join. Then, start creating new geometry to cover the join and bridge the gap (see Figure 7-4). Select pairs of edges that roughly line up on either side of the join and create faces between them (**F**).

3. You can then add some loop cuts (CTRL-R) across this face to split it into more even-sized quads.

4. Grab the new vertices this creates and release them again to snap them to the surface. Repeat the process to continue filling in the gaps, joining new faces together and trying to keep the topology as even and grid-like as you can.

5. Repeat the above steps for all of the joins between the roots and the trunk.

6. Finally, close the open ends of the roots. It's also worthwhile at this stage to adjust the density of edge loops around the roots and trunk, deleting some (**X ▸ Edge Loop**) in areas where they are too dense and adding them in sparser areas (CTRL-R).

Retopologizing the Bat Creature

While the original Bat Creature's base mesh was a good start, it lacked the necessary topology to support all the features of the head and more detailed

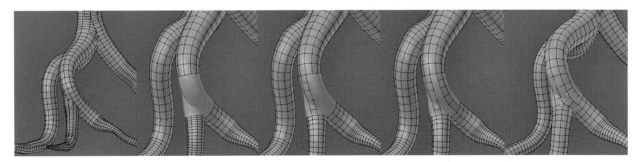

Figure 7-4: Retopologizing the curve-based trees into a single mesh using Blender's Snapping tools. After I duplicated the original curve-based tree and converted it to a mesh, most of the work was done, leaving only the joins between roots and the trunk to be filled in.

anatomy. Additionally, the wings were initially constructed and sculpted as separate pieces. Now, I needed to create a final mesh with more detailed topology that combines the two parts.

Decimation

Before using retopology, I needed to deal with the fact that the full sculpt was in the millions of polygons and was getting unwieldy. Of course, this was the reason for retopologizing it, but still, it would be good to have a stand-in mesh that captures the details with a lower polygon count for me to draw my new topology over. The answer is decimation.

Decimation is a process whereby a high-poly mesh is automatically simplified by collapsing small edges and polygons to reduce the model's complexity while losing as little detail as possible. Blender has a Decimate modifier, but it's a little slow and not always effective, so I often use another open source application called MeshLab (*http:// www.meshlab.sourceforge.net/*). To use MeshLab on a Blender sculpt, take the following steps:

1. Export your object as a wavefront object (*.obj*) file (**File ▸ Export**), making sure that the

Selected Only and **Apply Modifiers** options are checked so that all modifiers are applied (including Multires) and that the details of your sculpt are preserved. This will create a fairly huge *.obj* file that contains your high-poly sculpted mesh.

2. To import your sculpt into MeshLab, just run the program and then use **File ▸ Import** to import your mesh in *.obj* format.

3. MeshLab has a huge array of options for processing meshes, but for our purposes, we'll use the Quadratic Edge Collapse Decimation tool (**Filters ▸ Remeshing ▸ Quadratic Edge Collapse Decimation**). This brings up a menu allowing you to specify a target polycount for your mesh, among other options (see Figure 7-5).

4. Set the target poly count to around 150,000 and turn on **Planar Simplification** in the options. Then run the filter. After a short wait, you should be presented with a much lower polygon count version of your sculpt that still encompasses much of the detail. You can export this from MeshLab using the File menu and then re-import it back into Blender.

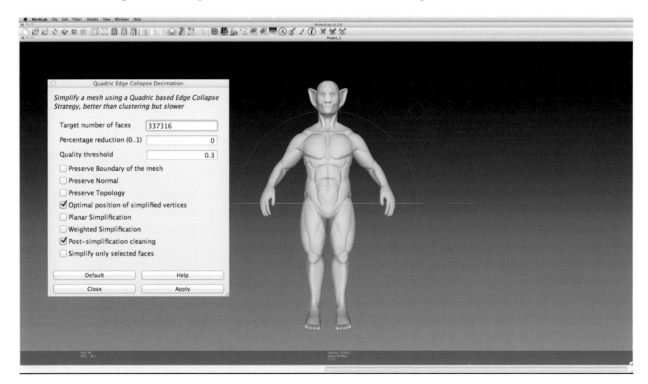

Figure 7-5: Decimating sculpts in MeshLab. The Quadratic Edge Collapse Decimation tool allows you to set a target poly count, to which MeshLab will then reduce your mesh by merging close-together vertices.

Retopologizing the Body

With the sculpt decimated and re-imported back into Blender, I could start laying some new topology over it. I began by adding a new plane in Object mode and applying a Mirror modifier to it. Then, I turned on Projection in the Snapping tools buttons. Next, I grabbed my plane in Edit mode and scaled and positioned it where I wanted to start my retopology from (the torso, in this case).

> ✿ At this point, I thought carefully about what density of polygons I wanted in the final model. Scaling the first plane up or down and working to this scale made a big difference in the final poly count of the retopologized mesh. I generally tried to work at a similar scale to most of the important details of the original mesh.

With a starting point set, I began extruding (**E**) from one edge of my original quad along the forms of the model (see Figure 7-6), following the outline of the ribcage and torso muscles. This created a face loop that ran along an important form within the model. By filling in the surrounding areas and creating further face loops along other forms, we can work toward completely retopologizing our sculpt with topology that supports the forms we have sculpted. This creates a more efficient mesh for capturing the fine details when we subdivide it and makes it easy to unwrap and rig if we desire to later.

As I progressed over the model, many of the same general positions for face loops that I used in the base mesh were useful again. While overall the topology was more complex, creating face loops that ran around the armpit and shoulder and around the arms, legs, and neck resulted in clean, easy-to-modify topology (see Figure 7-7). Also, because the mesh was still broadly symmetrical, I only needed to retopologize half the body and use a Mirror modifier to fill in the other half.

For some areas, like the face, I began to shrink the polygons in order to pack more into the area's smaller, more detailed forms. I created loops that ran around the eyes, nose, mouth, and outside of the ears (see Figure 7-8). These loops both supported the forms of the face so that they weren't lost or softened too much when subdivided and added extra density to these areas to allow for the addition of more details with the Multires modifier. (For specific tips on face topology, see "Head Topology" on page 106.)

To create a mouth cavity, I extruded back from the edge loop surrounding the mouth and filled in the hole (see Figure 7-9). When we return to sculpt on this retopologized mesh, we'll need to resculpt this area, but the mouth will now be able to be opened and posed.

For objects like the wings, where it can be difficult to see into tight areas, it can be handy to switch to perspective view (**5**), which allows the camera to be moved in and around tight spaces. It can also be useful to restrict the view with ALT-B. This lets you select a part of your model to show in the 3D Viewport, allowing you to see a small area without other parts of your model getting in the way, as shown in Figure 7-10.

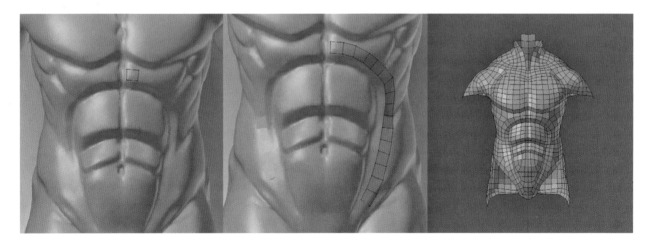

Figure 7-6: Begin by creating a single important face loop quad by quad. Then, move on to others and fill in the areas in between.

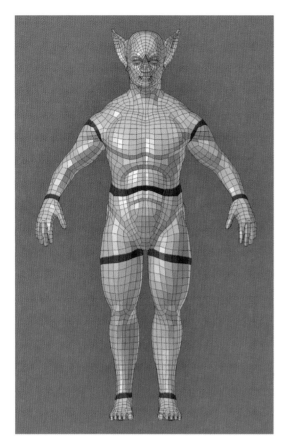

Figure 7-7: Important face loops. A good tip when doing retopology is to view your new mesh on its own by pressing / (forward slash) to view just the selected objects. This will let you see how your retopologized mesh is progressing before pressing / to return to global view and continue modeling.

Figure 7-8: Retopologizing a face to create new topology that follows the sculpted forms

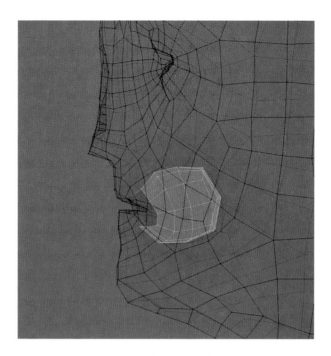

Figure 7-9: Adding a cavity for the mouth

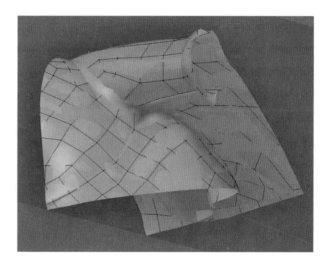

Figure 7-10: Restricting Blender's view to a small selection (ALT-B) makes it easier to work on tight areas. Hit ALT-B again to return the display to normal.

Creating new topology that bridges the join between the wings and body is as simple as continuing to retopologize over the join (see Figure 7-10, which shows the mesh covering both the wing and shoulder of the Bat Creature). Doing so allows you to create a single mesh that combines the wings and body (see Figure 7-11).

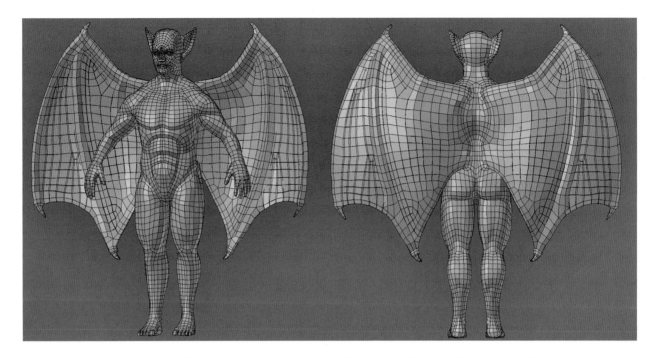

Figure 7-11: The retopologized body mesh, now incorporating both the wings and body and with enough detail to capture the broader features of the face and musculature

Retopologizing the Spider Bot

My goal for the Spider Bot was to turn the rough sculpt into a smooth, hard-surface model. To do this, I needed to replace the original, simple topology of the base mesh with a denser mesh, tailored to the shapes of the body. Additionally, retopology allowed me to embellish as I went along, turning parts of the model into hollow shells, adding holes, or adding supplementary details to the retopologized surface.

Beginning with the body, I added a plane (SHIFT-A) as before, with Snapping turned on and set to project new geometry onto the surface of the sculpt. Next, I added a Mirror modifier to my plane and began following the major lines across the surface (see Figure 7-12). The final step was to fill in quads to complete the rest of the surface, while

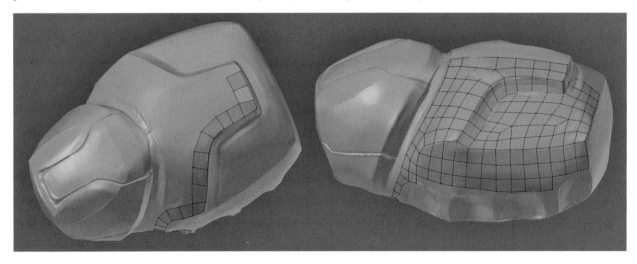

Figure 7-12: Retopologizing the body. Note how the polygons flow around the edges of the sculpt. Later, we'll add support loops to refine the edge to make it sharper and cleaner.

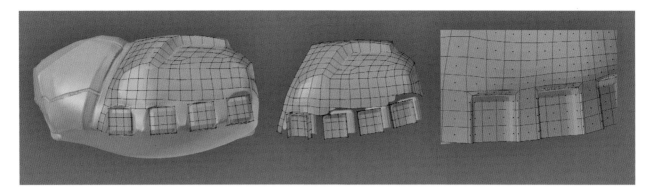

Figure 7-13: Replacing some areas of the sculpt with new, cleaner geometry. Here, cubes are placed by hand and subdivided a couple of times before being connected to the retopologized geometry.

trying to keep the size and distribution of polygons even. To smooth out any dents in the surface, you should select an area you've already retopologized—avoiding edges and corners—and use the Smooth tool a few times to even out the distribution of geometry.

For some parts of the sculpt, I wanted to replace the rough forms sculpted freehand with more precise geometry. To do this, I simply added a primitive, such as a cube or cylinder with approximately the right shape, and moved it into place. For example, in Figure 7-13, I added cubes to form the sockets for the legs, deleting their front and bottom faces and subdividing them to give the right shape while adjusting the surrounding geometry to fit them in.

To further refine the model, I added support loops around its main hard edges (see Figure 7-14). You can do this using tools like Loop Cut (CTRL-R), Subdivide (W ▸ **Subdivide**), and Edge Slide (CTRL-E ▸ **Edge Slide**), or you can use the **Inset Faces** operator, which adds an edge loop around the selected faces with a constant thickness. Combining these operators lets you build up support loops around the key hard edges of your model.

You can add embellishments to the retopologized mesh in several ways. For example, the piece on the left in Figure 7-15 was created by duplicating (SHIFT-D) some of the faces of the retopologized mesh in Edit mode and moving them up (with snapping turned off) to create a new piece. Then, by extruding the new part to give it some thickness and adding some support loops around the edges, I created a raised area on the surface of the model. The circular element on the head in Figure 7-15 was made by creating a new circle, projecting the circle onto the surface of the model with Blender's Snapping tools, and then turning off snapping and extruding out to create a raised area. To flatten the top of it, I scaled the central part along its normals by changing the transform orientation for the 3D manipulator widget

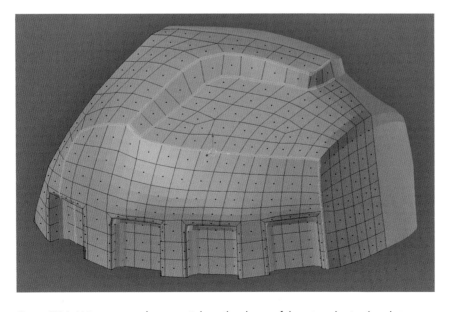

Figure 7-14: Using support loops to tighten the shape of the retopologized sculpt

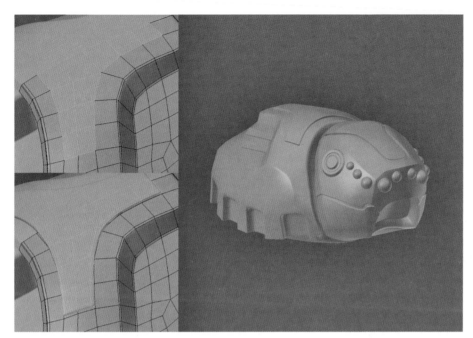

to Normals and then using S ▸ Z ▸ Z ▸ 0 to scale the selection along the surface normals to zero, making it perfectly flat.

I repeated the same process for the abdomen (see Figure 7-16) and the legs (see Figure 7-17). In some areas, my sculpt had lumps or areas that didn't quite polish well enough while sculpting, so I had to tweak things a bit once retopology was finished in order to get nice clean edges.

Because I sculpted only a couple of variations for the different leg pieces, I had an easy time when retopologizing. Each unique piece was retopologized only once (as shown in Figure 7-17) and then duplicated as linked duplicates to create the copies needed for the legs. As in the case of the body, I also used a Mirror modifier to mirror the leg pieces across their axis of symmetry.

Duplicating Groups of Objects

Because I didn't really need to copy the legs to the other side of the body properly at this stage, I added all of the leg pieces to the left side of the body as a group (CTRL-G in Object mode) and then created another instance of this group (SHIFT-A ▸ Add ▸ Group Instance ▸ *Name of group*). The result was a noneditable, duplicate instance of all the objects in the group. I then scaled this group by –1 on its

x-axis to flip it to the other side of the body. Later, I could use the Make Duplicates Real operator (CTRL-SHIFT-A) to convert this group to real geometry (still as linked duplicates of the original objects), but for now, this was a convenient way to preview the entire model without creating unnecessary objects (see Figure 7-18).

Tips for Retopologizing

In summary, here are some general tips to follow when retopologizing your models:

- Model the important edge loops first and then fill in the rest.

- Use support loops or creasing to tighten edges.

- Use Blender's retopology tools to add extra embellishments to your model.

- Try to keep an even polygon density, unless you are specifically adding more detail in a certain area.

- Pay attention to the silhouette of your model. Usually you will be looking at the area you are retopologizing face on, so be sure to look at it from other angles to see that it works.

- Try to work with larger polys where possible. Don't use more than you have to!

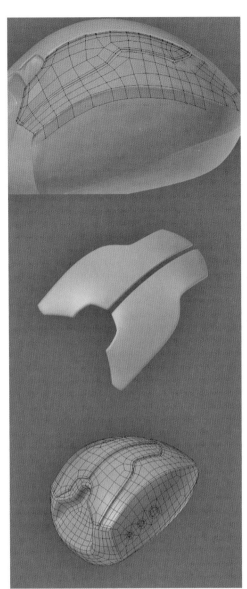

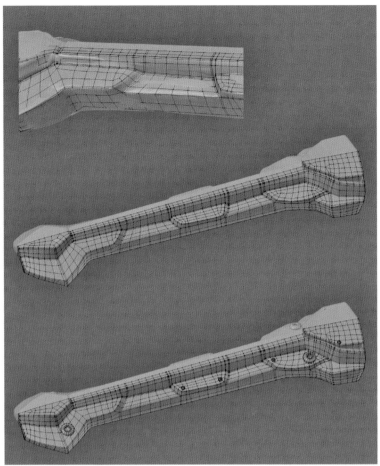

Figure 7-17: Retopologizing the legs. For some areas, I had to either clean up the retopologized mesh manually or simply model new areas, such as the underside of the legs, from scratch. Some extra embellishments, like rivets and so on, I placed by hand.

Figure 7-16: Retopologizing the abdomen. The part in the middle was separated from the main body of the abdomen to break up the shape of the abdomen a bit, giving it a more interesting appearance.

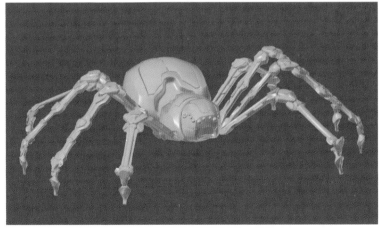

Figure 7-18: The combined elements of the Spider Bot that required retopology, with the legs in place. The legs are mirrored to the other side of the body.

Head Topology

The head is such a complex subject that it deserves some special attention here. While there is no one topology for every conceivable head, there are some important principles to consider. Mainly, when retopologizing a head, you should concentrate on creating face loops around the key features of the face, particularly the mouth and eyes, which will make it easy to deform the face into familiar shapes (see Figure 7-19). These principles apply whether you are retopologizing a sculpted head or modeling one from scratch.

By constructing the important areas of the face with nice topology first, it's easier to join the rest of the head together. In general, I begin with the eyes and work down from the nose into the mouth. Then, I work backward through the cheeks, forehead, and ears. Lastly, I cover the rest of the head

and on down the neck. By first building outward from the most important and complex parts of the head, you'll have to sort out fewer problems with the topology in the areas that matter most.

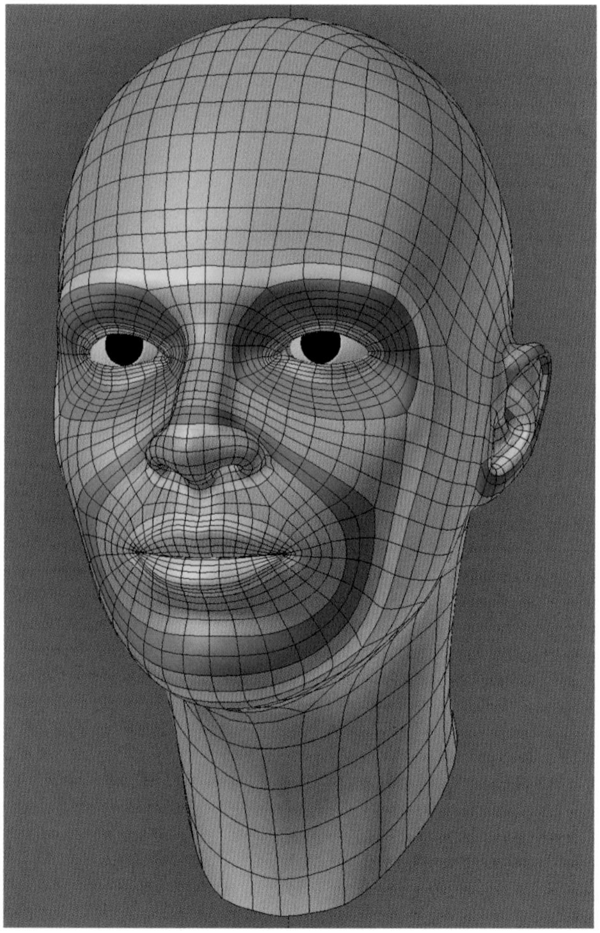

Eyes

When creating or retopologizing a head, there should almost always be a clean ring of face loops around the eyes (see Figure 7-20). These face loops should extend out from the outline of the eyelid to encompass the brows, the outer area of the bridge of the nose, and the upper surface of the cheekbones. This ring will make it easy to close the eyes or raise the eyebrows or cheeks, and it mirrors the underlying anatomy of the face: The *orbicularis oculi* muscle surrounding the eye circles the eye in exactly the same fashion as this ring of face loops.

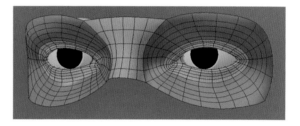

Figure 7-20: The eyes. Adding edge loops around the eyes makes them much easier to edit, pose, and rig. Note the tear duct in the inner corner of the eye, where the gap between the upper and lower eyelids has been bridged. To create the eye socket, the innermost loop around the eyelids is simply extruded back and then optionally filled in to close up the hole.

Mouth

As with the eyes, the *orbicularis oris* muscle encircles the mouth and is responsible for widening and narrowing it (see Figure 7-21). To make it easy to produce common motions of the mouth, we'll create a ring of edge loops around the mouth in the same way. This ring will also make it simple to define the outline of the lips and deform them easily.

Nose/Nasolabial Fold

The complex features of the nose are the nostrils and its tip. By incorporating face loops that run around these areas, the rest of the nose becomes relatively easy to define.

Figure 7-19: The head, with the major face loops highlighted

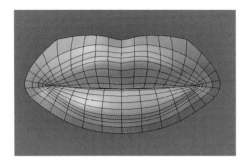

Figure 7-21: The mouth. Note at the corners of the mouth that the edge loops on the surface of the lips bunch up and flow around inside the mouth. Try to keep the same edge or face loop flowing around the outline of both the upper and lower lips. The easiest way to do this is to start with this edge loop and work inward.

The nasolabial fold is an important feature of the nose and is most obvious in snarling or older faces. Adding a face loop that runs over the bridge of the nose and down the sides of the mouth, connecting under or at the chin, allows us to define this area (see Figure 7-22). The bridge of the nose is formed simply by bridging across between the loops encircling the two eyes.

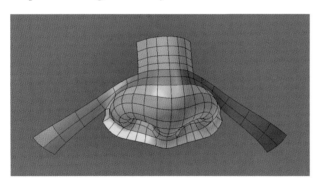

Figure 7-22: The nose. Here, the face loops running along the nasolabial fold and over the bridge of the nose are highlighted in blue, and a face loop running around the nostrils and the tip of the nose is highlighted in green. It is also useful to create face loops around the inside of the nostrils.

Ears

Ears are highly variable from person to person, but their overall construction is reasonably constant. Because the ear is mainly cartilage with no musculature or articulation, it is a pretty static feature of the head and thus a good place to hide awkward triangles if necessary. By defining the helix and

antihelix (the outer and inner curved parts of the ear, shown in blue and green respectively in Figure 7-23) with edge loops that run down into the earlobe, we can make it easy to define the ear's overall structure. The other main feature of the ear is the ear canal. In addition, it is sometimes handy when constructing the ear to try to have a single edge loop encircling the ear to make it easier to attach the ear to the head. One way to do this is to construct the ear as a separate mesh initially and then create a loop around the outside before placing the ear and connecting it with the head.

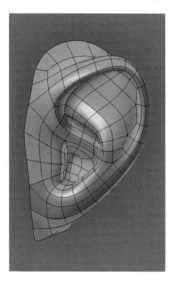

Figure 7-23: The ear

In Review

In this chapter, you've learned how to retopologize meshes with arbitrary topology, be they high-poly sculpts or a collection of separate primitives, to create smooth, clean topology that subdivides well. We've discussed ways to use Blender's Snapping tools to retopologize meshes, as well as alternative methods, such as the Bsurfaces add-on and the Shrinkwrap modifier. We moved on to using these tools to retopologize the meshes we created in earlier chapters with new, better topology.

In Chapter 8, we'll unwrap this new topology to provide it with texture coordinates before baking and painting textures for our final models in Chapters 10 and 11. The improvements that we've made to our models in this chapter will make that process easier and will also improve our render times when we reach Chapter 14.

8

UV UNWRAPPING

In this chapter, we'll UV unwrap the models created so far (where necessary). *UV unwrapping* describes the process of creating a set of 2D coordinates for the faces of a model, which we can then use to apply textures to the model. Creating UV coordinates is akin to cutting up the surface of your model (along lines called *seams*) and spreading it out flat (see Figure 8-1). As you know, a mesh in Blender is made up of vertices joined together to form edges and faces. Each vertex in a model has its own set of spatial coordinates in the three spatial dimensions of the 3D Viewport: *x*, *y*, and *z*. These coordinates determine its position in 3D space. Similarly, UV coordinates are a separate set of 2D coordinates for the points of a model that allow you to map a 2D image to the surface of your mesh.

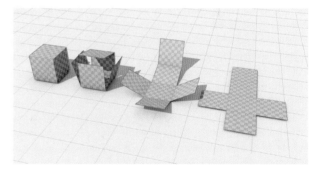

Figure 8-1: UV unwrapping is akin to taking a 3D object and spreading it out flat on a 2D surface. This results in your mesh having a set of 2D coordinates that can then be used to map a 2D image to your object.

Other Kinds of Texture Coordinates

UV coordinates are only one way of mapping an image to an object in Blender. Blender also has a number of procedural coordinates that you can use to assign textures by applying some kind of

projection to your mesh. These have the advantage of being automatic and are useful for a wide range of applications, but they lack the precision of UV unwrapping, which allows you to specify exactly which points on the mesh correspond to the parts of an image.

Editing UV Coordinates

To edit UV coordinates, we use Blender's UV Image editor along with the 3D Viewport. In general, when working with UV coordinates, it's useful to switch to Blender's UV editing layout using the drop-down menu in the Info editor header (see Figure 8-2). This brings up the UV Image editor shown on the left and the 3D Viewport on the right.

It's helpful to add a Properties editor between the UV Image editor and the 3D Viewport by right-clicking the border between them and choosing Split Area. When you set the new area as a Properties editor, you can access the Object Data tab for switching between different UV coordinate sets and the Render tab for accessing Texture Baking controls.

The UV Grid

We'll use the UV Grid in the Image editor to determine which portion of a texture or image is applied to part of a mesh. The grid has coordinates that run from 0 to 1, with the origin at the bottom left. By default, these coordinates are multiplied by the size of the image you select in order to give a number in pixels. If you have no image selected, Blender will assume the grid is 256 pixels across and give coordinates on that scale. You can turn this feature off by pressing **N** to bring up the Properties region of the UV Image editor and checking **Normalized** in the Display panel, which will then give UV coordinates between 0 and 1. The UV Image editor follows the same conventions as the 3D Viewport: You can move, rotate, and scale any selected vertices using the same keys as in the 3D Viewport, and you can use the **X** and **Y** keys to constrain operators to the horizontal and vertical axes of the UV grid. By default, a mesh will not have any UV coordinates, so there will be nothing to select until you unwrap it.

When you map an image to a mesh using its UV coordinates, the image is scaled to fill the UV grid, and each point of the mesh is then mapped to the corresponding point in the image. Beyond the edges of the UV grid, the image is repeated or extended so that UV coordinates outside the grid are mapped to part of the image as well. This allows you to repeat a *tileable texture* (one that can be repeated side by side and top to bottom without any discontinuity) over the surface of your mesh by unwrapping the mesh to be much bigger than the UV grid. Conversely, you can unwrap a whole mesh (or even multiple meshes) so that all the UV coordinates fit within the UV grid

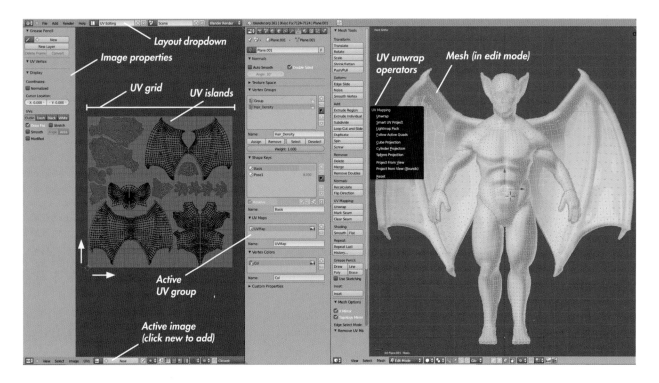

Figure 8-2: A slightly modified UV Image editor layout. You can save this as the default layout by setting up your windows like this in a new .blend file and choosing Save User Settings from the File menu.

and then use a single (nontiling) image to uniquely texture each part of the object's surface. Both options are shown in Figure 8-3.

Figure 8-3: Two options for UV unwrapping. Top: Packing all of an object's faces into the UV grid to texture each part uniquely. Bottom: Tiling an image over an object's surface.

When creating objects with fairly repetitive or homogenous textures, such as brick walls or soil, tileable textures can save you a lot of time. On the other hand, when creating characters and other unique objects, you'll need to pack an object's UVs onto a single grid in order to texture each part differently.

Unwrapping Tools

To start unwrapping a model, you'll need to be in Edit mode (press TAB to switch into it if you aren't already there). You'll probably also want to switch to Edge Select mode in the 3D Viewport header, as tagging edges with UV seams is easiest when you can select edges directly. To begin unwrapping your object, press **U** in the 3D Viewport, which will bring up several operators for unwrapping your object, as shown in Figure 8-2. These operators are as follows:

Unwrap This is probably the most useful UV unwrapping method. Blender will try to unwrap your mesh by flattening it as if it were made from stretchy fabric, while also trying to minimize the distortion that this flattening inevitably causes.

(In order for this process to work for a closed mesh, you'll need to mark some UV seams on your mesh.)

Smart UV Project This will automatically project your mesh by first projecting the largest chunk possible from one angle, excluding invisible faces or ones that point away from that viewport. It will then project progressively smaller, more difficult parts, splitting them into different UV islands as it goes. This effect can work reasonably well for simple meshes, but when used with more complex shapes, it often produces a lot of little islands that can be difficult to work with.

Lightmap Pack This special UV unwrapping option for baking lighting to textures projects each individual polygon in a mesh to a separate rectangular UV island. The Lightmap Pack option uses up the UV coordinate space very efficiently, which makes it useful for baking lighting textures for game engines but not very useful for practical texturing.

Follow Active Quads This follows the active quad (the one highlighted when you have multiple faces selected in Face Select mode—usually the most recently selected one) and unwraps the faces radiating out from it in an even grid. This option works particularly well for meshes with grid-like topology (that is, no poles), such as pipes, cylinders, flat(ish) grids, and the like. It works best when you unwrap one quad first as a perfect rectangle with 90-degree corners: 1) Unwrap with **U ▸ Unwrap**; 2) select each edge of the unwrapped quad in the UV Image editor and scale it so it's perfectly horizontal/vertical; 3) unwrap the rest of the mesh by selecting it with CTRL-L, which selects anything connected to your current selection; 4) use the **Follow Active Quads** unwrap operator to get a nice even unwrap. This option, though, doesn't work well for meshes with more complex topology.

Cube Projection This option projects the faces of your mesh as if on the surface of a cube. It's useful for roughly cube-shaped objects.

Cylinder Projection This option works like Cube Projection but acts as if the mesh is cylindrical.

Sphere Projection This option also works like Cube Projection but acts as if the mesh is spherical.

Project from View   This option projects your mesh as it appears in the 3D Viewport. It's particularly useful for projecting a small, flat part of your mesh before pinning it and then projecting the rest using the Unwrap operator.

Project from View (Bounds)   This option works like Project from View, but after it projects the meshes, it stretches the UV coordinates to fill the whole UV-coordinate space.

Reset   This option stretches each face across the whole UV-coordinate space.

Seams

Imagine trying to flatten out a beach ball. Even once you deflate it, you can't stretch it out so that each part of the surface is flat on the ground without making at least one cut to the ball, and the more you carve it up, the less you have to stretch and distort it in order to flatten it out. Something similar is true when using the Unwrap operator to unwrap a mesh. In order for the operator to work, you'll need to mark edges as *seams* where the mesh will split. Ideally, you should mark as few seams as possible so that you won't have to paint across too many seams when it comes to texturing, but you also need to mark enough so that your mesh will not be distorted by the UV unwrapping. Distortion in this case arises from Blender having to warp and stretch the geometry in order to lay it out flat. When you use the distorted UVs to map an image to the 3D object, the texture will look stretched out as well.

To mark UV seams, select edges in Edit mode and use CTRL-E ▶ **Mark Seam** to mark the edge as a UV seam. To quickly select the shortest path between two edges (a good way to select a long string of edges for marking), select one edge, then press CTRL and right-click the edge you want to use as the end point. You can also press ALT and right-click to select an entire edge loop at once, allowing you to mark multiple edges at the same time. Shortcuts like these will make tagging multiple edges at once much quicker.

In general, you should try to hide your UV seams in areas where they won't cause problems and where they will minimize the amount of stretching in your unwrap. Valleys and creases in your mesh are good places to hide seams, as is any area that won't get too much attention. Try to mark seams symmetrically to make it easier to understand your unwrap and to allow you to copy and paste elements of your texturing later (if your unwrap is symmetrical, too). Finally, split your mesh into sensible islands (groups of faces bounded by seams). For example, in the case of the Bat Creature, I split the torso, wings, head, arms and legs, and hands and feet into separate sections, as you can see in Figure 8-4.

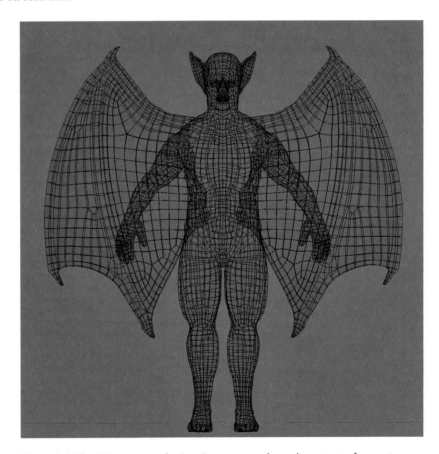

Figure 8-4: The UV seams on the Bat Creature are shown here in wireframe view. While some seams are (unavoidably) in visible areas, such as around the outside edge of the wings, most are hidden in less conspicuous areas, like the inside of the legs and down the back of the ears and neck. Hiding your seams like this makes cleaning up seams in textures easier later on.

Pinning Vertices

Unwrapping your mesh with the Unwrap operator may not give you exactly the unwrap you want; for example, one area might be scrunched up or have a proportion that's not to scale. To fix this, you can pin vertices in the UV Image editor so that they won't move when you re-unwrap the mesh (shortcut **E** in the UV editor or **U** in the 3D Viewport) by selecting a vertex or vertices and pressing **P** to pin them. (Pinned vertices will be highlighted in red.) Now when you re-unwrap, Blender will keep the pinned vertices in place and stretch the rest of the unwrap to allow for this. To unpin vertices, select them and press ALT-P.

One important reason to use pinning is to establish a symmetrical unwrap. To do this, unwrap your mesh and then select a string of vertices running down the middle of the mesh and align them in the UV Image editor so that they are in a straight line (running in the appropriate direction). An easy way to do this is to scale them to zero on the *x*- or *y*-axis and then pin them (**P**). Now press **E** in the UV editor to unwrap again. This gives you a more symmetrical unwrap, as shown in Figure 8-5.

Pinning can also be used to fix areas on large meshes that unwrap on top of one another, as often happens with long, tube-like meshes, where the UV unwrap may coil around undesirably. To fix this problem, pin one vertex from each end of the mesh so that the vertices sit farther apart in UV space, then unwrap the mesh again.

Finally, when unwrapping a mesh with a lot of different pieces, it can help to pin entire UV islands as you finish with them so that you can move on to unwrapping other pieces without disturbing the ones you're happy with. Blender will re-unwrap anything you have visible in the UV Image editor by default when you re-unwrap, so this is a good way to keep finished parts of your unwrap safe.

Packing

When unwrapping characters and other unique objects, it's often helpful to pack all of the UV islands for your mesh into a single grid. To do this automatically, you can use the Pack operator (CTRL-P), but you can usually do a more efficient job of packing UV islands yourself simply by moving, scaling, and rotating them like puzzle pieces. To speed up the selection of whole islands, switch to Island Selection mode in the UV Image editor using the buttons in the header.

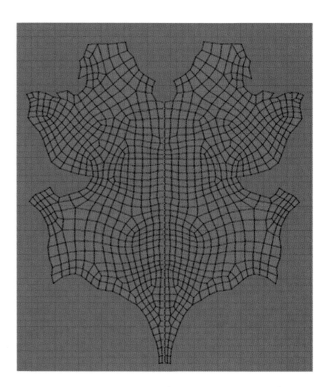

Figure 8-5: To get a symmetrical unwrap on the torso of the Bat Creature, I did a normal unwrap and then pinned the vertices down the center of the chest in a vertical line and unwrapped again. The result is a symmetrical UV island that will be simpler to texture later.

When packing UV islands, be sure to keep the scale of the islands similar. To average the scale of any UV islands you have selected, use CTRL-A or scale the islands manually. It's much easier, though, to see whether islands are scaled correctly once you have a UV test grid assigned (see "Testing Your UV Coordinates" on page 114).

Assigning UV Textures

There are many ways to display textures on your models. For one, you can use Blender GLSL materials to create advanced materials with Texture options that respond to lighting and transparency. For simpler applications, though, such as previewing how a single image will be mapped to an unwrapped object, you can assign that image to your model in the UV Image editor. To do so, take the following steps:

1. Select the object and enter **Edit mode**.
2. Select all of the faces and unwrap them if you haven't done so already.

3. Select the image you want to assign to the mesh from the image drop-down menu in the header of the UV Image editor. Alternatively, you can open an image with **Image ▸ Open Image**, or create one with **Image ▸ New Image**.

4. To see your image in the 3D Viewport, go to the Display panel of the Properties region and enable **Textured Solid**.

Testing Your UV Coordinates

To make sure that your UV unwrap works well and that areas are not becoming too distorted, apply a UV test grid to see the effects of your unwrap on your mesh (see Figure 8-6). To do so, follow the steps below:

1. In the UV Image editor, with your object in Edit mode, click **Image ▸ New Image** to apply a new image to your mesh and check the **UV Test Grid** option. This will generate a test grid pattern and assign it to the UV coordinates of your mesh.

2. Turn on **Textured Solid** in the display options of the Properties region in the 3D Viewport. You should see a checkerboard pattern applied to your mesh.

You should now be able to easily see problem areas in your unwrap, such as areas with awkward stretching or parts of the mesh that are too big or too small. You can then fix these areas in the UV Image editor and see the changes in real time in the 3D Viewport.

Unwrapping the Bat Creature

As you've seen in the preceding discussion, I unwrapped the Bat Creature and packed it into a single UV tile by first tagging seams and then unwrapping with the Unwrap operator (see Figure 8-7). For the torso, I made the unwrap more symmetrical by selecting the line of vertices that ran down the middle of the front of the torso in the UV Image editor, scaling them on the x-axis to zero (**S ▸ X ▸ 0**), pinning them, and then unwrapping again (**E**). Next, I averaged the scale of all of the islands, packed them into the UV grid, and scaled up the head slightly to give it more texture space relative to other areas (because it's the part of the body likely to get more attention).

Figure 8-6: Checking your UV unwrap with a UV test grid image. This grid will help you to identify areas that have not unwrapped well, as well as ones that are out of scale with the rest of the unwrap.

Finally, I unwrapped the fingernails and teeth onto the same layout, fitting them into the remaining gaps between the other islands.

For the eyes, I unwrapped only the inner mesh simply by positioning the 3D Viewport to look at the eye straight on and using the Project from View (Bounds) operator. Later on, I will tweak the UVs of the eye mesh to fit the texture I will paint for it. See Chapter 11 for more on unwrapping and texturing the eyes.

Unwrapping the Jungle Temple

The Jungle Temple had many separate elements, and rather than go through them all, I'll just cover the most difficult ones. (The objects in the Jungle Temple not discussed below are simply unwrapped using variations on the techniques discussed earlier.)

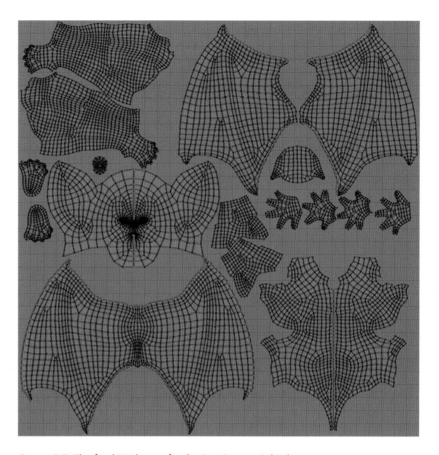

Figure 8-7: The final UV layout for the Bat Creature's body

Stone Blocks

There were an awful lot of stone blocks in the Jungle Temple, so I didn't want to have to texture each individually. Instead, I wanted to be able to unwrap them all relatively quickly and reuse the same textures for each. My quick and dirty solution was to use the Select Sharp operator in Edit mode to select the sharp edges of the blocks (Select ▶ Sharp Edges from the 3D Viewport header) and then mark them as seams (see Figure 8-8). Next, I used the Unwrap operator to unwrap all the blocks at once. I manually removed some seams in areas like the damaged stone and at the edges of some blocks where I wanted the texture to wrap around rather than having an obvious seam. I only placed seams manually on the blocks in the scene's foreground, and I unwrapped these manually to make sure they unwrapped nicely.

Trees

In the case of the trees, I added seams down their backs (the sides facing away from the camera) and around the joins between the trunk and the roots. I then unwrapped them using Unwrap. Next, I selected a string of vertices in the UV Image editor that ran down the middle of the root or trunk, aligned it with the vertical axis, and pinned it. Unwrapping again gave me nicely aligned UV islands.

The technique described above is useful when unwrapping something like tree bark that has a texture with a strong grain or directional pattern because all of the pieces will align with the direction of the grain. I packed both trees into the same UV space (see Figure 8-9) to allow me to texture them both at the same time later on.

Figure 8-8: Placing seams automatically for the blocks in the Jungle Temple scene. I selected the edges of the stone blocks with Select Sharp and then marked them as seams and unwrapped them.

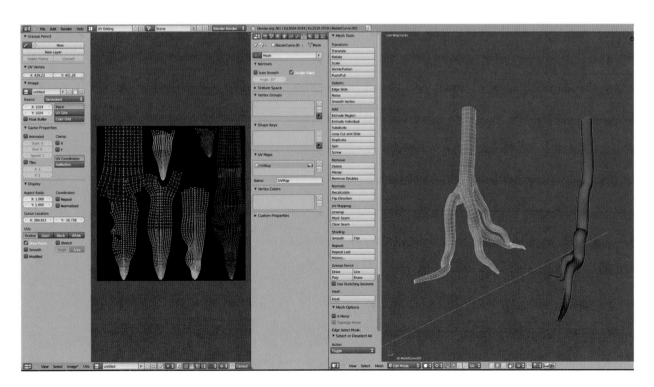

Figure 8-9: The UVs for the tree objects. The active object appears as editable UV islands, while other selected (but not active) objects appear gray in the UV Image editor.

Multiple UV Maps

You can add multiple UV-coordinate sets to an object and edit them independently. This is good for making use of multiple textures in complex materials and when texture painting. When texture painting, you can use one UV set to neatly pack your UV islands for your final texture and use another to assign seamless textures or photos to clone texture information from. In subsequent chapters, I will sometimes refer to creating extra UV sets for purposes like these.

For the trees, I created a second UV coordinate set to match up with a tileable bark texture, saving the first UV set to use for baking ambient occlusion and the final texture maps. To create this second set, I opened the Object Data tab of the Properties editor and clicked the + icon in the UV Maps panel to create a new UV set. You can choose between your existing UV sets from this panel and edit whichever is active. To unwrap the second UV set for my tree, I used the Follow Active Quads operator for the parts of the trees with approximately cylindrical topology and unwrapped and packed

them so that they filled the width of the UV grid (see Figure 8-10). Later, this would allow me to tile a texture multiple times around and along the length of the trunk and roots without creating too many seams where the textures didn't match.

Sharing UV Space Between Objects

Just as you'll usually want to combine all of a single object's UV islands in the UV grid, when it comes to unwrapping multiple objects for texturing, you may want them all to share the same UV space so that they can all use the same texture. Doing so will save you time when painting textures and memory when rendering. To see the UV coordinates of multiple objects in the UV Image editor at the same time, select the objects and then enter Edit mode for the one you want to edit. In the UV Image editor, turn on **View ▸ Draw Other Objects**. The UV coordinates for the selected objects will now be visible in gray (though only the current object will be editable), allowing you to align multiple objects on the same UV grid (see Figure 8-11).

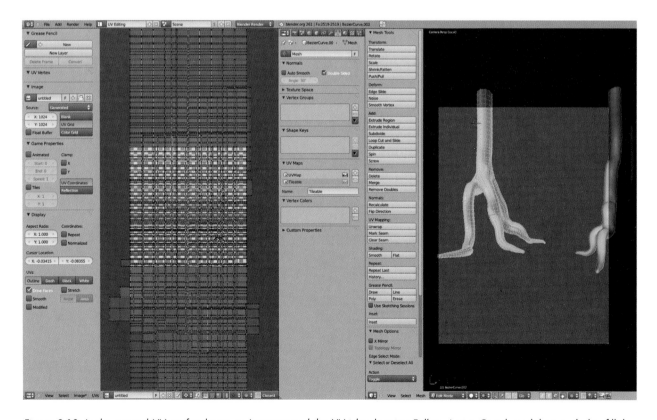

Figure 8-10: In the second UV set for the trees, I unwrapped the UV islands using Follow Active Quads and then scaled to fill the width of the UV grid. Later, this will be used for aligning tileable textures along the length of the trees and their roots.

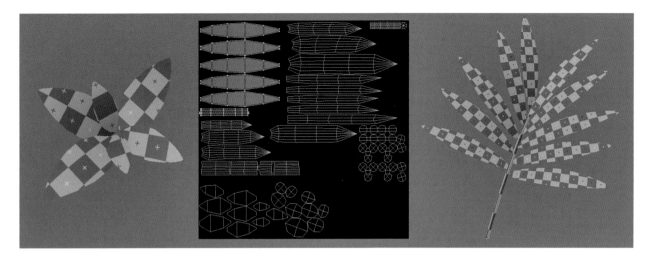

Figure 8-11: UV coordinates for the various leaf objects. Most were unwrapped to share the same UV coordinates.

Leaves and Grass

Flat meshes with open edges are particularly easy to unwrap because you don't have to mark any seams. I simply used Unwrap on all the leaves in my scene, unwrapping them all to share the same UV space (see Figure 8-11). This excludes the IvyGen leaves, which were automatically unwrapped by the IvyGen add-on already. For the cylindrical elements, such as the stems of the grass, I marked seams as needed, unwrapped one face (making sure it unwrapped as a rectangle), and then selected the rest of the mesh (CTRL-L) and unwrapped using Follow Active Quads.

Statue

For the statue mesh, I marked seams by hand around all the major parts and unwrapped using the Unwrap operator. Figure 8-12 shows the results. You could try using Smart Unwrap, and you might get what you need for a mesh like this, but unwrapping by hand will always give you more control.

The Rest of the Elements

The other elements in the Jungle Temple scene were all pretty straightforward and followed the same strategies used so far. Some elements, like the water, didn't need UV textures because they will use entirely procedural materials instead. (Chapter 9 will deal with creating procedural materials that don't require textures, such as water and glass.)

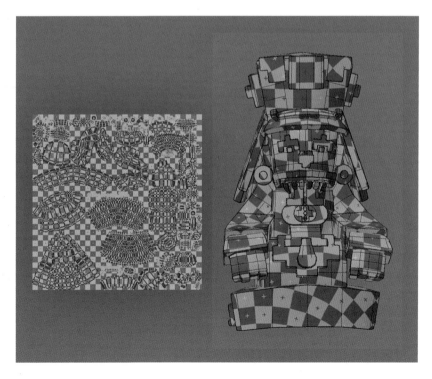

Figure 8-12: The statue UVs, unwrapped and packed into the UV grid

Unwrapping the Spider Bot

For the Spider Bot, I did my best to squeeze the model's entire UV unwrap onto a single texture (see Figure 8-13), excluding a few parts that would receive only procedural materials. Because much of the model used similar materials, it was easy to edit the whole texture at once. By starting with the big elements, like the body and the legs, and then squeezing the smaller parts into the gaps in between, I could produce a very efficiently packed set of UVs, ensuring that important elements got the texture real estate they needed. You can always check that the different parts unwrap with the right scale and without stretching using a UV grid texture (see Figure 8-13).

Applying Modifiers and Duplicates

In previous chapters, I used modifiers to model and retopologize the Spider Bot's body and legs symmetrically. By doing so, I reduced the amount of work required and duplicated some of the parts for the legs. While I could have kept the leg pieces as duplicates, it was better to apply some of the modifiers at this stage, especially Mirror modifiers, because otherwise the textures would be mapped to both sides of the objects symmetrically. This would result in some obvious symmetry down the middle of the objects; worse, if I were to use any text or graphics in my textures, they would appear on the mirrored side of the mesh backward! For this reason, I applied the Mirror modifiers assigned to many of the Spider Bot's constituent objects.

Unfortunately, Blender won't allow you to apply modifiers to objects that share their mesh data with other objects. This makes applying modifiers to the model difficult when, as for the Spider Bot, I have used linked duplicates to copy parts of the model, like the legs, which now have many objects that share the same mesh data. To get around this, use the Mesh from the Curve/Meta/Surf/Text operator (ALT-C), which will apply any modifiers to an object and convert them to proper geometry. Because you want to apply only the Mirror modifier, not the Subdivision Surface modifier, remove all but the Mirror modifier first and then use the operator. You will then need to remove the Mirror modifiers from the other duplicates because they will now be using the already mirrored mesh data.

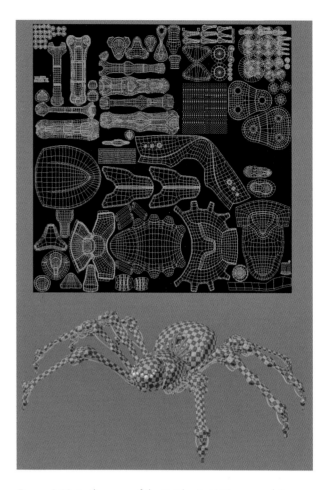

Figure 8-13: In the case of the Spider Bot UVs, most of the unwrapping was done with Unwrap. Once I unwrapped it, I packed all of the UV coordinates for the model to occupy the same space. (You only need to unwrap each duplicate part once. So, for example, the parts of the legs don't all need to be unwrapped separately, as long as the duplicates all use the same mesh data.)

Sharing UV Space Efficiently

For certain areas, I shared the UV space for similar parts (see Figure 8-14). For example, for the mechanical elements beneath the legs, I placed all of the UV islands on a patch at the top-right corner of the UV grid. Doing so will cause errors when baking textures, but by painting a generic texture over these areas, I can texture multiple parts of the model without using as much UV space. (Since these parts are relatively hidden, the lack of unique textures on these areas won't make too much of a difference.)

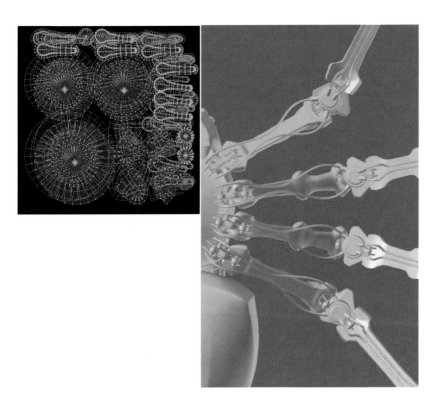

Figure 8-14: Some mechanical elements of the Spider Bot were unwrapped to share the same portion of the UV grid. The small mechanical joints below the legs (right) were unwrapped to a small corner of the UV grid (left).

Making sure that all objects are assigned roughly the same amount of UV space according to their size is more difficult for multiple objects because the Average Islands Scale operator (CTRL-A) works only on UV islands within a mesh. However, by using a UV grid texture and enabling Textured Solid in the 3D Viewport, you can judge the scale of an object's UV coordinates and adjust them accordingly.

In Review

This concludes unwrapping the models I created in earlier chapters. We've looked at how to tag seams to unwrap meshes and how to refine the results of Blender's unwrapping. We've also learned how to pack UV coordinates for meshes together to make it simple to texture multiple objects with one image. In Chapter 9, we'll move on to adding particle systems to some of our projects to create fur and grass before baking and painting textures in Chapters 10 and 11 and creating materials in Chapter 12. In these later chapters, we'll apply images to the UV coordinates we created in this chapter in order to bake and paint on textures that we can then use as the inputs for materials.

9

HAIR AND PARTICLE SYSTEMS

Blender's particle systems are a powerful tool that you can use to create both static and dynamic hair and animated particle effects. They can also be used to populate your scene with instanced objects in order to create grass and other foliage. In this chapter, we'll use Blender's hair particles to create fur for the Bat Creature and to create grass for the Jungle Temple scene.

When you add a particle system to an object, the system is initially set up as a dynamic one that spawns point particles that are then simulated using Blender's physics engine. In this chapter, though, we'll mostly use the "hair" type for particles to create strands that are emitted from the surface of your mesh by default (see Figure 9-1). These strands will respond to physics and can be combed over the surface of your model and be procedurally modified to look like hair, fur, grass, or a variety of other materials. You'll learn how to move from the default system shown in Figure 9-1 to creating realistic hair and fur that we'll add materials to in Chapter 12 and then render in Chapter 14.

Particles for Hair

In order to make Blender's basic particle system resemble fur or hair, we need to give it some guidance. First, we determine where and how we want the fur to grow, after which we can comb the resulting hair for more control over how it looks. But rather than do this for hundreds of thousands of hairs on a body, we'll define a few hairs by hand as parent particles and then have Blender fill in the rest with child particles automatically. These stages are represented in Figure 9-2: First, the particle system is added ❶; then, the hair is restricted to some areas with a vertex group ❷; next, it's combed ❸; and finally, child particles are added ❹. You then have a basic render ❺.

Choosing an Object to Add Hair To

One question to think about when creating the hair or fur for a model is what mesh you want to assign the particle system to, as this can be approached in several ways. The simplest option is to just add a

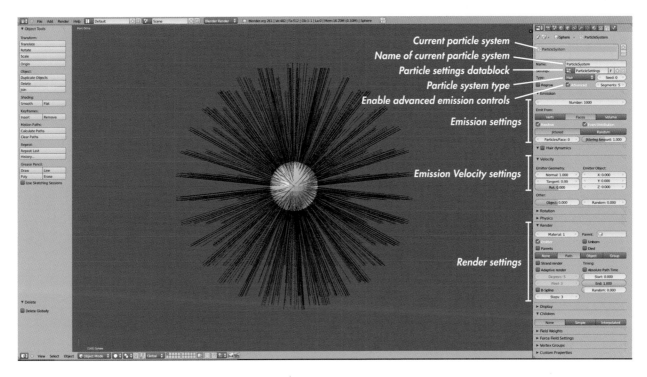

Figure 9-1: The standard particle system in Blender with the particle system type set to hair

Figure 9-2: Hair particle systems at different stages

particle system to the mesh you have modeled and intend to texture and render later. However, this means that you can no longer edit your mesh (at least beyond moving vertices), as changes to the vertex order of your model will corrupt the hair.

In the case of the Bat Creature, the final render will be done using a mesh created by applying some of the multires subdivision to the model and leaving the rest to be re-created using a displacement map. Because this will require creating a new mesh, I could either wait until that stage before creating the hair or create the hair system using a different mesh, which I would keep in the *.blend* file for the final render later. The latter option allows me to work on a "safe" mesh, which I can then use to work

on the fur—the mesh won't change if I make further changes (within reason) to the "skin" model later. I will use this mesh only to hold the hair for the character, and its surface will not be rendered.

Creating a Scalp

A similar strategy can be useful when creating a haircut for a character. While we might wish to make all kinds of changes to the model for a head, the shape of the skull is likely to remain reasonably static. In order to keep the hair separate, then, it is often useful to create a "scalp" object to which the hair can be added by duplicating the head mesh and deleting any parts that aren't needed (see Figure 9-3). The particle system for the hair can then be added to this object.

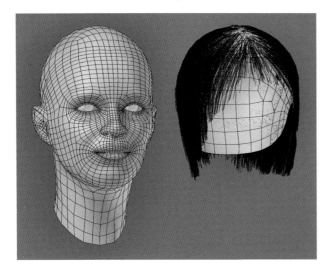

Figure 9-3: Creating a scalp to hold the particle system for a character's hair. This allows you to keep modifying the model for the head without disturbing the hair. Here, the two are shown side by side, but generally they would be on top of one another.

For the Bat Creature, I created a new mesh to hold the particle system by duplicating my sculpted high-resolution mesh and applying the Multires modifier at level 1. To do this on a mesh that has shape keys, use the Convert to Mesh operator (ALT-C ▸ **Mesh from Curve/Meta/Text**). This applies all modifiers and shape keys to the mesh.

Vertex Groups for Hair

By default, particle systems emit particles from all over the surface of an object. In order to restrict hair to specific areas of a model and control the length and behavior of the hair, we use vertex groups. A *vertex group* is a subset of the vertices in a mesh, like the legs of a character or a specific part of a wall. You can assign vertices to these groups either in Edit mode or Weight Paint mode.

Vertices can also be partially assigned to a group, with their weighting for the group (that is, how strongly they belong to it) given any value between 0 and 1. This allows for smooth gradients and blending between vertices that are and are not assigned to groups.

Once created, vertex groups can be used to control the effects of modifiers, to make it easy to quickly select vertices in Edit mode, and to influence particle systems. By using vertex groups, we can "paint" hair placement in Weight Paint mode and then assign the vertex group to the particle settings to tell Blender to create particles only where we want them.

Weight Painting

Blender offers two methods of editing vertex groups. The first is to manually assign weights to a group in Edit mode, using the buttons in the Object Data tab of the Properties editor and the tools in the Properties region of the 3D Viewport (press **N** to bring this up). This method is useful for defining more precise groups, like the ones we used in Chapters 4 and 6 to restrict the effect of the Displace modifier.

But if your goal is to produce smoother, less precise groups with more variation and randomness, Blender's Weight Paint mode tools (shown in Figure 9-4) are a better option. Entering Weight Paint mode (CTRL-TAB, or use the mode drop-down menu in the 3D Viewport header) allows you to paint vertex weights using brushes.

The standard brush tools in Weight Paint mode are as follows:

Mix Replaces the current weighting with the weight specified by the brush. This is the standard brush for painting vertex groups.

Blur Blurs vertex weights between neighboring vertices and is useful for smoothing transitions.

Add Adds to the vertices' weight.

Subtract Subtracts from the vertices' weight. This brush is useful as an eraser.

Multiply Multiplies the vertices' current weight by a particular value. Set the weight to 0 to use this as an eraser; use higher values to reduce vertex weights without completely removing vertices from the current group.

Lighten Replaces the vertices' current weight with the weight you specify for the brush if the new weight is greater.

Darken Replaces the vertices' current weight with the weight you specify for the brush if the new weight is less.

Blender's default brushes work pretty well, so you probably won't need to make your own, though you can do so in much the same way as described in Chapter 6.

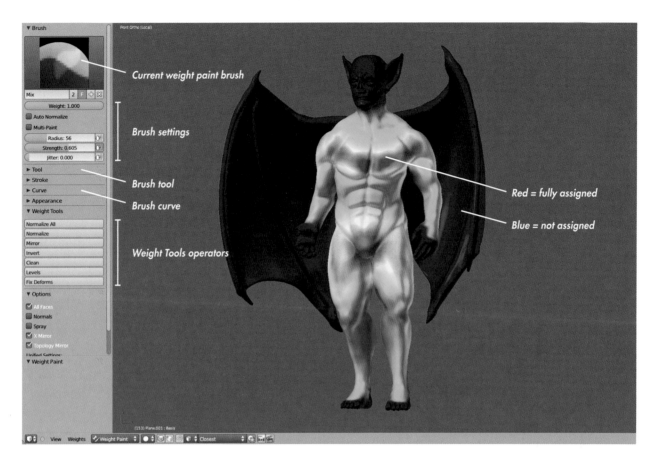

Figure 9-4: Weight Paint mode. Red areas represent vertices fully assigned to the current group, and blue areas represent vertices that are not assigned to the current group.

Hair Density

To control where the Bat Creature's hair will grow, I needed to paint a vertex group that defined where I wanted hair and where I didn't. I began by adding a new vertex group that I'll call *hair density*. Then in Weight Paint mode (CTRL-TAB), I began assigning areas I wanted to be furry to the group using a Mix type brush. I could remove areas using the Subtract brush and smooth the transition between hairy and hairless areas with the Blur brush. (Because I am editing only the hair density for now, the boundaries of the vertex group will still have long hairs. To make the hairy regions fade out into shorter hairs, I will create a second vertex group in a minute to control the hair length.)

Figure 9-4 shows my hair-density group: Areas on the upper body and upper legs are fully assigned to the group, areas like the arms and lower legs are only partially assigned, and areas like the wings and face that are to remain hairless are not assigned at all.

To completely remove part of a mesh from a vertex group, you can use the Subtract brush in Weight Paint mode, but it's easier to do this precisely in Edit mode. To do so, use the Object Data tab of the Properties editor to edit vertex groups and manually add or remove vertices by selecting them in Edit mode and pressing the Assign or Remove buttons. For example, for the Bat Creature, I manually selected the wings and removed them from the density (and length) vertex group to be sure the wings wouldn't grow hair.

Hair Length

The hair-length vertex group (see Figure 9-5) controls the length of the hair by defining how long the hair created by our particle system will grow, relative to the maximum length we choose in the Particle System settings. This group is similar to the hair-density group, except that I assigned the chest and pelvis much more than other areas, giving them the longest hair, and I blurred the weights more significantly between areas to produce a smooth transition in hair length.

When painting the length group, you can paint outside the bounds of the hair-density group without fear because hair will not grow outside the density group. This allows you, for example, to grow long hair right up to the edge of the density group, if you wish.

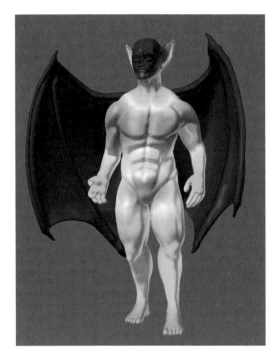

Figure 9-5: The hair-length vertex group

Adding a Particle System

Having added the basic hair vertex groups, I next created a particle system to "grow" the hair. To do so, I went to the Particles tab of the Properties editor and added a new particle system using the + icon on the right. (You can add additional particle systems to the same object and switch between them using the selector at the top of the Particles tab.)

Adding a new particle system brings up a whole slew of panels, like the ones shown earlier in Figure 9-1. I began modifying some of these. First, I changed the particle system type from an emitter of dynamic particles to a hair system by changing the type setting to Hair. This change initially caused the mesh to look like a crazy hairball. To turn the hair particle system into something useful, I used the vertex groups I created for hair

length and density to restrict the hair growth. Then, I assigned the settings for the particles and combed and cut the hair to make it look the way I wanted. To make going through these stages easier, I'll first discuss the main panels for particle systems when creating hair-type particle systems. These are discussed below in the order they appear in the Particles tab of the Properties editor.

Particle System Properties

At the top of the Particles tab in the Properties editor, you'll find a panel showing the existing particle systems assigned to the active object. Below this are a few basic options that define what sort of particle system you are creating:

Type (Hair/Emitter)   Set this to *Hair* for creating hair and fur. The Emitter type is for creating dynamic, point-particle stems.

Advanced   Turn this on for greater control over particle emission.

Segments   This determines how many control points are used per strand of hair in order to control the shape of the hair. More control points mean you can incorporate more twists and bends into your project. For short hair and fur, the default value of 5 is fine, but for longer haircuts, consider turning the value up.

Emission Panel

This panel controls how many particles are emitted from your mesh and their distribution.

Number   Determines the number of particles the particle system will generate. If you use child particles in the settings, the total number of particles will be this setting multiplied by the number of child particles. Keep this in mind when setting up a hair particle system because for the same final number of particles, you could create lots of parents and fewer children, or fewer parents and more children. In general, you want to have to edit as few strands as possible, while maintaining control over the look of the hair over the surface of the mesh. So when adding hair to a simple head, Blender's default of 1,000 might be a little high, but for larger areas (for example, when covering a whole creature in fur), you might want to increase this value. For the Bat Creature, I chose a value of 2,000.

Emit From (Verts/Faces/Volume) Determines where hair particles are emitted from, such as from the vertices of the mesh, scattered over its faces, or from inside the volume of a closed mesh.

Random Emits particles randomly, ignoring the order in which you created the faces of your mesh. Leave this set to *Random* for hair.

Even Distribution Scales the number of particles emitted from each face according to the face's area. Leave this checked, or large faces will appear sparsely populated with hair when compared to smaller faces.

Jittered/Random, Particles Per Face, and Jittering Amount These settings control how the emission locations for particles are generated. The default values almost always work well.

Velocity Panel

The settings in the Velocity panel basically determine how long your hairs will be and in what direction they'll point. The random and normal values are most important here. *Normal* values cause hair to point straight out from the surface, while *random* values make the hair point in random directions. Combining the two will allow you to point the hair generally away from the head with the normal value, while keeping a little roughness with the random value. The other settings in this panel can be useful if you want the hair to point in a specific direction (such as straight up, using the *Z* value).

Rotation

The Rotation panel isn't particularly important when working with strand-particle hair, but if you set the render type for the particle system to Object or Group, you can use the settings here to add random rotation to the objects as they are generated. This feature is a great way to prevent particle systems that use the Object render type from looking too repetitive by making it more difficult to recognize repeated objects.

Render

This panel contains settings for how your particles will be rendered in the final image. These settings, listed below, will interact with the material we apply to the particles later on in Chapter 12.

Material This determines what material slot (in the Materials tab of the Properties editor) the hair particles will use. For example, if your first material slot for the object is the skin material for your model, you could set this to 2 and use the second slot to define the hair material.

Emitter When this setting is checked, both the hair and its emitter mesh will render; when unchecked, only the hair itself will render. This setting is useful to disable if you are using an object other than your "skin" object to generate hair or if you're generating objects with a particle system and you want to render only those instanced objects.

Parents If you are using child particles, this setting will cause the parent particles to be rendered along with the children.

None/Path/Object/Group This setting determines which renderable geometry the particle system will use for particle generation. The default setting of *Path* is used to create particle hair, but a particle system can also be used to create other kinds of geometry. Setting this to *Object* will turn each hair particle into a duplicate of the object chosen in the box that appears, and setting it to *Group* will choose objects from a group and duplicate them in the same way. These options are useful for making grass or for populating a surface with extra details, like rocks or debris. The *None* option will cause particles not to be rendered.

For hair, choose the Path option, which brings up the following additional settings that determine how particle hair will be rendered:

Strand Render This uses Blender's custom strand primitive to render hair and fur in a way that produces much faster results. The downside to this rendering method is that it's not compatible with ray-traced shadows, so you will need to use spot lamps with buffer shadows instead.

Adaptive Renderer This option for rendering hair is compatible with ray tracing and optimizes the hair geometry, simplifying bends in the hair so that long, straight sections use less geometry than more complex, curved parts of strands. This keeps the total amount of geometry used for hair to a minimum and thus can speed up renders.

Degrees The strand renderer renders hairs in a sequence of straight sections, and this value determines how many degrees the underlying curve must bend through in order to create a new section. Smaller values will result in smoother-looking hair but will take longer to render as they will generate more sections.

B-Spline This method uses a Bézier-like curve to render hair strands, resulting in much smoother curves but with some loss of detail in the shape of your edited hair as the curve is smoothed out.

Steps This method determines how many sections in total are generated for the hair curve, expressed as the number of times the hair is subdivided. For example, a value of 3 will make the hair twice as smooth (twice as many sections) as 2, and a value of 4 will make the hair curve twice as smooth again.

Display

This panel works like the Render panel but defines how your particles appear in the 3D Viewport. Turning these settings down can often speed up the 3D Viewport when working with complex particle systems, while turning them up can give you a better feel for what your rendered particles will actually look like.

None/Rendered/Path These options allow you to determine how particles appear in the 3D Viewport. Setting this to *Rendered* will use the display type used for the render. *None* prevents the particle system being drawn at all in the 3D Viewport, and *Path* draws particles as paths regardless of the render type.

Display (Percentage) This option sets the proportion of the total number of hairs visible in the 3D Viewport. Lower settings will reduce the strain on your machine when working with complex hair systems.

Size, Velocity, Number These options will draw the corresponding datum for each particle on screen next to that particle datum (that is, the particle's size, velocity, or ID number).

Color (Material/Velocity/Acceleration/None) This option is more relevant for emitter particle systems. Leave it set to *Material* for hair particles.

Steps This option determines how many subdivisions are used to draw the hair in the 3D Viewport (as in the render options). Set this higher if you need to work on complex hairstyles or lower if you need a more responsive 3D Viewport.

Children

Here, we get to the most powerful aspect of particle systems. Child particles work by treating each original parent particle created by the particle system as a guide for creating further particles. Not only does this let you define relatively few particles and then create a great many more, but it also allows you to add novel features, like clumping, twisting, and even braiding, to the hair around the parent particle guides, making your hair look more varied and interesting.

None/Simple/Interpolated Simple particles are a basic option that creates a basic bundle of child particles around each original parent, all of which follow the same path as their parent. Simple children aren't attached to the mesh surface, and they don't use vertex-group inputs to influence how they are generated. Other than in basic hair systems, simple children don't usually look as good as interpolated children. This is because interpolated children are generated from the surface of the mesh just like parent hairs, and then they interpolate their paths from the various parent particles around them. Interpolated children generally give nicer results, so assume for this chapter that we are using interpolated child particles.

Display Determines how many child particles to create and display in the 3D Viewport.

Render Determines how many child particles to create at render time.

Seed Lets you choose the random seed for use in generating child particles. If you have a few child particles that you really don't like, try changing this value.

Virtual Parents Creates extra virtual parent particles before generating children, which gives the children more targets to clump to or kink around, making the hair look more varied.

Clump Causes child hairs to clump together around their parents, making the hair look matted or spiky. Negative values cause hairs to puff out toward the ends instead. The *shape* value determines how far up the hairs start to clump.

Length   Determines how long the child particles grow as a proportion of the parent particle length. The threshold value below this setting allows some particles to reach the full length, while others are cut down to the shorter value specified by the Length setting.

Parting Controls   These options only appear if Virtual Parents is set to 0. Turning up the parting (cap) amount forces child particles to pick a side when interpolating between parents that point in different directions. As you might imagine, this is useful for parting hair (though as we will see later, there are other ways). The *min* and *max* values determine the range of angles or distances between parent hairs that child particles will part over.

Roughness   You can apply three kinds of roughness to the child hairs. The *Uniform Rough* setting roughens up the hair depending on location, affecting all hairs in a local area in the same way. The *size* value determines the scale of these perturbations. The *Endpoint Rough* setting randomizes the endpoints of the hairs, pushing them farther apart (much like the opposite of the Clump setting). The *Random Rough* setting roughens the hairs independently, with the *size* value determining the scale of perturbations and the *threshold* value determining what proportion of hairs are left unaffected by this roughening. (Random roughness is good for adding stray hairs or for making hair look frizzy.)

Kink (Nothing/Curl/Radial/Wave/Braid)   These options (shown in Figure 9-6) add secondary patterns to the way the child hairs follow the parents. *Curl* causes the hair to form curls, *Radial* makes the hairs move periodically closer and farther apart, *Wave* adds waves to the hair, and *Braid* makes them form a three-stranded braid. The settings below these choices determine the amplitude and frequency of this secondary pattern, as well as how it is affected by clumping and distributed along the hairs using the *shape* value. The *flatness* value causes the hairs to flatten together when taking on these secondary shapes.

Figure 9-6: Different kink settings applied to the children of a single parent particle. Left to right: No Kink (but with Clump turned on so that the strands come to a point), Curl, Radial, Wave, and Braid.

Vertex Groups

In this panel, you can assign various vertex groups to control the settings over the surface of a mesh. This panel is where we apply the vertex groups we created earlier in order to control the density and length of our initial parent hairs before combing and cutting them (see Figure 9-7).

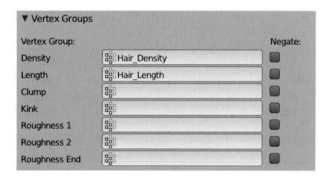

Figure 9-7: Using vertex groups to control hair length and density. You can add vertex groups for the other properties later on, but this is all we need for now.

Using vertex groups to control particle systems affects both the initial generation of parent particles and the later distribution of child particles. However, once you start editing the parent particles in Particle mode, you can add or remove particles and edit them independently of the properties defined by vertex groups using the Particle mode brushes, as discussed in the next section.

Particle Mode

Having set up a basic hair system, you can edit it in Particle mode (see Figure 9-8), using a variety of tools that let you grow, comb, cut, and smooth your hair or fur, as well as add or delete hairs.

You can switch to Particle mode from the mode drop-down menu in the header of the 3D Viewport. Once in Particle mode, the hair particles in the currently selected particle system become editable. (At the same time, you will no longer be able to edit the Particle Emission settings in the Properties editor, unless you click Free Edit at the top of the Particle Settings tab to scrap your edited particles and start again.) Similar to Sculpt mode, Particle mode brings up a list of brushes in the Tool Shelf on the left of the 3D Viewport, along with some options for how these brushes affect your particles.

Shaping Your Hair

In Particle mode, I began shaping and styling the hair for the Bat Creature using Blender's particle brushes. I first used the Comb tool to flatten the hair and get it to flow along with the contours of

the body (see Figure 9-8), adding some peaks and scruffy areas as well. By default, when you comb hair in Particle mode, it's deflected by the emitter mesh, making it easy to comb it along the mesh's surface. (You can turn this off using the *Deflect Emitter* option from the Tool Shelf, if you wish.) If the hair in an area gets a bit too flat, use the Puff tool to fluff it back up. (The Puff tool causes the hairs to repel one another and generally spread out.)

To control the length of the hair strands, the Length and Cut tools are the most useful. The Length tool allows you to grow or shrink hairs to adjust their length, while the Cut tool cuts them back away from the brush as you make strokes with it. The Cut tool will also completely remove a hair if you cut it right down to the base, so this is a useful technique for getting rid of awkward hairs that are causing your child particles to behave strangely. (If it's difficult to see the base of a strand, try switching to wireframe view and zooming in.)

You can also add extra hairs using the Add brush, which creates new hairs wherever you stroke. Turning on the *Interpolate* option (usually advisable) causes new hairs to follow the direction of surrounding ones that already exist, which comes in handy

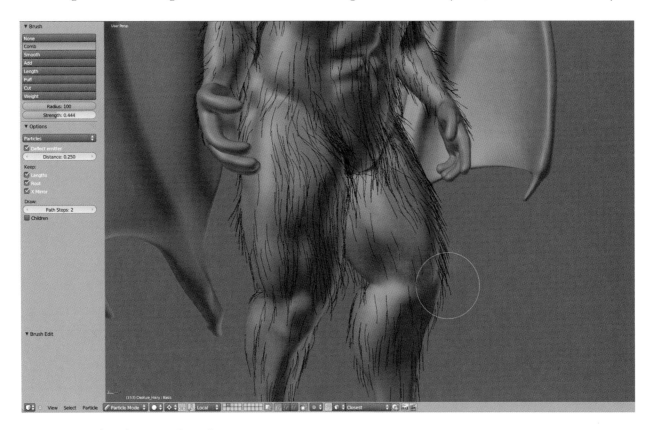

Figure 9-8: Combing fur in Particle mode

when adding extra hairs to an area you have already combed. For example, with the Bat Creature, I added some extra hairs to the ears and around the feet and hands to better define the flow of the hair around these areas.

Styling Tips

Be sure when styling to rotate the model frequently to see it from different angles. As you rotate it, think about the silhouette you are carving out as well as the direction the hair is pointing and use the Cut tool to trim stray hairs that disrupt the silhouette. If you cut any hairs too short, you can use the Length brush to grow hair back out.

You can select and manipulate individual or multiple hairs as you would in Edit mode, using the right mouse button to select and the **G**, **S**, and **R** keys to grab, rotate, and scale strands. You can also switch between different selection methods in Particle mode, selecting either the whole hair or individual points along it or just choosing to comb and cut the overall path. This is analogous to being able to choose between selecting vertices, edges, or faces in Edit mode. Selecting hair strands can be useful for dealing with tricky areas, as the brush tools will work only on selected strands, allowing you to select specific particle hairs that are causing issues and comb or cut them in isolation.

Another useful trick is to press **L** to select hairs under the cursor. Hold down **L** and wave the mouse over an area to select a few hairs at random. Then, comb them independently. This works well for roughening up hair and adding volume.

Child Particles

Once you have the basic hairstyle roughly in place, turn on **Child**

Particles in the Particles tab to see what effect it has on the look of your hair. Set the child type to **Interpolated** and set the **Display** number of particles to about **50**. (The Render number can be a lot higher, but keep in mind how this will affect the total number of hairs and thus your render times.)

For the Bat Creature, I set Virtual Parents to 0.3 and Clump to 0.5, and I added a very small amount of Random, Endpoint, and Uniform Roughness (around 0.001 to 0.01 for each, as these are sensitive settings). Turning up the virtual parents gives the child particles more parent strands to clump around and prevents the hair from looking too patchy. Adding some roughness makes it look less neat and smooth.

I also added some variation to the particle length using a Length setting of 0.5, and I set the threshold value to 0.15 to produce hair of different lengths and to give a more natural look to the fur (see Figure 9-9).

> *Returning to Particle mode will hide your child particles by default, but you can turn them on in the draw options in the 3D Viewport Tool Shelf by checking the Children option.*

When working on hair systems, it can be useful to render occasionally, as the shading of hairs in the 3D Viewport can look flat and ambiguous. You may want to skip to Chapter 12 for a discussion of materials for hair and then create a quick render setup for use while you are working on hair (see Figure 9-10). See Chapter 13 for how to light the scene and Chapter 14 for more on rendering.

Figure 9-9: Particle settings for the Bat Creature

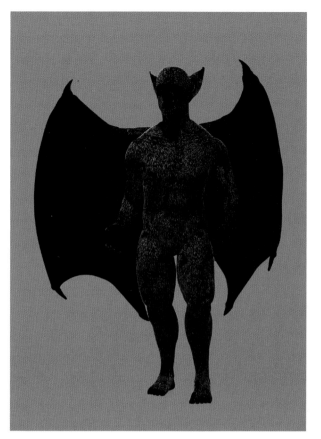

Figure 9-10: The fur for the Bat Creature. While the 3D Viewport gives a good estimate of what the hair is doing, a render will really show you what areas need attention. Here, I set the skin of my character to black to see the hair on its own and rendered it with a simple three-point light setup. (See Chapter 12 to learn how to set up materials and Chapter 13 for lighting.)

Figure 9-11: The Peach Fuzz particle system for the Bat Creature adds fine hairs covering most of the body.

Peach Fuzz

I also decided to add a second particle system to my Bat Creature to incorporate some short hair that covered more of the body, like the head, ears, and some of the wings. I made this in exactly the same way as the first system. I started by adding another new particle system to the same object as the first, this time with a much shorter length. Then, I created a vertex group to limit this hair to the body, head, and the beginnings of the wings. I didn't need a length vertex group this time, as the hair was all very short. Next, I combed the hair to follow the contours of the body and added child particles to increase the hair density. The resulting particle system can be seen in Figure 9-11.

Complex Haircuts

The hair for the Bat Creature was pretty simple, so let's look at a character with a more complex hairdo. The character in Figure 9-12 uses several different particle systems, each of which covers different areas of the overall hairstyle. Each system is restricted to its own area by a separate vertex group, allowing it to be edited separately.

Creating hair this way makes it easier to iterate through different styles and create more complex hair because you can edit individual aspects without worrying about their effect on others.

Figure 9-13 shows a character that makes full use of this strategy with different hair particle systems that all use different settings. For example, the braids in the beard are single parent strands that use the Braid Kink setting for children, while other systems use different kink settings. This technique is often useful when creating a hairstyle with a parting of some kind because splitting the hair into two particle systems makes it much easier to comb outward from the parting on either side.

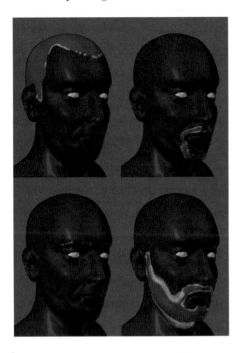

Figure 9-12: Using different particle systems with unique Density vertex groups allows more control over the look of each. Here, I have created separate vertex groups for the hair, goatee, eyebrows, and stubble.

Figure 9-13: Multiple particle hair systems combine to create the full effect. Here, five different hair systems are used to create the final hairstyle on the bottom right. Each can be combed and have its settings adjusted separately, allowing considerably more control.

Controlling Particles with Textures

While so far we have focused on using vertex groups to control particle hair properties, Blender can also use texture input to control aspects of particle systems in the same way that we use vertexes. To use a texture this way, first assign a particle system to your mesh, switch to the Textures tab of the Properties editor, and click the **Particle Textures** icon (see Figure 9-14). Now you can add textures and use them for the same inputs as you would vertex groups, including the density and length of hair for hair particles, as well as clump, kink, and rough values. (Values such as time and velocity are used for dynamic point particle systems.) By default, white will be mapped to 1.0, and black to 0.0 for these values.

Controlling particle systems with textures allows you to use Blender's procedural textures to add variation to how a hair or fur system looks. For example, by using a cloud texture to affect the rough value of the fur for the Bat Creature, I could quickly add some randomized roughness to the creature's hair, without having to edit vertex groups manually.

> *Textures can also be used to affect the look of particles through Blender's materials, as you'll learn in Chapter 12.*

Other Uses for Particle Systems

In addition to modeling hair and fur, Blender's particle systems are useful for numerous other tasks. For example, for the Jungle Temple, I used a particle system to create patches of grass on the ground, using the Group render type to duplicate a few different grass objects many times.

Grass for the Jungle Temple

While I placed most of the plants in the Jungle Temple scene by hand, I used a particle system to generate some grass around my scene. While hair strands on their own can look a lot like grass with the right materials, I chose to create models for the individual blades of grass. Then, I used a particle system to scatter them around the scene, as shown in Figure 9-15.

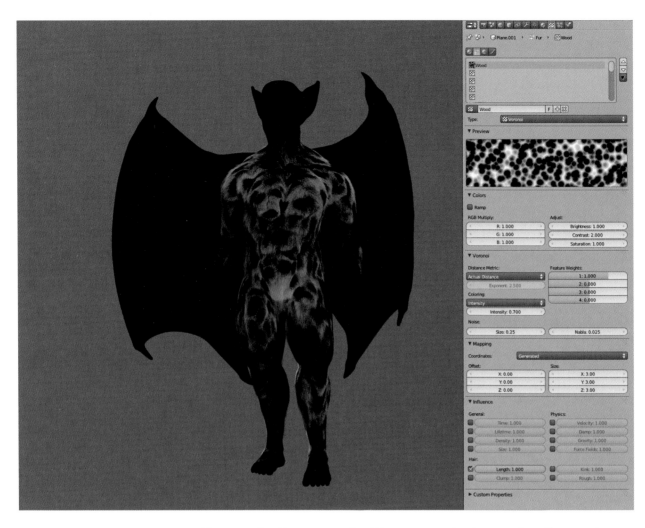

Figure 9-14: Using a texture to control hair particles. Here, a procedural Voronoi texture has been used to affect particle length. You can use both procedural and image textures to affect particle properties.

Figure 9-15: Simple grass models. These are all just planes and cylinders that are subdivided, stretched, and grabbed with proportional editing to form them into the stems and leaves of the grass. Each is a separate object with its origin at the base of the plant.

Figure 9-16: The density vertex group for my grass particle system, shown here with grass growing on the assigned areas

Creating a Grass Particle System

To create grass this way, I needed some models for different blades or clumps of grass and then a particle system (added to my ground mesh) that would duplicate and scatter these models around the scene. First, I created a few different grass models (see Figure 9-15) and added them all into a single group (CTRL-G). Next, I added a new particle system to the ground mesh in my Jungle Temple and created a vertex group for the grass density and length (as I did for the hair) to place the grass in just a few key areas (see Figure 9-16). Then, I set the render type for the particle system to Group and chose my grass group as the group to use (the Dupli Group setting). Finally, I enabled the Use Count option to determine how each member of the group was duplicated so that the small grass models repeated more often than the larger ones (see Figure 9-17).

To give the grass duplicates some random rotation, I used the rotation properties (see Figure 9-17). By setting the rotation axis to Normal and the random values to 0.15 for the rotation axis and 1.0 for the rotation phase, each grass element gets a bit of random rotation, making it look more unique (see Figure 9-18). Similar variation can be achieved for the scale of the objects with the Random Size setting in the particle systems physics properties (see Figure 9-17).

Object Rotation and Particle Systems

It should be noted that in order for the grass particle system to work correctly, the grass meshes need to be rotated so that the stems of the grass point along Blender's y-axis. This is because, although the z-axis is treated as the "up" direction in Blender's global coordinates, for particle systems, the y-axis of an object points along the length of the strand.

The easiest way to rotate the grass objects correctly is to select them in Object mode and (assuming you initially modeled them pointing upward with respect to everything else in the scene) press **R ▸ X** to rotate the objects around the global x-axis and enter **–90** degrees to specify the amount of rotation. This should leave your grass pointing along the y-axis of the scene. Press CTRL-A and select **Rotation** to apply this rotation to the objects' geometry.

Figure 9-17: The particle settings for the grass system. To give different orientations and sizes to the duplicated blades, I used the rotation settings and the Size and Random size options. I used the Use Count option to repeat some objects in the group more often than others.

Figure 9-18: The grass particle system in the final Jungle Temple scene

Hair and Fur Tips

Here are some final tips for working with hair particle systems.

Split up complex tasks. For complex haircuts, split the hair into different systems that you can comb and cut separately. Use different settings to get the effect you need.

Keep an eye on particle counts. As an example, human hair has an approximate density of a few hundred hairs per square centimeter, but you don't always need to reach this value. When rendering your hair, try various numbers of children to see what looks best.

Experiment. Hair is tough to get right. Sometimes the only way is to try a number of different settings to see what works best. Getting a quick render of your hair will often provide useful insight.

Materials make a difference. Chapter 12 features some materials geared specifically for particle hair. If you're tearing your hair out wondering why your fur doesn't look right, it might not be the particle system's fault. Make sure you have a good material on your hair system to help it look its best.

In Review

In this chapter, we've looked at ways to create particle hair and fur systems and discovered other uses for Blender's hair particles, such as for procedurally scattering objects, as we did for grass. In later chapters, we'll return to hair and fur, as we discuss what materials to apply to create nice looking hair (see Chapter 12), how to light strand particles (see Chapter 13), and how to get the best results when rendering hair (see Chapter 14) by rendering it as a separate render layer.

10

TEXTURE BAKING

Having modeled, sculpted, retopologized, and UV unwrapped our models, we're now ready to create textures and materials for them and then move on to lighting and rendering. In this chapter, we'll focus on baking textures—creating procedural textures using the geometry, lighting, and materials of objects in our scene. For example, we'll bake the normals of a high-poly sculpted mesh into a texture map or bake the shadows that a mesh receives in the cracks and grooves of its surface into a texture to mimic dirt and dust. Textures like these can then be used to aid in texturing and creating materials later.

In this chapter, we'll discuss the various types of procedural texture maps that Blender is able to bake, their uses, and how to bake them. In Chapter 11, we'll move on to combining these baked textures with hand painting and other techniques in GIMP and Blender, cleaning them up and combining them with other texture sources, such as photos. Then, in Chapter 12, we'll cover

how to plug all these kinds of maps into Blender's materials system to create realistic materials for rendering our models with.

Images and Textures

First, a little terminology: The terms *image* and *texture* are often used interchangeably. In most circumstances, this is fine, but I shall try to avoid confusion here by explaining my terminology. An *image*, for our purposes, is a picture, perhaps in the form of an image file, like a *.jpg* or *.tiff* file or a file generated within Blender's UV Image editor with no specific file type assigned to it yet.

A *texture* in Blender can be any kind of input used to affect the look of a material applied to an object. A texture can be an image, but a texture may also be procedurally generated or taken from a video, point cloud data, or something even more obscure. But because we frequently use images as the input for textures, it's often convenient to refer to "an image used to affect a material's diffuse color" as a *diffuse texture* for short.

In general, when I refer to baking textures, I mean an image *used* as a texture. As this would rapidly become tedious to read, I'll often instead use the term *texture* more loosely—particularly as the process of baking images is so frequently referred to as *texture baking*.

The term *map* when used in the context of textures (such as *texture map*, *diffuse map*, and *displacement map*) refers to an image used for a UV unwrapped object—one in which each point on the object can be mapped to a point on the image.

In this book, I often talk about *assigning* an image or texture to an object. Assigning an image to an object is different from assigning a texture.

Assigning an Image

When I assign an image to an object, I link that image with the object's active UV coordinate set. This causes the image to be displayed on the object when using the *Textured Solid* shading option in the 3D Viewport (found under Display in the 3D Viewport Properties region). It also means that when baking images, this will be the image that is baked to.

To assign an image to an object's UV coordinates, select the object in the 3D Viewport and press TAB to enter Edit mode. Hit **A** to select all, then in the UV Image editor (I'm assuming here that the object has already been unwrapped), use the drop-down menu in the Editors header to select an image to assign to the active UV set.

To create a new image and assign that instead, use **Image ▸ New Image** to create a new image to bake to with the size and properties you specify.

Assigning Textures

Textures are assigned to materials, which are then assigned to objects or parts of objects. Textures are used to affect how an object will be rendered and also as inputs for some modifiers. To assign a material to an object, go to the Materials tab of the Properties editor to choose a material from the drop-down menu at the top of the tab or create a new material with the **+New** button. You can then assign textures to this material in the Textures tab in the same way.

Texture-Baking Controls

To bake a texture (technically, an image—from here on I will use the two terms less rigorously) in Blender, use the Bake panel in the Render tab of the Properties editor (shown in Figure 10-1). This contains all of Blender's settings and tools for baking texture maps, including the following:

Bake This button bakes images for the currently selected objects, using the bake settings you've defined.

Bake mode These settings are used to set what kind of map you are baking.

Clear This option clears the texture and replaces it with black before baking.

Margin This option extends the baked textures out beyond the edges of the UV islands by the number of pixels you set to prevent seams showing on the mesh.

Selected to Active This option enables baking from one mesh to another.

Distance and Bias These settings determine how far Blender will look for the surface of the other mesh when baking from Selected to Active.

In order to bake a texture, Blender needs two inputs:

- A mesh with UV coordinates that you want to bake textures for. This must be selected as the active object, and the UV coordinates you want to bake to must be the active set.

- An image to bake the texture to, assigned to the object's active UV coordinate set.

With these inputs in place, click **Bake** in the Bake panel to have Blender render the texture. Blender should render the map type dictated by the Bake Mode setting (see Figure 10-1) and take the following into account when baking:

Selected objects Blender will bake textures for any selected objects that have UV coordinates with an image assigned to them. You can bake multiple textures at once, as well as baking multiple objects.

Other objects on currently visible layers Unselected objects will not be baked, but when baking lighting or other maps that are affected

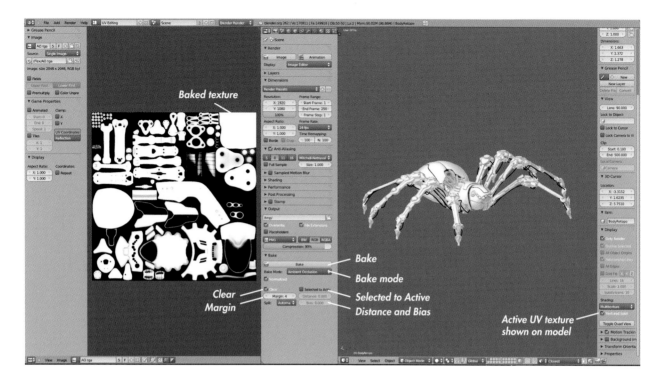

Figure 10-1: Texture-baking controls while working in the UV editing layout we created in Chapter 8. The UV editing layout is useful because it allows us to access our baking controls through the Properties editor, the baked images through the UV Image editor, and the objects in our scene through the 3D Viewport, all in one layout.

by the selected object's surroundings, Blender will take into account the other objects (meshes, lights, and so on) that are on the currently visible layers. To bake the lighting for an object in isolation, place it temporarily on its own layer, along with the lights you want to affect it.

> *Baking is currently supported only when you use the Blender Internal renderer. If you don't see any baking options, make sure that you have Blender Internal selected as your render engine from the Info Editor header (see Figure 10-1).*

Texture Map Types

You can bake several different map types, some of which are more important than others. Here's what Blender has to offer:

Full Render This does a full render, including textures and lighting of your surface. The resulting texture is exactly how your model will look in your final render, mapped to the object's UV coordinates.

Ambient Occlusion This renders ambient occlusion for the object, taking into account any other visible, renderable objects on the currently active layers. Ambient occlusion is a self-shadowing effect that creates dark areas in the corners and crevices of objects. It's useful both for mimicking the effect of more complex lighting, as well as for creating a rough map of areas where dirt and dust are likely to accumulate. This kind of map is often very useful when creating textures and materials (see Figure 10-2).

Shadow This renders the shadows from lights in the scene into a map.

Normals This takes the normal vector of the object's surface at each point and records it as an RGB value. This is done in a variety of ways, depending on the normal space option you choose. Different normal spaces record the normals of the mesh relative to different coordinate systems. For example, the *Camera* option records them relative to the camera; *World*, according to world space; *Object*, according to the object's local coordinates; and *Tangent*, according to the surface normal of the baked object itself.

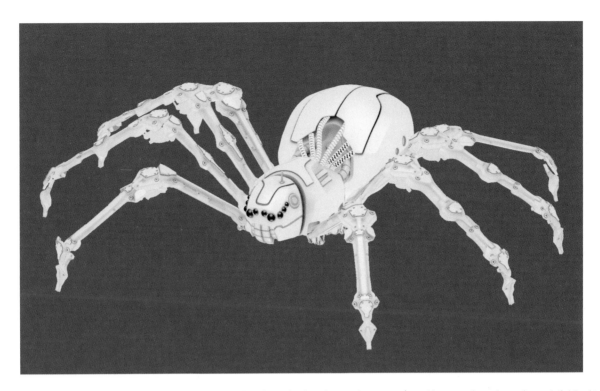

Figure 10-2: An ambient occlusion map, baked and applied to the mesh as a texture (the eyes here have been left black)

Of these, Tangent is probably the most important; it lets you bake the normals of one mesh to the surface of another by enabling the Selected to Active setting, selecting your source mesh (or meshes) and the target, and then baking. This renders the normals of the source mesh relative to the selected target mesh. This map can then be used to distort the surface normals of the mesh when it is rendered, giving the impression (when the map is applied as part of the object's material) of having a lot of detail in the surface when in fact the underlying geometry can be much simpler. (See Figure 10-3 for an example of this effect.) Tangent space normal maps are particularly useful because the normals are recorded relative to the surface of the mesh itself, so they work even when the mesh is distorted from its original shape by modifiers or further editing, so long as the UV coordinates remain the same.

Textures This bakes the diffuse color of any materials and colors applied to the mesh. This can be useful for baking procedural colors and textures into a UV map.

Displacement This converts the distance between two meshes into a black-and-white image. Black represents negative displacement, mid-gray represents zero displacement, and white represents positive displacement. Use the Selected to Active option to bake from a source mesh (or meshes) to the active mesh.

The Displacement map is generally used as an alternative to normal maps, and this map can then be used as the input for the Displace modifier or the Displace setting of a material to deform a mesh into the shape of the source mesh (see Figure 10-3). Alternatively, a baked displacement map can be used as a *bump map* for a material. (Bump maps work like normal maps, giving the impression of surface detail by altering the shading of the surface, but they require only black and white input.)

Normal maps are a very efficient way to give the impression of detail, but they don't affect the silhouette of the mesh or the casting of shadows because no *real* geometry is displaced. Displacement mapping creates real detail by deforming the mesh but requires you to subdivide the mesh to provide sufficient geometry to deform. In Figure 10-3, a group of spheres has been baked to a normal map (8 bit) and a displacement map (32 bit). These maps have then been

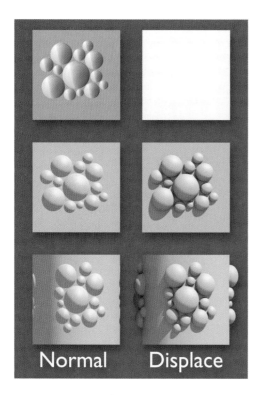

Figure 10-3: Normal mapping vs. displacement mapping

Specular Colors   This bakes the color of specular reflections of a material into a texture and is useful for baking procedural values to an image texture.

Specular Intensity   This bakes the amount of specular reflection of a material into a texture. It's useful for baking procedural values to an image texture.

Each kind of texture map has a purpose from time to time, but in this chapter, we'll focus on ambient occlusion, texture, normal, and displacement maps most often. Of the texture maps, these maps are the most useful for use with painted textures and for rendering detailed final models.

Baking Textures for the Bat Creature

In the case of the Bat Creature, my aim was to create textures for the skin and to bake a displacement map for rendering the final model with a Displace modifier in order to capture all the details I sculpted earlier. In this section I'll discuss how I baked maps for ambient occlusion and displacement to help with this. I'll also cover baking a normal map as an alternative to displacement maps, one that renders a lot more quickly though at the cost of some accuracy in representing the fine details.

Baking Displacement from Sculpt to Final Mesh

Because I continued sculpting on the retopologized mesh, I could just render the final mesh directly. But this isn't always desirable, because the Multires modifier can sometimes get corrupted and displaying its effects in the 3D Viewport can be slow and unwieldy. A better solution would be to bake a displacement map using either the high-poly sculpt, which can then be applied as part of a material, or the Subdivision Surface and Displace modifiers to reconstitute the high-poly details of the mesh only when it is rendered, leaving it simple and quick to work on in the 3D Viewport.

To bake the displacement for the Bat Creature, I first selected the body of the creature (the high-poly sculpt), duplicated it, and then applied the Multires modifier at level 3. This is the mesh I'll use as the final body mesh for rendering. (I'll add the hair that I created in Chapter 9 to the final scene as a separate object.) This captures most of the detail already, but I'll use a displacement map to capture the highest resolution detail.

applied to a plane and a cylinder. The normal-mapped objects capture a lot of the shading with much lower polycounts, but they don't affect the actual shape of the mesh or cast shadows. The displacement-mapped objects are much more realistic, but they have to be subdivided in order to capture all the details.

Alpha   This bakes the alpha transparency of the mesh to a texture. It's useful for baking procedural values to an image texture.

Emission   This bakes the emission color and amount of a material into a texture. As with the texture map, this can be useful in baking procedural emission colors into an image texture.

Mirror Colors   This bakes the color of ray-traced reflections for a material into a texture. It's useful for baking procedural values to an image texture.

Mirror Intensity   This bakes the amount of ray-traced reflection for a material into a texture and is useful for baking procedural values to an image texture.

Next I needed to add a Subdivision Surface modifier to match the level of subdivision between the top level of the multires mesh and the new, soon-to-be displaced mesh. I added the modifier and set the number of subdivisions to 2.

Then, in Edit mode, I selected the whole mesh, and in the UV Image editor, I added a new image for the displacement map to be baked to. This image needed to be a 32-bit float image in order to capture all of the details of the displacement without creating artifacts. I set its size to 4096×4096 pixels, more than enough to capture all the details of the sculpt. I selected the original multires mesh and my new final mesh. As shown in Figure 10-4, I made sure that Selected to Active was enabled and Normalize was unchecked, and I set the Margin setting to 4 to give a 4-pixel border around the UV islands, reducing the chance of artifacts around UV seams. (The other settings were left at their defaults.)

At this point I was ready to bake my texture, so I clicked Bake in the Bake panel and set Blender to work baking my texture. This baked the displacement between my high-poly sculpt and my subdivided final mesh into a displacement map holding all of the detail of the high-poly sculpt. Once finished, I saved this as a 32-bit OpenEXR image to preserve all the information present in the displacement map by pressing F3 while in the

UV Image editor and setting the format (in the bottom left of the file browser editor) to EXR (see Figure 10-5). You can choose Float (Full) to use 32-bit values. Setting the Codec to ZIP will keep the file size a bit smaller.

Bit Depth and Textures

I've touched on bit depth briefly, but now I'll explain it a bit further. *Bit depth* refers to the number of bits (that is, the length of a number in binary) that is used to store the red, green, blue, and alpha (RGBA) values for each pixel in an image. The more bits used to store each number, the more distinct levels there are, and the greater the range and subtlety of colors and brightnesses that can be stored in an image.

Most image formats (such as *.jpg* and *.png*) use 8-bit color, which is fine for simply displaying pictures on screen or even for storing simple diffuse textures. But if you plan on performing more complex manipulations on your images, such as using them for displacement maps or altering their colors and exposure, you'll start to see artifacts appear.

For such demanding use cases, you can use higher bit depths (either 16 or 32 bit) for images, which give you a greater range of values to work with. Using higher bit depths will prevent ugly artifacts from appearing in your renders and displaced

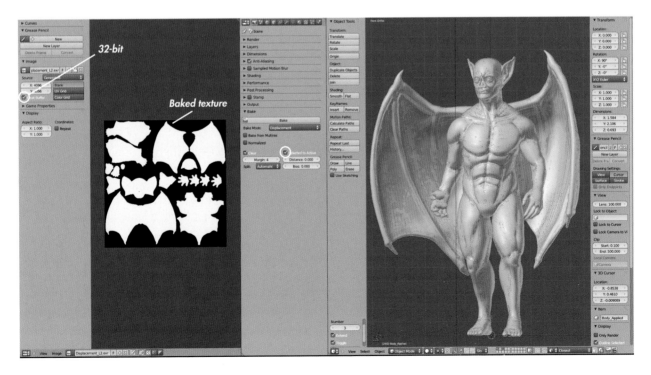

Figure 10-4: Settings for baking the displacement map for the Bat Creature

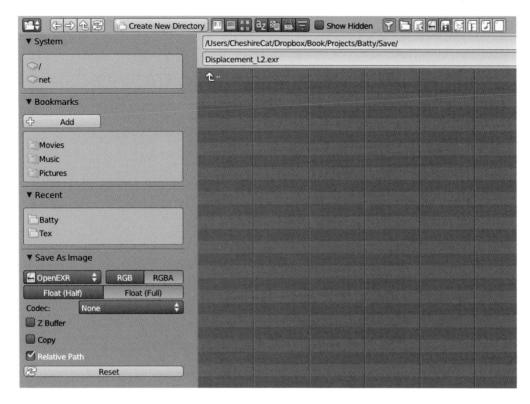

Figure 10-5: Saving the displacement map as a 32-bit OpenEXR image

meshes. The OpenEXR (*.exr*) format is a good choice for saving high-bit-depth images. For low-bit-depth images, I generally use the Targa (*.tga*) format.

During the baking of texture maps, most types of textures can be saved in 8-bit formats. That said, displacement maps should almost always be saved as 32-bit images to avoid stepping artifacts when applying them to your models. Stepping artifacts can be seen in Figure 10-6; the input for a Displacement modifier has been baked in Blender and saved as both an 8-bit *.tga* file (applied using a displacement modifier, center) and a 32-bit OpenEXR image (right). The center image shows the artifacts that can result from using a displacement texture with insufficient bit depth.

Figure 10-6: Displacement maps usually need to be saved in a high-bit-depth image format because lower bit depths don't store enough information and can result in stepping artifacts. (Here the effect has been exaggerated significantly.) Left: A cloud texture, the original source of our displacement map. Center: Using an 8-bit displacement map, showing stepping. Right: Using a 32-bit displacement map, no stepping.

Applying the Displacement Map

To make sure that the displacement map worked correctly (and to apply it to our model for use in our final renders), we can apply it to our duplicated model using the Displacement modifier. Having added a Subdivision Surface modifier to the duplicated body object, we have the geometry we need, so we can simply add a Displacement modifier to the object as well.

To assign the displacement map, we use the *image* we baked as input for a *texture*; this texture can then be assigned as the input for the displacement modifier. (Here, I'm using the more rigorous definitions that I discussed at the beginning of this chapter.)

The easiest way to create and modify a texture block is to add a material to the model, if you haven't already (we created a MatCap material in Chapter 6 that we no longer require; we can either use this or create a new one), and then add a new texture to this material using the Textures tab of the Properties editor by clicking the **+New** button with an empty texture slot selected. Give the texture a useful name like *Body_Displacement*, then set the type of this texture to **Image** or **Movie**. In the Image panel that appears, open your displacement map.

Now return to the Modifiers tab and, in the Displacement modifier, use the texture drop-down menu to select the texture you just created. Leave Direction set to **Normal** and set Texture Coordinates to **UV**. A strength of **1.0** should give the correct amount of displacement. Adjusting the View Subdivision Levels setting on the Subdivision Surface modifier will let you see more or less of the detail generated by the displacement map.

Baking Normal Maps

While we won't use one for our final renders, normal maps are a useful and quick-to-render alternative to displacement maps. They are frequently used in game engines because they are fast enough to use in real-time applications. They can also be used with the Blender Internal renderer to give the impression of extra detail without requiring such dense geometry.

The process of baking a normal map is very similar to baking a displacement map. First, you assign a new blank image to your duplicated mesh (it doesn't need to be 32 bit). Then, select the sculpt first and then the duplicate. We don't need to apply a Subdivision Surface modifier to the duplicate

this time because the silhouette of our character is broadly fine and normal mapping doesn't require extra geometry (it doesn't physically displace the mesh). Next, from the Render tab of the Properties editor, set the Bake mode to **Normals** and Normal Space to **Tangent**, enable **Selected to Active**, and click **Bake** (see Figure 10-7).

The resulting map will be a bluish texture, with other colors denoting areas of the sculpt that face in different directions relative to the normals of the unsubdivided duplicate mesh. This texture may later be applied as part of the object's material to give the effect of mimicking the surface forms of the sculpted mesh (see Figure 10-8). See "Adding a Normal Map" on page 194 to learn how to apply normal maps as part of a material.

Baking Ambient Occlusion

In addition to the displacement map, we also want to bake our ambient occlusion map from our high-poly sculpt onto the final mesh. This process is simpler than producing the displacement map:

1. Select the sculpt and then the final mesh. Set the Bake mode to **Ambient Occlusion**.

2. Select **Normalize** to ensure that the ambient occlusion map uses the whole range between black and white to store the occlusion.

3. To get the best-quality ambient occlusion map, adjust Blender's world lighting settings in the World tab of the Properties editor, which contains all the settings for ambient occlusion and environment lighting (see Figure 10-9). (See Chapter 13 for more on these settings.) Enable **Ambient Occlusion** (set to **Multiply**) from the Ambient Occlusion panel.

4. In the Gather panel, turn the Attenuation Distance down to **0.2** and enable **Falloff** and set it to **1.0**. This causes only close-together geometry to cause shadowing and speeds up rendering.

5. Set the samples to **24** to reduce the noise in the results.

Having saved a displacement map externally, you can simply bake over the displacement map image, remembering to save it as something different once the ambient occlusion map is baked. Click **Bake** and let the ambient occlusion map render (see Figure 10-10).

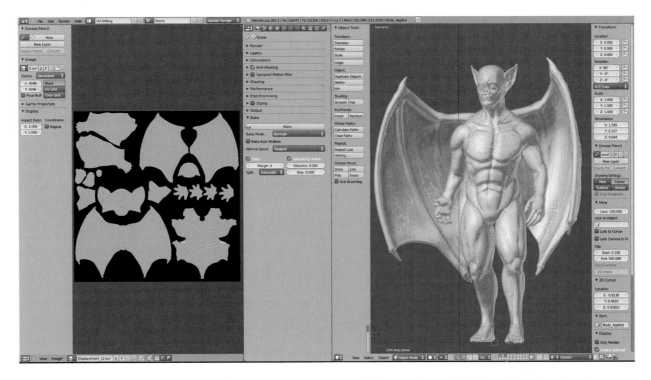

Figure 10-7: Baking a normal map. Normal Space is set to Tangent, and the normals are baked from the sculpted mesh to our final model—this time without subdivision. Some artifacts are present in the bake, but these can be corrected later in GIMP (see Chapter 11).

Figure 10-8: The normal map applied as part of the material, previewed in the 3D Viewport using GLSL shading. The artifacts from the bake can be seen on the wing as black areas, but this can be fixed later in GIMP simply by painting over them.

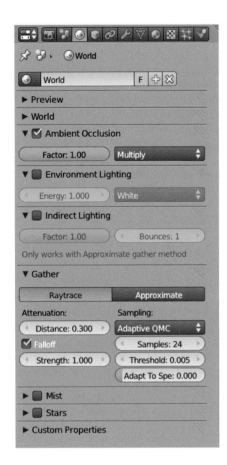

Figure 10-9: Ambient occlusion settings for baking ambient occlusion maps.

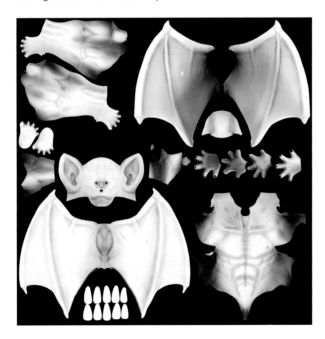

Figure 10-10: The baked ambient occlusion map. This contains some artifacts from baking that we'll remove later by hand.

To make sure that the ambient occlusion map came out okay, turn on **Textured Solid** in the Display panel of the Properties region in the 3D Viewport. This displays the texture assigned to the mesh on the model, allowing you to see the effect of the ambient occlusion map. When you're happy with the bake, save it as a *.tga* image. (You don't need to use a high-bit-depth format this time, as the ambient occlusion map will work fine with 8-bit color.) There may be one or two artifacts, but you can paint these out later in GIMP once you begin texturing.

Baking Textures for the Spider Bot

For the Spider Bot project, I didn't need to bake displacement or normal maps; the point of retopology in this case was to eliminate the roughness from the sculpts and end up with the smooth forms the retopologized model now has. The model would still benefit from an ambient occlusion map, though, which will be useful during the texturing process. To save time when painting colors for the textures, it will also help to assign some basic materials with different colors to the parts of the model and then bake these colors into an image to serve as a guide when painting textures.

Baking Maps for Multiple Objects

In Chapter 8, I packed the UV coordinates for most of the Spider Bot model onto a single UV grid so that I'd require fewer texture images later on. Next I needed to bake the maps for all of the objects together. To do this, first make sure they all have the same image assigned to their UV coordinates. If so, you could simply select all of the objects for the Spider Bot that share the same UV coordinates and click Bake to bake all of the selected objects at once.

But what if you want to be selective about which parts of the model are visible when baking different objects? Or if you wish to be able to correct parts without rebaking the entire model? By default, Blender will clear the texture every time you click Bake, preventing you from baking multiple times with different objects selected. To prevent this, turn off the Clear setting in the Bake panel, and Blender will replace only the parts of the image assigned to the selected objects. This will allow you to bake objects one at a time, in groups, or all at once, adding to the texture map as we go along.

This selective technique comes in handy for pieces like the legs. Because some of the leg components overlap slightly, if they were baked together, the overlapping areas would come out black when we bake our ambient occlusion map. And if we were to later re-pose the legs, these black regions might show through.

To avoid baking in shadows from overlapping objects that may not always be there, use Blender's layers. Blender bakes objects only on the currently visible layers, so we can isolate the parts we want to include each time on a single layer and then bake them. To do so, take the following steps:

1. Select the objects you wish to bake and press **M** to bring up a menu that allows you to pick which layers the object should be visible on.

2. Select a new empty layer (check the layers icons in the 3D Viewport header to see which ones are occupied) and press ENTER to put the object on that layer.

3. Jump to the selected layer in the 3D Viewport, either with the selector in the header or using the keyboard shortcuts (1 through 0 on the keyboard for layers 1 to 10, ALT-1 through ALT-0 for layers 11 through 20).

4. Now select the mesh and bake the ambient occlusion map for that object alone, as shown in Figure 10-11.

This selective process allows you to progress through each object in the model, baking the ambient occlusion as you see fit, whether for a single component or for small groups. For example, for the head section of the Spider Bot, I baked the antenna and extra parts of the head along with the head mesh and kept the wires at the back of the head/body segment on the same layer while baking (though I baked these separately). I baked the legs as individual pieces, isolating each type of leg part on its own layer before baking. The final bake after progressing over the whole model is shown in Figure 10-12.

For areas like the joints on the underside of the Spider Bot's body, which share the same UV space, I couldn't bake a proper UV map. Instead, I just filled that area with white in GIMP after I saved the image. (See the top right corner of the ambient occlusion map in Figure 10-12.)

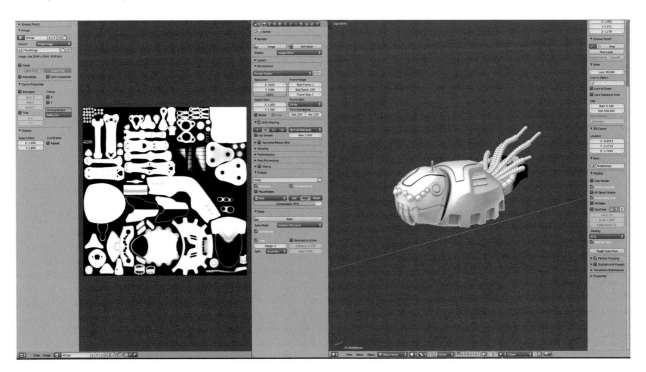

Figure 10-11: Baking the ambient occlusion map for the head and body segments of the Spider Bot. Only selected objects are baked, and only objects on layers that are currently visible are taken into account by the baking process.

Figure 10-12: The final baked ambient occlusion texture for the Spider Bot

Baking Diffuse Colors and Textures

In order to get a rough feel for the colors I wanted the Spider Bot to have and to bake these into a map to serve as a guide for the texture painting process, I needed to create some basic materials and assign them to the different parts of my model. These materials didn't need to be complex; in fact, I needed only to adjust the diffuse color setting. (I'll discuss more complex materials in Chapter 12.)

To create a few basic materials:

1. Go to the **Materials** tab of the Properties editor (with an object selected) and click the **+New** button to create a new material.

2. Click the name *Material* to rename it something more useful, like *Basic_Fill_01*, and then set the diffuse color to a mid-gray color.

3. Create more materials by duplicating this first one (click the + icon next to the material's name) and set these to different colors.

When working with the new materials, I began by choosing three colors: one principal color for most of the model, a secondary color, and a highlight color for small details. I then started assigning these materials to the different objects that made up the Spider

Bot using the Materials tab of the Properties editor, though it's even easier to accomplish using an add-on called Material Utils.

Material Utils Add-On

The Material Utils add-on is a quick way to modify materials assigned to your models. It's particularly useful for working with scenes that use a lot of materials or ones with multiple objects that share the same materials.

To enable the add-on, open Blender's User Preferences Editor (you can bring this up by going to **File ▸ User Preferences**) and under Add-Ons, search for and enable **Material Utils**. This adds a new keyboard shortcut (**Q**), which brings up a menu that you can use in either Object or Edit mode to assign materials to meshes (see Figure 10-13). In Object mode, the add-on allows you to assign materials to an entire object (or to multiple objects if more than one is selected), while in Edit mode, it will assign a material only to the part of the mesh you have selected.

For the Spider Bot, I quickly applied the same material to every object in the model by selecting them all with **A** and then using Material Utils (**Q**) to assign one of my basic materials to all of them. Then, I began selecting individual pieces (and also dropping into Edit mode with TAB to select parts of meshes, as in Figure 10-13) and assigning other materials from the three I created. My overall goal was to keep one main color, one secondary color, and a highlight color for small or interesting parts

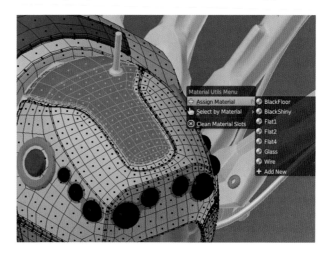

*Figure 10-13: Assigning materials with the Material Utils add-on (**Q**) greatly speeds up adding materials to your scene, particularly for scenes with a lot of objects.*

of the model. For certain objects, like the wires and eyes, I created unique materials by first making the existing material datablock for that object unique (by clicking the number next to the materials name at the top of the Materials tab) and then adjusting it as necessary. After assigning materials, I began changing the diffuse colors of my materials in search of a combination that worked, as shown in Figure 10-14.

Baking a Texture Map

Having established my color scheme, I was able to bake the colors to a texture map. Using a texture to define the color of the objects, rather than different materials, allowed me to use fewer materials to render my model and simplified the process of tweaking materials later on.

To bake the texture map, I returned to the Bake panel of the Render tab in the Properties editor, set the Bake mode to Texture, and then clicked Bake. This baked the colors of the various materials I assigned into a single texture (see Figure 10-15). Because there is no interaction between the meshes to consider this time (as there was when rendering ambient occlusion), I can bake the meshes all at once by selecting them all before baking.

It's worth pointing out here that you can bake more complex material colors and textures as well. For example, you can bake image textures into the UV unwrapped texture for an object or bake procedural materials into images. Figure 10-16 shows the result of adding a procedural wood texture to one of the flat materials for the Spider Bot before baking, which gives it a zebra-striped pattern.

Texturing the Jungle Temple

In the case of the Jungle Temple, most of my textures were tileable to some degree, or they were repeated on meshes in multiple locations. This meant that baking maps for things like ambient occlusion would be less effective because a map baked for a mesh in one location may not have quite the right effect when repeated in another. In the end, the only mesh I baked maps for was the statue (see Figure 10-17), for which I created an ambient occlusion map for the object by itself. I did this by putting the statue on its own layer while baking, just as I did for the parts of the Spider Bot model above.

Figure 10-14: After iterating through different color ideas for the Spider Bot, I eventually settled on a white, gray, and green version.

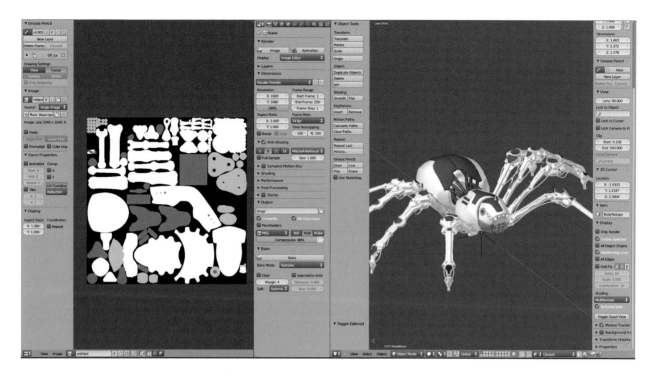

Figure 10-15: Baking simple materials into a texture map

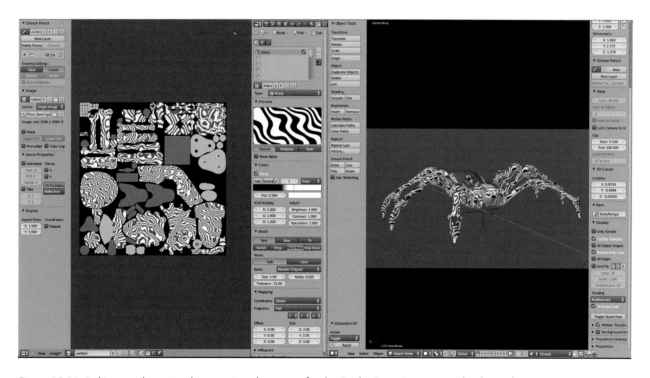

Figure 10-16: Baking a zebra-striped pattern into the texture for the Spider Bot using a procedural wood texture

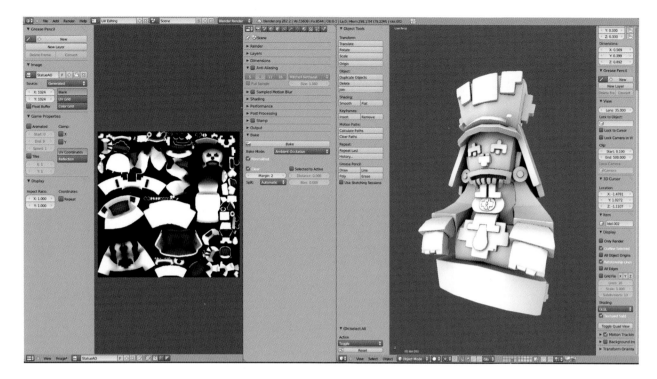

Figure 10-17: Baking the ambient occlusion map for the statue in the Jungle Temple scene

General Tips for Baking Maps

Baking larger textures will allow you to capture more detail but will also take more time. When deciding what size textures to bake, consider how much detail your model has and how much will be present in the bake beforehand in order to optimize the resolution of the texture you use.

In general, a good rule of thumb to follow for displacement maps is that the size of the map in pixels need not be much bigger than the polycount of the mesh. So if you are baking about a 1M poly sculpt, a 1024×1024 pixel map will probably suffice. For other texture maps, consider the size that an object will appear in the final render. If an object will appear only a few hundred pixels high in the final render, its texture map should be about the same size. On the other hand, if an object appears close-up at a high resolution, then bigger textures will be needed.

In the case of particularly simple textures, like the flat colors we baked for the Spider Bot, you can make the image much smaller while baking and

scale it up in an image editing program like GIMP later (making sure to increase the margin setting to prevent seams).

When creating images to bake to, set bit depths appropriately. Displacement maps require 32-bit images, while other texture types typically only require 8-bit (or 16-bit if you plan to manipulate them heavily). Blender can bake either 8- or 32-bit images, but remember the bit depth you end up with is also determined by the file format you save to. Use OpenEXR for high-bit-depth images and *.tga* or *.png* files for 8-bit images. Additionally, remember that GIMP can only edit 8-bit images (for now, that is— future versions are likely to incorporate support for high-bit-depth images), so if you plan on painting textures in GIMP, the extra depth is of little help.

When baking ambient occlusion or lighting, consider isolating the pieces you are baking on one layer to get more control over the results. And finally, it can be helpful to change the world settings (or settings for lamps if you're baking lighting) to achieve higher-quality baked textures. (See Chapter 13 for more on world and lighting settings.)

In Review

In this chapter, we've discussed baking textures into images using Blender's baking tools and the kinds of maps Blender will allow you to bake. I used these techniques to bake maps for my various projects: For the Bat Creature, I baked displacement and ambient occlusion maps, and for the Spider Bot, I baked ambient occlusion and some block colors to aid with texturing later. While I didn't need to do a lot of texture baking for the Jungle Temple scene, I did create an ambient occlusion map for the statue.

In the next chapter, we'll combine the textures we've baked with other ways of creating textures, from painting and cloning textures directly in Blender to painting in GIMP and combining photo textures to synthesize new ones.

11

TEXTURE PAINTING

In the previous chapter, we used Blender to generate textures automatically; in this chapter, we'll shift our focus to creating textures by hand. Using a mix of hand painting, working with photo textures, and utilizing the textures we created in Chapter 10, we'll bring color and texture to the objects in our scenes. We'll also cover creating such images as specular, hardness, and alpha maps, which we'll use in Chapter 12 to influence other aspects of the materials we make, such as their shininess, smoothness, and transparency. We'll look at creating both tileable textures that can be used on multiple objects and unique textures that are UV mapped to specific objects using a mix of both Blender and GIMP.

Let's begin with a look at the tools available.

Texturing in Blender

In Blender, we can paint in 2D, using the UV Image editor, and we can paint directly on objects in 3D, using Texture Paint mode in the 3D Viewport. This gives us a great degree of flexibility in how we paint

our models. The brushes work across both the UV Image editor and Texture Paint mode, making texturing with Blender straightforward and consistent.

Once you select a mesh that has been unwrapped and assigned an image in the UV Image editor, you can switch to Texture Paint mode in the 3D Viewport. (Use the mode drop-down menu in the header, as shown in Figure 11-1.) By default, you'll see the texture on your mesh and be able to paint on it using Blender's texture brushes.

Blender offers several brush types that you can use to paint textures on your model:

Draw, Brush, and Texdraw   These all offer the same basic functionality, allowing you to paint directly on your mesh with the color specified by the color picker.

Clone   This brush allows you to clone texture information from one part of your model to another or from one UV coordinate set to another. With the Clone option turned off in the Project Paint settings (see "Project Paint" on page 154), the brush will take the texture information lying

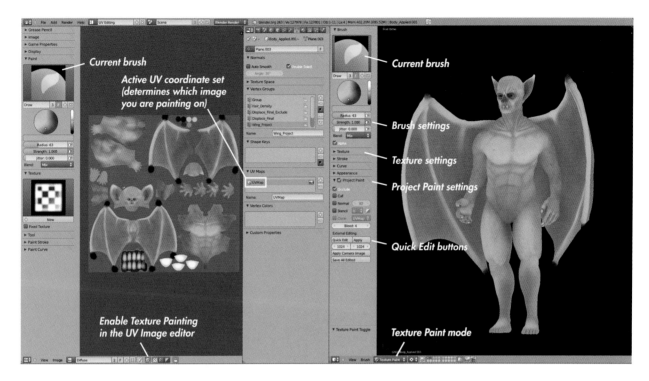

Figure 11-1: Texture Paint mode in Blender. Here, I've used the modified UV Unwrapping Layout created in Chapter 8. This layout allows me to paint textures in the 3D Viewport (right), to see and edit the resulting image in the UV Image editor (left), and to edit materials and settings in the Properties editor.

under the 3D Viewport cursor and copy it to where you paint, allowing you to clone from one part of the model to another within the same texture. With the Clone option turned on in the Project Paint settings, the brush will instead clone texture information from the *same part of the mesh* but from the texture assigned to a *different UV coordinate set* (the one chosen in the Project Paint settings).

Smear This will smear your texture in the direction of the brushstroke. It can be used to blend colors and to smudge out mistakes.

Soften This blurs the texture under your stroke, reducing noise and fine details.

These brush types can be duplicated and modified just like Blender's sculpt brushes, allowing you to create a variety of brushes tailored to your needs. Also, as in Sculpt mode, you can apply textures to your brush using the Texture panel of the Tool Options region. The texture you apply will then multiply with your brushstrokes while you paint.

Project Paint

Blender has two ways to paint textures in Texture Paint mode. The older, legacy method, while useful, has significant limitations. The newer Project Paint method offers a more advanced set of tools, including ones that allow you to mask and clone textures using other UV coordinates and images and to paint only on surfaces visible from your viewpoint. When enabled, Project Paint gives you the options shown in Figure 11-2. I discuss these options below in the order in which they appear on the Project Paint panel.

Figure 11-2: The Project Paint panel has a variety of options for controlling how Blender's texture brushes work.

Occlude This prevents painting "through" the mesh onto surfaces behind visible ones.

Cull This prevents painting on faces that face away from you.

Normal This blends out the strength of your strokes depending on whether they are facing you (as with Cull, but with a smooth fade-out). You can control the limits of this fade out using the *Angle* setting to the right of the checkbox.

> ❧ *The above options are on by default, but it can be useful to turn them off to quickly paint large parts of your model with a single stroke.*

Stencil This allows you to use an image mapped to the object's UV coordinates (which can be a different set from the one you are painting on) to mask the effect of your brushstrokes. This setting can be used to restrict the area you are working on or to simplify adding texture to your model, as you'll see later in this chapter. To the right of the stencil checkbox, you can select which UV coordinate set (and thus which image) to use for masking and whether to invert the mask.

Clone This allows you to clone texture information from one UV map to another. (Your brushstrokes will clone to the image assigned to the active UV set from the one selected in the drop-down menu next to the checkbox for this option.) This setting lets you, for example, project your model onto a photo with one UV coordinate set and then clone that to another, more neatly laid out UV map for further texturing. (We'll use this option later for the Jungle Temple.)

Bleed This determines the amount Blender bleeds textures outward from the edges of the UV islands when you paint over a seam. This prevents seams from appearing in your texture, similar to the Margin setting for texture baking.

Quick Edit This is very useful when texturing, particularly for cleaning up seams and texturing tricky areas where you might want the extra tools available to you in a 2D painting program like GIMP. Quick Edit takes a snapshot of your model from the current viewpoint and opens it in the image editor of your choosing. (To choose your image editor, open the File

tab of Blender's user preferences under Image Editor; then, simply set the path to GIMP or whatever image editor you wish to use.) You can then paint your texture in the image-editing program and save it. Clicking Apply in Blender will project that texture from the viewpoint it was originally taken from. (You don't need to worry about moving the camera; Blender will remember that setting.) Later in this chapter, we'll cover using this feature to fix seams.

Apply Camera Image Like Quick Edit, this projects an image from the camera's current viewpoint. It will bring up a drop-down menu of any images you have already opened in Blender for you to choose from, and it'll then project your chosen texture onto your model.

Save All Edited This saves any textures that you have edited while working in Texture Paint mode, though they must have already been saved once manually or Blender will not know where to save them. Generally, it's better to remember to save manually anyway so that you can keep track of which textures you have worked on already.

Painting in the UV Image Editor

You can also paint textures in Blender's UV Image editor. To do so, click the paintbrush icon in the header of the UV Image editor region. You can then paint on the current image in the UV Image editor using the same brushes as in the 3D Viewport. By using the 3D Viewport and UV Image editor side by side (as in Figure 11-1), you gain a lot of control when painting textures.

> ❧ *Later we'll render some of the projects in this book using Blender's Cycles renderer, but while texture painting, it's easier to leave the renderer set to Blender Internal. This is because Cycles can cause Blender to behave a little strangely when texturing objects with multiple UV coordinate sets.*

Texturing in GIMP

While we can paint in 2D in Blender, GIMP offers a much wider array of painting tools, such as selections, masks, layers, and filters. This variety of tools makes GIMP (or another image editor, such as Photoshop) indispensable for working on textures. In particular, the ability to work with layers makes it much easier to create textures as nondestructively as possible, building up one layer and then adding details in a new layer over the top.

The ability to work in layers also allows you to combine baked textures with your hand-painted textures easily. For example, you can add an ambient occlusion texture over another layer of your texture map to add shadowing. GIMP also has a more advanced brush system, making it easier to paint detailed textures. (I covered the basics of painting in GIMP in Chapter 2, so we'll cover only the more texturing-specific aspects of GIMP in this chapter.)

Creating Brushes for Texturing in GIMP

GIMP's brushes are easy to edit and are capable of creating a wide variety of looks. When texturing, it can often be useful to create custom brushes that aid in quickly building up texture. In particular, when used as clone brushes or as paintbrushes, brushes with a speckled or grungy look are often useful in blending between different colors and textures.

For example, let's create a grungy-looking brush that will come in handy when texturing the Jungle Temple. Its effect can be seen on the right of Figure 11-5. To create it, we start with a photo texture from CGTextures (*http://cgtextures.com/*) and then refine it into a brush that can be exported as a default GIMP brush, which can be used again and again for texturing or painting in GIMP.

GIMP brushes are image files that are used to control the shape of a brush. RGB (color) images are used as is (more like a stamp than a brush) and will not inherit the brush color. Black-and-white images interpret black as the shape of the brush and white as transparent, and they take their color from the color you have selected in GIMP's color picker. To create a GIMP brush, all we have to do is create a black-and-white image and save it in one of GIMP's brush formats (*.gbr* or *.gih*—I'll discuss the difference between these in a second).

1. Start with a photo of some paint splatter from CGTextures (see Figure 11-3) and choose **Colors ▸ Desaturate** to convert the image to black and white, selecting the **Luminosity** option for desaturating the image in order to give more variation in brightness.

Figure 11-3: The image we'll be using as our brush texture

2. Next, identify a square area that might make a good brush and select that area with the Rectangular Select tool (**R**; press and hold SHIFT while dragging to make a square selection). Copy this area (CTRL-C) and paste it as a new image (CTRL-SHIFT-V), which you'll soon save as a new brush.

3. While you've already desaturated the image, it's still encoded using RGB colors, so switch to using black and white values with **Image ▸ Mode ▸ Grayscale**.

4. Next, make a few tweaks to the new image, painting out some of the splatter that clips the edge of the canvas. The texture is now ready to save, as shown in Figure 11-4.

Figure 11-4: A portion of the photo, copied and pasted into a new image and tweaked a little around the edges

Adding Variation to a Brush

You could stop here and export the brush as a *.gbr* brush file, but when used as a brush, it would simply repeat this one image over and over. To give the brush more variation, repeat the steps above, adding more layers to the brush image, and then save it as an animated *.gih* GIMP brush. This brush will use a different layer of the brush image each time it paints part of the stroke, making the stroke look more varied. To do this, take the following steps:

1. Select more regions of the original image and copy and paste them as new layers into the brush image (CTRL-V, then click **New Layer** in GIMP's layers dialog). After doing this a few times, you'll have five different layers with different splatters on them.

2. Export this as a *.gih* brush file to GIMP's brushes folder[1] (select **File ▸ Export**, set the file type to *.gih*, and then click **Save**).

3. GIMP should give you a dialog that lets you define how your brush is set up. You can stick with the defaults if you have placed each "frame" of your brush on a different layer; just be sure to change the brush's description to something helpful and check that the Cells setting is the same as the number of layers in your image. If you wish, you can adjust the default offset of the brush or the distance between each brush mark placed on the canvas

when you make a stroke. For heavy, painterly brushes, choose a small value, but for this grungy-looking brush, a wider spacing is more appropriate—say around 40.

4. With these settings in place, click **Export**. Now if you click **Refresh Brushes** at the bottom right of the Brushes dialog, you should be able to select the new brush and start testing it out. Its effects at the moment are shown on the left in Figure 11-5.

5. You've created an animated brush with a few different shapes, but notice that they repeat quite frequently (left image of Figure 11-5). To fix this, you can tweak GIMP's brush dynamics to vary the brush some more along the length of the stroke.

> ❧ *This assumes that you have a pressure-sensitive pen tablet (highly recommended) for painting. If you don't have one, you can still use the brush dynamics settings, such as Velocity, Fade, and Random, to add effects to your brushstrokes. But obviously pen pressure does not apply to mouse clicks.*

6. To tweak GIMP's brush dynamics, open the Brush Dynamics dialog (**Windows ▸ Dockable Dialogs ▸ Paint Dynamics** and click **New Dynamics**, the second icon on the bottom left of the dialog). This opens the Paint Dynamics editor (see Figure 11-6), where you can use the mapping matrix (the large grid of checkboxes) to set the brush's behavior. The top row of the mapping matrix

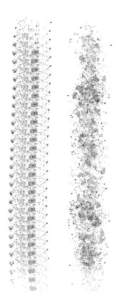

Figure 11-5: Left: Our new brush with GIMP's default brush dynamics. Right: The same brush with GIMP's brush dynamics set to randomize the size and rotation of the brush.

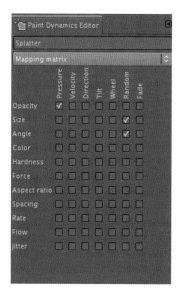

Figure 11-6: The Paint Dynamics editor, shown here with settings for the dynamics of my grungy brush. Checking a box in the mapping matrix makes the variable in the corresponding column affect the brush property in the corresponding row.

---

1. You can find this location or add a new location for brushes from GIMP's preferences (File ▸ Preferences) under Folders ▸ Brushes.

lists all sorts of inputs that can be used to drive the brush's behavior, and the left side of the matrix lists the brush settings these inputs can be used to affect. Set Pressure to affect the brush's opacity and Random to affect the size and rotation of each brush mark. With these dynamics in place, you now get a nice random, grungy-looking brushstroke that you can use for all sorts of textures (see Figure 11-5, right line).

Texturing the Bat Creature

I wanted textures to make the Bat Creature look like a creature of the night: patchy, purplish skin and discolored nails, with some extra wrinkles, freckles, and veins to add some details on top of those I sculpted. To create them, I built up my textures in stages, first blocking in basic colors and then smoothing and refining them before adding the details.

I started by painting some flat colors in Blender's Texture Paint mode. I then saved my work and opened it in GIMP for finer texturing—for example, I combined my painted texture map with the ambient occlusion map I baked in Chapter 10. I then used GIMP to manipulate and supplement the diffuse texture to create specular and hardness textures.

To begin blocking in my colors, I dropped into Edit mode and assigned a new blank image to the mesh for the Bat Creature (the mesh used for baking textures in Chapter 10, not the high-res sculpted mesh). The New Texture dialog lets us choose a color to fill the new image, so I set it to a muted pinkish purple—a sort of unhealthy skin color that might befit a denizen of the night.

Next, I established an overall palette of colors for my texture in the UV Image editor, selecting an unused space not mapped to any part of the mesh (see Figure 11-7). I chose a darker purple for use in shadowed areas, like the area under the eyes; a lighter yellowish color for bony areas; a dark, saturated red for veins and areas with a lot of blood flow; and a darker and lighter version of the original base color to act as shadows and highlights. (We're not painting lighting into our texture; I'm talking only about lighter and darker skin coloration in different areas.) I also chose a light contrasting color to act as a highlight in some areas. I painted a little of each onto my image so that I could color pick from them for use later, either in the UV Image editor or when painting in the 3D Viewport.

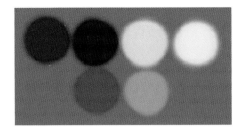

Figure 11-7: Choosing some initial colors to paint the Bat Creature's skin makes it easy to return to the same colors again and to maintain a consistent color palette.

Materials and UI Setup for Painting

When in Texture Paint mode, Blender will by default show the texture you are painting on applied to your mesh in the 3D view, with Blender's default solid shading. As with sculpting, however, we can use Blender's GLSL Shading mode to display the texture in different ways by adding simple lights to the scene (see Chapter 13 for more on lighting) and a simple material to the mesh (see Chapter 12 for more on materials).

For the Bat Creature, I added a simple material to the bat object, which I named *Body_TexturePaint*. In the Textures tab of the Properties editor, I added a new texture to this material, set its type to Image, selected my painted image that I had already assigned to the object's UVs, and set the mapping type for the texture to UV.

Adding a Light

To make the object visible in GLSL Shading mode, we need to add a light, so in Object mode, I created a new Hemi lamp to light my object. Switching into Textured Viewport mode (make sure that shading is set to GLSL in the Display panel of the Properties region), I could see that this lit the Bat Creature from above only, so I duplicated the lamp and rotated it 180 degrees to light the object from below. Next, I decreased the intensity of the new duplicate to around 0.3 in the Lamp's Object Data tab in order to leave a little difference between the lighting from above and below the character. I also turned off the specular component for the lamps (see Figure 11-8) so that my mesh wouldn't look shiny.

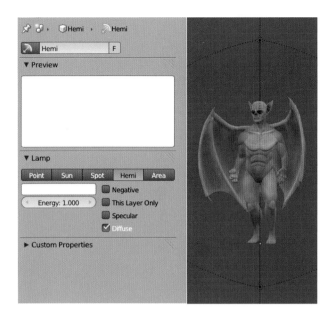

Figure 11-8: Adding simple lighting and materials to make texture painting in GLSL mode easier. Here, I've added a couple Hemi lamps and turned on GLSL shading.

✿ *If you find painting in Blender becoming unresponsive, create a lower-res mesh to paint on by duplicating the sculpted mesh and applying the Multires modifier at a lower level. Because this lower-res mesh shares the same UV coordinates, you can paint on it and apply the textures to the higher-resolution model later.*

Laying Out Basic Textures in Blender

I could now start laying out some basic textures on my model. Using the Standard brush in Texture Paint mode, I sampled from my palette of colors in the UV Image editor and then painted on my model in the 3D Viewport.

I began by using anatomical features as a guide for colors, making bony areas lighter and yellower; recessed areas, like the eyes, dark and purple; and the back darker. I made areas with a lot of blood flow or thin skin, like the wings and ears, redder and slightly highlighted some of the muscles on the torso and legs with lighter colors. I worked with Occlude turned on in Project Paint, but Normal and Cull turned off, as these settings allow you to paint smoothly on the mesh even at side-on angles. At this stage, the aim is only to establish a rough idea of the colors you want.

Switching to GIMP

With my basic colors laid out, I needed more advanced painting tools to start blending colors and adding details. Thus, it was time to move to GIMP. I saved my texture in Blender as a *.tga* image (press F3 in the UV Image editor to save the active image). I then loaded the saved image in GIMP and began cleaning up and smoothing out the colors I had painted in Blender, fixing artifacts and filling in awkward areas. This process is best done with the Paintbrush tool, using a relatively large, soft-edged brush to simply color pick (use CTRL-click to do this without switching away from the Paintbrush tool) from existing colors and blend areas together (see Figure 11-9). (Another way to blend colors is to use the Smudge tool and a grungy-looking brush, like the one we created earlier in this chapter, to blend back and forth between two areas, mixing their colors.)

To add detail to my texture, I incorporated the ambient occlusion map I baked in Chapter 10. Using File ▸ Open as Layers, I opened my baked ambient occlusion map as a new layer on top of my painted texture.

I cleaned up this layer a bit, as I had done for the rough diffuse color. For cleaning purposes, I used GIMP's brushes and color picking, blending areas that didn't look right with the Paint tool or using the Clone tool to fill in areas while preserving texture.

Layer Modes and Opacity

Initially, our ambient occlusion map is imported as a normal layer on top of the texture, completely replacing it. To rectify this, we can use GIMP's layer-blending modes to find a more appropriate way to blend the two.

GIMP's Layers dialog shows each layer in your image (see Figure 11-10, with the Ambient Occlusion layer selected and its blend mode set to Multiply). At the top of the dialog, a drop-down menu lets you choose the Selected Layers blending mode. Different blending modes have different effects: *Normal* lays one over the other, *Multiply* multiplies the values of each pixel in the two layers together, and *Add* adds them together. The Overlay mode causes the layer to brighten or darken the layers below it, depending on its value—dark values make areas darker, light values make them lighter, and mid-gray has no effect. Experiment with a variety of layer modes when combining images to find the one that works best. To combine the ambient occlusion map with my painted colors, I set the mode to Multiply.

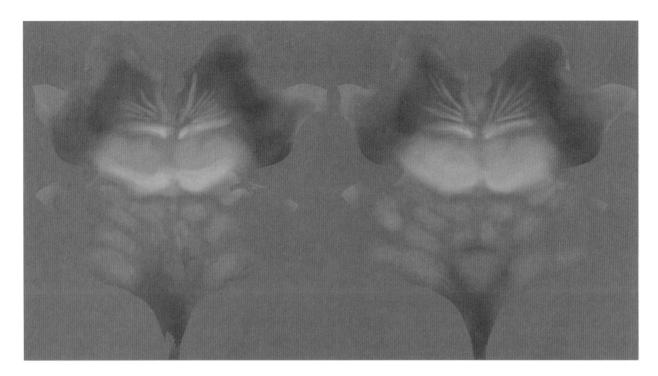

Figure 11-9: Cleaning up our texture in GIMP: part of the roughly painted texture created in Blender (left); after blending together and painting areas in GIMP (right)

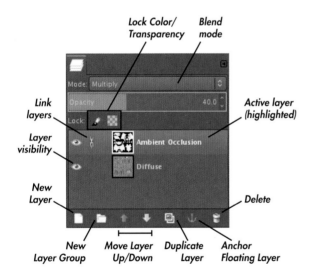

Figure 11-10: GIMP's Layers dialog. At the top, Mode and Opacity set the layer-blending mode and opacity. Beneath these selections are options to lock the color and alpha of layers. Each layer has options to toggle its visibility and link layers (so that they stay aligned when moved, scaled, or rotated).

You can control how much one layer blends with another with the layer's Opacity setting (see Figure 11-10). Because my Ambient Occlusion layer darkened the underlying texture quite a lot, I reduced its opacity to about 40 percent. The result of the ambient occlusion layer at this opacity is shown at the top left of Figure 11-11.

Adjusting Colors

GIMP has a variety of tools for manipulating the colors of an image, both from its wide array of filters and from the Colors menu. For example, you can adjust the exposure of an image—its hue and saturation—and the brightness of each channel using curves or sliders, among a wealth of other options.

At the moment, our texture for the Bat Creature looks rather gray because the black-and-white ambient occlusion texture is multiplied on top. To fix this, we can adjust the curves on the Ambient Occlusion layer to introduce some more red, making the shadows more saturated and redder. To do so, take the following steps:

1. Choose **Colors ▶ Curves** with the Ambient Occlusion layer selected, which brings up the Curves dialog.

Before curves　　　　　　　　　　　　　　　**After curves**

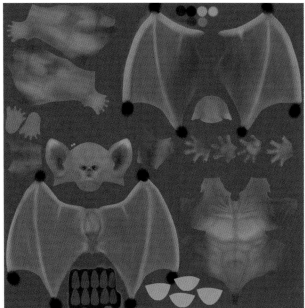

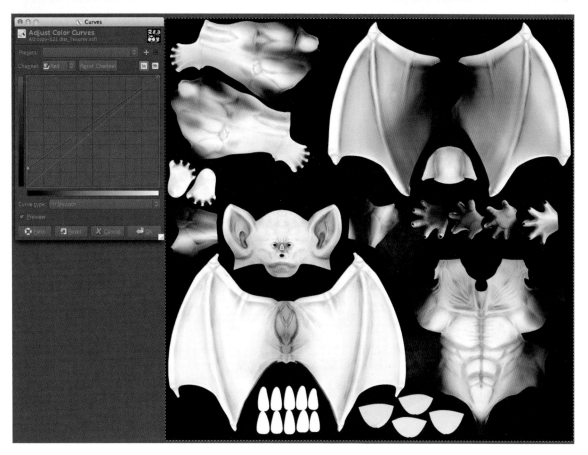

Figure 11-11: Incorporating the ambient occlusion map into our texture. Top left: The ambient occlusion texture multiplied over the rough diffuse texture at 40 percent opacity, before any alteration. Bottom: Adjusting the colors of the ambient occlusion map with the Curves tool, to make it redder. Top right: The reddened ambient occlusion map multiplied over the diffuse texture at 40 percent opacity.

2. This lets you modify the values of each channel (red, green, blue, and alpha) in an image using a curve function.

3. To add red to the darker portions of the image, select the red channel from the Channel drop-down menu, grab the bottom left point of the curve, and drag it upward (see Figure 11-11, bottom).

4. Click **OK** to apply the curves, and the ambient occlusion map now gives nice saturated crevices and shadowed areas to the skin (see Figure 11-11, top right).

Saving and Exporting Back to Blender

The texture isn't finished yet, but it's important to save often, and doing so can be a useful way to see how our current work-in-progress texture looks in Blender on the model. GIMP distinguishes between saving (CTRL-S) in its native *.xcf* format, which preserves layers and other information, and exporting images to other formats, such as *.jpg* or *.tga* (CTRL-E). We need to do both so that we have the GIMP file with all its layers available for further editing as well as an image that we can use in Blender.

First, I saved my image as a *.xcf* file, and then I exported it as a *.tga* image. To open this image in Blender, I selected my Bat Creature object, switched to Edit mode, and in the UV Image editor, used Image ▸ Replace Image to swap the old, roughly painted texture for the new one. (Remember to do this for the material, too—though if you used the same image for the texture as you applied to the mesh, it should update automatically.) You should then see your updated texture on your mesh. You could now start painting in Blender again, but I opted to stay in GIMP for the moment.

Adding Details

Back in GIMP, with our ambient occlusion now working well alongside our painted texture, we can start adding more details. I used a mix of hand painting and photographic textures.

To start, it's handy to build up some texture using photos, followed by adjusting and supplementing the existing texture with some hand painting. To that end, I grabbed some elephant-skin photos from CGTextures, with some wrinkles and skin

texture that complemented my texture nicely. I opened them as layers in my texture image file and scaled them so that the scale of the wrinkles in the texture roughly matched those of the Bat Creature.

I used the Move tool to spread out the textures on my image, knowing that their precise placement wouldn't be important for the time being. I then created a new layer (SHIFT-CTRL-N or Layer ▸ New Layer) and set its blending mode to Overlay. Next, by dragging the layer's icon in the Layers dialog up or down, I placed it between my original color texture and my Ambient Occlusion layer in the layers stack.

Using the Clone tool (**C**), I first set the clone source (CTRL-click) to one of the skin textures, making sure it was selected in the Layers dialog first. Then, I switched to my new layer and began cloning the skin texture in various areas (see Figure 11-12). I frequently switched between the different skin textures to find areas that would suit the different parts of my creature's skin. I also used the Flip (SHIFT-F) and Rotate (SHIFT-R) tools to flip and rotate the skin images to see whether they worked better in different orientations before cloning. To get at areas hidden by the skin images, I toggled their visibility using the eye icon in the Layers dialog or simply moved them to one side with the Move tool.

With a first layer of detail built up from photo images, I hid the photo textures and started working on some hand-painted details (see Figure 11-13). First, I added some veins to the wings on a new layer using the Paintbrush tool and a soft-edged brush. Next (on another new layer), I added some spots to the skin in areas like the shoulders, temples, and back in both darker and lighter colors. The Grunge brush I used earlier works well for this with the spacing (found in the Brushes dialog) turned up higher, as does a simple, small, hard-edged brush for painting specific spots. Keeping different kinds of details on different layers makes it easy to mix and combine them in different ways and comes in handy when creating specular and other kinds of maps.

Nails and Teeth

The nails and teeth of the Bat Creature are included in the same UV map as the body. For the nails, I painted a dark purplish color with some brighter yellowish highlights. For the teeth, I used a yellow color with some brown near where the teeth would meet the gums, as shown in Figure 11-14.

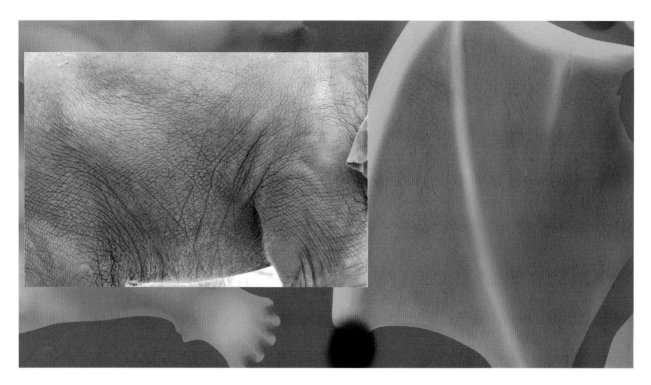

Figure 11-12: Cloning in texture from photographs with the Clone tool. I added the photograph as a new layer; then, on yet another new layer (set to Overlay), I cloned from the photo to create some skin detail for my texture.

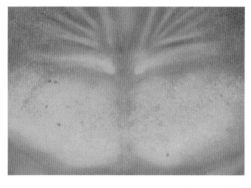

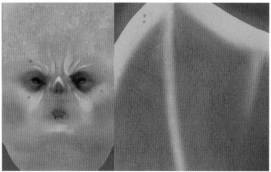

Figure 11-13: Some close-ups of hand-painted details

Figure 11-14: The nails and teeth

Fixing Seams

With my texture for the skin nice and detailed, I headed back to Blender to check that it worked okay and then started fixing any seams in the texture. To do this, I exported my skin texture from GIMP and replaced the old skin texture in Blender with the new exported version.

There were bound to be some artifacts in the texture along UV seams, where I had painted over the edges of a UV island in GIMP. To fix these, use Blender's Quick Edit feature:

1. To fix a seam on one part of your model, navigate the 3D view to an angle where the seam is clearly visible.

2. To make sure that no shading is visible on screen, set the viewpoint display mode to **GLSL** and set the material to **Shadeless** in the Materials tab of the Properties editor.

3. In Texture Paint mode, set the Quick Edit resolution to **1024** and click **Quick Edit** from the Tool Shelf (see Figure 11-15 ❷). This opens a screenshot of that view in GIMP, which we can then start painting over.

4. For best results, scale up the screenshot in GIMP, using **Image ▸ Image Size**, and set the new size to **2048**. Then, create a new transparent layer on which we will fix the seam (the reason for this will become clear shortly).

5. Using the **Clone** tool, start cloning from the layer below to cover the seam; the Grunge brush shape works well for this. (Turning on **Sample Merged** in the tool options will let you sample from all layers when you set the source, rather than having to switch layers first.)

6. With the seam painted out, disable the original layer, leaving only the newly painted layer that covers the seam. Use CTRL-E to export the image and save over the original exported image from Blender.

7. Back in Blender, click **Apply** to apply the painted-over image to your texture (see Figure 11-15 ❹). Because you saved only the areas of the image that covered the seam, only these areas are replaced. Repeat this process for any further seams on your model and then save the new fixed texture as a new image.

Reconciling Fixed Seams and Layered Images

This process fixed my seams, but because I fixed the texture in Blender, I had only a single-layer image as a result. To get back to a layered format, I opened the corrected image in GIMP as a new layer in my texture file, on top of my other layers. I wanted to be able to keep my old layers visible where possible, so I needed to mask this layer to show through only in those areas where I fixed the seams. To accomplish this, do the following:

1. Set the new fixed layer's blend mode to **Difference** in the Layers dialog. The result of this blend mode is the difference between the colors on this layer and the pixels below, meaning that different areas look bright and unchanged areas remain black. Overall, it may look very dark at the moment because the differences are slight, but you'll fix that shortly. You can use the result as the basis for a mask that shows only the fixed parts of the new layer.

2. Right-click on the top layer in the Layers dialog and select **New Layer from Visible**. This creates a new layer that is a composite of all the layers below, merged into one. In our case, this is the difference between the fixed layer and the original layered image. Using the Levels tool (**Colors ▸ Levels**), you can increase the values of this layer to create something we can use as a mask. The Levels tool takes the current layer as the input and uses the settings you provide to adjust the values of the layer. You simply want to take any pixels that aren't 100 percent black—areas where the fixed image differs from the original—and make them white. To do this, set the right-hand endpoint of the input gradient so that it's close to the left-hand end by dragging it to the left (see Figure 11-16) and click **OK**.

3. The results may look slightly noisy and have some odd-looking colors, but the colors don't matter because we'll be using only the brightness of this layer as a mask. To smooth things out a bit, use the Gaussian Blur filter (**Filters ▸ Blur ▸ Gaussian Blur**) to blur the layer by about 10 pixels.

4. Next, copy this new merged layer and use it as a mask for the fixed texture. Press CTRL-A to select all and CTRL-C to copy the layer to the clipboard.

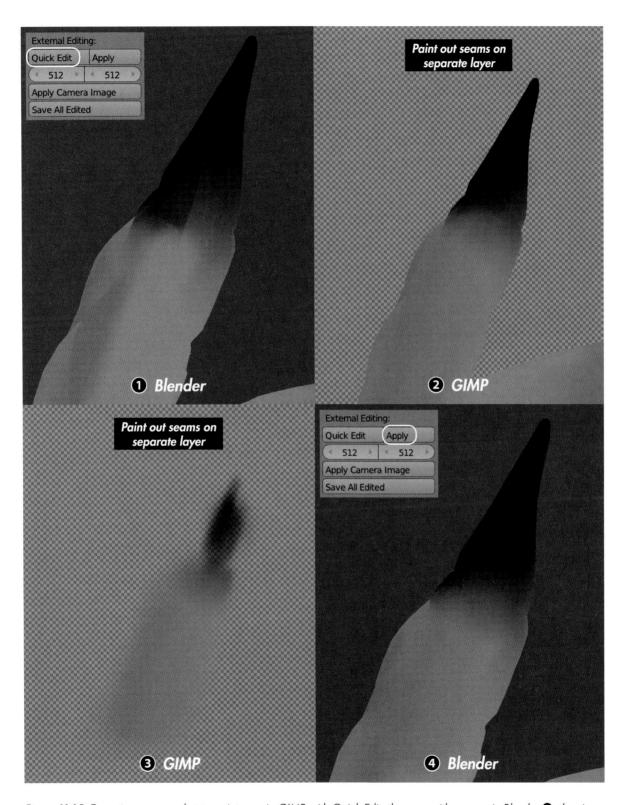

Figure 11-15: Exporting a screenshot to paint over in GIMP with Quick Edit: the area with a seam in Blender ❶; the view exported from Blender to GIMP with Quick Edit and painted over on a new layer ❷; the new layer on its own, which will be saved over the original export ❸; and the exported image applied to the texture, back in Blender, using the Apply operator ❹

Figure 11-16: Altering the values of a layer with the Levels tool. Note how the handles for the input levels have been bunched up at the left side of the graph to increase the brightness of all but the darkest values to white.

5. Disable the merged layer's visibility in the Layers dialog and set the Blend mode for the fixed layer back to **Normal**. Then, to add a layer mask to the fixed layer, right-click on it and choose **Add Layer Mask**. Choose white as the color of the layer mask and then click **Add** to create it.

6. Press CTRL-V to paste in the mask we created from the merged layer as a "floating" layer— one you can continue working on and moving around before anchoring it and applying it to the layer you pasted it into. Since we don't need to make any changes to it, press CTRL-H to anchor it.

Our fixed image is now masked so that only the areas that differ from the original texture show over the layers below. This more or less completes the creation of our diffuse texture (see Figure 11-17), so save the image as an *.xcf* file and export a new *.tga* image of the diffuse texture.

Layer Masks

A *layer mask* is a black-and-white image that determines how a layer in GIMP mixes with the layer below it. White areas are applied 100 percent if the overall opacity of the layer is also 100 percent (otherwise the two are multiplied together), black areas are completely masked out, and values in between blend between the two extremes.

When you add a mask to a layer (as we did above), it appears to the right of that layer's thumbnail in the Layers dialog. To edit the new layer mask, click its thumbnail, and you can paint on it just as you would on a normal layer (except that it allows only black and white values, so tools and filters that work with RGB colors are not available).

Click the thumbnail for the layer to go back to painting normally (the thumbnail of the active layer or mask is outlined in white). You can apply the effect of a layer mask by right-clicking the layer in the Layers dialog and choosing **Apply Layer Mask**. This will apply the mask to the layer itself, making masked areas transparent.

Creating Specular and Hardness Textures

With our diffuse texture painted and the seams cleared up, it's time to create our specular and hardness textures. The *specular texture* defines the color and intensity of our creature's specular reflections: Dark areas will look matte, and bright areas will look shiny. The *hardness map* determines how soft the highlights are: Low values create soft, spread-out reflections, and high values create smaller, more intense highlights.

To create these textures, we can duplicate and modify the layers of the diffuse map. We'll work in the same GIMP *.xcf* file to create these textures, which will give us ready access to the layers we've already created.

Layer Groups

To make it easier to manage creating specular and hardness textures, I used *layer groups* to organize my layers. Layer groups allow you to group layers and expand and collapse those groups in the Layers dialog, making it simpler to keep things organized. To create a layer group, right-click on a layer in the Layers dialog, and choose **New Layer Group** or click the folder icon at the bottom of the dialog. You can then drag other layers onto the group layer to assign them to the group. To organize my textures for the Bat Creature, I created three layer groups: one for the diffuse texture, one for my specular texture, and one for hardness (see Figure 11-18).

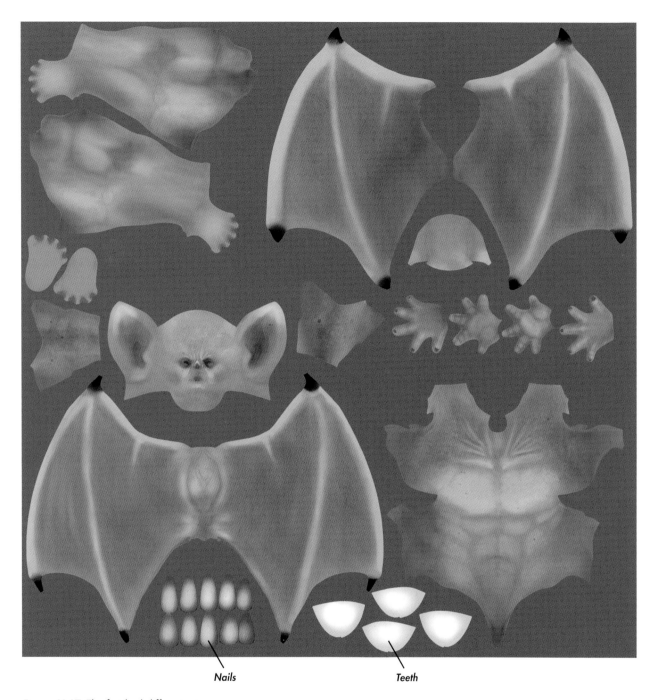

Figure 11-17: The finished diffuse texture

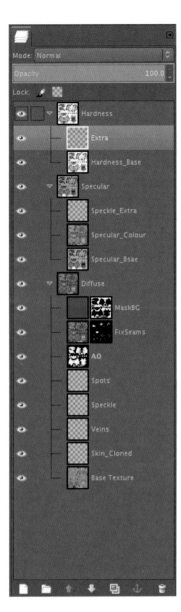

Figure 11-18: Organizing layers with Layer Groups

Specular Map

For the specular map, I first created a new layer from the visible layers (Layer ▸ New Layer from Visible) and placed it in the layer group for my specular map. I inverted the colors of the texture (Colors ▸ Invert) and then tweaked the levels (Colors ▸ Levels) to give the layer some more contrast. Next, I changed the color of the layer using Colors ▸ Hue and Saturation and shifted the Hue slider to give it a more bluish tint (see Figure 11-19 at ❸). Although this already gave a pretty good specular texture, to get more variation, I duplicated the layers I created earlier for the diffuse map with speckles and spots on them and placed them in the layer group for the specular map, adjusting their colors appropriately.

Next, I started tweaking some areas to get the right level of specularity. For example, I wanted the lips and the area around the eye to look moist and shiny, and I wanted the torso and arms to look more matte and dry. I could have started painting over using a basic brush, but doing so would have lost a lot of the texture I'd already worked to create. Instead, I was able to preserve some texture by using a different Brush mode. The Brush mode can be set from the Tool Options dialog. Brush modes have the same options (normal, multiply, addition, and so on) that Blend modes for layers have. A good way to tweak the values in an image without losing detail is to use the paintbrush with the Brush mode set to Overlay and to use black to darken areas and white to brighten them.

In certain areas, I wanted to keep some texture while getting rid of very dark or light values, and here the Lighten Only and Darken Only brush modes came in handy. I used Darken Only and a midvalue color to get rid of overly bright areas without losing darker elements of the texture, and vice versa. Figure 11-20 shows the finished specular texture.

Hardness Map

To create the hardness texture, I first made a New From Visible layer from the diffuse texture. (You can turn off the visibility of the specular texture layer group to make the diffuse texture visible again.) Next, I inverted the layer, adjusted the levels, and began tweaking by hand with the Paint tool, just as I did above. Because the hardness texture benefits from more variation, I created a new layer and painted in more speckles over the body (both lighter and darker ones). Figure 11-20 also shows the finished hardness texture.

Texturing the Eyes

With most of the texturing done, I moved on to texturing the eyes. For this I made a new image, which I painted by hand by taking the following steps:

1. Create a new image that is 1024×1024 pixels in size (**File ▸ New Image**). Then, to get a guide for the middle of the eye, create two guidelines through the middle of the image, horizontally and vertically. To do this, click **Image ▸ Guides ▸ New Guide by Percent.** To create guidelines for placing the pupil, repeat this once for the vertical guide and once for the horizontal one, each at 50 percent of the image's height or width.

2. Fill the first layer with a yellowish color and then create a new layer for the iris. To get the correct shape, use the **Ellipse Selection** tool (**E**) and click and drag from the center of the image to draw out a circle. Holding down

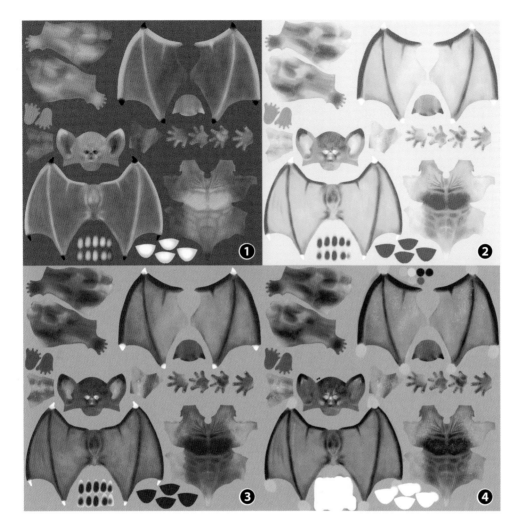

Figure 11-19: Creating the specular map by tweaking the diffuse map: diffuse map ❶; invert colors ❷; adjust levels, hue, and saturation ❸; and paint extra details ❹.

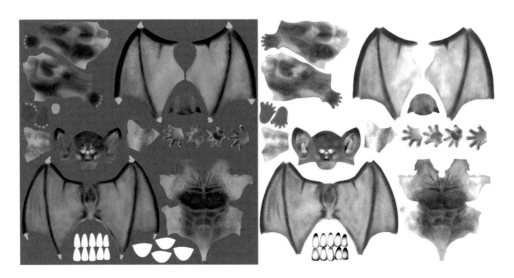

Figure 11-20: The finished specular texture (left) and hardness texture (right)

CTRL makes the selection expand from the center, and holding SHIFT constrains the selection to be circular.

3. Draw out a circular outline for the outside of the iris and then subtract the pupil shape from the middle of the iris selection (hold down CTRL before clicking and dragging). This time, I created an elliptical shape to give the eye an evil look.

4. Feather (**Select ▶ Feather, 20 Pixels**) the selection to give the iris a more gradual transition into the rest of the eye. Then, convert the selection into a layer mask by right-clicking on the layer in the Layers dialog, selecting **Add Layer Mask**, and under **Initialize Layer To**, choosing **Selection**. This creates a layer mask with your selection that allows you to paint on the layer itself (select it in the Layers dialog first) without losing the shape of the iris (see Figure 11-21).

5. Fill the iris with black using the **Fill** tool and then use the **Paint** tool and a large, soft brush to add color. I began with a bright orange and then added elements of red, green, and purple to build up different colors (use low pressure if you have a tablet, or set the brush opacity low). I left the edges of the iris black.

6. Now add color around the outside of the eye (the *sclera*) on the layer below the iris. I painted a lighter yellow here and mixed it with a darker, reddish brown. I also filled the pupil with black on this layer. My eye texture now looked like Figure 11-21. I saved this texture as a *.tga* file.

Because I decided to change the shape of the pupil slightly in my texture, I also tweaked the shape of the pupil on my model by selecting the pupil's vertices and scaling them up on the z-axis. I slightly adjusted the UV map, too (see Figure 11-22).

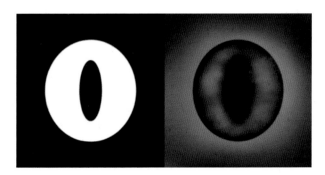

Figure 11-21: The mask for the iris, created using the Elliptical Select tools (left) and the eye texture (right)

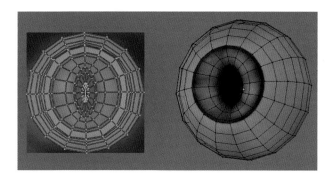

Figure 11-22: Adjusting the pupil to fit the texture. Left: The adjusted UV coordinates. Right: The eye in Edit mode with the texture applied.

Texturing the Jungle Temple

The textures for the Jungle Temple scene required a different approach. This project has a number of objects that require very similar textures, so texturing each one individually would be time consuming and unnecessary. Instead, I chose to use tileable, seamless textures to cover much of my scene and to supplement these with details in key places. Tileable textures allow a single texture to be used across multiple models.

Hardness vs. Roughness

For the Bat Creature, one of the texture types I created was a hardness texture, which will be used to define which areas of my materials have sharp, small specular reflections and which parts have blurry, more spread out specular reflections. To define these areas, the texture is mapped to the hardness value of the material's specular shader. Dark areas of the texture then result in soft, blurry specular reflections, and bright areas result in sharp, hard specular reflections.

However, this is only the case when rendering in Blender Internal. When rendering with Cycles, materials are created differently (as we will see in Chapter 12). And instead of a hardness value, specular shaders now have something called a *roughness* value. This works in the opposite way to a hardness value, but defines roughly the same thing. For a roughness texture, bright areas denote soft, blurry reflections, and dark areas denote sharp reflections. Keep this in mind when creating your textures.

Creating Seamless Textures with GIMP

To create a seamless texture, the edges of the image must align with one another, and the features of the image must continue smoothly across the boundary. It helps to make sure that the texture doesn't have features that repeat too obviously when tiled (large, distinctive features are easily noticed when they repeat often). We also want to make the image square so that we won't have to scale an object's UV coordinates when applying the seamless texture.

To create a seamless rock texture for the stone blocks of the walls and floors, I began with a rock texture from CGTextures. First, I increased the size of the image to make it square with Image ▸ Canvas Size. Next, I used Layer ▸ Add Alpha Channel to give the layer a transparent background, which we'll fill shortly, and Layer ▸ Layer to Image Size to match the size of the layer to the image.

Now we have to fill in the remainder of the image and make its edges align with each other. To do this, I used the Offset tool and the Resynthesize filter. First, I offset the image by 50 percent on the *x*- and *y*-axes (Layers ▸ Transform ▸ Offset), choosing the x/2 y/2 option and clicking Offset. This shifted the image and repeated it, placing the edges against one another, as shown in Figure 11-23 at ❷. The new edges now matched up because they were in the *middle* of the image previously.

To fix the areas where the edges met, I used GIMP's Resynthesize feature to fill selected areas seamlessly. To create a selection, I used GIMP's Quick Mask feature (CTRL-Q) to paint my selection directly with GIMP's paint tools. Areas painted white are selected, while areas painted black are unselected. While working in Quick Mask mode, an image will be highlighted in red, but selected areas will appear as normal. I pressed CTRL-Q to enable quick masking and roughly painted a white stripe down the seams where the image edges met, and filled in the gap left in the middle. Then, I pressed CTRL-Q again to convert my quick mask to a selection.

Next, I used Filters ▸ Map ▸ Resynthesize to fill the selected area. I turned on Make Horizontally Tileable and Make Vertically Tileable, and kept the texture source as the current layer. After running the filter, I offset the image again by a different amount (a third in each direction) and resynthesized any remaining problem areas. The result is the texture shown on the right of Figure 11-23 at ❹. This texture will now tile seamlessly.

Testing the Texture

To test the texture, create a duplicate of the image in GIMP (CTRL-D) and scale it way down (for example, to 512×512). Then, use **Filters ▸ Map ▸ Tile** to create a tiled version of the texture. If any areas show obvious repeats, remove them by going back to the full-size texture and selecting and resynthesizing any trouble spots. Once you're happy with how the texture tiles, save it as a *.tga* file.

To test your texture in Blender, select an object and then assign the image to it in the UV Texture editor. Switch to **Textured Viewport** shading and set the shading type to **Multitexture** in the display panel of the Properties region so that you can see the image assigned to the object. You may need to scale the UVs up or down or tweak the texture a bit to get the best results.

Creating Additional Textures

I repeated the process for producing a seamless texture to create a second rock texture, a bark texture for the trees, and a dirt texture for the ground, as you can see in Figure 11-24. I also created specular maps using the same techniques to modify and supplement the diffuse maps that I used for the Bat Creature. For the bark texture, I didn't make the texture square since I would be wrapping it around the trunk of the tree. Instead, I opted for a narrow, tall texture. This results in a more efficient use of texture space, as the texture will repeat often along the length of the tree while only once around the circumference of the trunk.

To make different textures—like the two rock textures—work better together, you can use GIMP's Hue-Saturation and Curves tools. By adjusting the hue and saturation of an image, you can make the overall coloration of one texture more similar to the other, and by using the Curves tool, you can brighten or darken the image to make the range of values of the two textures more similar. For example, the two rock textures in Figure 11-24 initially had quite different colors and levels of brightness, but I adjusted them to make them look more similar. This makes it much easier to blend these two textures later on when creating further textures and materials.

Texturing the Ground and Trees

To create textures for the ground and the trees in my scene, I made heavy use of Blender's Project

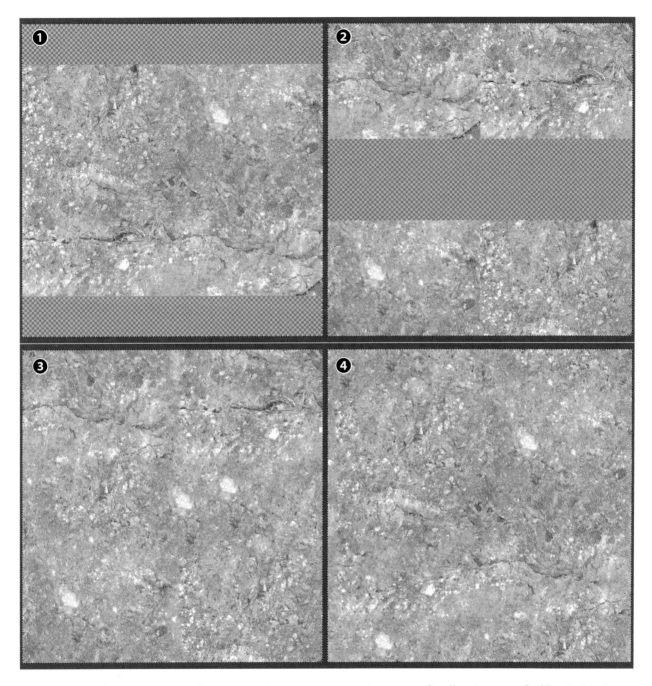

Figure 11-23: Making an image seamless: Increase the canvas size to make it square ❶; offset the image ❷; fill in the blanks and fix the seams with the Resynthesize filter ❸; and re-offset to check the texture and resynthesize any problem areas ❹.

Paint tools to mix together the seamless textures I created in GIMP. This approach allowed me to quickly build up more unique textures by using the generic tileable texture I had already created as a starting point.

Ground Texture

While I now had a seamless texture for the ground, it wasn't particularly unique or tailored to the scene. To create a more interesting ground texture, I chose to project the existing seamless texture to a unique

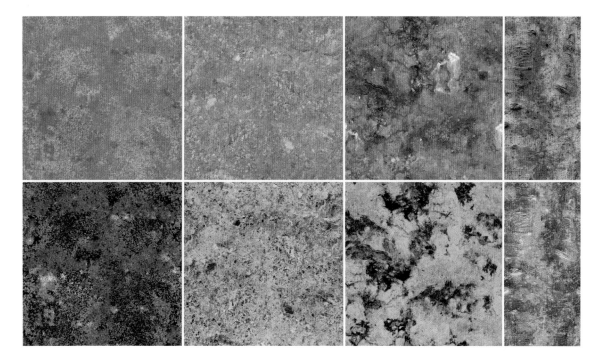

Figure 11-24: Seamless textures for the Jungle Temple scene, from left to right: dirt, two rock textures, and a bark texture. The top textures are diffuse maps and the bottom textures are specular maps.

unwrapped one and then to embellish it with some extra details. To accomplish this, take the following steps:

1. Create a second set of UV coordinates, unwrapping the floor mesh to fill the new UV space as well as possible. Then, add a new blank image to the new UV set.

2. Use the **Clone** tool to clone the seamless texture. I set the seamless soil texture as the image for the old UV coordinates and then selected my new set.

3. In Texture Paint mode, use the **Clone** brush to clone the seamless texture onto your new unwrap. (Make sure that you also have Clone turned on in the Project Paint options and that the old UV map is set as the source for the cloning.)

4. To mix in a second texture, replace the old UV coordinate sets image with a different soil texture and repeat the cloning process again, this time adding only some small patches.

5. Finally, repeat the process using a mossy rock texture to add some stony patches to the ground. The final texture is a lot more distinctive and diverse, as shown in Figure 11-25.

Tree Textures

To modify the texture for the trees, I began with a seamless bark texture and then blended in mossy and muddy elements to make the texture more interesting (see Figure 11-26). This time, however, I projected the first seamless texture in Blender and then saved the image and switched to GIMP to add elements from other photographs. This let me use different brushes to clone together bits of different images and split my texture into layers while working. I then created specular and roughness maps for the tree from the diffuse map.

Texturing the Statue

For the statue in the Jungle Temple scene, I wanted the more hidden parts to look mossy and overgrown and the exposed parts to be bare rock. To accomplish this, I could have cloned in the mossy areas by hand, but instead, I chose to use the ambient occlusion map I baked earlier, which is already darker in the crevices, as a mask.

To do this in Blender, I duplicated the UV coordinate set for the statue and assigned the ambient occlusion texture to it. Then, I used this UV set as

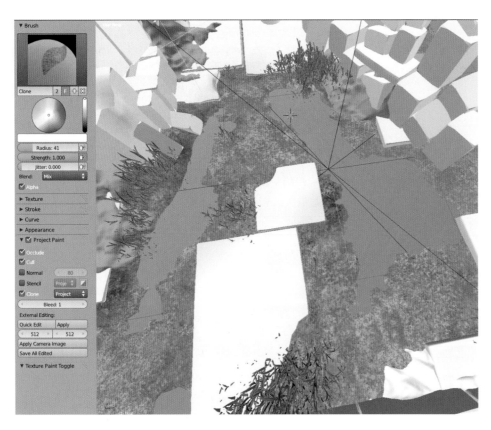

Figure 11-25: Projecting seamless textures to a unique texture map in order to combine them and create something unique. Here, I'm using the Clone brush to clone from a seamless texture to my unique UV map.

Figure 11-26: Texturing the trees. I began with a seamless bark texture and then blended in other textures in GIMP.

a mask layer for cloning a mossy texture over a rock texture, as follows:

1. Duplicate the original UV map twice by clicking the + icon in the UV Coordinates panel of the Object Data tab in the Properties editor. Rename each set so that you'll know which is which. As the names for my sets, I chose *Paint* for my final painted texture, *Mask* for my mask image, and *Cube*. I would use the Cube UV set for projecting my seamless textures, so I re-unwrapped the statue in Edit mode using the **Cube Project** option to give an unwrap with nice consistency between parts of the model.

2. Assign your seamless rock texture to the Cube UV set, scaling it to suit the details in the rock. Then, switch to your Paint UV set and use the **Clone** tool (make sure Clone is turned on in the Project Paint panel) to clone the rock texture from the Cube project UV set to the painted texture.

3. To mix in the second texture, use the Project Paint **Stencil** option. Switch to Edit mode and assign your ambient occlusion map to the Mask UV set by selecting the **Mask UV** set in the Object Data tab of the Properties editor. Then, assign a different rock texture to the Cube UV set, but this time use a moss-covered rock texture.

4. Now return to texture painting on the Paint layer (again selecting it in the Properties editor to make it the active UV set). Switch on **Stencil** in the Project Paint panel, choosing your mask UV set from the drop-down menu beside it. Then, with the **Clone** brush, paint the second rock texture over the original one. The effect of the brush is automatically masked according to the ambient occlusion map, allowing you to easily paint only on the exposed areas, as shown in Figure 11-27.

After saving the resulting image as a *.tga* file, I used the ambient occlusion map in GIMP to lighten the exposed areas of the texture by opening the painted texture and adding the ambient occlusion map over the top (using Open as Layer). Setting the ambient occlusion map's blend mode to Overlay and reducing its opacity subtly lightened the exposed areas of the statue and darkened the crevices, as shown in Figure 11-28.

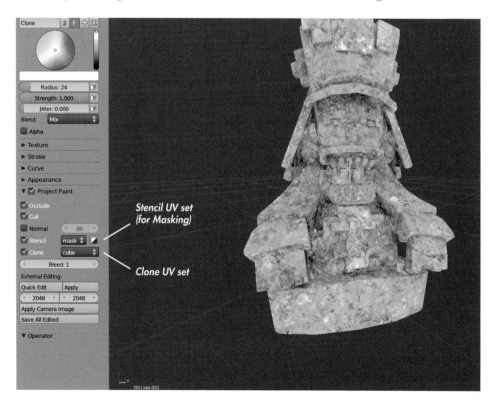

Figure 11-27: Using the Project Paint Mask setting to mask the effect of the Clone brush allowed me to mix textures according to an ambient occlusion map.

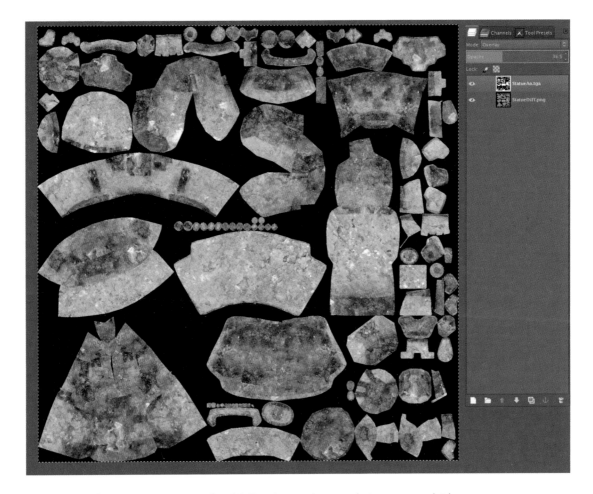

Figure 11-28: The statue texture opened in GIMP with an ambient occlusion map overlaid on top

Texturing to Camera

When it came to the rocks and soil in the foreground of the Jungle Temple scene, tileable textures wouldn't give quite the level of control I wanted. For this part of my scene, I opted to paint the textures for the ground and rocks as they appeared from the camera viewpoint. To do this, take the following steps:

1. Put the foreground rocks and soil on the same layer (use **M** to move objects to a different layer and **P** in Edit mode to part the selection from the current object if necessary).

2. Switch to **Textured** view (with the shading set to **Single texture** in the properties region) and assign your seamless textures to the UVs of your objects.

3. Use the **Render Active Viewport** button (the camera icon) in the 3D Viewport header to render the current view to an image (see

Figure 11-29). Then, save this as a *.tga* image. (In order to be able to mix my rock textures together, I assigned my second rock texture to the stones and saved a second viewport render.)

4. Open these in the same document in GIMP (open the first normally and then open the second using **Open as Layers**). Next, begin blending the two by adding a new layer mask to the top layer and painting in black areas to let the layer below show through.

5. Then, to soften the boundaries between the mud and rock, create a new layer and mix them together slightly using the **Clone** tool and your **Grunge** brush (see Figure 11-30), saving the image as a *.tga* file.

Later on, this texture will be projected from the camera and used as part of the material for the foreground objects.

Figure 11-29: Rendering the view to an image

Figure 11-30: Editing the textures projected from the camera view. I filled in the background to prevent it from creating artifacts near the image boundary where the texture wraps around at the bottom. Then, I blended the textures on the objects in the foreground.

Texturing the Leaves

For the leaves in the Jungle Temple scene, I wanted to create three textures: one for the color of the leaves, one for the specular map, and one for their transparency. I would use the transparency (alpha) map to make the parts of the mesh that are not actually part of a leaf transparent, thus giving the leaves detailed outlines without using geometry. This is doubly important for the leaves I generated with IvyGen, as these are just flat planes.

Collecting the Leaf Images

I began by collecting leaf images that were roughly the shape I wanted. Then, I opened them in GIMP and selected the rough outline of the leaf with the Scissors tool, placing points around the edge of the leaf to trace its outline automatically. I could then refine this using Quick Masking and the Paintbrush tool with a hard-edged brush, painting with black or white to remove or add parts of the leaf selection. I used the leaf selection as a layer mask (Layers ▸ Mask ▸ Add Layer Mask and choosing Selection) to mask out the background of the leaf image.

Alpha Map

The next step was to create the alpha, color, and specular images. To create the alpha texture, I clicked the layer mask, pressed CTRL-A to select all, and pressed CTRL-C to copy the mask to the clipboard. Then, I clicked New Layer and pasted in the mask, now visible as a normal layer. Figure 11-31 shows the finished alpha map.

Diffuse Map

For the diffuse map, I added a uniform color background and got rid of any specular highlights in the photo to make it more suitable to use as a texture. For the background, I created a new layer and filled it with a green to match the leaf color so that when the material blended into transparency, there would

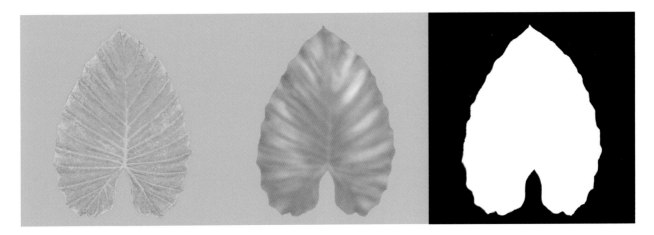

Figure 11-31: The textures for a single leaf, from left to right: diffuse, specular, and alpha. These textures are used on my IvyGen mesh.

be no color change around the edges. I duplicated the leaf image layer and placed it on top of this background.

To remove the specular highlights, I used the Dodge/Burn tool (SHIFT-D) set to burn (hold CTRL or change the settings in the Brush Tools palette) with a large, soft brush. I brushed lightly over the highlights to dim them (use a light pressure if you're using a pressure-sensitive tablet, or simply set the Exposure setting of the Dodge/Burn tool down low if you're using a mouse). To fix any areas that become oversaturated, I used the Paintbrush tool with a color from a good part of the texture. Then, I set the blend mode of the brush to Saturation and painted over any oversaturated areas to bring them in line with the rest of the texture. (Figure 11-31, left, shows the diffuse texture.)

Specular Map

For the specular color, I duplicated my masked leaf image and used the Hue-Saturation tool to desaturate it a bit. Then, I shifted the specular color slightly toward yellow. I also painted in some highlights on smooth areas of the leaf and then blurred the texture slightly. You can see the specular texture in Figure 11-31 (center).

This completed the textures needed for a single leaf, so I saved each as a .tga image and then saved an .xcf file with my layers. I used this single leaf as my texture for the leaves generated by IvyGen. For the rest of the leaves in my scene, I wanted to combine as many as possible into one image so that I wouldn't have to manage too many textures. So I repeated the cutting-out process for as many leaf

images as I needed, skipping the specular textures for the time being. Later, I combined all these leaves onto a single map so it would be easier to do the specular map afterward.

Combining Leaves onto a Single Texture

For most of the foliage in my scene, I packed all of the leaves onto the same UV map. (In Chapter 10, I baked a color map from the material color of the leaves to serve as a guide.) To make it easier to assemble all my leaves into one texture, I applied the layer masks that I had created earlier to the diffuse layer of each leaf texture. I then saved each of these leaves as images and opened them as layers on top of the guide image I baked in Chapter 10.

Next, I started arranging the leaves to fit the map, using the Move, Scale, and Rotate tools. After getting a leaf roughly in place, I used the IWarp tool (Filters ▸Distort ▸IWarp) to warp the leaves to more accurately fit the shapes I needed (see Figure 11-32). IWarp allows you to move pixels around your selection fluidly in order to reshape areas of an image. For the leaves, I used the Move Deform mode in IWarp to fit the outline of the leaves to the shapes I needed. I repeated this, duplicating some of the leaves to cover each space that needed a leaf texture. For the unwrapped stems, I cloned from the bigger leaves to fill in the whole region with a rough green texture. The diffuse texture for all the leaves combined into a single texture is shown in Figure 11-33. I then created the specular map for my grouped-together leaves the same way I did for the individual leaf.

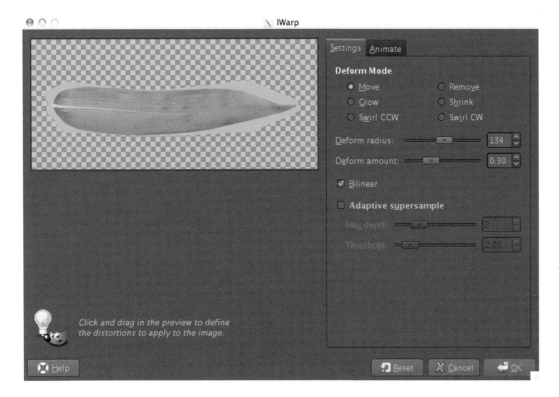

Figure 11-32: Using the IWarp filter to warp the shape of a leaf

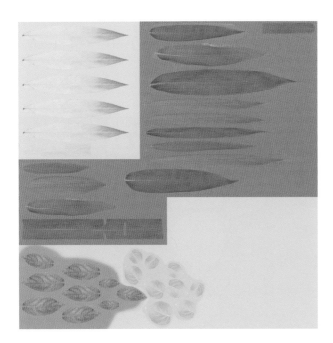

Figure 11-33: I merged the textures for several of my leaves onto a single image to keep the number of textures in my scene down.

To get an alpha texture again, I simply merged the leaf textures into one layer and then right-clicked the layer in the Layers editor and chose Alpha to Selection. Then, I created a new black layer and filled the selection with white to get my alpha image. Finally, I exported each of my diffuse, specular, and alpha passes as *.tga* images and saved the GIMP *.xcf* file, too. The combined leaf textures can be seen in Figure 11-31. This completed almost all of the textures for the Jungle Temple. I created any remaining ones in much the same way as those described already.

Texturing the Spider Bot

Texturing the Spider Bot was a bit simpler than texturing was for the other two images because this project relies largely on procedural materials. I made a UV texture that covered the body in order to take some of the hassle out of creating different materials later and to allow me to add some detail to the model.

Creating Three Textures

I began with my baked color map in GIMP and scaled it up to 4096×4096 pixels. Then, I opened my baked ambient occlusion map as a layer, scaled it to fit, and set its blend mode to Multiply at 40 percent opacity in order to add some subtle shadowing to the texture.

I needed to make three textures: diffuse, roughness, and specular. Because I wanted the body's green areas to be shiny, I made the green area much darker for the diffuse texture and bright green for the specular texture. For the body's white areas, I did the opposite: dark gray on the specular map to make it less shiny and light on the diffuse.

For the roughness map, I made the green areas (of the diffuse map) dark to give sharp, glossy reflections, and I made the white areas bright to give softer highlights. You can see the three textures in Figure 11-34. To keep my textures organized, I created separate layer groups for each of the diffuse, specular, and roughness maps, just as I did for the Bat Creature.

Adding Decals

To make things a bit more interesting, I decided to add some decals to the Spider Bot. To make decals, I drew a few simple designs using 2D curves in Blender and rendered these in black and white. Then, I opened these as layers over my existing texture file in GIMP.

To make the background of the decals transparent, I used Colors ▸ Color to Alpha and selected the background color as the color to remove. I selected individual decals and spread them out over the body by selecting them and then scaling, moving, and rotating them into place. (It can be easier to do this if you split up each decal onto its own layer by selecting it and pressing CTRL-SHIFT-L to float the selection and CTRL-SHIFT-N to convert it to a layer. Then, you can scale and rotate it independently of the other decals. Once it's in place, you can merge the details back onto the same layer.)

To get a better feel for the placement of your decals, you can mark in roughly where you want them in Blender's Texture Paint mode. Then, save the image as a guide to use in GIMP. Once I had the decals laid out, I set their opacity to 60 percent for the diffuse map.

To make the decals stand out, I worked them into the specular and roughness maps too. I duplicated my decal layer from the diffuse map and placed copies in my layer groups for the specular and roughness maps. For the specular map, I used Colors ▸ Invert to make the decals white, which would make them shinier on the eventual material. For the roughness map, I made the decals black once again to give them sharp reflections (see Figure 11-34).

With my textures complete, I saved a GIMP *.xcf* file with all my layer groups and then exported *.tga* files of my diffuse, specular, and roughness maps.

Figure 11-34: Textures for the Spider Bot, from left to right: diffuse, specular, and roughness. I incorporated some decals into the textures to make them more interesting, making sure to add them to the roughness and specular maps as well.

In Review

In this chapter, I've covered using both Blender and GIMP to create textures, starting with our baked textures as a foundation and building up layers of detail and different images. We've used Blender's Texture Paint mode, cloned textures in both Blender and GIMP, and used seamless textures both on their own and as a basis for creating more distinctive textures.

For the Bat Creature, I built up my textures mainly by hand, blocking in simple colors in Blender and then refining these in GIMP, painting in extra details and supplementing them with elements from photographic textures, and then jumping back to Blender to clear up seams.

For the Jungle Temple, I created a variety of seamless textures, which formed a foundation for creating further textures for unique objects. By creating a range of tileable, reusable textures first, I achieved consistent textures across multiple elements in the scene and sped up the texturing process.

For the Spider Bot, I focused on creating relatively simple diffuse, specular, and roughness textures that I will later use to create some fairly complex materials. I used my ambient occlusion map and the solid color map I generated in Chapter 10 as a starting point and then created and added decals to embellish the design of the Spider Bot without crowding in too many details.

In Chapter 12, we'll create materials for use by both Blender's Internal renderer and the new Cycles renderer, using the textures created in this chapter as inputs. We'll look at the different ways to apply textures when working with the two renderers and the similarities and differences in creating materials with the two render engines in mind.

12

MATERIALS

In Chapters 10 and 11, I created textures that specified the diffuse colors for the models, as well as other parameters, like reflectiveness, smoothness, and specular colors. Now we'll look at combining these image textures with procedural textures and shaders to create materials for the scenes that look both interesting and convincing.

This chapter will cover how Blender's materials work and how to incorporate textures into these materials. Let's look first, though, at Blender's two default render engines for rendering images, Cycles and the Blender Internal renderer, as they will significantly impact how we set up our materials.

Render Engines: Blender Internal and Cycles

The *render engine* is how Blender creates a final image using all of the information in your scene—objects, materials, lights, and settings. Blender has two render engines. The older one, the Blender Internal render engine, is a very robust (if slightly old-fashioned) renderer that uses various tricks and

techniques to create the final render, eschewing absolute physical accuracy for speed and flexibility. However, this lack of physical accuracy doesn't mean that Blender Internal can't render realistic-*looking* images. It can quickly render scenes with a variety of complex materials to create a final look anywhere between a highly realistic aesthetic and a very non-photo-realistic and stylized one. This makes Blender Internal a highly flexible renderer, well suited to animation.

Cycles is Blender's new render engine, which is still in active development. Unlike the internal engine, it focuses on creating more realistic simulations of light and uses more physically correct models for materials and lights. As a result, it can deliver very realistic images, including effects that are difficult to achieve in Blender Internal, such as the complex refraction of light in glass and other transparent objects, multiple reflections of light bouncing around a scene, and the physically correct emission of light from objects. The tradeoff is that (at least as of this writing) Cycles renders scenes—even those with simple lighting—more slowly than Blender Internal. And because Cycles is in active development, it lacks certain important features, like subsurface scattering (see "Subsurface Scattering" on page 194 for more information) and the ability to render hair and fur.

I'll use both renderers in this book. Which renderer I choose for each project has a significant impact on how I define my materials, because these two render engines work in different ways and require materials to be set up differently. For the Bat Creature, I'll use Blender Internal to render realistic skin with subsurface scattering, as well as the fur. And for the Spider Bot, though either renderer would do, I'll use Cycles to create some nice glossy, reflective materials. For the Jungle Temple project, I'll use Cycles to allow me to experiment with lighting and get direct feedback, thanks to Cycles' interactive render preview (discussed in "The Cycles Render Preview" on page 200).

Before examining the differences in creating materials for the two different render engines, let's take a brief look at a few general principles that will come up as we discuss materials. These principles center mainly on the various ways a surface can interact with light by reflecting, refracting, or absorbing it.

Reflection

We see objects because our eyes detect the light that bounces off them. The appearance of a surface is thus determined by the precise way in which it interacts with light, which is in turn determined by the structure and composition of the material.

In the real world, matte surfaces, like rock and rubber, have a rough structure on a microscopic scale. Light bounces off them in all directions, and as a result, the light you see reflected looks much the same no matter which direction you look at the surface from. This is called *diffuse* reflection.

In contrast, polished surfaces are relatively smooth, even at microscopic scales. This means that you'll see a perfect reflection when you look at the surface, and as you move your viewpoint, what is reflected will change. This is called *specular*, or *mirror*, reflection. The differences between diffuse and specular reflection are shown in Figure 12-1.

In the world of CG, however, we often take shortcuts to achieve the look of real materials. For example, consider specular reflections: While it's possible to render mirror reflections, doing so is

Figure 12-1: Diffuse (left) vs. specular (right) reflection (Cycles renderer)

slower than rendering diffuse reflections because there are simple algorithms to approximate the effect of diffuse reflections. So rendering diffuse reflections can be extremely fast, but rendering mirror reflections requires processor-intensive ray tracing. To get around this problem, we sometimes consider only the most obvious things that a surface can reflect, like bright lights. For example, if you were to look at a shiny metal surface in bright light, you might overlook mirror reflections of the surrounding environment due to the very bright reflection of the light source itself. Specular reflections work this way in Blender's Internal renderer: The renderer creates only highlights from light sources rather than making the surface reflect other objects around it (see Figure 12-2). This shortcut often does the job, and when more accurate reflections are needed, you can turn them on as well (by enabling ray-traced mirror reflections) at the cost of extra rendering time.

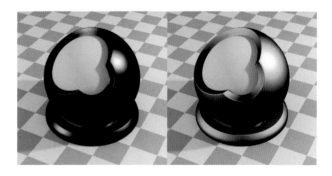

Figure 12-2: Blender Internal's approximated specular reflections (Blender Internal renderer). Often these are referred to as specular reflections, while more realistic (mirror) specular reflections are referred to as glossy reflections. Left: A material with only specular reflections and a hardness of 15. Right: A hardness of 100.

Transmission and Refraction

In addition to reflecting light, surfaces like water or glass also *transmit* light (allow light to pass through them). In the real world, a part of the *incident light* (light hitting the surface) is usually reflected, and the rest is transmitted and bent slightly (*refracted*). The light is bent because as it enters a different medium, its speed changes. This bending of light results in a distorted image when you look through a transparent material. The amount of distortion depends on the object's *index of refraction (IOR)*, which determines how much the direction of a ray of light is altered at the boundary of the object (see Figure 12-8 on page 189), and the shape and thickness of the object. For some objects, this effect is significant—for example, when you look through a lens or a glass of water, you'll notice considerable distortion. Other times, the effect is minimal—for example, there is little distortion when you look through the thin glass of a window.

Z Transparency

We can use Blender to simulate transmission and refraction of light using ray-traced transparency. But we can also cheat by ignoring refraction and simply rendering whatever is behind an object. This is called *Z Transparency*. This technique works well with objects like windows, where the refraction is minimal. Figure 12-3 compares ray tracing with Z Transparency.

Z Transparency is also useful for rendering thin surfaces with holes or complex outlines, where the mesh can be left simple and a texture can be used to

define transparent—or, in this case, nonexistent—areas of the surface. These areas can then be rendered completely transparent (invisible), which will make the surface appear more complex than its geometry alone would allow (see Figure 12-4).

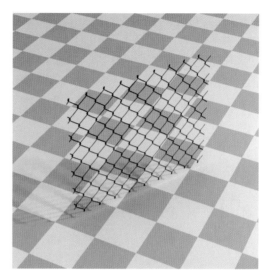

Figure 12-4: Using Z Transparency to give this wire fence material a more complex appearance without requiring extra geometry (using the Blender Internal renderer). This material has been applied to a single plane. (The Transparent Shadows option has been turned on for the floor material to create accurate shadows.)

Light can interact with a surface in still more complex ways, such as scattering beneath the surface or exhibiting translucency or anisotropic reflection, which is the type of reflection produced by brushed metal. We'll examine these other types of interaction as we move through this chapter.

Blender Internal Materials

Blender Internal is Blender's default render engine, and you can create materials for Blender Internal using the Materials and Textures tabs of the Properties editor. You can find the properties of materials in the Material tab (and the textures and aspects of a material they can be used to affect) in the Textures tab.

Blender Internal's materials are pretty modular, allowing you to add and combine different material properties—such as specular reflections, mirror reflectivity, transparency, and subsurface scattering—simply by turning on the relevant options from the different panels in the Material

Figure 12-3: Ray tracing vs. Z Transparency (using the Blender Internal renderer). Left: Z Transparency with an alpha of 0.25 and specular highlights. The specular and slight diffuse visibility make this material visible. Right: Ray-traced transparency with an IOR of 1.5. This image is more realistic but will take much longer to render.

tab (Figure 12-5), without having to start from scratch. Notice in the figure that all of the materials assigned to the active object are in the panel at the top of the tab. Below, in the Preview panel, is a preview of the active material, followed by other panels containing the Materials settings. I'll discuss the relevant panels in the Materials tab (when using Blender Internal) here.

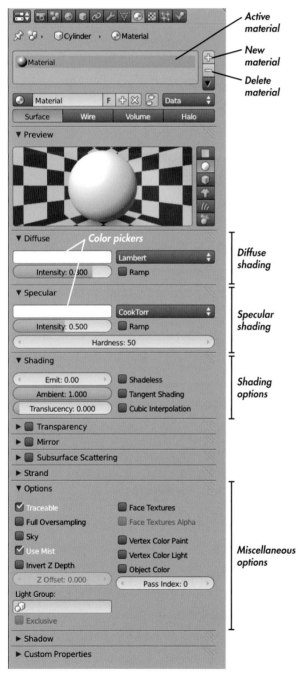

Figure 12-5: The Materials tab when using the Blender Internal renderer

Diffuse This panel contains the settings for the diffuse color and shading of a material. The color picker (see Figure 12-5) allows you to set the diffuse color of the material, which is then multiplied by the *intensity* value. The drop-down menu to the right lets you set the diffuse shader model, which affects the falloff of the material's diffuse color from light to dark at different angles. The default Lambert shader model is usually fine, though the Oren Nayar shader model can be used to mimic surfaces with a rougher microscopic structure, like clay or stone. The other shader models here are more exotic and rarely useful.

Specular The settings in the Specular panel are similar to those in the Diffuse panel, except that they control an object's *specular shading* (a loose approximation of specular reflection, as discussed earlier in "Reflection" on page 184). The *hardness* entry determines how broad or tight these reflections are (see Figure 12-6). Materials with a high hardness value have sharp, bright highlights, while those with a low hardness value have softer, more spread out highlights.

Shading The following options affect a material's overall shading:

Emit This causes an object to appear bright even when it is not lit and can even cause an object to cast light on other objects when it is used with certain World settings.

Ambient This determines whether an object receives ambient illumination (using the Ambient Color setting in the World Settings tab).

Translucency This causes an object to appear lit on both its front and back, making it look translucent, like thin paper or a leaf.

Shadeless This completely eliminates the effect of light on an object; the object will get its color and brightness entirely from its diffuse color and textures.

Tangent Shading This alters the shading of a surface to more closely resemble that of brushed metal or other materials with a "grain" or directionality to their microscopic structure. The direction of the grain is taken from the object's UV coordinates, so the grain will be aligned with the *v*-axis in UV space. In other words, it will be aligned vertically in the UV Image editor, so ensure you have unwrapped the object appropriately when enabling this option.

Cubic Interpolation   This alters how the surface blends between light and shadow, usually with smoother-looking results though often slightly darker.

Transparency   Turn on the Transparency checkbox to render a material with transparency. This panel offers three ways to render transparent objects, using the surface's alpha value. The simplest, *Mask*, simply blends the material into the background where the color is transparent. *Z Transparency* is slightly more sophisticated, rendering whatever is behind the transparent object. *Ray-traced Transparency* calculates proper refraction. Choosing Ray-traced Transparency brings up a variety of options that allow you to set the index of refraction of the material and the glossiness and amount of filtering done by the material.

Mirror   Enable Mirror to turn on rendering ray-traced reflections. The settings in this panel let you define the amount (*Reflectivity*) and sharpness (*Glossy Amount*) of ray-traced reflections.

Subsurface Scattering (SSS)   This option controls the effect of light scattering under the surface of a material commonly found in skin or wax. I'll discuss this in more detail in "Subsurface Scattering" on page 194.

Options   This panel contains some miscellaneous options. For example, the *Traceable* setting controls whether an object is taken into account when rendering ray-traced shadows and reflections. I'll cover these when they come up, and you can look up any I don't mention on the Blender wiki (at *http://wiki.blender.org/*).

Shadow   This panel controls how an object receives and casts shadows. For example, the *Cast Only* option makes an object appear invisible except for any shadows it casts. *Shadows Only* renders a material's shadows as the only nontransparent parts. (This is particularly good for creating shadows that you can then composite into another image.)

Figure 12-6: Different levels of hardness affect the look of specular reflections. This checkerboard texture is used to control the hardness. (You could also vary hardness using a texture map.)

Cycles Materials

Unlike the Blender Internal renderer, which is packed with dirty tricks and approximations to make rendering quicker, the Cycles renderer uses more physically realistic models for materials. It combines realism with a node-based approach that focuses on building up complex materials from simple parts. You can still use the Materials tab of the Properties editor to edit Cycles materials, which gives an overview of the current material, but it's much simpler and clearer to use Blender's Node editor, as shown in Figure 12-7.

To create a material with Cycles, all you need is a Shader node and Material Output node. You can build out from there and combine other shaders, inputs, and textures to create a wide variety of materials. To add a node, use SHIFT-A and choose the node you want from the menu that appears, just like adding objects in the 3D viewport.

The BSDF (Bidirectional Scattering Distribution Function) Shader nodes control how materials work. These functions define how light interacts with a surface—for example, whether the material reflects light in a diffuse way, acts as a mirror, or transmits light like glass. You'll find the BSDF shaders under Shaders in the Add menu in the header, along with a few other options.

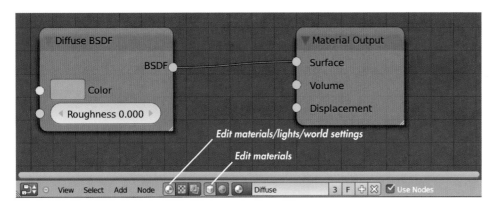

Figure 12-7: Editing a Cycles material in Blender's Node editor. On the right is the Material Output node; its Surface node is connected to the BSDF output socket of a Diffuse Shader node. The result is the diffuse material shown in Figure 12-1.

Cycles currently supports the following shaders:

Background This affects the world background rather than materials. (See Chapter 13 for more on world lighting settings.)

Diffuse BSDF This scatters light in all directions, creating a diffuse look.

Glossy BSDF This reflects light like a mirror. Increasing the *roughness* value makes reflections increasingly blurry.

Glass BSDF The Glass BSDF function transmits light as glass or any other transparent medium does. The *index of refraction (IOR)* determines how much the light is bent when it penetrates a surface. The higher the value, the more it is bent. Denser materials have higher IORs. For example, the IOR of glass is around 1.5, and the IOR of water is about 1.3. Diamond, a much denser material, has an IOR of around 2.4. The differences can be seen in Figure 12-8.

Translucent BSDF This scatters light in all directions from the back of the object, resulting in a translucent appearance, like that of a thin paper or leaf, with light transmitted through the material.

Transparent BSDF This allows light to penetrate a material without being refracted, as if there were nothing there. It's useful when combined with alpha maps. (See "Leaves" on page 207 for more on creating leaf materials.)

Velvet BSDF This reflects light somewhat like the diffuse shader, but it reflects light more when viewed from oblique angles. The result is a velvety appearance.

Emission This turns an object into a lamp that emits its own light.

Holdout This creates a "hole" in an image that goes through to the background color with zero alpha transparency. It's useful for compositing.

Mix Shader This allows you to mix two shaders with the proportion of mixing determined by the factor input. The Mix nodes allow you to combine shaders in numerous combinations to create all sorts of materials. For example, you could create a plastic-like material by combining a Glossy BSDF and Diffuse BSDF shader, as shown in Figure 12-9.

Add Shader This adds two shaders together. It's less flexible than the Mix node because you can't control the amount of mixing, but it works much the same way.

For more on these shaders and other Cycles documentation, visit *http://wiki.Blender.org/*.

Other Inputs in Cycles

Cycles allows you to use a wide variety of nodes that supply different data for use in your materials. You'll find nodes to input image textures and procedural textures as well as nodes to supply geometric information, such as surface normals and the position of the surface in 3D or UV space (allowing you to map textures to a surface). Combining these nodes can prove a powerful tool, as we'll see throughout the chapter.

Figure 12-8: Different indices of refraction. Left to right: 1.05, 1.5, and 2.5. As the IOR increases, the refracted light becomes more complex.

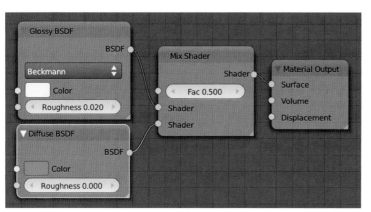

Figure 12-9: Combining shaders with the Mix node. Here I create a plastic-looking shader by combining an orange Diffuse BSDF shader with a white Glossy BSDF shader.

Texture Nodes

The Texture nodes are particularly useful for creating materials, and they can supply a variety of procedural and image-based textures for use on your materials. I'll use the image Texture nodes to apply the textures I created in Chapters 10 and 11.

The other nodes create procedural textures. For example, the noise texture creates multicolored clouds that are useful for adding random-looking detail to surfaces, and the waves texture creates repeating bands that can be distorted to look like wood grain. The checkerboard is a great texture for testing out material settings; for example, by

connecting a checkerboard node to the Fac input of a Mix Shader node, you can use it to compare two shaders (see Figure 12-10). We'll cover using textures with Cycles in more detail later in this chapter.

Nodes in Blender Internal

While I won't cover them in detail, Blender Internal also supports node materials. Although the principles are the same, these work slightly differently from Cycles nodes. Instead of shaders, you can use other materials as inputs and combine them to make new materials. Figure 12-11 shows two materials combined to create a third.

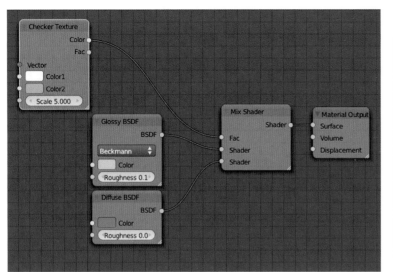

Figure 12-10: Controlling the mixing of shaders with a texture. Here, a checkerboard texture is used to control the mixing of a glossy and a diffuse shader.

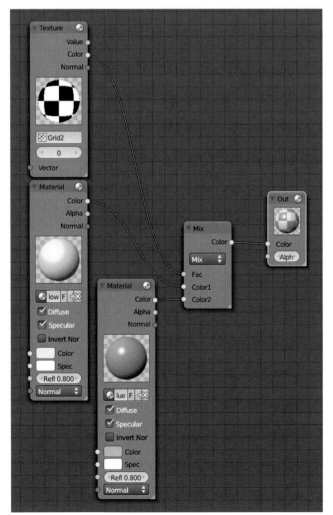

Figure 12-11: Blender Internal also supports node materials, though they work slightly differently. Here, two (non-node-based) materials have been blended (again using a checkerboard texture to control the mixing) to create a third.

Materials for the Bat Creature

Let's look at how to create materials, beginning with the Bat Creature and Blender Internal. For this project, I needed materials for the skin, fur, eyes, and teeth.

Skin

I began with the creature's skin. I added a new material to the Bat Creature object—that is, our final one with displacement, which I'll use for rendering. (Remember there are two copies of the Bat Creature in the scene: one copy that I'll use to render the body and another that I created in Chapter 9 to hold the hair.) To add a new material to the Bat Creature, I went to the Materials tab of the Properties editor and deleted any existing

material slots (by clicking the – button at the top of the tab). Then, I clicked +New from the material selector drop-down menu. I could then start creating the material. The beginnings of the material are shown in Figure 12-12.

So far, this was just a simple material; I merely tweaked the diffuse color and the specular intensity and hardness. I also switched the specular shading to Blinn, which gave softer highlights. Next, I needed to start incorporating my textures and refining the material.

To incorporate the diffuse texture, I switched to the Textures tab of the Properties editor, selected the first texture slot, and clicked +New to add a new texture. Then I set the Texture Type to Image. This added an Image panel to the Texture tab where I could open my diffuse texture.

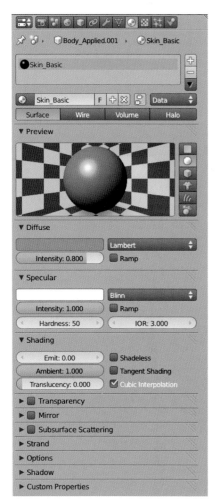

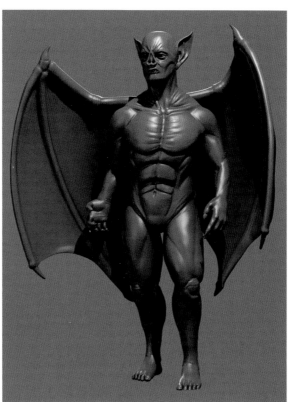

Figure 12-12: The Bat Creature material, shown without any textures or subsurface scattering. The rendered material is shown at the right. (See Chapters 13 and 14 for how to set up the lighting and render settings.)

Mapping Coordinates

To apply the texture to the mesh properly, I needed to tell the material to use the UV coordinates that I created in Chapter 8.

To do so, I could set the Coordinates option in the Mapping panel to UV. There are several other choices here, though, that are worth discussing. For example, the Generated option will create a procedural projection using the Projection setting below, which can be useful for applying seamless textures without having to unwrap an object. Generated coordinates project the surface of the object onto an imaginary shape—a plane, a cube, a sphere, or a cylinder—and use this projection to apply the texture. The result is shown in Figure 12-13.

We'll use some of the other options, such as *strand* coordinates, later in this chapter. We've already seen normal coordinates in action, when applying MatCap images for use with GLSL shading.

Influence

The Influence panel of the Materials tab is where we set which properties of the material our texture will affect. The panel lists all the material properties that textures can be used to control, such as normals; hardness; alpha transparency; and diffuse, specular, and mirror colors and intensities. For our diffuse texture, we'll stick with the default of Color, under the diffuse properties, which sets the diffuse color of the surface using the texture's RGB values (see Figure 12-14). I set the Blend mode for this texture to Mix, meaning it will replace the default diffuse color specified in the Material settings.

You can also use only the black-and-white value of a texture and ignore its color information by checking the RGB to Intensity option. This lets you choose a specific color to multiply this value within the color picker below it, for use with properties that still need colors. The Negative option inverts the texture before applying it to the model. The Stencil option can be particularly useful for combining procedural textures because it makes the texture act as a mask for the texture slots below: White areas of the texture will allow subsequent textures to be applied, while black areas will show only textures higher up in the texture slot stack.

Further Textures

Now, I'll continue to apply textures to my material. First, we'll look at the specular and hardness textures that I created in Chapter 11. To add the

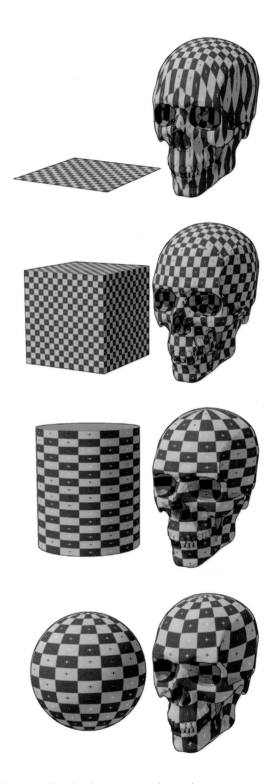

Figure 12-13: Blender's generated coordinates project an arbitrary shape onto your object to create a mapping for textures. Top to bottom: flat, cube, tube, and sphere projections. Here, cube and sphere do a good job because the shape of the skull is largely similar to these shapes.

Figure 12-14: Adding my diffuse texture to the skin material for the Bat Creature

specular texture to the material, I selected the next empty texture slot from the top of the Textures tab and clicked +New from the texture selector drop-down menu to create a new texture block. I set its type to Image. Then, I set the mapping to UV as before, but this time, under the Influence option, I set the texture to affect the specular color of the material. I set the Blend mode to Multiply so that the values from the texture were multiplied with the overall specular color of the material.

For the hardness texture, I set the texture to affect the material's hardness, and I enabled the RGB to Intensity option to make sure Blender would treat the texture as a simple brightness value rather than as three color values. (RGB textures can fail when used with inputs that don't require color information.) I set the Blend mode to Multiply.

Note that having a hardness value of 0 gives strange results, so either make sure the hardness texture contains no fully black areas, or set the influence of the texture to less than 1 to eliminate this issue.

This completed adding textures to my material. The current result is shown in Figure 12-15.

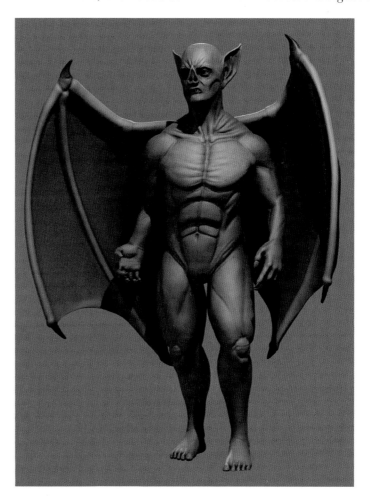

Figure 12-15: The material for the Bat Creature with textures added

Adding a Normal Map

Though I had finished adding textures to the material, you may remember that in Chapter 11, I also baked a normal map for the Bat Creature as a potential alternative to using displacement. At this stage, I could add the normal map in another image texture slot and set it to affect the Normals of the material in the Influence options. I also had to tell Blender that this is a tangent space normal map (not a bump map or an object space normal map), so in the Image Sampling panel of the Textures tab, I enabled the Normal Map option and made sure the Normal Map Space option just below was set to Tangent. The resulting material will use the textures to distort its normals when rendered, making it look more detailed even with subdivision and displacement mapping turned off.

As I *was* using displacement mapping, I didn't need to use my normal map at all, but it's a fair alternative if you want to keep render times low or if your computer is struggling with the poly count of the scene.

Subsurface Scattering

Subsurface scattering (SSS) is the effect of light bouncing around below the surface of a material, and it's common in materials like skin, wax, and marble. It results in the edges of shadows looking somewhat blurred, as light diffuses out from fully lit areas to areas in shadow. As the light scatters, some of it is absorbed, with the remaining light usually taking on the color of the underlying substance. In the case of skin, the flesh and blood below the skin cause the scattered light to appear an orange-red color.

To replicate this effect in Blender Internal, we can enable subsurface scattering for a material. This effect approximates the scattering of light within an object by precomputing the lighting over its surface and then blurring the shadows. It also causes light to scatter through thin parts of the model. This produces a nice effect when combined with lighting the subject from the back (as I will light the Bat Creature in Chapter 13).

Enabling subsurface scattering in the Materials tab of the Properties editor gives you a lot of options to play with. The settings for subsurface scattering are as follows:

IOR   This is the index of refraction of the material. High IORs result in slightly softer boundaries between light and dark.

Scale   This is the most important setting, because it determines the scale of the scattering effect as a ratio between Blender's units in the 3D Viewport and real-world scales. If you've built your scene to a scale of 1 Blender unit = 1m, then a value of 0.001 is "correct," though you can set this to whatever value achieves the desired results (see Figure 12-16).

Scattering Color   This determines the color of light scattering. Its effect depends largely upon how you set the color blend (as discussed below). When the color blend is set high, it colors all of the scattered light with the color you choose, generally turning your whole mesh that color. When the color blend is set to 0, it has the opposite effect, causing the scattered light to take on the *inverse* color—that is, the color on the opposite side of the circle in the color picker (see Figure 12-17).

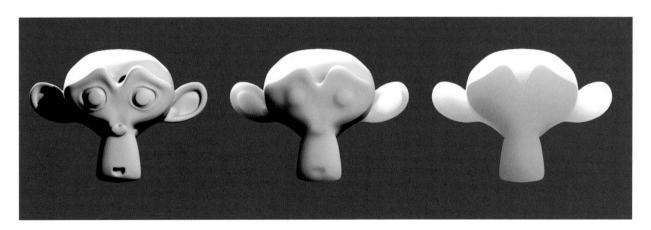

Figure 12-16: The effect of different scale values on subsurface scattering. Left to right: Scale values of 0.01, 0.1, and 0.5.

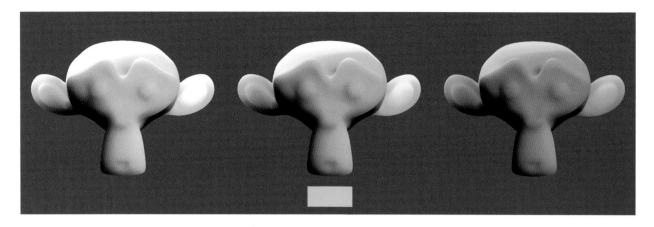

Figure 12-17: The effect of different color blend settings on subsurface scattering. Here, the same bluish color is used as the scattering color for all three materials, but different color blend values are used. Left to right: Color blend values of 0.0, 0.5, and 1.0.

RGB Radius　In many materials, some colors of light scatter farther than others. For example, in pale skin, red light scatters farthest, green scatters about half as far as red light, and blue scatters about a quarter as far as red light. These settings let you define the relative scattering distances for red, blue, and green light.

Blend (Color/Texture)　These settings determine how much the scattering color and diffuse texture spread out. I generally set both of these very low, if not to 0, because the results are more pleasing. High color blend values tend to cause the scattering color to wash out any other colors in the material (see Figure 12-17), and high texture blend values cause the texture to look blurry.

Scattering Weight (Front/Back)　This adjusts the relative amount of scattering from the front and back of the model. Increasing the back scattering weight causes light to scatter through thin parts of the model more noticeably, which is often desirable. Setting the front value to 0 causes the material to scatter no light from the front of the surface, making it black for all but back scattered light, as shown in Figure 12-18. (This is sometimes useful in node material setups.)

Error　This value determines the quality of the SSS effect. Lower values give more accurate results but at the cost of longer render times. The default value is usually fine.

For the Bat Creature, I set the SSS settings as shown in Figure 12-19. I set the scale relative to the size of the creature, which I created at a 1m = 1 Blender unit scale, and chose teal for the scattering color, which together with a color

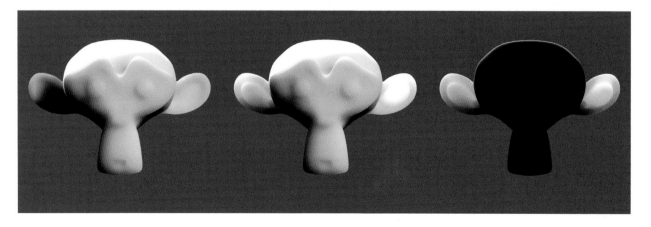

Figure 12-18: Front and back scattering. Left to right: Front scattering only, front and back scattering, and back scattering only.

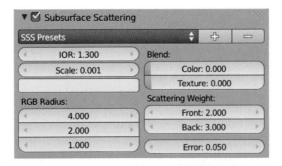

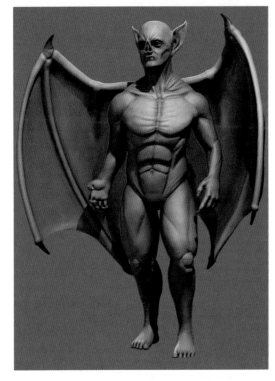

Figure 12-19: The SSS settings for the Bat Creature's skin. Combined with the lighting from behind, subsurface scattering causes the wings to glow with light scattering through them.

blend set to 0 gave a nice orange scattering. I set the back scattering weight high to allow light to scatter through the wings. This completed the skin material for the Bat Creature.

Teeth, Nails, and Eyes

To create the materials for the teeth and nails, I started by duplicating the material I created for the skin, toning down the SSS effect, and increasing the overall specularity to make these areas shinier.

To duplicate a material, assign it to an object. Then, in the material selector drop-down menu,

click the + icon to make a new material by duplicating the one currently assigned. You can then modify the duplicate leaving the original unchanged. This is useful when creating a material similar to one you have already made.

For the eyes, I created two new materials. Recall that when I modeled the eyes in Chapter 5, I created them as two separate parts: a cornea object that forms the outer surface of the eye and an inner part that would become the eyeball itself. Having unwrapped and textured the inner part, I set up a material similar to the skin material, with slightly less red subsurface scattering. I also turned specular reflections for this material off (by setting the specular intensity to 0), as the specular reflections for the eye will come from the cornea object. I applied the eye texture I painted in Chapter 11 as the diffuse texture for the material.

For the cornea, I needed a shiny, transparent material that wouldn't cast a shadow on the inner eye object. To produce this, I created a new material assigned to this object. Then, I turned on transparency in the Material settings and set it to Z Transparency, with the alpha for the material set to 0. These settings make a material transparent, with the exception of any specular and mirror reflections, if they are present. I turned the specular and hardness of the material up quite high, and to prevent the material from casting shadows, I disabled Traceable in the Options panel and Cast Buffer shadows in the Shadows panel. The two materials for the eyes can be seen in Figure 12-20.

Fur

Materials for fur are a little more complex than regular materials and require a bit of knowledge about lighting and rendering. I'll cover the material aspects here and some of the lighting aspects in Chapter 13.

In Blender Internal, strand particles can be rendered either like any other material or using Blender's Strand rendering option. Blender's Strand rendering option offers a much faster way to render hair and fur, but it isn't compatible with ray-traced shadows. Instead, it allows only for the rendering of shadows using spot lamps with buffered shadows.

To enable strand rendering, use the Render panel in the Particles tab of the Properties editor (see Figure 12-21). For the Bat Creature, I opted to use strand rendering. In Chapter 13, we'll discuss creating an appropriate lighting setup for use with this setup.

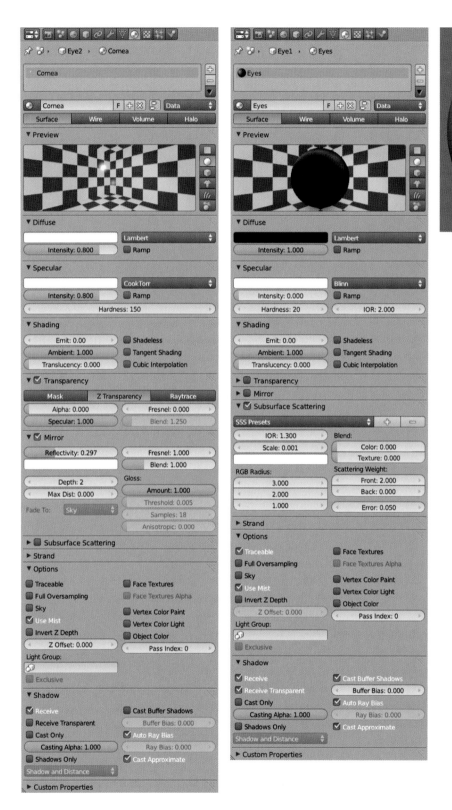

Figure 12-20: The two materials for the eyes. The specular highlights come from the material applied to the cornea mesh. The rest are from the inner eye mesh.

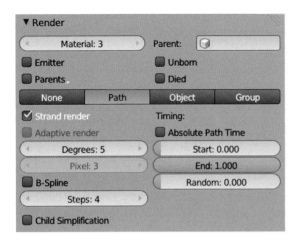

Figure 12-21: Enabling strand rendering from the Particles tab of the Properties editor

Next, I specified the Strand options for the material. In the Strand panel of the Materials tab, you can specify how thick the strands will be and their shape, among other options:

Size (Root/Tip/Minimum)   This determines the thickness of the particles at the root and tip of the hair. The Minimum setting specifies the minimum width of a strand in pixels that Blender will render.

Blender Units   By default, the thicknesses you specify using the Size setting are specified in pixels. This can be problematic if you have a lot of particles at different distances away from the camera, as they will be rendered with the same width in pixels, making the faraway ones look too thick. Turning on Blender Units lets you specify particle width in Blender units instead.

Tangent Shading   This option uses the strand's tangent direction rather than its normal for shading, which generally gives better results.

Shape   This modifies the transition between the width of the root and the tip of the strand. The default value of 0 gives a linear transition. Negative values result in a spiky shape, while positive values make the strand look more rounded at the end.

Width Fade   This setting causes the strand to fade across its width, but only when strand rendering is enabled.

UV Map   This allows you to overwrite one of your UV coordinate sets to provide a UV map for the strands. In turn, this lets you UV map an image to all your strands for texturing, but it works only with strand rendering disabled.

Surface Diffuse   This setting causes the diffuse shading of the surface to blend with the strand shading over the specified distance.

Strand Coordinates

As mentioned above, we can texture strand materials by using the UV map override. A simpler option, however, is to use the strand coordinates for mapping when applying textures. While this only gives a one-dimensional coordinate along the length of the strand, this is usually enough for thin strands anyway.

For the Bat Creature's fur, I first set up a simple material using the settings shown in Figure 12-22. Notice that I enabled Z Transparency and set the Alpha to about 0.7. For the Strand settings, I enabled Blender Units and then set the Root and Tip sizes to 0.00125 and 0.0001, respectively. (These values are small because the hairs need to be very thin, and their widths are now given in Blender units.) I also turned on Tangent Shading and set Width Fade to 1.0.

Next, in the Texture settings, I used Blender's procedural blend texture to add a fade to the hair's alpha along its length, making it become transparent toward the tip. I added a new texture to the material's first texture slot and set its type to Blend. Then, I began adjusting the colors of the blend texture by first enabling the Ramp option in the Colors tab and then adjusting the colors that the procedural texture used. I clicked Add to create a couple more stops along the gradient and then set the colors to fade from transparent black to opaque white and back (see Figure 12-23). Finally, under Mapping, I set the texture's coordinates to alpha, and under Influence, I set the texture to multiply with the material's alpha and its specular intensity.

I did something similar for the hair color. I created a new blend texture in the next Texture slot, but this time I set up a blend from black to white (both alpha 1.0). Again, I mapped the texture to the strand coordinates and set it to multiply by a factor of 0.8 with the strand's diffuse color, which made the base of the strands a little darker, thus faking a bit of shadowing.

Next, I added a cloud texture, which I set to modify the material's color—this time influencing the diffuse color with a factor of 0.8, with the Blend

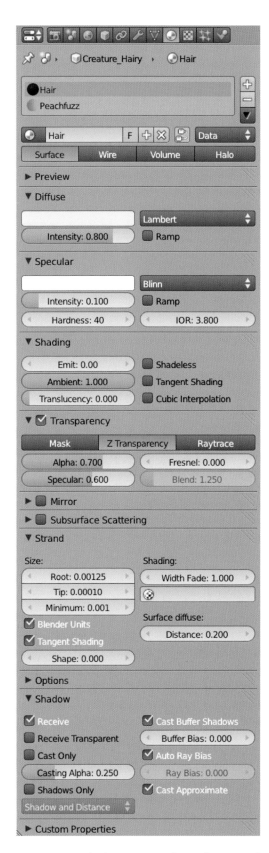

Figure 12-22: The basic settings for my fur material

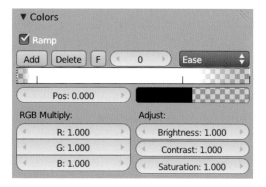

Figure 12-23: Modifying the colors of a procedural blend texture

mode set to Multiply and its mapping set to UV. I turned the scale of the cloud texture down to the absolute minimum, essentially turning the texture into black-and-white noise and giving each hair a slightly different brightness. This completed the hair material, with the resulting hair seen in Figure 12-24.

Figure 12-24: The hair material

Peach Fuzz

I set up a very similar material for the peach fuzz particle system. For this material, I decreased the size settings for the strands to make them thinner and reduced the overall alpha of the material to make the hair look wispier. The resulting material can be seen in Figure 12-25. It mainly shows up around the edges of the body, which is just what I wanted.

This completed my materials for the Bat Creature.

Figure 12-25: My peach fuzz hair provides a more subtle effect; it adds a bit of a halo of fluff around brightly lit parts of the model.

Materials for the Spider Bot

For the Spider Bot, I chose to use Blender's Cycles renderer because it allowed me to create some nice shiny materials to complement the model. I began by creating a single material to apply to all the (textured) parts of the Spider Bot mesh. You can use the Material Utils Script to do this quickly: Simply enable it in Blender's Add-Ons menu (**User Preferences ▶ Add Ons**) and use the shortcut **Q** to assign materials to all your selected objects at once. By default, when you create a new Cycles material for an object, Blender will assign a diffuse BSDF shader, like the one shown in Figure 12-26. The default material will be a plain matte white.

Editing Node Materials

To edit Cycles materials, use Blender's Node editor, keeping it visible alongside the 3D Viewpoint with a render preview of the scene (a major advantage over Blender Internal that I'll discuss shortly). To allow

space for the Node editor as well as the preview, I split the default layout once by right-clicking on the bottom edge of the 3D Viewport and choosing Split Area. Then, I split the left-hand area in two, horizontally.

Once I split up the work area, I made one of the new areas into a Node editor and the other into a 3D Viewport, with its Display Method set to Rendered. In the Node editor header, I selected the materials icon in the left-hand group of icons and the cube icon in the right-hand group (see Figure 12-27) so that the Node editor would display the node tree for the current material. This gave me a workable layout for editing Cycles materials.

The Cycles Render Preview

When the Display method for a 3D Viewport is set to Rendered, Blender will continuously render and update a Cycles render of the current view in that viewport (as in Figure 12-26). This technique is a great way to get instant feedback on how the materials and lighting in your scene will look.

 *While we haven't covered lighting yet, it's helpful at this stage to add some basic lights to the scene so that the rendered preview will reflect the final look. Jump to Chapter 13 for more on lighting, or simply add a couple of lights to the scene by pressing SHIFT-A in the 3D Viewport, choosing **Lamps ▶ Point**, and adding a point light. Adjust the brightness of the light using the Strength setting in the Object Data tab of the Properties editor. Add a couple of basic lights to the scene just to help work on materials, or create a more finished lighting setup.*

Adding Textures

Next, I started combining further shaders into my material. I began by adding a Glossy BSDF shader (SHIFT-A ▶ Shaders ▶ Glossy BSDF) and using an Add Shader Node to blend the glossy and diffuse shaders by connecting both of the shader output sockets from the Shader nodes to the Add node and by connecting the Add node output socket to the Material Output node (see Figure 12-27).

Next, I started incorporating my textures, beginning with my diffuse map. I added an Image Texture node (SHIFT-A ▶ Textures ▶ Image Texture) and opened my diffuse map by clicking the folder icon in the node. I connected the color output of this node to the color input of my Diffuse Shader node.

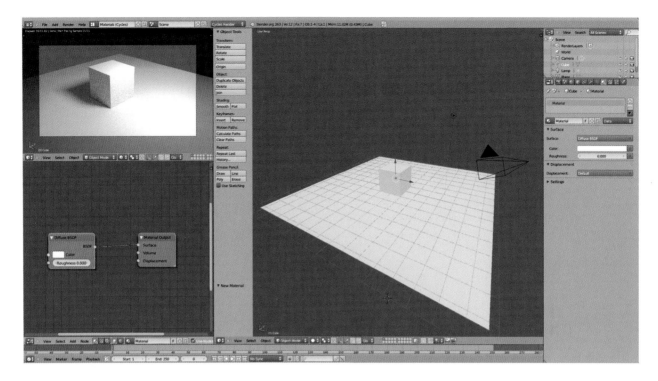

Figure 12-26: My screen layout for editing Cycles materials

I did the same for my specular color map, connecting it to the color input of the Specular Color node. By default, the mapping for these textures is the active UV coordinate set, so you don't strictly need to define this manually. But because it can help to know what coordinates a texture uses, I added a Texture Coordinates node to the scene and connected its UV output to the vector (blue) input of my Image Texture nodes. Doing so tells

these nodes to use the active UV map as the source of their texture coordinates. The node setup so far is shown in Figure 12-27.

Socket Types

Now that I have a reasonably complex node setup for the material, let's talk about node sockets. Node sockets are the little colored circles that denote the

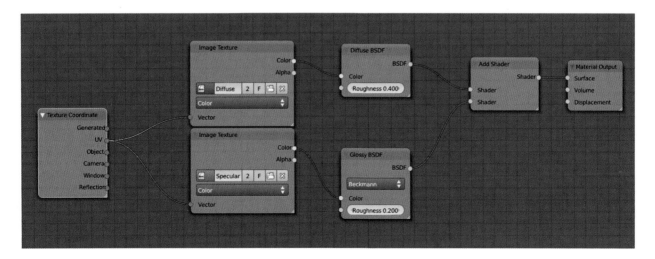

Figure 12-27: The evolving node setup for the Spider Bot material

inputs and outputs of a node and that allow nodes to be connected by clicking and dragging a connection from the output socket of one node to the input socket of another. Notice in Figure 12-27 that the sockets we used to connect nodes all have matching colors—green with green, yellow with yellow. The colors need to match because different output sockets pass different types of data and different input sockets expect different kinds of data. Some may require color information, some only a single value. Others may require vector information, like texture coordinates or normals.

Node sockets are color coded to clarify what a node expects as input and what it creates as output:

- Blue sockets are for vector data. They can carry multiple values, such as UV coordinates (two dimensional) or position data (three dimensional).

- Green sockets are for shaders. They carry all the information that determines how a material interacts with light.

- Gray sockets are for value data. They carry a single numerical value.

- Yellow sockets are for color data. They carry RGBA values (red, green, blue, and alpha).

Certain types of sockets can be mixed and matched. For example, value sockets can be used as the input for color sockets, and Blender will simply treat the value data as a black-and-white image. Color sockets can also be attached to value inputs, and Blender will use the overall brightness of the color as a value input. However, shader sockets are more complex and can only be connected to other shader sockets.

Roughness Map

In Chapter 11, I created a roughness map for the Spider Bot. In Cycles, I can connect this map to the roughness input for the Glossy BSDF node to control how blurry or sharp the reflections from the material should be. Dark areas will have sharp reflections, while light areas will have blurry ones (remember, this is the opposite of a hardness map).

To accomplish this, I added a new Image Texture node, loaded in the roughness map, and connected its output to the Glossy nodes roughness input. As a result, bright areas of the texture had blurrier highlights, and dark areas had sharp, glossy highlights.

I also set the color space of the Image Texture to Non-Color Data from the drop-down menu in the Image node to indicate that this node was not being used as a color image, ensuring that Blender wouldn't perform any gamma correction on this node.

Adjusting Inputs

To get the most out of my textures without having to edit them in GIMP, I tweaked them using Blender's nodes. For instance, to darken the diffuse colors a little and make the reflections from the glossy shader a little sharper, I added a Color Mix node, setting its type to Multiply, its factor to 0.5, and its second color input to black.

When this Color Mix node is dragged over the connection between an Image Texture node and a Shader node, Blender adds it to the chain automatically. (The connection will be highlighted, and the new node will be inserted when you drop it.) I did this for the connection between the diffuse map and the Diffuse BSDF shader to darken the texture slightly.

For the Glossy BSDF shader, in order to sharpen up the reflections, I needed to reduce the values of the input to the roughness shader. I accomplished this by adding a Math node between my roughness image Texture node and the roughness input of the glossy shader. I set the operation of the node to Multiply and set the second value of the node to 0.5. This halved the values from the roughness image before passing them to the Glossy Shader node so that the overall roughness of the input to the shader was halved, giving sharper, more glossy reflections.

For the shiny green areas of the mesh, I added some variance in color based on the angle of the surface to the camera. This gave the material a nice iridescent look. I accomplished this by adding a Geometry Input node (SHIFT-A ▶ Input ▶ Geometry) to provide the surface normal as an input and a Normal node to take the dot product of this input with the view direction. I then used this dot product output to modify the hue of my specular color map with a Hue Saturation Value node. By using the dot product output of the Normal node, I got a value (rather than a vector) that varied with the surface normal of the material. When this value was used to affect the hue input of the Hue Saturation Value node, the color of the material was subtly shifted as the surface of the material tilted away from the camera. You can see the node chain I used in Figure 12-28. It's a somewhat complex setup, but seeing it laid out and testing it for yourself should help you make sense of it.

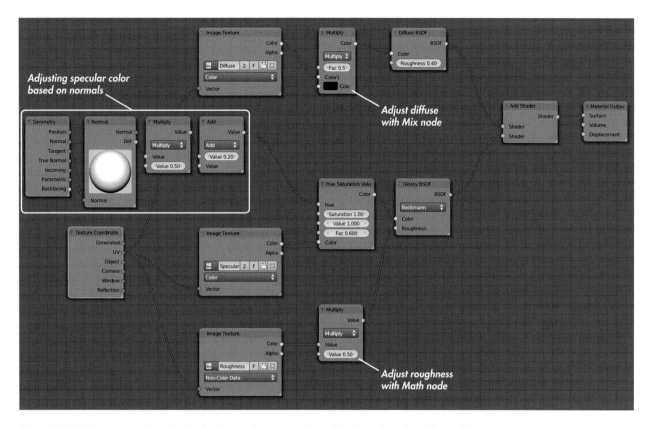

Figure 12-28: The material for the Spider Bot, with some nodes added to adjust the effects of the textures

Other Materials

I still needed to make a couple of materials for the Spider Bot: a shiny material for the eyes (I used a simple glossy shader set to dark gray, with a slight roughness of 0.05) and a material for the wires (I combined a glossy shader and a diffuse shader with a Shader Mix node). You can see these materials in Figure 12-29 and the finished Spider Bot material in Figure 12-30.

Materials for the Jungle Temple

I used the Cycles renderer for the Jungle Temple scene as well. This scene needed a variety of materials: leaf materials for the foliage, generic materials for the rocks and soil, and a couple of unique materials for the objects I textured individually, such as the foreground stones and the statues.

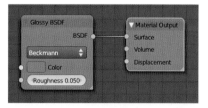

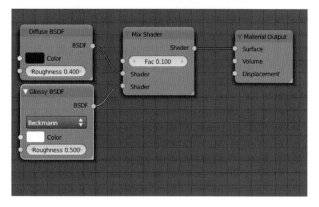

Figure 12-29: The extra Spider Bot materials. Top: The eyes, a simple glossy material. Bottom: The wires, a Diffuse BSDF shader with a rough Glossy BSDF shader mixed in.

Figure 12-30: The look of the finished Spider Bot material. See Chapters 13 and 14 for information on lighting and rendering.

Ground

The ground material was probably the simplest to create. It's simply a mix of a Diffuse and a Glossy BSDF shader, using my painted textures as inputs for the colors. Because I felt my original textures made the material look a little light, I used a Gamma node to darken them slightly without losing too much contrast (see Figure 12-31).

Stone Material

For my stone material, I wanted to combine the two different stone textures I made in Chapter 11, allowing each to show through in different areas, to give a bit of variation in the look of the material. To do so, I started by creating a basic shader that mixed a diffuse and glossy shader together using a Shader Mix node. I controlled the amount of mixing with a Layer Weight node, using its blend output. The Layer Weight node blends from 0 to 1 depending on the normals of a mesh: Surfaces facing the camera get low values, and ones facing away get high values (the exact values depend on the output used—facing or fresnel). Using the Facing output of this node to control the blending between the glossy and diffuse shaders produced some shiny highlights around the edges of objects with a more diffuse look when viewed straight on, as shown in section ❶ of Figure 12-32.

To create a patchy distribution for the different stone textures, I combined a couple of Voronoi Texture nodes with different scales and then used these to control the mixing between the different textures for the rocks for both the specular and diffuse maps, as shown in Figure 12-32 ❷. I also used some Map nodes to scale up the texture mappings for my rock textures to make them match one another and fit the scale of the scene, which you can see in Figure 12-32 ❸.

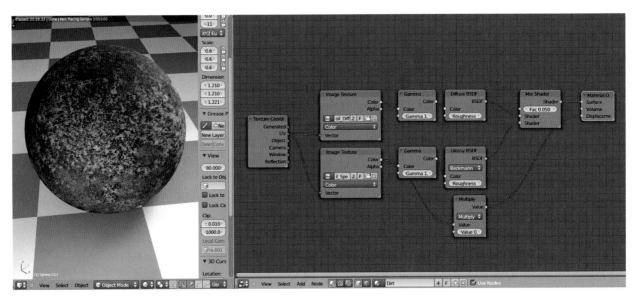

Figure 12-31: The soil for the Jungle Temple scene

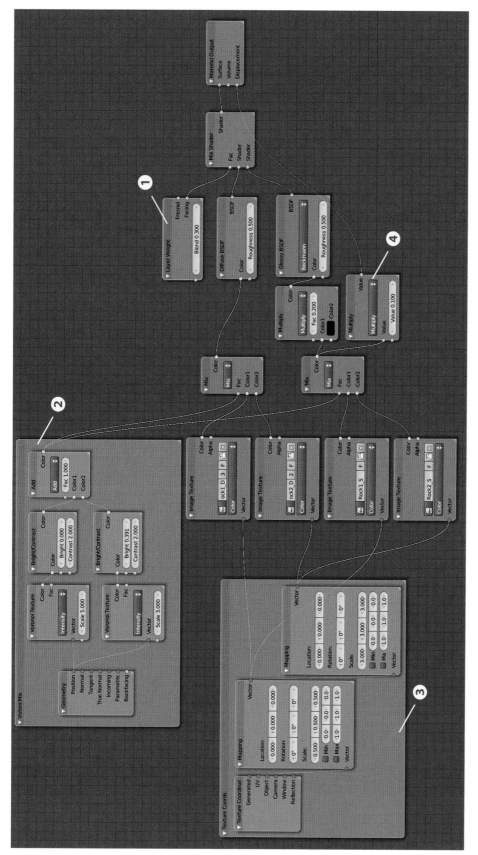

Figure 12-32: My rock material setup is somewhat complex. A Layer Weight node ❶ is used to blend between the specular and diffuse shaders. Two Voronoi textures added together ❷ control the mixing of my rock textures (two for diffuse colors, two for specular). The textures themselves are scaled using some Map nodes ❸, and the specular colors are also used for displacement ❹.

Displacement

Cycles currently supports the use of a black-and-white input (or converting an RGB input to just a single value) to mimic the effect of small bumps in the surface of a material. This is often referred to as *bump mapping* in other render engines. Cycles does not yet support normal maps.

To add a bit more of a textured look to the surface of my rocks, I used the specular colors (the two mixed together) as the displacement input for the Material Output node, though I used a Multiply node to scale down their values to reduce the effect, as shown in Figure 12-32 ❹. The finished rock material is shown in Figure 12-33.

Statue

The statue material is basically just a copy of the generic stone material, except that it uses the textures I painted for the statue. To create it, I applied the stone material to the statue and then clicked the + icon in the material selector drop-down menu to make a new material using the current one. Next, I deleted (**X**) the extraneous nodes from the material in the Node editor and replaced them with my textures (see Figure 12-34).

Figure 12-33: The rock material

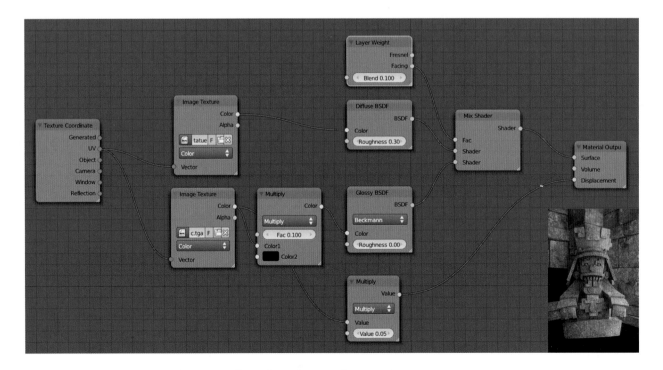

Figure 12-34: The statue material is very similar to the rock material, except that it uses its own textures.

Leaves

For the leaves, I wanted a translucent material so that leaves illuminated on one side would appear bright when viewed from the unlit side as well. To achieve this, I mixed a Translucent BSDF shader with a Diffuse BSDF shader and mixed in specular highlights on top to make the leaves shiny. The leaf meshes had to be transparent in order to make the areas of the mesh that weren't part of the leaves invisible. I accomplished this by mixing the result of all the nodes so far with a Transparent BSDF shader, using the alpha map from Chapter 11 to control the mixing (see Figure 12-35).

Foreground Rocks and Soil

In Chapter 11, I created a hand-painted texture for the foreground objects from the camera's perspective. To use this, I needed to create a unique material for these objects. I began by duplicating the material I created for the statue and then replacing its texture inputs with the ones I created for the foreground objects.

To map the textures to the models correctly, I snapped the 3D Viewport to the camera view (NUMPAD 0) and UV unwrapped the foreground objects using the Unwrap ▶ Project from View operator for each object to which the material was applied. This projected the objects' UV coordinates to match the camera's perspective and so allowed me to use the UV coordinates as the texture coordinates. The material nodes for this material can be seen in Figure 12-36.

Puddles

For the puddles, I needed a water material that would let some light penetrate the surface and show some reflections. The glass material alone would do the job (using an IOR value of 1.33, equal to that of water), but to get a bit more control over how much light would penetrate the surface and the strength of the reflections, I blended Transparent, Glass, and Glossy BSDF shaders. I mixed in the glossy shader using a Layer Weight node connected to the Mix node to get a bit of extra reflection at low viewing angles.

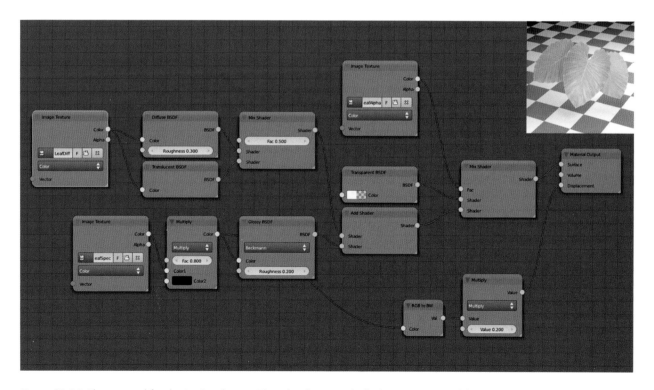

Figure 12-35: The material for the IvyGen leaves. The other leaves, which share textures and the same material, were created in the same way.

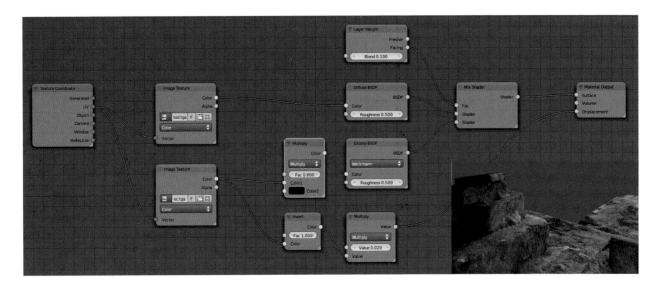

Figure 12-36: The material for the foreground rocks and soil

To produce ripples in the surface of the water, I created a Waves Texture node (SHIFT-A ▶ Texture ▶ Wave Texture) and connected it to the displacement socket on the Material Output node to create some distortion in the water's surface. By default, the Waves node gives straight, repeating waves, but by setting the wave type to Rings and increasing the distortion value, you can get some nice ripples (see Figure 12-37).

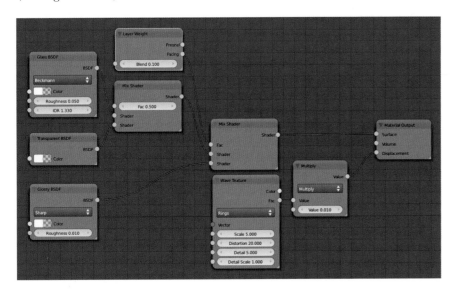

Figure 12-37: The water material, created by mixing Transparent, Glass, and Glossy BSDF shaders and using a wave texture to provide some displacement

General Tips for Creating Materials

Here are some general principles to keep in mind when creating materials in your projects. Chiefly, they involve paying attention to the real-world equivalents of the materials you are trying to replicate and constructing your material accordingly:

Keep reflection amounts sane. Make sure that the total amount of light your object is reflecting is sensible. When using the Add node to combine shaders in Cycles, it's possible to create a material that reflects more light than it would realistically receive in the first place by adding too many shaders together. Similarly, in Blender Internal, keep in mind that the diffuse and specular reflection amounts (plus the light absorbed by the object) should roughly add up to 1—for example, a diffuse intensity of 0.6 and a specular intensity of 0.3, leaving some absorbed light to spare. Otherwise, your material will look unrealistically bright next to other materials.

There are no perfect materials. No material reflects 100 percent of all light, and no material absorbs 100 percent either. Try not to make any materials that are completely dark or completely white (unless you are doing so for a good reason).

Use saturation in moderation. The color of a material is rarely 100 percent saturated, even for brightly colored materials like plastics. Most everyday colors are less than 85 percent saturated, so keep the colors of your materials in a sensible range to make them believable.

Keep it simple. Try to avoid making complex materials to ensure shorter render times. For example, in Blender Internal, try to use ray-traced reflections only when really needed.

Supplement materials with procedural textures. Blender's built-in procedural textures are a great way to supplement materials by using them as bump maps or to blend other textures. Doing so can add a lot of variation to your materials while preventing you from having to laboriously hand-paint textures.

In Review

In this chapter, we started with a look at Blender's options for creating materials, both for the Blender Internal renderer and Cycles. Because these two render engines require different approaches when creating materials, we explored their different options and requirements. Then we moved on to creating materials for the three projects. For the Bat Creature, I created Blender Internal–compatible materials for the body, fur, eyes, nails, and teeth. For the body, I created a material with subsurface scattering to mimic realistic skin, and for the fur, I covered the different options for fur materials and rendering. I used Blender's strand shader to render the fur and examined ways to apply textures to fur.

For the Spider Bot and the Jungle Temple scene, I created materials for rendering with Cycles, using Blender's Node editor to create a range of different materials by combining Shader nodes and using textures to supply their inputs.

The projects are now ready to be lit and rendered. In Chapter 13, you'll learn about different lighting setups and how to use lighting in both Blender Internal and Cycles.

13

LIGHTING

Lighting is perhaps the aspect of an image that most impacts how we perceive it. Lighting can change the tone of an image and make characters and scenery look either dark and sinister or warm and inviting. In this chapter, I'll work on lighting the projects I've built so far using a variety of techniques, including both Blender Internal's array of lighting options and Cycles' more physically accurate methods for creating different kinds of lights.

Blender Internal vs. Cycles Lighting

Both Blender Internal and Cycles have a wide variety of powerful tools for lighting. Blender Internal supports a range of lights that behave in different ways, as well as two methods for rendering shadows—using either shadow buffers or ray tracing—both of which will be discussed shortly.

Cycles uses only ray tracing for lighting, and its results are more realistic than those of Blender Internal. It also supports the emission of light from meshes, allowing you to create lights of any shape. But while Cycles is the more realistic lighting

renderer, neither Cycles nor Blender Internal is the right choice for everything, and both have advantages. For example, Blender Internal's lights are quick to render and offer a wide variety of uses and styles, while Cycles offers a reliable and realistic way of working with lights that doesn't require much tweaking to produce good results. We'll use both renderers in this chapter as we light the Bat Creature for rendering in Blender Internal and the Spider Bot and Jungle Temple for rendering in Cycles.

Lighting in Blender Internal

Blender Internal uses Blender's lamp objects to light a scene. To create a lamp, press SHIFT-A in Object mode and choose one of the following under Lamp:

Area   This creates a square- or rectangular-shaped lamp that emits light from all over its area. Area lamps support ray-traced shadows and are well suited for creating soft shadows and studio-style lighting, but they can slow render time significantly because they require more samples than other lamp types to produce noise-free results.

Hemi   This lamp lights the entire scene in a diffuse way, similar to outdoor light from the sky. Because it doesn't support shadows, it's very quick to render but of limited use.

Point   This creates a point light, which emits light in all directions from the lamp's center. It supports ray-traced shadows and is a good general purpose lamp.

Spot   Spot lamps are like a spotlight at a theater or a flashlight. They emit light in a cone from their origin, making them a good tool for lighting specific areas. They support both ray-traced shadows and shadow buffers. Shadow buffers produce shadows without ray tracing and are generally significantly faster to render. This makes them very versatile and useful for scenes that need a high degree of control over lighting.

Sun   This lamp lights an entire scene from one direction, just as the sun might. It supports ray-traced shadows.

The settings for each lamp can be altered from the Object Data tab of the Properties editor, which has a lamp icon when a lamp is selected as the active object. You can adjust a lamp's brightness and *falloff*—the distance over which the strength of its light fades—as well as the settings for shadows, colors, and so forth. While different lamps—particularly spot lamps—have certain unique features, they generally share the same settings. The settings for a point lamp are shown in Figure 13-1 and discussed below.

Light Color   This color picker lets you choose the color of your light.

Energy   This determines the overall intensity of your light.

Falloff   Available only for point and spot lamps, this controls the distance and curve over which the strength of the light fades. The drop-down menu lets you specify the falloff curve for the fade (choose Inverse Square for realistic falloff and experiment with the others). *Distance* lets you specify the overall distance for the fade— the higher the setting, the farther the light will spread. The *Sphere* setting causes the intensity

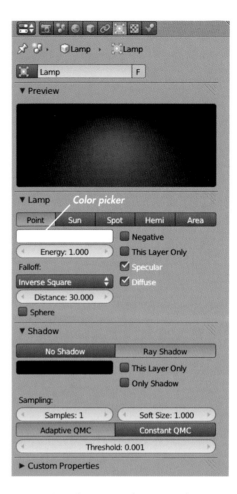

Figure 13-1: The settings for a point lamp

of the light to fade to zero over the determined distance rather than tapering off indefinitely.

Negative   This turns the light into an *"anti" lamp* that removes light from the scene instead of adding it. This setting can be useful for creating dark corners or hiding areas of a scene in shadow.

This Layer Only   This causes lights to illuminate only objects on their same layer. This setting can be useful for lighting individual objects.

Specular/Diffuse   These settings let you control whether a light will contribute to specular and diffuse reflections. It can be handy to turn off a lamp's specular reflections in order to add soft illumination to an area without creating highlights. By turning off diffuse reflections, you can position a light to place highlights precisely without changing the overall diffuse lighting.

Shadows in Blender Internal

Blender offers two ways to render shadows: ray tracing and shadow buffers.

Ray Tracing

The first method uses ray tracing to determine the parts of a mesh in shadow. Ray tracing "fires" rays out from the camera for each pixel in an image and draws them to the surface the pixel is facing. Further rays are drawn to the lights in the scene to determine whether that point is in light or shadow: If a ray can be drawn to the light without intersecting another object, the point is lit; otherwise, it is in shadow.

When there are multiple lights or soft shadows, multiple rays must be cast per pixel, increasing render times. The same goes for ray-traced reflections and transparency, where rays may be reflected or refracted multiple times. Ray tracing can produce crisp, pixel-perfect shadows as well as soft shadows, and it's more accurate but generally slower than shadow buffers.

Shadow Buffers

The other method uses shadow buffers and is only available for spot lamps. Shadow buffers take advantage of the spot lamp's restricted cone of illumination to create a map of which areas are in shadow over the range of angles that the lamp covers. Essentially, Blender creates a basic render of the scene from the lamp's point of view: Areas that can be seen from the lamp's viewpoint are lit, while areas that cannot are in shadow.

Shadow-buffer shadows are generally faster to render than ray-traced ones and are also compatible with the strand renderer for hair. In fact, the deep shadow-buffer option for spot lamps is ideally suited to rendering shadows cast by hair. But getting accurate buffered shadows, which you do by increasing the resolution of the shadow-buffer map, can use a lot of memory, and the borders of low-resolution buffered shadows can look jagged (see Figure 13-2), so be sure to set them up correctly.

Common Shadow Options

In the Shadow panel of the lamp settings, the following options are common to both ray-traced and buffer shadows.

Shadow Color This option lets you set a color for the shadow. Of course, in reality, shadows have no color, so this is actually a trick designed to help change the aesthetic of your lighting. Leave it set to *Black* for normal (uncolored) shadows.

This Layer Only This causes only objects on the same layer as the lamp to cast shadows, though objects on any layer may be lit by the lamp as long as the corresponding option isn't turned on in the Lamp panel.

Only Shadow This causes the lamp to cast only shadows, meaning that you will need other lights in your scene to light your objects. This option can be used to create a shadow in a specific place without affecting the overall look of your lighting.

Ray-Traced Shadow Options

Enabling Ray Shadow for a lamp gives the following options:

Samples This determines the number of samples taken per pixel for soft shadows in order to determine the amount of shadowing. Higher sample numbers give less noisy results. Setting Samples to 1 gives hard-edged shadows regardless of the Soft Size setting.

Soft Size This setting is designed to produce soft shadows by spreading out the area the light comes from. The larger the soft size, the softer and less defined shadows become. Larger sizes require higher numbers of samples to produce noise-free results.

Adaptive/Constant QMC This sets the sampling method used to determine whether a point on a surface is in shadow. For *Constant QMC*, the number of samples taken is always that specified by the Samples setting. For *Adaptive QMC*, fewer samples may be taken for areas that are obviously either in or out of shadow. The *threshold* value dictates the level of certainty required to determine how many samples are needed: Higher threshold values are more tolerant and faster, but they can produce noisier results.

Shadow-Buffer Options

Opting for shadow-buffer shadows for spot lamps gives the following options:

Buffer Type (Classical/Classic-Halfway/Irregular/Deep) The specifics of these types are quite technical (you can find the details with a bit of googling), but the differences are really pretty straightforward.

Classical These buffers are the simplest and can suffer from biasing artifacts (see Figure 13-2).

Classical-Halfway These buffers improve on Classical and suffer less from biasing artifacts.

Irregular These shadow buffers always produce crisp, clean shadows with no aliasing, but they can't be used to produce soft shadows, and the shadows they create don't show up in ray-traced reflections.

Deep These shadow buffers are the most advanced and can store transparency information, allowing for partial shadowing from transparent objects. They are ideal for rendering shadows from materials like hair and fur, as well as volumetric materials.

Filter Type The filter type used to blend shadow borders. *Gauss* gives the smoothest results.

Soft This sets the softness of your shadows in terms of the size of the lamp used to cast shadows. Larger values give softer shadows but require more samples.

Bias This adjusts how the shadow buffer is calculated. It's used to prevent artifacts that are caused by faces at a low angle to the lamp casting shadows on themselves (see Figure 13-2). Higher values reduce bias artifacts but can cause some parts of a mesh not to cast shadows where they should, so set this as low as you can without introducing artifacts.

Sample Buffers This determines the number of shadow buffers that are rendered. Higher values give better anti-aliasing of hard-edged shadows, but more buffers use more memory, so tread carefully.

Size This sets the resolution of the shadow-buffer map (see Figure 13-3). The higher the value, the greater the detail that can be captured in the map and the more memory required for rendering. If you want soft shadows, you won't be able to see that much detail in them anyway, so use high resolutions only for harder shadows.

Clip Start/End These settings define the range of distances over which objects will cast shadows in the shadow buffer. Objects outside this range

Figure 13-2: Shadow-buffer biasing artifacts are shown here with a low shadow-buffer size to exaggerate the effect. Increasing the Bias value avoids these artifacts, but high settings can cause you to lose shadows that should be there.

will still be lit by the spot lamp but will not cast shadows. The extent of this range is displayed in the 3D Viewport as a solid line extending outward from the lamp's center between the clip-start and clip-end distances (see Figure 13-4).

Autoclip Start/End Turning on these options leaves it to Blender to set the clip-start and clip-end distances automatically based on the vertices visible from the point of view of the lamp.

Lighting in Cycles

In Cycles, lighting is broadly similar to that of Blender Internal but with fewer options. Setting up lighting in Cycles is easier because you get instant feedback from the render preview. Lights in Cycles are node based and consist of shaders, just as with materials. In fact, Cycles allows you to incorporate the emission of light into materials *and* lamp objects. We'll discuss both here.

Figure 13-3: The shadow-buffer Size setting affects the definition of shadows and reduces aliasing of shadow borders. Here, some very overstretched shadow buffers are shown in increasing resolutions.

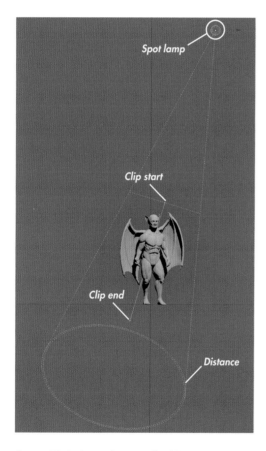

Figure 13-4: A spot lamp in the 3D Viewport showing the clipping range

Lamp Objects in Cycles

Cycles supports most of the same lamp types as Blender Internal, except for Hemi lamps. Adding a new lamp object in Cycles adds a standard emission shader connected to the lamp's output node,

as shown in Figure 13-5. This shader can be used to adjust the intensity and color of the light. To adjust the softness of the shadows the lamp generates, use the lamp's Size setting in the Object Data tab of the Properties editor.

❀ *Avoid setting the size of a lamp to 0, as this can cause "fireflies"—a kind of noise consisting of single bright pixels. If you want sharp shadows, just set the size to something very small but not 0.*

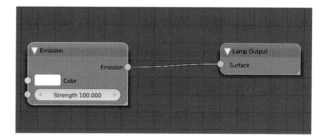

Figure 13-5: The emission shader is used for both lamp objects and mesh-emitter objects in Cycles.

Mesh-Emitter Objects in Cycles

Cycles supports the emission of light from materials, meaning that you can turn any mesh into a light by applying a material that contains an emission shader. This feature is great for creating unique lighting setups and for lights that appear in glossy reflections. (We'll look deeper into this when lighting the Spider Bot.) In the case of mesh emitters, you can combine emission shaders with other shaders using the Add and Mix nodes (as discussed in Chapter 12).

World Settings and Ambient Light and Occlusion

In Chapter 10, we baked ambient occlusion maps for our projects. Ambient occlusion maps are textures that mimic the effect of light coming from all around an object that is occluded, or blocked, by parts of the object itself. This effect is similar to what we see in the sky on a sunny day. The main source of light is the sun, but light also scatters throughout the atmosphere so that it comes from all directions and even illuminates the shadows. (This effect is even more apparent on an overcast day when the lack of direct sunlight means things are lit more evenly from all directions.)

To achieve the effect of light coming from a scene's surroundings, we can use Blender's World settings, accessible from the World tab of the Properties editor. These settings determine the look of your scene's background and how the background contributes to the scene's lighting. Both Blender Internal and Cycles support world lighting, though in slightly different ways.

World Settings in Blender Internal

Blender Internal's World settings are shown in Figure 13-6. The most important ones are as follows:

Horizon Color/Zenith Color/Ambient Color
By default, the sky in a scene will simply be the *Horizon Color*. The *Zenith Color* is used when Blend Sky is turned on, rendering the background as a gradient from the horizon color to the zenith color. The *Ambient Color* is a fixed color that is added to the lighting of every surface in the scene, brightening the shadows, but the effect is very unrealistic, so it's best to leave this set to black.

Paper Sky/Real Sky *Paper Sky* applies any texture or blend applied to the background to the camera coordinates. This can be useful when you have a background photo or image that you want to use as is, without distortion. *Real Sky* creates a background with a real horizon in the plane of the scene's global coordinates so that any textures remain static as the camera is rotated and any blend in the sky occurs from the "real" horizon upward (and downward). Real Sky is useful when panoramic or mirror-ball textures are used as backgrounds.

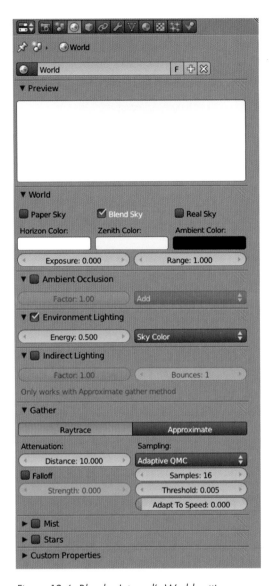

Figure 13-6: Blender Internal's World settings

Ambient Occlusion We encountered ambient occlusion in Chapter 10. Ambient occlusion lights or adds shadows to a surface based on the surrounding geometry. Areas with geometry around them that blocks light will be darkened, while the exposed parts of a mesh will remain well lit. The Ambient Occlusion option can be set to *Add* or *Multiply* with the other lighting in the scene. Additive ambient occlusion brightens the existing lighting, while Multiply adds shadows. Multiply is the more "realistic" option and is more suitable to most scenes. (The environment lighting settings offer better tools for adding further light to the scene anyway.)

Environment Lighting This adds light to a scene, coming from all directions (though blocked by nearby geometry, as with ambient occlusion). The Environment Lighting setting can be used to mimic scattered light from the sky in an outdoor scene or to approximate the effect of light bouncing around and illuminating a scene. The color of the environment lighting can be set to white, to the sky color (where it will use the horizon color or both the horizon and zenith colors if you have a blend sky), or the sky texture if you are using a background texture.

Indirect Lighting This setting allows Blender Internal to simulate the effect of light bouncing repeatedly, and thus illuminating more of a scene, before entering the camera or eye. The result can be color bleeding, where the color of a brightly colored diffuse material is reflected onto nearby objects (as shown in Figure 13-7). The method is only compatible with the Approximate Gather method (discussed below). The *Factor* setting affects the strength of this effect, and the *Bounces* setting determines how many times light may bounce off a surface and still be rendered.

Gather (Ray Trace and Approximate) These settings let you choose between Blender Internal's two options for rendering world lighting. As with lamps, *Ray Trace* takes multiple ray-traced samples per pixel to determine the amount of world lighting. This process gives more accurate results, typically at the cost of extra render time and noise (if the number of samples is set too low). The *Approximate* setting does not require ray tracing and is noise free, but it can produce other artifacts, such as overocclusion in some areas. Turning up the number of passes and setting the error value lower gives better results but takes more time to preprocess when rendering. Alternatively, using the Correction parameter reduces the strength of the occlusion to compensate for the artifacts. When using the Approximate Gather method, turning on Pixel Cache generally gives much faster results.

Attenuation The *Falloff* setting under Attenuation causes ambient occlusion, environment lighting, and indirect lighting to fade out over a certain distance, reducing the effect of far away geometry on a surface and lightening the surface. Falloff also speeds up rendering because calculating the lighting for a surface point only requires taking nearby geometry into account. The *Strength* setting determines how strong the attenuation is, while the *Distance* setting (only with the Ray-Trace Gather method) determines the range of the falloff.

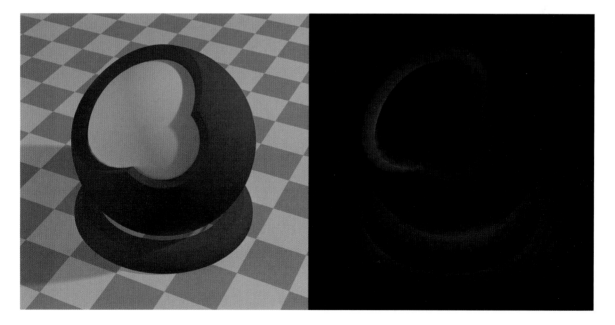

Figure 13-7: Color bleeding from indirect lighting. Here, the red sphere reflects red light onto its surroundings. This is most visible on the gray inner sphere. This is a subtle effect, so indirect light alone is shown on the right. The surroundings also contribute indirect light, shown as grayish colors in the image on the right.

World Settings in Cycles

In Cycles, World settings are node based and use the same shader system as do materials and lights. The World settings use the Background Shader node exclusively, which lights the scene and sets the background color or texture (depending on the inputs you supply it with) and the strength of the lighting that the background contributes. The standard background node tree is shown in Figure 13-8.

You can influence the color of the background as with other materials by using textures, images, and colors. Particularly useful for this are the Sky Texture and Environment Texture nodes. The Sky Texture node creates a procedural sky, using the direction you set by dragging the sphere input of the node, with the level of atmospheric scattering determined by the Turbidity setting. This effect works particularly well when combined with a sun lamp with a yellow-orange (sunlight) color to get some basic outdoor lighting (see Figure 13-9).

Cycles also supports ambient occlusion, which can be used to add white ambient light to a scene, with occlusion based on the distance between faces. You can turn this effect on in the World tab of the Properties editor by using the Ambient Occlusion tab.

Also in the World tab under Settings is the option to sample the background as a lamp. Enable this when using a textured background, particularly when using HDRI (high-dynamic-range image) maps for background lighting to dramatically speed up rendering (see Figure 13-10).

Lighting the Bat Creature

For the Bat Creature, I wanted dramatic lighting to make the character look dangerous and foreboding. I needed some dark shadows and stark lighting that wouldn't give too much away. To create this effect, I used a three-point lighting setup, which is commonly used to light characters and portraits. Additionally, I needed to set up my lights to create good shadows with the creature's hair and to light the creature from behind so that light would be seen scattering through the skin of the wings (using the subsurface scattering material we created in Chapter 12).

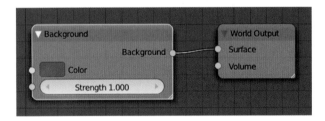

Figure 13-8: The standard node tree for World settings in Cycles

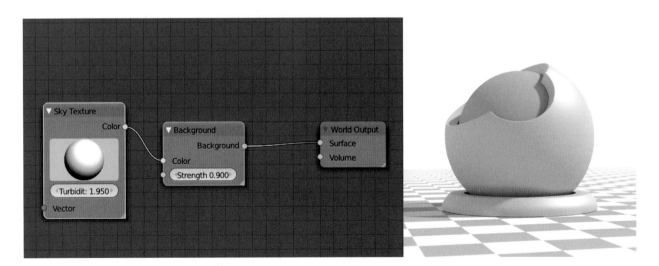

Figure 13-9: Combining the sky shader for the background with a sun lamp gives a decent approximation of outdoor lighting. Left: The sky shader. Right: Illumination from the sky combined with a sun lamp.

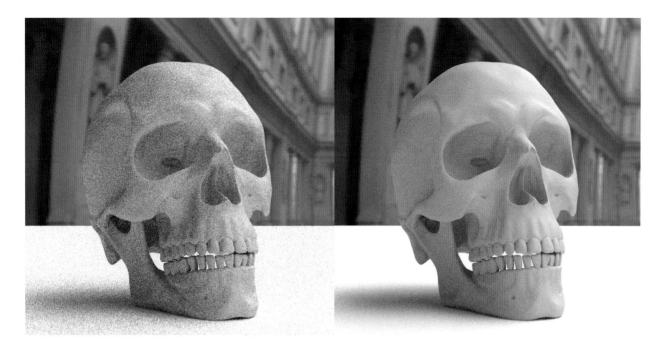

Figure 13-10: Turning on Sample as Lamp for backgrounds with texture information speeds up reduction of noise while rendering. Here, an HDRI map has been used to light the scene. Left: Sample as Lamp turned off (30 passes). Right: Sample as Lamp turned on with map resolution set to 256 (again, after 30 passes).

Three-Point Lighting

Three-point lighting is considered the "standard" lighting setup for a lot of portraiture and cinematography because the use of three lights achieves a pleasant, natural look that can be adapted to many circumstances with good results.

The Key Light

The first of the three lights—the *key light*—is the main source of light in a scene and is generally placed so that it lights the subject from the side and slightly above to provide some interesting illumination.

For the Bat Creature, I added a spot lamp above and slightly to the left (from the camera's perspective) of the character, as shown in Figure 13-11. The key light would provide most of the illumination, so I set its intensity quite high (to about 12) and the distance low (around 3) so that the intensity of the light would fade relatively quickly. I gave the light a bluish tint, as shown in the figure.

Figure 13-11: The effect of the key light

The Fill Light

The next light—the *fill light*—is placed opposite the key light, usually illuminating the subject from the other side and generally adding some subtle light to the shadows cast by the key light. Because I wanted the Bat Creature to have really dark shadows, I set the intensity of the fill light to 0.5 and its distance to 6. I set its color to a reddish hue to contrast with the blue key light. The effect of the fill light is shown in Figure 13-12.

> While the fill light usually comes from the opposite side of a subject, I placed the fill light to the character's right (camera left) because the Bat Creature's left wing (camera right) shields the body.

The Back Light

The back light (sometimes called a *rim light*) lights a subject from behind, usually adding a subtle highlight around the edges of a subject on one side. This light was especially important for the Bat Creature because it provided scattered back lighting through the wings and ears. I set its intensity high (to 10) and its distance to 10 to give the light enough brightness to shine through the wings (see Figure 13-13). Together, the key, fill, and back lights produce the final lighting, as shown in Figure 13-14.

Positioning the Lights

Positioning the three lights involves thinking about what aspects of your model you want to light and where you want the light to come from and then exercising a bit of trial and error. To help with the process and to get quicker feedback on how your lights look (without having to render each time), use Blender's GLSL shading mode to see how your lights will look in real time in the 3D Viewport (see Figure 13-15). This works particularly well for spot lamps as GLSL also supports buffered shadows, meaning the GLSL preview will look pretty close to your final renders. Turn on this shading mode by going to the 3D Viewport header and setting the shading to **Textured**. Then, look in the Properties region under Display and set the shading type to **GLSL** (press **N** to bring up the properties region in the 3D Viewport). You can then move your lights around as you please and get instant feedback on how they look.

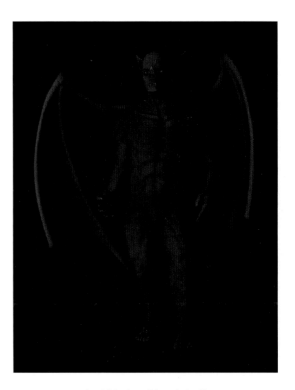

Figure 13-12: The fill light adds subtle illumination to the shadows.

Figure 13-13: The back light provides highlights around the outline of the character (that is, on the shoulders and the back of the head). In this case, it also scatters light through the wings and ears.

GLSL shading supports all but area lights, though it only renders shadows for spot lamps with buffered shadows.

Clay Renders and Material Override

Another way to get a feel for how your lighting is working is by rendering your scene and applying the same material (usually a flat, diffuse one) to every object. Often called a *clay render*, this lets you see how the lighting is working in isolation and can be useful for checking whether an issue with your renders is due to lighting or materials.

To quickly set up a clay render, use the Material Override option in the Render tab of the Properties editor. Create a new, flat, gray material (just use the default material and turn down the specularity) and assign it to the Material Override option in the Layers panel to render the scene without textures and materials, as shown in Figure 13-16. Press F12 to render. (See Chapter 14 for more on rendering.)

Figure 13-14: All three lights contribute to the final lighting.

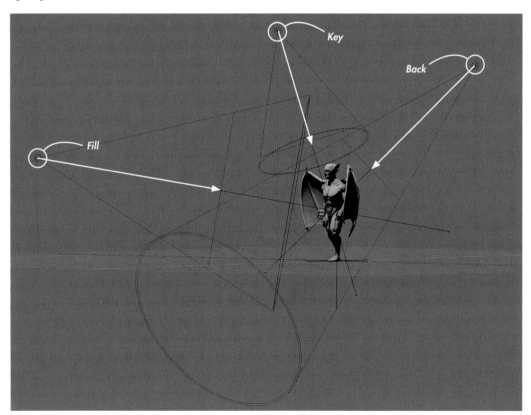

Figure 13-15: Positioning lights using GLSL shading for feedback

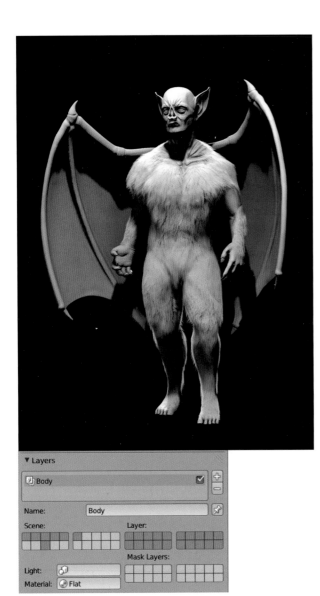

Table 13-1: Settings for the Shadow Buffer Spot Lamps in the Bat Creature Scene

	Key	Fill	Back
Filter type	Gauss	Gauss	Gauss
Soft	12	30	10
Bias	0.2	0.2	0.2
Sample buffers	1	1	1
Size	2048	2048	2048
Samples	16	16	16

Lighting the Eyes

Eyes are a critical part of most characters, and it's important to make sure they're lit as you want them. Sometimes this can mean cheating by adding some separate lighting to the eyes to get the look you want. For the Bat Creature, I placed the two eye objects on their own layer (press **M** to move objects to other layers) and pointed a Hemi lamp at them. I set the lamp's intensity low (to about 0.05) so that the lighting would come predominantly from the existing spot lamps. Then, I turned off the light's Specular option to prevent it from contributing to specular reflections. Next, I turned on This Layer Only in the lamp's settings so that the lamp would light only the eye objects, adding a bit of extra illumination to the eyes to help them stand out more.

Floor Shadows

While I didn't create a backdrop for the Bat Creature, I knew some shadow around his feet would improve my final render. To produce the shadows on their own, I used the Only Shadows option for materials. I added a plane to the scene and assigned a new material to it. Then, in the materials settings, I turned on Transparency (set to Mask), and in the Shadows panel, I turned on Only Shadows. This new material (shown in Figure 13-17) then renders as just the shadows cast by other objects, with the rest of the mesh rendering completely transparent. Later on, this will allow me to easily composite these shadows onto the background of the final render. I scaled the plane up to pick up all the shadows from the Bat Creature, using the GLSL shading mode as a guide.

Figure 13-16: A clay render of the Bat Creature using the Material Override setting. Here, I've created a material called Flat and assigned it to the material override in the Render Layers panel. This technique lets you see the lighting of your model in isolation.

Shadows and Fur

While ray-traced or buffered shadows would both be appropriate for most of the Bat Creature, our fur has more specific lighting requirements. For best results, use deep shadow buffers on each of the key, fill, and back lights and adjust the other settings as shown in Table 13-1.

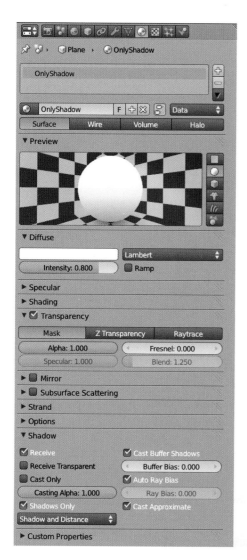

Figure 13-17: Using an Only Shadows material to cast shadows on the floor, shown here on a white background

World Settings for the Bat Creature

I didn't need to do much in the way of World settings for the Bat Creature since I would be compositing in a simple background later; I just needed to turn on Ambient Occlusion. To do so, I enabled Ambient Occlusion in the World tab of the Properties panel and set it to Multiply with a factor of 1.0. For the Gather method, I chose Approximate. I set the number of passes to 1 and turned on Falloff with a strength of 1. These settings work well with hair, and using them meant that I wouldn't have to do any ray tracing when rendering since I was using buffer shadows for the rest of my lighting.

This completes lighting the Bat Creature. We'll return to rendering it in Chapter 14.

Lighting the Spider Bot

We'll be rendering the Spider Bot with Cycles. For this project, I wanted bright, dynamic lighting to show off the character's shiny surface. I accomplished this with a mix of mesh lights and lamp objects. Since I wouldn't be using world lighting, I set the color of the world background to black in the World tab of the Properties editor, and I set its intensity to 0 before continuing.

The principal lighting for the Spider Bot comes from the right from a point-lamp object with an orange color and high strength, as shown in Figure 13-18. This lamp is supplemented by a mesh light overhead that is composed of multiple planes with a light-emitting material. To create this light,

I added a new plane object and moved it above the scene. Then, I duplicated the face several times in Edit mode, using Blender's snapping tools (set to Increment) to keep the planes aligned in a grid. I then scaled the whole array of planes along the x-axis to make them rectangular.

To make these planes emit light, I assigned a new material to them, and in the Node editor, I added an Emission Shader node and attached its output to the Material Output node (see Figure 13-18). I gave the Emission shader a bluish color and set its strength to 10. Because these lights are meshes, not only do they light the scene, but they also show up in the reflections on the Spider Bot's shiny green surfaces, particularly on the back, as seen in the figure.

It's simple to tweak the strength and color of lights in Cycles, thanks to the render preview shading mode of the 3D Viewport, which can give instant feedback on how your lighting looks as you adjust lights. (For more on the 3D Viewport render preview, see Chapter 14.)

Lighting the Jungle Temple

The Jungle Temple required a more complex lighting setup, but again, we have the Cycles render preview to give instant feedback on how our lighting looks. For this scene, I wanted to create a nighttime atmosphere with a bright, fiery orange light coming from the entrance to the temple.

World Background

Because I would be lighting the Jungle Temple scene without world lighting, I set the world background color to black with 0 intensity.

Temple Entrance Lighting

Let's start with the light coming from the temple entrance, as this is the light source with the most impact on the scene. I used a couple of light sources to create this lighting. The first is a mesh emitter at the end of the tunnel (out of sight of the camera); I assigned red and orange emission materials to it to provide orangish light throughout the tunnel and a bit beyond. I set the intensity of these emission materials to about 40.

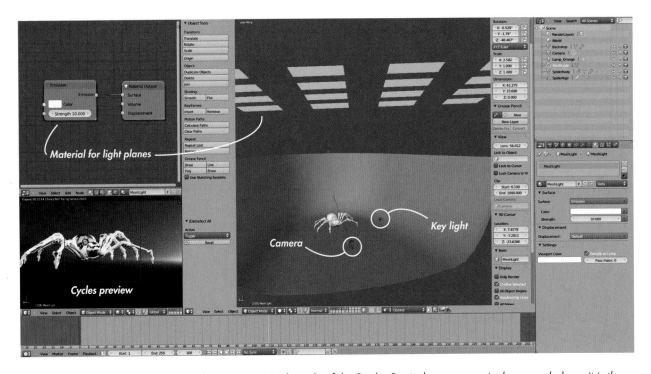

Figure 13-18: Adding lights to the Spider Bot scene. To the right of the Spider Bot is the orange point lamp, and above it is the grid of mesh lights with their material visible in the Node editor on the left. The Cycles render preview is a great way to get instant feedback on your lighting.

To help spread this light further into the surroundings, I created a point-lamp object with a yellow-orange color nearer the mouth of the tunnel. I gave it a high intensity to light more of the surrounding areas and set the point-light size to 1.5 to give soft shadows. These lights can be seen in Figure 13-19.

Fill Lighting

To add further light, I created a soft (large size) point lamp hovering over the middle of the scene to provide some general lighting. I also added a harder (small size) light behind the camera and off to one side to illuminate the foreground objects a bit. I gave both lamps a bluish color, which lent the scene a blue, moonlit look where it was not illuminated by the orange light from the tunnel. (Blue and orange also oppose one another nicely.) These lights can be seen in Figure 13-20.

Back Light

I also added some illumination from the right, coming from behind the temple, to highlight the leaves and give a slight rim light to the rocks of the temple walls. This light comes from two lights: a long, shallow mesh light that illuminates mainly the backs of the leaves and a point light that provides some extra illumination from this direction (see Figure 13-21). The overall effect is shown in Figure 13-22.

A Note on Soft Shadows

While soft shadows look nice, they can really bump up your render times. I ended up using quite a few lamps with soft shadows for this scene, and as a result, it took quite a while to render. This isn't really a problem for stills, but bear it in mind if you want to render an animation or if you want quick results, and consider using lights with harder shadows or having some lights that don't cast ray-traced shadows at all.

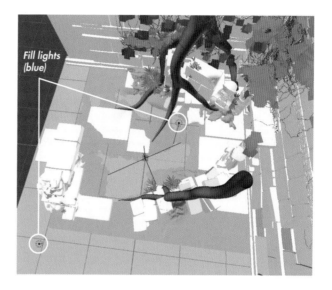

Figure 13-20: The temple entrance lighting combined with some blue fill lighting

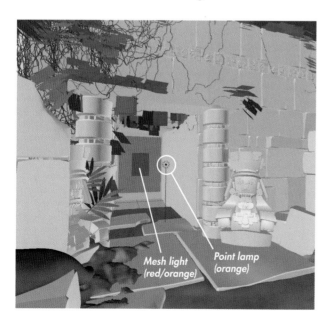

Figure 13-19: The lighting of the temple entrance

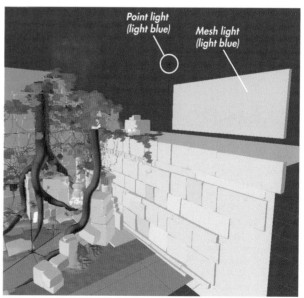

Figure 13-21: The back lighting from one mesh light and a point lamp

General Lighting Tips

Lighting makes a big difference to the feel of an image, and you can do a lot with lighting to change how your subject is perceived. Here are some tips to make your lighting render more efficiently and work better artistically.

Experiment. I tried a lot of different lighting setups for all of my projects. For the Jungle Temple scene, I tried both daylight and nighttime lighting, and for the Bat Creature and Spider Bot, I experimented with many directions and colors. Coming up with something good requires experimentation.

Use test renders and previews. Use Blender Internal's GLSL shading and Cycles's render preview for real-time previews of your lighting. Do test renders to make sure your lighting works.

Less is more. Try to use fewer lights where possible to simplify the process of tweaking your lighting and to make it easier to see which lights most influence your image.

Shadow settings. While it can be tempting to turn up all the settings for your lamps to try to get the nicest shadows, it's often not necessary to do so. Experiment and try to minimize the use of settings that increase render time significantly, such as shadow samples and shadow-buffer

Figure 13-22: The lighting for the Jungle Temple scene. This will later be tweaked with some compositing in Chapter 14.

Back light

Orange light from tunnel

Blue fill light

sizes. For example, soft shadows don't need high-resolution shadow buffers, and crisp, hard-edged shadows don't need lots of samples. Once you have lighting you like, try to determine which settings you can turn down without affecting the look of your lighting in order to speed up renders.

Make the most of shadow buffers. The resolution of a shadow-buffer lamp is spread out over the lamp's cone. To make the most of it, restrict the lamp by reducing its angle to cover only the model (go to Size under Spot Shape in the Object Data tab) and to make sure that you're not wasting any of the shadow buffer's resolution on areas that aren't casting shadows.

Use opposing colors. Use color theory to your advantage when lighting. Often, opposing colors (pairs of colors on opposite sides of the color wheel, such as orange and blue or green and purple) work well when used as opposing key and fill lights (see Figure 13-23). Natural light often follows this example: Sunlight is orange, while scattered light from the atmosphere is blue.

Directional lighting and characters. The direction you choose to light a character from can change the way it's perceived. Lighting from above often looks regal and dignified, while lighting from below looks scary and menacing. A few examples are shown in Figure 13-24.

In Review

In this chapter, we looked at lighting for both Blender Internal and Cycles, beginning with a discussion of the different types of lamps that Blender offers and their functional differences in Blender Internal and Cycles. We examined different methods for dealing with shadows, both ray traced and buffered, and explored their advantages and disadvantages. We also looked at Blender's World settings and how they impact lighting.

For the Bat Creature, we covered creating a three-point light setup to give dramatic flair to the model and looked at how best to set up shadows for characters with hair. For the Spider Bot and Jungle Temple projects, I lit the scenes using a mix of lights and mesh-emitter objects to create dynamically lit scenes. When I worked with lighting in Cycles, the Cycles render preview came in handy for getting real-time feedback on the effect of our lights. And even in Blender Internal, I used GLSL shading to get some rudimentary feedback on the lighting and shadows in the scene.

In the next chapter, we'll render the scenes and do some final color correction and compositing for our projects. I will cover render options for both Cycles and Blender Internal and how best to optimize render times while getting the best possible renders. We'll look at node-based compositing using Blender's compositor, as well as creating backgrounds and doing final tweaks in GIMP.

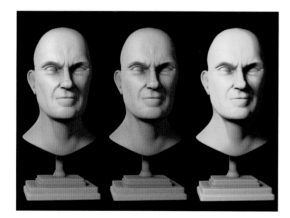

Figure 13-23: Opposing colors often make for pleasant lighting schemes. Left to right: Orange key light and a blue fill, blue key light and an orange fill, green key light and a purple fill.

Figure 13-24: Lighting direction changes how we perceive characters. Left to right: Lighting from above looks dignified, lighting from below looks spooky, and a rim light from behind gives an ominous silhouette.

14

RENDERING AND COMPOSITING

In this chapter, we move into the final stages of the projects as we turn each of the scenes into rendered images and tweak them to look their best. We begin by looking at Blender's render settings, both for Blender Internal and Cycles, to determine how to get the best render in the shortest time possible. Following that discussion, I'll cover using Blender's node-based compositor to further refine, adjust, and grade these renders into final images. Finally, we'll make a few tweaks to the renders in GIMP.

The Render Tab

We touched on the Render tab of the Properties editor when we used it to bake textures in Chapter 10. In this chapter, we'll examine the other settings available in this tab. Many of these depend on which renderer is being used—Blender Internal or Cycles—so we will look at each in turn.

Rendering with Blender Internal

The Render tab in Blender Internal is shown in Figure 14-1. Let's look at the settings available in each panel.

Render Panel

This contains buttons for rendering your animation and playing back the results.

Image/Animation   These buttons render the current frame (F12) or every frame in the range set by the Frame Range settings in the Dimensions panel as an animation (CTRL-F12). You can play back the rendered animation with the play button.

Display   Display lets you set where the rendered image will appear. The Image editor option will render the image in an available UV Image editor if possible, or it will temporarily switch one of the other editors into a UV Image editor during rendering if necessary. The other options allow you to render full screen, in a new window, or in the background (Keep UI).

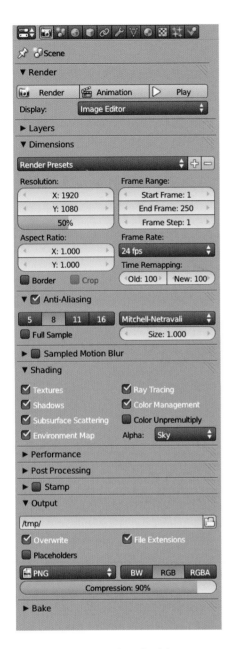

Figure 14-1: The Render tab of the Properties editor, shown here in Blender Internal

Layers Panel

The Layers panel contains tools and options for creating different render layers and for choosing which scene layers contribute to your final renders. At the top of the panel, the Layer selector lets you select the render layer to work on. Use the checkboxes on the right to enable or disable rendering particular layers; use the + and – buttons on the right to add or delete render layers.

Name   This allows you to name the selected layer.

Scene/Layer/Mask Layer   These three sets of checkboxes let you choose which scene layers are used in your final renders and how. Enabling a layer under Scene turns the layer on in the 3D Viewport (just as the layers checkboxes in the 3D viewport header do). Layers must be checked under Scene to be renderable. Enable layers under Layer to make them render for the currently selected render layer; you can have multiple layers turned on under Scene, but only those checked under Layer will be rendered. Layers checked under Mask (but not under Layer) will mask out geometry on other layers, as shown in Figure 14-2.

Light   The Light option lets you specify a group of lights to be treated as the only lights in the scene when rendered.

Material   As discussed in "Clay Renders and Material Override" on page 221, the Materials option lets you override the materials for a scene with a single material when rendering. We used this option in Chapter 13 to produce a clay render of the Bat Creature project in order to test the lighting.

Include   This offers a number of checkboxes that detail the types of surfaces and effects to be rendered with this layer. For example, you can turn on or off the rendering of z-transparent materials, fur, or solid materials.

Passes   Within a layer, Blender can render other kinds of information and split up aspects of an image into different passes, such as shadows, environment lighting, and z-depth (the distance from the camera). This pass then contains only that data that can be used in compositing the final image. For example, you could use the z-depth pass as the input for a Defocus node to create depth of field, or you could use an ambient occlusion pass to add extra shadows to an image. Use the checkboxes under Passes to enable or disable various passes. Some passes can be excluded from the main render pass by toggling the camera icon to the right of the pass's name.

Dimensions

This panel lets you set the dimensions in time (frames) and space (resolution) of your render or

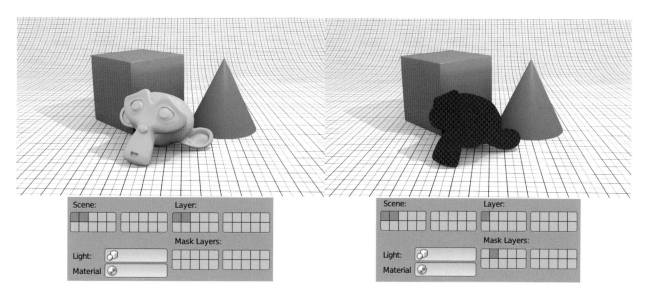

Figure 14-2: Using layers as mask layers. Here the monkey object is placed on layer 2, with everything else on layer 1. On the left, both layers are checked under Layer, and everything renders as expected. On the right, layer 2 is used as a mask layer instead, so you see a transparent hole where the monkey head obscures the other objects.

animation. The Resolution settings let you choose the size of your final render, while the Frame Range settings are used to specify the number of frames in your animation. Aspect Ratio sets the aspect ratio for the pixels in the image (some video formats use nonsquare pixels, but for stills, always use square 1:1 ratio pixels).

You can use the Border and Crop settings to render a small patch of your image rather than the whole thing. To do so, switch to the camera view in the 3D Viewport (NUMPAD 0). Then press SHIFT-B and drag out a rectangle over the area you wish to restrict the render to. This will automatically enable the Border setting. Use the Crop setting to reduce an image's dimensions to the size of your border region; otherwise, the remaining area will be filled with black.

Anti-Aliasing and Motion Blur

Aliasing is an artifact in a pixel-based image where sharp boundaries may look jagged due to the finite resolution of the image (see Figure 14-3). Aliasing is often most obvious on the outlines of objects or shadows, but it can also crop up in textures or specular highlights. Anti-aliasing addresses this problem by taking multiple subsamples of each pixel with slightly different offsets and blending them, resulting in a smoother-looking boundary, as you can see in the figure.

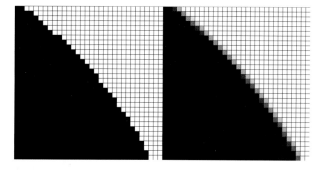

Figure 14-3: Anti-aliasing reduces the appearance of jagged edges in renders. Left: No anti-aliasing. Right: Anti-aliasing turned on with the number of subsamples set to 8.

Use the numbers on the left of the Anti-Aliasing panel to determine how many samples will be taken (more samples will result in smoother renders but longer render times). The drop-down menu on the right sets the type of filter used to blend the samples: The default of Mitchell-Netravali gives good results without taking too much sharpness out of the render, but when working with higher-resolution images, try Gaussian. Use the Full Sample option to make Blender maintain each sample separately, even during compositing, which can help with aliasing issues at the compositing stage.

Sampled motion blur is similar to anti-aliasing in that multiple samples are taken per pixel but at different times rather than different locations. This results in motion blur for fast-moving objects once the samples are blended together. (Essentially, the image is rendered multiple times, and the results are blended.) The number of samples is determined by the Motion Samples setting, and the amount of time in frames over which the samples are taken is determined by the Shutter setting.

Shading

The Shading panel lets you turn on and off different rendering options, including Textures, Shadows, Subsurface Scattering, Environment Mapping, and Ray-Tracing options. To speed up renders, turn off unneeded shading options.

The Alpha drop-down menu lets you choose how to render the background of your image. Sky renders the sky colors and textures set in your global settings. The Straight Alpha and Premultiplied options render the background of your image as transparent. In the case of Premultiplied, the RGB values of transparent or partially transparent pixels are multiplied by the alpha value on output. This method of encoding alpha values is also referred to as *associated alpha* and is required for some image formats, like TIFF and PNG. It's also useful for compositing because combining images this way gives better results, though Blender's compositor has tools for working with both premultiplied and unpremultiplied alpha. Straight Alpha skips this step and renders unassociated alpha images instead.

If the above discussion on different methods of encoding alpha values seems complex, it's because it is. I've covered it only very briefly here, but it's actually a pretty deep topic. For more information, try searching http://www.blender.org/ and the Blender wiki for Color Management.

Performance

The Performance panel contains a number of options that can affect how fast Blender will render and how much impact rendering will have on your computer's resources. Blender splits up images to be rendered into multiple tiles, which are then rendered individually. The most important settings are Threads and Tiles. When set to Fixed, these settings let you specify how many tiles will be rendered at once (up to twice the number of processor cores you have).

The Tiles settings determine how the image to be rendered is broken up into tiles along the x- and y-axes. Tiles are rendered one at a time per thread,

meaning that if you have eight threads, you will be able to render eight tiles simultaneously.

Tweaking the Tiles settings can make a big difference in your render times. Using too few tiles can mean that processor threads are left idle once all available tiles are being rendered, even if there is plenty of your image left to be rendered. Using too many tiles uses more memory without speeding up the render. The optimum number of tiles is generally between 16 (4×4) and 64 (8×8), with more complex scenes benefiting from more tiles.

The other settings in this panel are even more technical and can usually be left at their defaults. For more on these settings, try *http://wiki.blender.org/*.

Post-Processing

The Post-Processing settings determine the post-processing effects applied to your image. The relevant ones are the checkboxes that turn on Compositing and the Sequencer (Compositing should be turned on). Dither adds subtle variation to the colors of pixels, preventing color banding in images with smooth gradients. The Edge setting draws cartoon lines around an image's geometry, with the strength of the line effect determined by the Threshold setting and the color of the lines determined by the color selector directly below the Threshold setting.

Stamp

The Stamp settings let you stamp your image with data about the render, such as the time it was rendered, the filename, the frame number, and so on. Stamp is often useful when rendering animations, but it's not of much use to us for our projects.

Output

The Output settings determine where the output of your renders is saved and in what format. Animation frames are saved automatically, but single-frame images must be saved manually. The default output directory (*/tmp/* on Mac and Linux systems or the Temp folder on Windows) determines where animation frames are saved, but you can change this to a directory of your choosing. The output format is determined by the drop-down menu, which includes options for what color information to save (black and white, RGB, or RGB and alpha).

Bake

These settings are discussed in detail in Chapter 11.

Rendering with Cycles

Many of the Render tab options remain the same in Cycles, so I will just cover the important differences here.

Sampling

The Sampling panel determines how many samples to calculate for each pixel in the image, which is the main way Cycles determines the quality and noisiness of your final image. The Render and Preview options determine how many samples to render for each pixel in an image before terminating the render. (Use Render for proper renders and Preview for the Cycles preview in the 3D Viewport.) More passes will result in less noise, but the number of passes required to get a noise-free image will vary widely according to the contents of your scene. Seed sets a random value for Cycles to use for sampling, and different seeds will produce different noise patterns.

You can use the Clamp option to prevent *fireflies*, which are overly bright pixels caused by noise from bright lights or specular highlights. To do so, set the maximum brightness (the *clamp* value) for a sample to a nonzero number (a value of around 3 works well). This keeps overly bright samples from throwing off the average value of a pixel too much, though it comes at the cost of some accuracy in rendering. (If you leave this at the default of 0, this feature will not be used.)

Light Paths

The Light Paths panel supplements the options in the Samples panel, allowing you to go deeper into how Cycles renders your scene. Specifically the Light Paths panel lets you determine what types of rays to render and how many bounces to calculate before terminating a ray. More bounces give more accurate (and slightly brighter) renders, at the cost of extra render time.

The Transparency, Light Paths, and Bounce settings define the maximum number of light bounces that Cycles will calculate for each type of interaction with light. The Max setting sets the overall maximum number of bounces, while the other settings restrict specific types of rays to fewer bounces. The Min setting for Transparency and Overall Bounces enables early termination of refracted rays, resulting in faster rendering with the loss of some accuracy.

The No Caustics and Shadows options let you turn on and off caustics and ray-traced shadows to speed up rendering. Caustics are rays that have been reflected or refracted by glossy surfaces that then contribute to diffuse illumination. Examples include the bright patterns of sunlight in a swimming pool and light focused by a magnifying glass onto a surface.

Film

You can use the Film panel's Exposure setting to change the exposure of your render to either brighten or darken scenes overall. (However, it's best to change the settings on your lamps instead for finer control.) The Transparency checkbox determines whether your background renders as transparent or uses your global settings. The drop-down menu on the right sets the pixel filter type (with the width of the filter below it). Smaller widths produce sharper-looking edges but can cause aliasing. Larger widths give smoother renders at the expense of a small amount of blurring.

Layers

Cycles works much the same as Blender Internal when it comes to layers, but it supplies a different range of passes. Cycles will split up each kind of light ray (diffuse, glossy, and transmission) into separate passes and can split up those passes further into direct and indirect passes. These features can be useful when compositing.

Balancing Render Time and Quality

When rendering any CG scene, the aim is to get the nicest render possible in the shortest amount of time. This can be tricky given the number of variables you can change, all of which affect how long an image will take to render. Still, there are some general principles.

Start simple and be organized. Organize your objects onto layers to make it easier to render different aspects of the scene. Also, make sure you don't have any unneeded objects in your scene on visible layers when rendering.

Experiment. If your renders are slow, try changing one setting at a time to see what most affects your render times. For example, change a render setting or the number of samples on a lamp. Or enable or disable some aspect of a material, such as subsurface scattering or ray-traced reflections. Changing one thing at a time will let you see exactly what makes the most difference, whereas changing multiple settings forces you to guess which one altered your render time. If you find that something in particular is slowing down your renders without contributing much to the final image, get rid of it.

Minimize surplus geometry. Once you have the camera angle that you want, start getting rid of objects that won't be seen in your render by deleting them or temporarily shifting them to other layers. This will reduce the amount of geometry Blender has to keep track of when rendering and will speed up your renders! This trick is often helpful when working with environments.

Simplify lighting. Try to simplify the settings on your lamps and see whether you can eliminate some. In particular, look at the shadow settings: Will a smaller shadow-buffer resolution really make much difference, or does a ray-traced lamp need quite so many samples?

As you become more familiar with Blender, you'll soon learn which settings impact render time for different aspects of scenes. In the meantime, the time you spend experimenting and simplifying your scene will almost always speed up render times.

The Compositor

You've pressed F12 to render, and your image is finished, right? Not quite. Now it's time to post-process the final renders using Blender's compositor and GIMP. Blender's compositor is node based and uses the Node editor (which we explored in "Editing Node Materials" on page 200). In this section, I'll show you how to use the compositor to apply effects such as depth of field, bloom, and color grading and to combine separate render layers into one final image (see Figure 14-5). I'll also show you how to use GIMP for painting and touch-up.

Rendering and Compositing the Bat Creature

I wanted to show the final Bat Creature on a dark background with a little color grading. To facilitate this, I split the rendering into two layers: one for the fur and one for the rest of the body. I planned to create a simple, dark-colored background in the compositor with a slight vignette to darken the corners and keep the focus on the bat.

Render Layers

As the first step toward splitting the Bat Creature into two *render layers*, I split my scene into four *scene layers*. On (scene) layer 1, I placed the body (with Subdivision Surface and Displace modifiers) and the teeth and nails. On layer 2, I placed the eye objects, along with the Hemi light I created to light just the eyes (using the This Layer Only option for the lamp). On layer 3, I placed the duplicated body that I had used to create the hair (with Emitter turned off in the Render panel of the Particles tab so that only the hair rendered). Finally, on layer 4, I placed my lamps, the camera, and my floor plane.

Next, I set up two render layers. On the first, I disabled Strand under the Include settings of the Layers panel. For the other, I disabled Solid so that normal meshes wouldn't be rendered while my strand hair would. I named the first layer *body* and the second *strand*.

For the body layer, I enabled an ambient occlusion pass under Passes in the Layers panel. The result when rendered was two separate layers, as shown in Figure 14-4. When looking at the render (choose **Render Result** from the image selector drop-down menu), you can switch between these layers using the drop-down menu in the header of the UV Image editor.

In the Layers panel, the options and settings you choose apply only to the currently selected render layer. In other panels of the Render tab, options apply across all render layers. I set the Alpha option in the Shading panel to Straight Alpha and turned off Ray Tracing to speed up renders. (I didn't need to use ray tracing since I was using buffered shadows for my spot lamps and approximate ambient occlusion.) I set the render size to 2200×3000 pixels in the Dimensions panel, and pressed Render (F12) to start rendering.

Compositing the Passes

After rendering, I used Blender's compositor to combine the layers. I wanted to achieve certain effects with the compositor, in the following order:

1. Add some extra ambient occlusion to the body render layer.

2. Combine the body and fur layers into one image with a plain background.

3. Soften the lighting in the image using a bloom effect.

Figure 14-4: The two render passes for the Bat Creature

4. Apply some basic color grading to the image.
5. Add a vignette to the image.

These effects (as with all things in the compositor) need to be applied in a particular order. Because each node is processed in the order it is connected, changing the order in which you apply nodes to your image can make a big difference. To begin compositing, make sure that Use Nodes is enabled and that you are editing the compositing nodes (not a material or texture). The default compositing node tree should look like Figure 14-5.

The initial Render node will use the first render layer you created in the Layers panel, which in my case was the body layer. I added a second Render Layer node (SHIFT-A ▸ Input ▸ Render Layer) to hold my strand render layer, selecting it from the drop-down menu at the bottom of the Render Layer node.

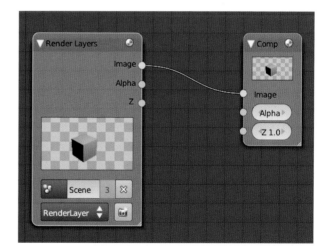

Figure 14-5: The default node tree for Blender's compositor is pretty basic. Whatever you connect to the sockets of the Composite node will become the final output of your render.

Extra Ambient Occlusion

Next, I used a Mix node (SHIFT-A ▸ Color ▸ Mix) to increase the strength of the ambient occlusion effect on the body render layer. I set the Blend mode of the Mix node to Multiply and used the Image output of the body render layer as the first input. I used the ambient occlusion pass (from the socket labeled AO) as the second input.

To increase the effect, I darkened the ambient occlusion pass with a Curves node before multiplying it with the image. To do so, I added an RGB Curves node and inserted it between the ambient occlusion output of the Render Layer node and the Multiply node. To do this quickly, drag the node over the connection between two other nodes (you should see the connection highlight) and release it to insert it in a chain between the other two nodes.

Finally, I made the curve on the RGB Curves node a bit steeper (see Figure 14-6).

Combining the Body and Fur

Next, I added an Alpha Over node (SHIFT-A ▸ Color ▸ Alpha Over), connecting the body as the first input and the fur as the second. To get the correct results when compositing layers with straight alpha, which I selected when choosing the Render settings earlier (see "Render Layers" on page 234), I enabled Convert Premultiply for this node. This should produce the expected result without any dark fringing.

To place the Bat Creature on a dark gray background, I used a second Alpha node with an RGB node as the first input (set to gray) and my newly merged body and hair layers as the second input, as shown in Figure 14-6.

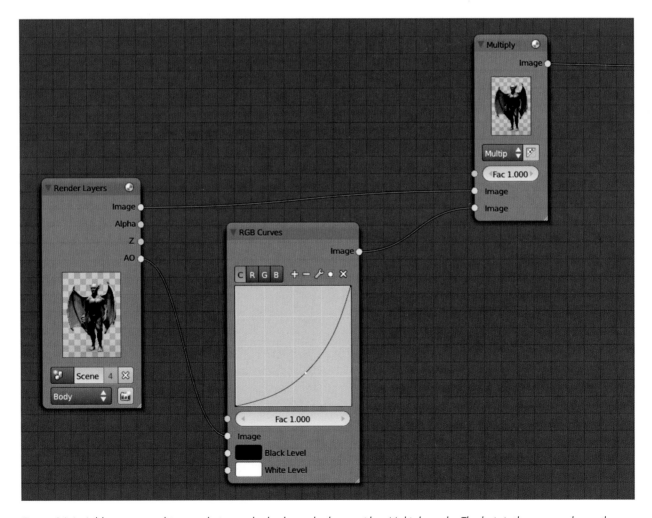

Figure 14-6: Adding extra ambient occlusion to the body render layer with a Multiply node. The hair is then merged over the top, and the composite is placed over a gray background using an Alpha Over node.

Bloom

Next, I added some bloom. *Bloom* is a common effect in both real and CG imagery, where light bleeds out from bright areas into darker ones, effectively lightening the image around darker areas. The real-world effect arises from imperfections in lenses, but I could mimic this by blurring my image and overlaying it on the original input.

To generate bloom, I created a Blur node (SHIFT-A ▶ Filter ▶ Blur) and set its type to Fast Gaussian. I also enabled the Relative option, which would allow me to specify the blur radius relative to the width of the image. This option is useful if you don't know what final resolution you want to use for your render, because the amount of blurring won't appear to change if you make the render smaller or larger. (It would if you defined the radius in pixels.)

I set the *x* and *y* radii to 2 percent and selected **Y** under Aspect Correction to make sure the blur had the correct aspect ratio. (This applies only when using relative blur.) Then, I used an Add node with a factor of 0.2 to subtly add the result of the blurred image on top of the original.

The initial effect was too bright, so I used another RGB Curves node to darken the darker regions of the image before it was blurred so that only the brightest regions would contribute to the bloom. The resulting node tree is shown in Figure 14-7.

Color Correction

Next, I applied some basic color correction using the Color Balance node. This node is really useful for applying a range of color-grading effects to your renders. First, I added the Color Balance node. Then, I connected my composite-in-progress to its image input and turned the factor down to 0.6. (The Color Balance node can produce a strong effect, so turning the factor down is an easy way to make it more subtle without having to make very small adjustments to the other controls.)

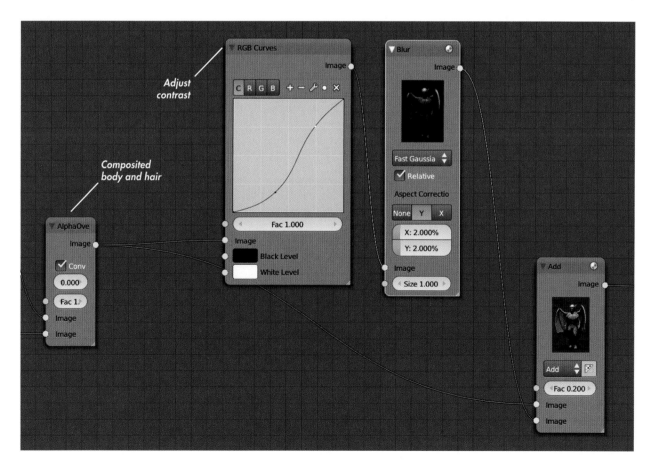

Figure 14-7: My bloom effect and the node tree responsible. The composited hair and body are first put through an RGB curves node to add some contrast, then blurred and added back on top of the original composite.

The Color Balance node has three sets of controls, each of which sets an RGB color. You can set each input by using the color wheel to control the hue and saturation and using the vertical slider to control the color. The color you select is shown below in the color picker. You can also click the color picker to use Blender's default color picker or to set RGB or HSV values manually.

The Color Balance node inputs are named *lift*, *gamma*, and *gain*, and they can be thought of as affecting the shadows, midtones, and highlights of an image. Thus, to give an image less prominent highlights, you could turn down the brightness of the lift input. To give it saturated red highlights, you could set the gain color toward red. In general, setting opposing colors for the lift and gain inputs often results in an image with nice color harmonies between the lights and darks.

In many Hollywood movies, the shadows are teal or blue, while the midtones and highlights are pushed toward orange—a color scheme that works well with the pinkish-orange of most lighter skin tones. For the Bat Creature, I opted for a slightly blue lift color and a slightly yellow gain color. The effect is shown in Figure 14-8.

Adding a Vignette

Next, I added a vignette to my image to slightly darken its corners and draw the viewer's attention to the center of the frame. To create this effect, I took the alpha channel of my body layer and ran it thought a lens distortion filter with a distort value of 1. This distorted the image into a circular shape with black corners, which was almost what I needed.

Then, I used a Blur node set to Fast Gaussian Blur with a relative radius of 50 percent to blur the output of the Lens Distortion node. This gave the image a soft gradient out from the middle, which I then overlaid onto the color-corrected render.

Finally, I added a Sharpen node with a very low Factor setting (around 0.05) to the end of the node tree and connected the output to the Composite node. The final node tree is shown in Figure 14-9, and the result is shown in Figure 14-10.

Compositing Feedback and Viewer Nodes

Creating a final composite from your renders can be a long process that requires some experimentation. To aid in the process, Blender automatically recomposites your final render when you change the node tree. An alternative way to get a feel for how your node setup is working is to use the Viewer node, a secondary output node that lets you view any stage in your node tree.

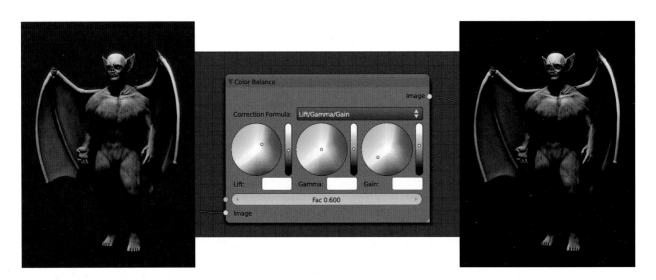

Figure 14-8: Adding color grading to the render of the Bat Creature. Left: Before grading. Middle: The Color Balance node. Right: After grading.

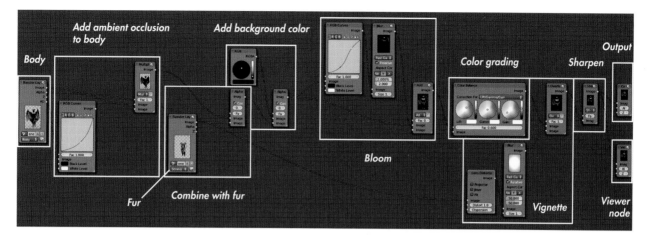

Figure 14-9: The compositing node tree for the Bat Creature

Figure 14-10: The composited output for the Bat Creature

To create a Viewer node, press SHIFT-A ▶ **Output ▶ Viewer** in the Node editor. Whatever is connected as the input for this node will then show up in the UV Image editor if you select **Viewer Node** from the drop-down menu or check **Backdrop** in the background of the Node editor header.

To quickly change which node the Viewer node is connected to, SHIFT-click any node in your setup. This allows you to easily go through your node tree, SHIFT-clicking each node in turn to see how it affects the composite. (You could create multiple Viewer nodes, but this method keeps your node tree clean.)

Organizing Node Trees with Frames and Node Groups

Node setups for compositing can become quite complex as you add more and more nodes. If you don't keep them organized, it can be difficult to come back later to determine what's going on in your node tree. To help with this, Blender lets you organize nodes as Frame nodes and node groups.

Frame Nodes

Frames are large, rectangular nodes with no inputs or outputs of their own; you place other nodes on top of them, which then "stick" to the frame node, allowing you to move collections of nodes together as one. You can label Frame nodes to mark the parts of your node setup (see Figure 14-11) by editing the node's name in the Properties region (**N**). To unstick a node from a frame, you can use the shortcut ALT-P, or you can use ALT-F to unstick the node and automatically grab it to move it around.

Node Groups

Node groups are different from frames. To create a node group, select one or more nodes and press CTRL-G to group them into a single node. The new Group node should contain all of the selected nodes with the inputs and outputs required by the group

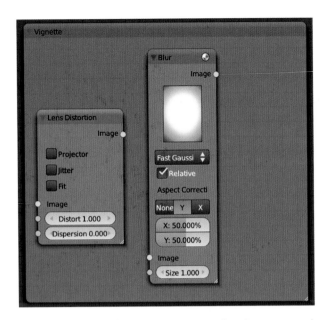

Figure 14-11: Using frames to organize nodes. Once assigned to a frame, multiple nodes can be dragged around together, making it easier to keep them organized.

as sockets. You can expand the group and look inside with TAB to modify its nodes and add extra inputs and outputs.

When you expand a node group, its inputs and outputs will be shown on the left and right sides of the group respectively (see Figure 14-12). To add an input or output, drag a connection from one of the nodes in the group to this border; to remove a connection, click the **X** next to it. Use the arrows next to each input or output to reorder them and tidy up the group.

Like all nodes, node groups can be duplicated and reused. Once duplicated, they behave like linked duplicate objects: A change within one instance of the group affects all instances the same way, which means that you can group commonly repeated chains of nodes and edit them all at once. Node groups can also be linked or appended from other *.blend* files, allowing you to reuse parts of your existing compositing setups.

Retouching in GIMP

Once you're happy with your composite, you can call it final and save it as an image. Formats like PNG, TIFF, and Targa are good for this, being lossless formats (for saving images without losing quality). For posting to the Web, you may want to use the JPEG format, which compresses images much more, giving you a small file at the expense of a small loss in image quality. For the Bat Creature, though, I opted to fix some things in GIMP before calling it final. I wanted to soften some of the specular highlights on the nails and lighten the eyes a bit. I saved it as a Targa (*.tga*) file (F3 in the UV Image editor) and opened it in GIMP.

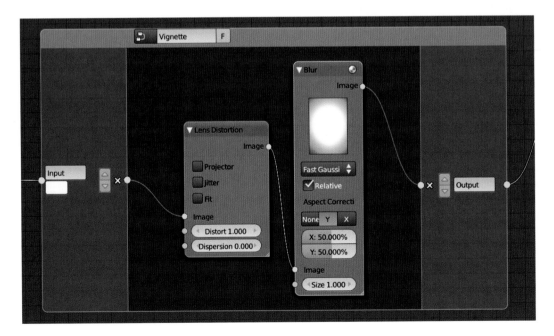

Figure 14-12: Working with node groups

To lighten the eyes, I created a new layer and set its Blend mode to Overlay. Then, I painted white over the eyes. I also added subtle highlights, painting some distorted reflections by hand on a separate layer (this time with the Blend mode set to Normal).

On the same layer as the reflections, I also darkened the highlights on some of the nails, picking colors from nearby areas with the color picker and painting over the bright highlights. (Make sure to turn on **Sample Merged** in the tool options to allow you to sample layers below the current one without switching to them.) Finally, on the original render layer, I used the Blur tool to slightly blur some of the hair on the feet in order to draw attention away from where it looked a bit too coarse.

In Figure 14-13, you can see the retouched eyes. Figure 14-14 shows the completed Bat Creature project.

Rendering and Compositing the Spider Bot

To finalize the Spider Bot, I wanted to add color grading to the lighting (from Chapter 13), show some depth of field to communicate the robot's small scale, and add some bloom.

Depth of field is a real-world phenomenon that happens with images seen through a lens, whether that's a camera or the human eye. Lenses can only focus perfectly on objects that are a certain distance away from them, a distance known as the *focal length*. Objects outside this distance become progressively more out of focus. The effect can be subtle (even not worth bothering with) or significant. In general, depth-of-field effects are most apparent when viewing objects at small scales.

Depth of Field in Cycles

There are two ways to create depth of field when rendering with Cycles. One is to use the Defocus node in Blender's compositor. This works with both Blender Internal and Cycles and will be used for the Jungle Temple scene later in this chapter. The other way is to use Cycles's "real" depth of field as a Camera setting when rendering.

To use real depth of field, do the following:

1. Select the active camera.
2. In the Depth of Field panel on the Object Data tab of the Properties editor, set a distance from the camera to the *focal plane* (the distance where objects appear in focus).

Figure 14-13: Retouching some areas of the composite in GIMP. I added some highlights to the eyes with one layer and brightened them overall with a second (with the Blend mode set to Overlay).

Figure 14-14: The retouched Bat Creature

3. Set an aperture size to determine the amount of blurring. This can be specified in terms of either a radius or a number of F/Stops. Higher numbers give more blur with radius or less with F/Stops. For the Spider Bot, I used radius to set the depth of field to about 0.3.

❋ *Cycles can also mimic the shape of an aperture like the one you might find on a real film or digital camera. To do this, set Blades to the number of sides of the aperture shape and set Rotation to rotate the shape.*

When setting the distance for the depth of field, you can either set a number manually with the Depth setting or specify an object using the selector under Focus. This causes the camera to ignore the Manual Depth setting and focus on the object's center instead. It's usually easiest to create an empty object, place it where you want the scene to be in focus, and then set this empty object as the depth-of-field target in the Camera settings.

To better visualize the depth-of-field distance, enable the Limits option in the Display panel of the Camera settings. Blender then displays a line pointing out from the camera (describing the clipping distances) with a yellow cross at the depth-of-field distance.

Render Settings for the Spider Bot

With depth of field set up, I was ready to render. I set the resolution of the render to 2600×3600, and in the Integrator panel of the Render tab, I set Render Samples to 1000 and Clamp to 2 to reduce the number of fireflies in the scene.

I wanted light to bounce around my scene and illuminate the shadows, but almost all of the scene is in direct light, so I didn't need to rely on bounced light too heavily. I set Max Bounces to 32 (with a minimum of 4 to allow early termination) and the three Light Paths settings to 32 as well. I didn't need any render layers or extra passes, so I left the Layers panel alone and pressed Render (F12).

Compositing the Spider Bot

Next, I added some color grading and bloom to my final render. While Cycles provides some different render passes, the process of compositing is essentially the same as when using Blender Internal. I added bloom as I did with the Bat Creature, using a Blur node to blur the image and an Add node to add the result back onto the image. Again, I

added an RGB Curves node before the Blur node to increase the contrast and slightly darken the image to be blurred.

For color grading, I added a Color Balance node: I chose a purplish color for the Lift Color and a greenish tint for the Gain. I set the Gamma to slightly bluish and brightened up the highlights of the image a bit by setting the value of the gain slightly higher than 1.0. (You can set numerical values for the RGB or HSV colors for Lift, Gamma, and Gain by clicking the color picker.) I then connected the output of the Color Balance node to the image socket Composite output node. The finished node tree is shown in Figure 14-15 and the resulting composite in Figure 14-16.

Rendering and Compositing the Jungle Temple

The Jungle Temple was a complex scene, and my Render settings had a much greater impact on render times for this project. I set the render size of the image to 2880×3840; the number of Render Samples in the Sampling settings to 5000; and Clamp to 3.0 to try to reduce noise a bit more quickly.

❋ *Although 5000 samples is a lot, I wasn't particularly concerned about how long my render took. Primarily, this high number was necessary because there were a lot of soft shadows in the scene. For good results with fewer samples, you can try turning down the Size setting on some of the lamps in your scene at the cost of harder-edged shadows.*

For bounces, I set the Max to 128 and Min to 8 to allow for probabilistic ray termination. Because I wanted to composite the final render on a background image of clouds and sky, I turned on Transparent under Film options.

I left the other Render options at their default and pressed F12 to render.

Background Required

When compositing the Jungle Temple, I wanted to add bloom, depth of field, and some color grading. But first I needed to composite my render over a background, which meant creating a background in GIMP and then importing it into Blender with an Image Texture node for further compositing.

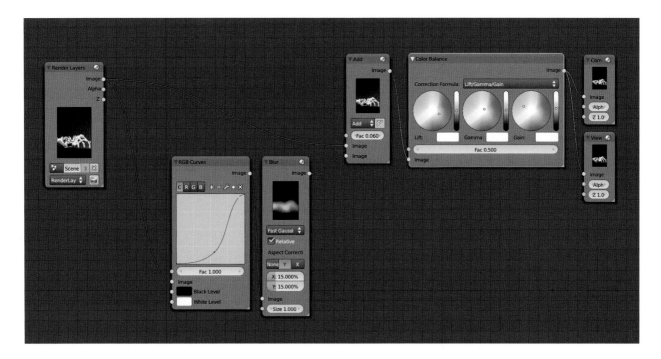

Figure 14-15: The node tree for compositing the Spider Bot

Figure 14-16: The composited Spider Bot

Painting the Sky in GIMP

To create a sky background, I first saved my uncomposited render from Blender's Image editor as a *.png* image with transparency (when saving, remember to choose **RGBA** next to the file type to save the transparency as well). Then, I opened the image in GIMP. To create a background for the top right-hand corner, I opened a sky texture from CGTextures as a layer (see Figure 14-17) and put it below the render in my layer stack. I then scaled and positioned the background to put a nice bit of cloud in the top corner (as you can see in the first image in Figure 14-17). To create a nighttime background, I used the Curves tool to really darken the clouds layer, while using the Hue-Saturation and Brightness tools (Colors ▸ Hue-Saturation) to reduce the saturation of the layer a bit so that the colors didn't look too saturated.

Next, I added some embellishments to the cloud image using the Dodge/Burn tool (set to Dodge) and added highlights to the edges of some clouds using a soft-edged brush. I also created a new transparent layer and set its Blend mode to Overlay. I then used this new layer to incorporate some extra colors around the clouds: a light blue around the edges of the leaves on the temple and some greens and yellows toward the corner. Throughout, my goal was to end up with a background that had a color palette similar to that of my rendered image.

Finally, I hid the render layer, saved the background on its own as an *.xcf* file (CTRL-S) so that I could edit it later, and exported it as a *.tga* image (CTRL-E). The background image and its various stages are shown in Figure 14-17.

Compositing the Temple

With my background created, I returned to Blender's compositor. First, I had to add my background behind my render. To do so, I used the Alpha Over node with the background as the first input and my render as the second (see Figure 14-18).

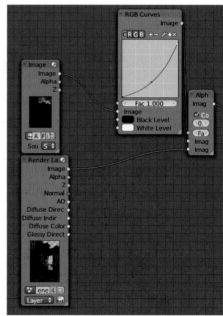

Figure 14-17: Creating a background for the Jungle Temple in GIMP, using an early, noisy render as a guide. The background was made with the same dimensions as the final image, but only the corner showing the sky is shown here. (The rest of the background image was black.) The render (on a separate layer) was hidden before saving the background.

Figure 14-18: Compositing the background in GIMP with an Alpha Over node. I also added a Curves node to darken it slightly.

Depth of Field

Next came some depth of field. When adding depth of field to the Spider Bot, I used physically correct, rendered depth of field. However, for the Jungle Scene, I used the compositor's Defocus node. This method gives slightly less accurate results than rendered depth of field, but it allows for more control over which areas are blurred and which are not and lets us change the focus *after* we finish rendering, which gives us more flexibility.

The Defocus node requires two inputs: the image to be blurred and a black-and-white mask that determines how much to blur different parts of the image. For the mask, you can use either the *z*-buffer directly (check the **Use z-buffer input** checkbox), or you can use any black-and-white image as a simple mask by leaving it unchecked. If you choose to use the *z*-buffer directly, Blender will use the camera's depth-of-field settings found in the Object Data tab of the Properties editor. Regions closer or farther than the depth-of-field distance will be blurred. If you turn this option off, Blender will use the value of the input to determine the amount of blurring so that white regions will be the most blurred and black the least.

For the Jungle Temple scene, I opted to use the *z*-buffer directly, but I added a Blur node (with a radius of 6 pixels) between the *z*-buffer output

and the *z*-input of the Defocus node to blur these values slightly. This method reduces the creation of artifacts on foreground objects, where objects that should be blurred appear to have sharp edges.

Adding Bloom and Vignetting

Next, I added some bloom. As with the other projects, I blurred the image and combined it back over the image with an Add Mix node. I applied some vignetting by taking the alpha channel of the render, distorting it with the Lens Distortion node, blurring it with the Blur node, and then overlaying this on top of the image. The nodes for these stages are shown in Figure 14-19.

Color Grading

To add color grading, I used two different nodes. First, I put the image through a Hue Correct node, which let me adjust the saturation (or hue or value) of specific colors within the image. Because I wanted to play up the oranges and greens before applying some extra grading, I adjusted the curve of the Hue Correct node by clicking the curve and dragging to add a new point, raising the profile of the curve in the orange and green areas, and lowering it slightly in the blues. This increased the saturation of the orange light from the temple entrance and the green of the leaves, making them more prominent. I ran the result through a Color Balance node, adding some blues to the shadows with a bluish lift color and some yellow and orange to the midtones and highlights with very slightly orange gamma and gain colors.

Finally, I added a Filter node at the end of the node tree, just before the Composite output node. I set this to Sharpen with a factor of 0.05 to add some very slight sharpening to the image.

This completes the compositing for the Jungle Temple scene. The complete node setup is shown in Figure 14-20.

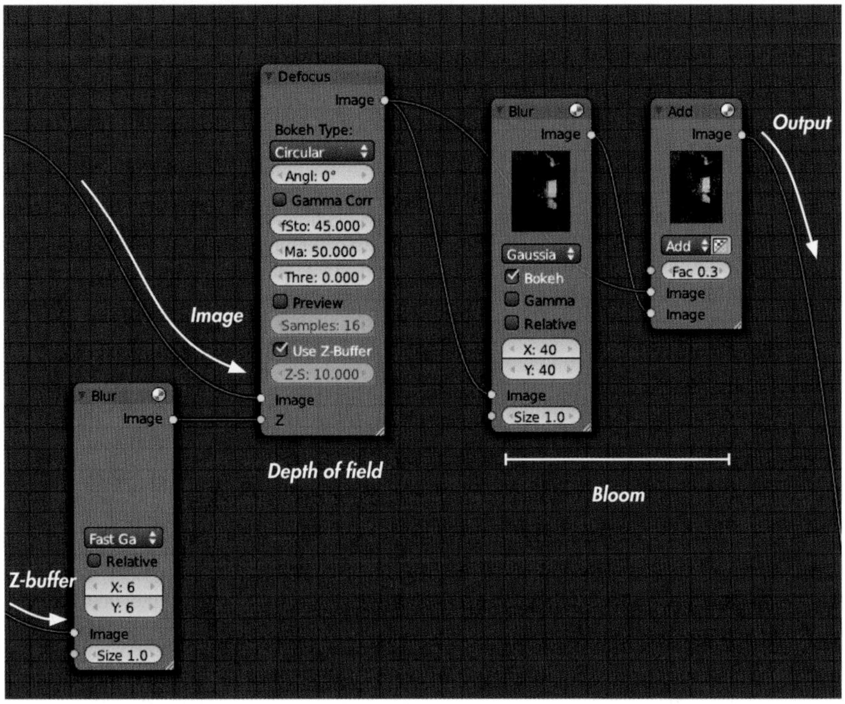

Figure 14-19: Adding depth of field and bloom to the composite

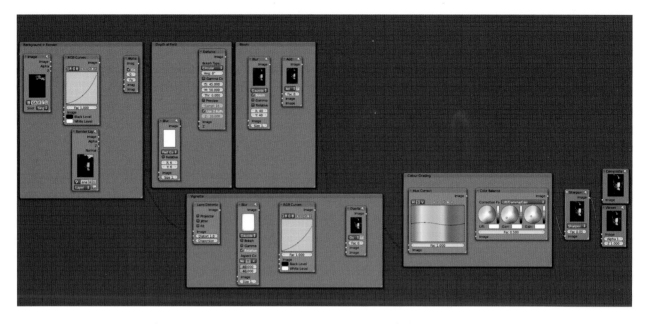

Figure 14-20: The node tree for compositing the Jungle Temple, organized with frame nodes

As a final adjustment, I opened the composite image in GIMP and cleaned up one or two remaining depth-of-field artifacts by hand with the Blur tool. I also cropped the image slightly to improve the composition. The result is shown in Figure 14-21.

In Review

This more or less completes each of the projects I set out to create for the book. In this chapter, I took the final scenes and rendered them using either Cycles or Blender Internal as render engines. Then I took the render output and used GIMP and Blender's compositor to tweak and refine these results into my final images. The result is renders of the projects that I can now call finished.

Of course, there's always another tweak that can be made, and in Chapter 15, we'll look at a few more things that could be done with these projects to take them further.

Figure 14-21: The final result for the Jungle Temple

15

GOING FURTHER

In this chapter, we look at some possible additions to the final projects, potential ways to develop them, and where to find the information on how to do so. Both Blender and GIMP have many uses beyond those discussed in this book. But as a full 3D animation suite, Blender has a number of features that we haven't had time to examine, so I'll concentrate on how we can use Blender to take our projects further.

For example, one Blender feature we can use to expand the projects is the Armature object, which gives models a kind of skeleton that allows them to be moved or posed. The process of creating an armature for a model and setting up the connections that make the armature control the mesh is known as *rigging*, and the resulting armature is known as a *rig*. Rigging can be complex. Covering it in full is well beyond the scope of this book, but I will briefly review the principles of rigging the Spider Bot. Once you have rigged your creations, you can animate them using Blender's animation tools. Like rigging, animation is a topic that would take a book of its own to cover, so I'll just suggest some ideas, as well as resources for further reading.

But first, let's look at some simple ways to add extra details to the projects.

Embellishments

It's often difficult to find the point where you're finally ready to call a project finished. Sometimes a project is just missing something—certain details or additional objects that would allow you to get extra mileage out of your creation. To that end, here are some ideas for extras we could add to the projects.

Adding to the Jungle Temple

The Jungle Temple scene already has a lot going on, but the color scheme is pretty simple. One way to dress it up would be to create a few flowering plants to add a splash of color here and there. I used face duplication (a way to duplicate one object over the faces of another) to add some flowers to the IvyGen mesh, and I increased the number of leaves to make the plant life more interesting. I created a new "branch" object consisting of a few leaves and flowers and then replaced the faces in the original leaf mesh with an instance of this object. Conveniently, this branch object also renders quickly: Cycles recognizes that each instance of the duplicated branch shares the same mesh data, so it stores the object only once, keeping the memory requirements for rendering reasonably low.

Creating the Branch Object

To create a branch, I began by subdividing a plane and giving it a slightly curved shape. This formed the basis of my leaf, which I duplicated a few times and arranged in an arching group of five leaves. I created a flower using a five-vertex circle, which I then filled in and extruded out to create the petals. Next, I unwrapped the flower and the leaf. I used the same texture and material for the leaves of the branch as before. For the flower, I used a flower photo from CGTextures. I created a texture and material from it as I had done for the leaves. I also modeled some basic twigs for the new leaves to attach to by creating a cube and extruding from it to roughly line up with the leaves. In the end, I created two branch objects: one with flowers and one without, as shown in Figure 15-1.

Figure 15-1: The branch objects I used to increase the complexity of the foliage in the Jungle Temple. Above: The branch objects in the 3D Viewport. Below: The branch objects rendered.

Duplicating with Face Duplication

To use the branch object to create some extra foliage, I turned on Face Duplication in the Duplication panel, which you can find in the Object tab of the Properties editor. To duplicate a branch, I parented it (selecting the branch, then the IvyGen mesh, and hitting CTRL-P) to the IvyGen leaf mesh. Then, I set the duplication type to Faces in the Duplication panel. This created a duplicate of the branch object for each face of the IvyGen mesh.

The objects must have the same origin or the duplicates will be offset from the parent mesh, so I selected my branch object and snapped my cursor to it (SHIFT-S ▶ Cursor to Selection). Next, I selected the IvyGen leaf mesh, clicked Origin operator in the 3D Viewport Tool Shelf, and selected Origin to 3D Cursor, giving the two objects the same origin.

Face duplication allows each duplicate to inherit the scale of the face it is duplicated from. I took advantage of this by enabling Scale in the Duplication panel and then adding some random variation to the scale of the IvyGen faces. To do so, I used Select ▶ Random in Edit mode to select a random sample of the faces in the mesh. Next, I scaled them down slightly with the Pivot Point set to Individual Faces in the 3D Viewport header (so the faces would scale down toward their centers). This scaled down a random selection of the faces. Then, I repeated the process—this time selecting different faces—and scaled them up a bit.

To create a mix between the two branch objects, I split the IvyGen mesh by selecting it, switching to Edit mode, and setting the selection method to Faces from the 3D Viewport header. Then, I used Select ▶ Random—again choosing 20 percent of the faces in the mesh (you can adjust the percentage in the Tool Options panel of the Tool Shelf)—and pressed **P** to part them from the mesh and turn them into their own object. Next, I parented the branch without flowers to the original IvyGen object and the branch with flowers to the new one, creating some branches with flowers and some without. The result is shown in Figure 15-2.

Creating Pebbles

To give the ground in the scene a little more variation, I used another particle system to scatter pebbles on the ground. I created a group of pebble objects,

Figure 15-2: Increasing the number of leaves by duplicating multiple branch objects for each original face in the IvyGen leaf mesh

Figure 15-3: A render of the Jungle Temple scene with some extra features added

as I did for the grass. Then, I added a new particle system to the ground, setting it up similarly to the grass system. This time, though, I used Simple Child particles to scatter the pebbles in small clusters around the scene. Figure 15-3 shows a render of the scene with the addition of the extra foliage and the pebbles.

Adding to the Bat Creature

I decided that the Bat Creature might benefit from having something to stand on, so I created a rocky plinth to give him a platform. I also experimented with adding a wispy cloud around his feet.

Creating the Rock

To create the platform (a rock), I first modeled a rough shape by scaling and extruding out from a cube. Next, I used Blender's sculpt tools and a Multiresolution modifier to sculpt this rough shape into a rocky one. The Clay Tubes and Scrape Flat brush from Chapter 6 were particularly useful for this purpose (see Figure 15-4). I used the seamless rock texture from Chapter 11 (that I created for the Jungle Temple project) on top of the sculpted details as a displacement map.

I made a material for the rock using the same rock textures I created in Chapter 11, and I added another light behind the rock to light up its top rim from the camera's perspective. I set this light to This Layer Only in the Lamps settings so that it would light only the rock, which was on its own

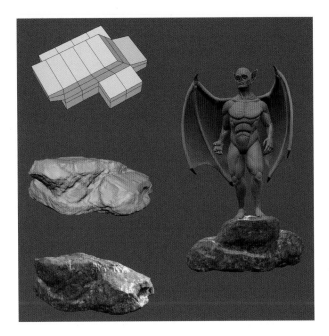

Figure 15-4: Creating the rock for the Bat Creature to stand on

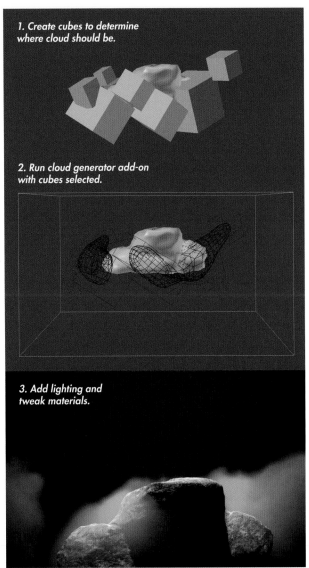

1. Create cubes to determine where cloud should be.

2. Run cloud generator add-on with cubes selected.

3. Add lighting and tweak materials.

Figure 15-5: Creating clouds with the Cloud Generator script

layer along with the lamp. I then shifted the camera down slightly and angled it up to give a different perspective on the Bat Creature, and I adjusted the positions of his feet to make him stand on the rock correctly.

Adding Clouds

To complement the mood of the image, I added some clouds around the rock. Blender has some fantastic tools for rendering volumetric materials like clouds. A full discussion would require its own chapter, but thankfully for our purposes, it's simple enough to say that a terrific add-on called Cloud Generator will do most of the work. Enable the add-on from the User Preferences editor.

To use the Cloud Generator script, I first sketched the rough volume of my cloud using cubes. Then, I used the Generate Cloud button, which can be found in the Tool Shelf, to automatically generate cloud objects with the rough shape of the cube objects selected and to set up appropriate materials (see Figure 15-5).

I left the generated material almost as it was made by the add-on, except that I turned on External

Shadows in the Lighting panel of the Materials tab and set the scale of the clouds texture belonging to the material a bit lower to give the cloud some more detail. I rendered the cloud on its own render layer and composited it into my image after adding the background in my comp setup (before the bloom and color grading were applied). The results are shown in Figure 15-6.

Figure 15-6: The finished clouds composited into my scene

Figure 15-7: Alternate renders of the Spider Bot, with different lighting and camera angles

Different Looks

Another way to get more out of a project is to consider some different looks for your final renders. This might involve finding new camera angles or trying different lighting schemes. I experimented with some different looks for lighting the Spider Bot, as well as different camera angles, as shown in Figure 15-7.

Rigging and Animation

Of course, the most dramatic way to take your projects further is to animate them. One simple way to animate a scene is to render a turntable by rotating the camera around the subject and keying its position and rotation as it moves in a circle. Another way is to render a fly-through, with your camera moving around the scene to show different points of interest. More complex animation—for example, animating your character's movements—involves creating rigs for any moving elements and then keying, or

storing, the different properties and positions of these elements through time.

Rigging requires adding an armature object to your scene and editing it to create a "skeleton" for your model. Next, you must bind your model to the armature, either by parenting the model's objects to specific bones or, preferably, by using the Armature modifier to assign different vertex groups within objects to the different bones of the armature. Once you've completed these steps, you can switch to Pose mode with the armature selected to begin moving and posing your model (see Figure 15-8).

In addition to creating bones to directly control parts of your model, you can also create constraints and helper bones to form a kind of user interface for your rig. These could include controls to make sure that limbs reach for a specific point automatically or controls to make the model perform certain actions. For example, in Figure 15-8, the bones shown highlighted in yellow and green are those that have had constraints applied to make posing the legs easier. This is a complex process, though. To learn more about rigging, look at the resources available from the Blender Foundation Shop and on the Blender wiki.

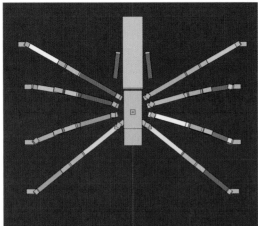

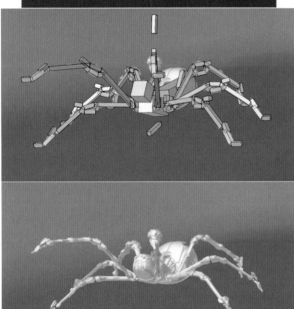

In Review

Over the course of this book, we have progressed from the initial inspiration for our projects to final images and beyond. After introducing Blender and GIMP in Chapters 1 and 2, we looked at how to gather, create, and use reference and concept art in Chapter 3, and moved on to blocking in the fundamentals of our scenes in the form of rough geometry and base meshes in Chapter 4. In Chapters 5, 6, and 7, we expanded upon these rough forms with further geometry and with Blender's sculpting and retopology tools. In Chapter 8, we unwrapped the models for texturing.

With the models laid out, we added further details with particle systems in Chapter 9 and textures in Chapters 10 and 11. In Chapters 12 and 13, we began turning our collection of models and textures into a renderable scene with materials and lighting, and in Chapter 14, we turned our *.blend* files into finished renders.

I hope that this chapter has given you a few ideas for ways you can enhance the finished projects in this book or your own projects. I've covered adding extra details to scenes and producing extra renders with different scenery or moods. I've also touched on the idea of animating and rigging projects, moving from the realm of still images into moving pictures.

Throughout this book, I've used my three projects to illustrate what powerful tools Blender and GIMP are and how their diverse range of functions can be used. Each tool has tremendous depth and can be daunting at first, but once you get to know the tools, they're fantastic for bringing your ideas to life. I hope you'll enjoy using the skills you've learned in this book to do just that.

Figure 15-8: Working with armatures. Top: The armature for the Spider Bot seen on its own from above, in B-Bone view (one of the display options for armatures). Middle: Posing the Spider Bot using the rig. Bottom: The posed Spider Bot shown on its own.

Once your model is rigged, you can begin animating your creation. By keying the transformations of the bones in your rigs, or storing their poses, and then moving through Blender's timeline, changing the rig's pose, and keying it again, you can build up a sequence of positions and poses for your rig to move through. When played back, your model will then perform the sequence of movements defined by the poses you created.

INDEX

V

VBOs (vertex buffer objects), 72
Velocity panel, for hair
  particles, 126
Velvet BSDF shader, for Cycles
  renderer, 189
vertex, 30
  count, 6
  extruding, 31
  hair particles emitted from, 126
  order, 76
  pinning for UV unwrapping,
    113
  positions in Local coordinate
    space, 9
  proportional editing and,
    43–44
vertex buffer objects (VBOs), 72
vertex group
  controlling modifiers with, 89
  for displacement control, 86
  for hair particles, 123, 128
    for hair density, 124
    for hair length, 125
Vertex option, for snapping, 36
vertical guides, in GIMP, 15
vertices. *See* vertex
Video Editing layout, 3
viewer nodes, compositing,
  238–239
viewport, snapping to specific
  angles, 5
vignette
  for Bat Creature, 238
  for Jungle Temple, 245
vines, IvyGen add-on for creating,
  59–61
virtual parent particles, 127
visibility, of GIMP layers, 160
visual path, 23
Volume option, for snapping, 36
volumes in sculpting, 77
  Bat Creature, 79
Voronoi texture, 133
Voronoi Texture node, 204

W

walls, 53–55
Warp operator, 44

water material, 207–208
Wave option, for hair
  particles, 128
wavefront objects, exporting
  object as, 99
Waves Texture node, 208
websites
  for Blender builds, 2
  CGTextures, 162, 171, 243, 248
  for GIMP, 13
Weight Paint mode, 123–125
Width Fade option, for strand
  rendering, 198
wings
  Bat Creature sculpting, 83
  modeling, 44–45
wireframe view mode, 5
wires of Spider Bot, modeling
  details, 61–62
World settings
  for Bat Creature, 223
  for Blender Internal renderer,
    216–217
  in Cycles renderer, 218
  for Jungle Temple, 224
World Settings tab in Properties
  editor, 5, 73

X

x-axis, 5
.xcf (GIMP) file format, 17,
  162, 166
x-coordinate, 5, 109

Y

y-axis, 5
y-coordinate, 5, 109

Z

z-axis, 5
z-coordinate, 5, 109
Z transparency, 185, 187
Zenith Color, in Blender Internal
  renderer, 216
.zmt format, 74
Zoom tool (GIMP), 15

Blender Master Class is set in New Baskerville, Futura, and Dogma. The book was printed and bound at Sheridan Books, Inc. in Chelsea, Michigan.

UPDATES

Visit *http://nostarch.com/blendermasterclass.htm* for updates, errata, and other information.

More no-nonsense books from **NO STARCH PRESS**

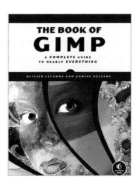

THE BOOK OF GIMP
A Complete Guide to Nearly Everything
by OLIVIER LECARME *and* KARINE DELVARE
JANUARY 2013, 676 PP., $49.95
ISBN 978-1-59327-383-5
full color

THE ARTIST'S GUIDE TO GIMP, 2ND EDITION
Creative Techniques for Photographers, Artists, and Designers
by MICHAEL J. HAMMEL
JUNE 2012, 320 PP., $39.95
ISBN 978-1-59327-414-6
full color

THE BOOK OF INKSCAPE
The Definitive Guide to the Free Graphics Editor
by DMITRY KIRSANOV
SEPTEMBER 2009, 472 PP., $44.95
ISBN 978-1-59327-181-7

THE BOOK OF AUDACITY
Record, Edit, Mix, and Master with the Free Audio Editor
by CARLA SCHRODER
MARCH 2011, 384 PP., $34.95
ISBN 978-1-59327-270-8

THE BOOK OF CSS3
A Developer's Guide to the Future of Web Design
by PETER GASSTON
MAY 2011, 304 PP., $34.95
ISBN 978-1-59327-286-9

ELOQUENT JAVASCRIPT
A Modern Introduction to Programming
by MARIJN HAVERBEKE
JANUARY 2011, 224 PP., $29.95
ISBN 978-1-59327-282-1

PHONE:
800.420.7240 OR
415.863.9900

EMAIL:
SALES@NOSTARCH.COM
WEB:
WWW.NOSTARCH.COM

ABOUT THE DVD

The accompanying DVD contains all the files for the projects in this book, including separate *.blend* files for each project (corresponding to each chapter in the book) and each project in its final state at the end of each chapter (where relevant). These resources should allow you to look in-depth at the workings of each project and to examine how each one takes shape. Also included are the textures used for each project, *.blend* files with some useful brushes for sculpting and MatCap materials, and a GIMP brush that you can use in your own projects.

The files are licensed under the Creative Commons noncommercial attribution (CC-BY-NC) license, with the exception of the textures, which are included with the kind permission of CGTextures (*http://www .cgtextures.com/*), a fantastic online resource for finding textures. These may not be distributed unmodified without permission from CGTextures.